P9-CFY-959

OUR HERITAGE IN PUBLIC WORSHIP

OUR HERITAGE IN PUBLIC WORSHIP

THE KERR LECTURES
Delivered in Trinity College, Glasgow
in 1933

BY

D. H. HISLOP

EDINBURGH: T. & T. CLARK, 38 GEORGE STREET
1935

PRINTED IN GREAT BRITAIN BY
MORRISON AND GIBB LIMITED
FOR
T. & T. CLARK, EDINBURGH
LONDON: SIMPKIN MARSHALL, LIMITED
NEW YORK: CHARLES SCRIBNER'S SONS

TO

THE VERY REV.

W. M. MacGREGOR, D.D.

PRINCIPAL OF TRINITY COLLEGE, GLASGOW

IN ADMIRATION AND AFFECTION

THIS BOOK IS DEDICATED

PREFACE

The substance of this book was given in Trinity College, Glasgow, in November 1933 as the Kerr Lectures, but I have added not a little which I had then to omit owing to the circumstance of their delivery. I chose the subject of these Lectures because of my belief in the importance of the question rather than because of any confidence in my ability to treat so high a theme.

The line of treatment I have adopted has made me indebted to many thinkers and liturgical scholars, and so deeply have I learned from others that I cannot always recognise their influence. My conscious debt is greatest to the works of Professor Will and Professor Heiler, to the books of Professor Hocking and Baron Von Hügel, and to the writings of Mr. Edmond Bishop. Owing to the lack of space I have been unable to add a full appendix as I desired, and since this is impossible I have incorporated in the text some details that otherwise would have found a suitable place in an appendix.

These lectures were delivered to the Divinity students of the Church of Scotland, and this, coupled with the fact that I hold orders in the same Church, doubtless colours my approach to the subject and leaves traces of practical application. But I write from the standpoint of one to whom the catholic tradition is precious and the catholic outlook fundamental.

I would acknowledge the great courtesy and kindness I received from Principal Macgregor and his colleagues in Trinity College, Glasgow, the consideration and forbearance which have been shown to me by the Kerr Lectureship Committee, and my warm gratitude to my friend, Rev. J. H. Leckie, D.D., the secretary of this committee, for his interest and goodwill. My friend, the Rev. W. A. Mill, has not only read the proofs with carefulness and prepared the Index, but has rendered me such constant help while my health was impaired that but for him neither would these lectures have been delivered nor this book published, and I would express my deepest thanks for his ungrudging and invaluable assistance.

Finally, I would acknowledge my obedience to the Catholic Faith, and express my earnest hope and fervent prayer that nothing I have written sins against the Faith once delivered unto the saints, nor offends against the Worship of God's most Holy Church where abides His Spirit.

D. H. HISLOP

EDINBURGH,
Lent, 1935.

CONTENTS

OUR HERITAGE IN PUBLIC WORSHIP

CHAPTER I

WORSHIP—TYPES AND VALUE

I

"Let us worship God" is a phrase familiar to our ears. What these words imply is the subject of the following lectures. It is obvious that, when such a resolve is made, there is the expressed intention to perform some act. Primarily worship is, on the human side, an act of faith, but this is not simply an act of individual devotion, it is the response of the Church to God's wondrous work of Revelation and Redemption. We too in our day and generation would join in this glad and adoring answer to God's exceeding grace.

Two facts, however, meet us on our way to worship: the one menacing to human society, the other baffling to our mind. The first is the existence in our world of a paganism open and unashamed, which repudiates religious faith and therefore denies the possibility and the value of worship. If it be true—as it has been said and I believe—that the only answer to an organised paganism, which like Antichrist seeks to do the work of Christ in another spirit and by a different method than Christ's, is the assertion of the visible unity of the followers of the Crucified and Risen Lord, the path to this union lies in the sphere of the soul's devotion and in the cultus rather than in doctrinal statement or ecclesiastical government. If the far-off vision of a Church of Christ that is the one Body of the Lord is to be realised, the first requirement is that we learn to understand and appreciate what is that unseen bond that links all souls in worship.

The second fact which is perplexing to the understanding is that to-day many whose souls are touched to the finer issues of life appear to feel no need for, nor find any meaning in, corporate worship. This would not be a problem if the instinct to worship were a special taste like the appreciation of primitive art. Then this fact could be accepted quite simply, just as we accept the fact that some people, like Charles Lamb, have no ear for music. Although individuals and races differ in their natural capacity for religion, our creed teaches that the Christian faith is something of common appeal, and therefore worship ought to correspond to a universal need and craving. Yet by the practice of to-day as well as by explicit criticism the tradition of public worship is set aside as a survival from an earlier era with little or no relation to the living issues of this generation. To many natures sensitive to the appeal of higher things the spirit of worship flows through purely individual channels; to these the earth and common face of nature speak rememberable things the divine service of the church does not, the ministry of art brings the sense of wonder and mystery, the great literatures of the world unveil hidden treasures of mind and heart, the intercourse of human life opens a communion with noble ideals of service, the feeling of the infinite enters within the gates of the soul in solitary experiences, and the warmth and guidance of sympathy are found through contact with human lives, but the public worship of the Church is to them a closed book. They have no religious feeling or experience of God that is common to others, or at least they are not conscious of it, and therefore the services of the church seem a meaningless relic of former days.

Unquestionably there is a mood and spirit of worship that is wider than either the corporate worship of the community or the habitual devotion of the individual. We must beware of regarding worship as something added to the activity of man's spirit in other spheres. "The worship of God," says Canon Streeter, "is not something different from the love of humanity, the passion for the beautiful and the devotion to the truth; it is what these actually are whenever, and in so far as, they are realised in their highest form, in their co-ordination and in their real meaning." If hearts alive to spiritual reality do not discover any place for the service and the ritual of the church, ought we not to consider whether the form and liturgy of her worship are adequate to the Church's high task of offering to the Creator the praise of His creatures, and are fitted to her sacred duty of developing and mediating the spirit of holy communion before the presence of the Eternal Father? Between the mood of this generation and the worship of the Church many obstacles seem to stand. Perchance it is possible that more clearly in her worship the Church can show the presence of that Living Christ to whom belong all that is true and noble in the life of this generation.

Within the Church we find a movement of the human spirit that is the antagonist of that godless paganism which denies all worship and the counterpoise of that individualistic experience which discards public worship. This movement has a triple tendency: (1) the first tendency is the emphasis on what is objective in religion—the recognition that worship is not simply the expression of subjective feelings. Something is sought for beyond and above human experience, and something definite and not vague is desired. There is a movement of the human spirit toward God as the Transcendent, high and lifted up, Who has revealed Himself in His wondrous grace. This is witnessed in the most diverse communions. The Roman Church emphasises more clearly the miracle of the Mass and defines more definitely the authority of the Church as the guardian of the faith given by God. The fundamentalists, so called, make more authoritative Holy Scripture as the Word of the Eternal God. The theology of Barth and Brunner is as marked a reaction from the subjectivity of Lutheranism as from the relativity of historical science. Religious experience is not the basis of our belief in God, but our subjective experience is the human reaction to the Divine Activity. There is the turning away from the hymns of pietistic devotion to the hymns that utter the great verities of the faith. In every communion, Roman and Reformed, there is the endeavour to affirm the absoluteness of God in contrast to the immanence of the Divine.

(2) The second tendency is a new emphasis on corporate devotion. The idea of the Church as the mystical Body of the Lord is specially prominent to-day. There is an attempt to include the

personal experience and piety of the individual Christian in the wider synthesis of the worshipping Church. The Benedictine liturgical spirit, as is its wont, led the way in the explanation of the Missal and in the spiritual interpretation of it to the worshipper, so that the devout soul may find in the ancient liturgical service the expression and inspiration of his piety, and thereby be part of Corpus Christi mysticum. In the Reformed and Lutheran communions the increased importance attached to the Sacrament is evidence of this same tendency to emphasise the social aspect of worship. Here too the human spirit reveals its desire to outstep the limits of individual devotion.

(3) The third tendency shows itself in the increased interest in liturgical form and order. As the first tendency was upward towards the sense of God as Absolute, and the second tendency was outward towards the recognition that the individual is part of a whole, so the third tendency deals with the means whereby communion with the Eternal is achieved and fellowship with others created. In each case the human spirit is searching for the objective. The liturgy of public worship is, then, the phenomenon through which men offer the soul's worship to the Most High and by which the corporate unity of the worshippers is expressed. In our own branch of the Church in Scotland, as in every other, this interest is to be found. I have mentioned already the liturgical revival within the Roman obedience. So also in the Orthodox Belief, in the Anglican communion, and in the Churches of the Continent, this matter is discussed. This is not simply the desire to make more beautiful and more adequate the communal offering of praise and prayer. There is implicit in this liturgical development the impulse to set worship beyond the mood and the emotion of the worshipper. The escape from temporal limitations into the sense of eternity is sought by making the form of worship wider and more stable. Of course this process may result in merely an antiquarian concern. With eyes fixed only on past forms men may seek to curb the expression of the living spirit. Such absorption in the past—be it the practice of the early Church, or the mediæval, or the ways of the sixteenth-century reformation—cannot solve the problems of our generation. Yet one would err

who saw here nothing but an attempt to dredge from the past its treasures and its curiosities. This awakened interest in former days is also the witness of the endeavour to make worship something which transcends the confines of our generation, and to find in worship something that is not at the mercy of passing time. Precisely because these ancient prayers and usages are not couched in the accent of our day, they are felt to give a sense of permanence within which the aspirations of the individual "cast upon this shoal and bank of time" find steadfastness and assurance. This interest in past worship is the response to the requirement of the future for it is the search for the abiding. It is the pursuit of the Eternal Spirit which endures above and within the spirit of each generation.

These three tendencies of the modern movement call attention to the fact that the worshipper in public worship touches what is beyond himself in three respects. The first objective aspect is the sense of God's presence, the Being to whom devotion is given is Other than the worshipper. Whatever be the level of man's spiritual life, worship means this experience of the Being Who is beyond. Without such an experience there cannot be worship. The second objective aspect is the presence of other lives, for worship in its origin and nature is a social act. The feeling of the individual worshipper meets with what is external to himself in the experience of worshipping with his fellows. The third objective aspect is the means through which the worship is offered. This may be a visible object like the cross or crucifix, may be the sacred elements of the Blessed Sacrament, may be the words of Holy Scripture or the music of psalm or hymn. It is in every case something visible or audible that is not himself. In the world of sense the worshipper feels something outside himself which is the medium of worship. These three objective aspects are related. The Otherness of God is represented to human experience in worship by the objectivity of other souls and by the externality of the media of worship. The liturgy or means of worship which is external to the self of the worshipper is the path of the soul to the Divine; yet it is not the path of one soul but of many souls. The worshipper finds his true self—the Christ that is in me, as St. Paul states it—through the discovery of this self in the experience of others. This discovery of the most real self stripped from the limitations of his cramping mortal existence each worshipper makes on the altar of Divine Grace. "The mystery of yourselves," St. Augustine profoundly says, "is placed upon the Lord's Table." Thus it is that the fellowship of other souls and the outer phenomena used in worship heighten and widen the sense of God as objective in religious experience. Social contact and the cultural object are instruments in public worship for creating and increasing the experience of God.

The liturgical revival we have already mentioned is, then, the effort to free the worshippers from individual subjectivity by emphasising the external modes of worship. I am well aware that the living faith of to-day can be sacrificed to what is deemed the correct expression of that faith. A method of worship may become an end in itself and the religious service simply a performance. Every form of worship demands a living personal faith to preserve it from formality. The task before the liturgical activity of to-day is to reconcile the spirit of worship with the organ of its expression, the soul of devotion which is native to the world of spirit with its embodiment which belongs to the world of sense. In presence of the antagonism between the inner and the outer, the reform of worship must seek to incarnate the spiritual in the sensible.

When we think of any reform in the method of worship there are three laws of liturgical development which must be borne in mind. (1) The first may be called the principle of survival. This law is found in the devotional development of every religion. The religious instinct is conservative and does not easily let go anything which has entered into the sphere of worship. Actions, gestures, usages, ceremonies, and prayers survive from either a lower level of religious insight or from an earlier expression of the faith. Within the Jewish religion Canaanite practices are found, and beneath the ensign of the Christian faith pagan elements survive. An illustration of this is seen in Hebrew religion in the ceremony of sprinkling blood upon the lintel. Originally this custom must have been to protect the household from malignant spirits that hovered around. Yet the practice lives on in the religion wherein Yahveh is a beneficent spirit toward His people. This act survives, but its original significance has disappeared.

(2) The second principle appears the antithesis of the first. It is the law whereby the living faith is ever freeing itself from dead tradition and conventional expression. The wine of the Spirit is ever bursting the skins of tradition. The repudiation of the golden calf which had been a means of worshipping Yahveh illustrates this second principle. We also find it at work in the prophetic criticism of Israel's ritual, and in the puritanic distrust of every form and ceremony. This principle might be termed the law of concentration, for all that is not impregnated with its own spirit is ruthlessly pruned away. The first principle may preserve what are meaningless survivals, the second principle working alone is in peril of scattering public worship into anarchy.

(3) The third principle harmonises the two former. We might call it the law of expansion. In its operation it preserves the old rite but attaches a new meaning to it. The Faith, ever seeking new forms of expression, adopts ceremonies, symbols, and rites which have sprung from alien sources. Old customs are illumined with a new light, foreign usages furnish fresh material whereby the spirit becomes incarnate in new forms. Again from the Hebrew Faith we find an illustration which is also a parable. The sacred stone once the object of worship becomes the table of stone on which is engraved the ethical law and which found its resting-place in the Ark of the Covenant. To-day we see in the history of liturgy the play and interplay of these principles, nor can we ignore their import. The task is laid upon the Church to-day of fashioning anew her divine service, but the final liturgy and full offering of human devotion await that Church of the future, One, Catholic, and Evangelic.

In such a situation we as members of the Church in Scotland find ourselves. We are warned that in view of God's future for his Church we may not neglect our past. We must needs recall that we belong to a Church that has passed through various phases in her history. What Meredith says of the individual life of man is true still more profoundly of the Church, and " If I drink oblivion of a day, so shorten I the stature of my soul."

(1) There was in Scotland the Celtic phase of the Church, wherein the kinship of the Irish and the Gallican devotions is evident, and wherein the expression of her worship is not untouched by the same influences that fashioned the rites of the Eastern Church. Within this period we move with the spiritual tides that have given to us the Divine Liturgy of St. Basil and St. Chrysostom in the Nearer East and have left the Mozarabic Rite of Spanish devotion.

(2) There is the Roman phase, with its characteristic contribution to devotional life. One of Rome's peculiar traits is the value she attached to uniformity of ritual. This uniformity is her distinctive method of seeking to declare the great and precious idea of Christian unity in worship.

(3) There is the reformed period alike Episcopal and Presbyterian. The second Prayer Book of Edward VI. of 1552 was in use in Scotland before Knox's Book of Common Order displaced it. Through this English book the influence of the daily services of matins and lauds enters our devotional life, and in Knox's book the specifically Calvinistic Scots service becomes our heritage. Puritan customs and Independent forms also touched our religious development. The record of the Church's public devotions in Scotland at one time or another has been in touch with almost every branch of the Universal Church. This, our Scots heritage, is wide as Christendom and is coloured by the devotion of almost every communion. By the story of her development is not the Church in Scotland called on to build the way to a worship that is at once Catholic and Evangelic? May it not be that a new phase lies before her wherein she will seek to express in answer to the needs of the modern world the full riches of her great inheritance?

II

Let us turn from the thought of how manifold and diverse has been the history of the devotions of the Church in this land to the elements that are in use in her present worship. Her service of to-day has an order and a sequence which call for historical justification as well as psychological consideration. The contents of her services are the spoken word in prayer, the reading of Scripture, preaching of the Word, and the singing of praise in psalm and hymn. When we look at this from a purely external standpoint we may say that as a means of worship the uttered word is the predominant feature. The element that belongs to the world of sense is sound, and the appeal is mainly through the sense of hearing. Speech is the medium through which the soul seeks to rise to the unseen, and hearing is the method through which the revelation of God draws near to the human heart. But the appeal is not only to the ear, there is also symbolism in the Presbyterian form. The celebration of the Holy Eucharist makes use of the eye and of touch and of taste as well as of the ear, as the means through which the eternal message of God's Being and the sense of His Presence are mediated to the soul. There are also gestures, such as the act of Benediction. In addition there is the Offering, which represents the rendering of our means and activity to God's Will and Purpose before the vision of His Grace. When we trace the inner meaning of these words, acts, these visible and tangible things, we discern that these external things of sense are the means whereby there is a meeting-place for the Eternal God and the human spirit and through which man's spirit can ascend and God's Spirit descend.

Bearing in mind the sensory features that belong to the Divine Service and the aim of worship which is communion between God and man, let us ask the question what worship involves. The answer is, that three things are concerned in this act. Something is uttered, something is depicted, something is done. Let us look at these in the reverse order.

Firstly, something is done. Public worship achieves something —it is not simply an expression of feeling; it is the performance of an act. An offering is made and this brings us to the idea of sacrifice. This thought of sacrifice goes far back to primitive times, even to the prehistoric age, it would appear. Man in the twilight of spiritual vision offers something to God or to the gods of his imagination. He hopes to win something from the unseen power by his act. *Do ut des* is the logic of the lowest forms. Man offers his sacrifice of beast or of first-fruits, and gives to God a share of what God gives to him. Sacrifice may be the attempt to placate the Divine will or to wrest favours from the Divine gratitude. It may also be the giving of man's will to the Divine through the external offering. From the untutored savage, who seeks to nourish his deity or to coerce or to cajole him by gifts, to the Christian's offering of himself upon the altar of God's sacrifice, we find the thought that something is achieved by this act. This thought of sacrifice, then, has entered into Christian devotion and has been purified from gross and blinded interpretations. There is the oblation which the Church offers to God consisting of the lives and wills of men awakened to spiritual reality and kindled to faith by the vision of Christ. The sacrificial idea in worship is the particular mark of the Roman communion, and by this idea her whole devotions are governed.

Secondly, something is depicted. The drama of the divine and human life is represented. The uplifting of the soul and the coming of the Deity are shown forth. The mood of the worshipper is bathed in an atmosphere of emotional expectancy. Here we have a form of worship—the mystery drama—that reaches far back into the beginning of things. It is the worship of primitive man impressed by the course of nature—the birth and death of the year, and the victory of life over decay in the resurrection of spring. Around the sowing and the gathering of the harvest a cluster of ceremonial practices gathers, and the growth of vegetation and the fertility of living creatures call to the deep in man. The cycle of human life beginning in mystery and ending in mystery arouses a feeling which finds utterance in ritual act. It is the recognition of the same rhythm in human existence and in the life of the earth. Let us not shut our eyes to the unethical possibilities of this worship. Pan with the goat's hoof is in it. Yet the shadow of the sacred falls across the face of creation. In historic times this approach to the Divine becomes in the Mystery religions a sacramental drama wherein the redemption of man's soul is sought through the coming of the Divine, and whereby through purgation and cleansing the soul receives the illumination of knowledge and wins union with the deity. Into the service of the Christian Faith this form has come.

The death and triumph of Christ are represented, and the story of God's saving Grace is recounted, while within the heart of the believer the work of redemption is repeated. To every form of Christian Worship there belongs something of this pictorial drama. Here too is the meeting-place of Divine activity and the human response. Traces of this are found in our service apart from Holy Communion. There are depicted in the praise, the Scripture lessons, and the preaching of the Word the wondrous Doings of the Lord which work in the soul of the worshipper corresponding moods and experiences. The Church of the East has specially concentrated on the use of this method in her public services. Every word and act and gesture are symbolic, and the Divine Liturgy depicts the story of the Creation and the Redemption. This aim of setting forth the Divine Drama of salvation gives direction to the whole devotions of the Orthodox Church.

Thirdly, something is uttered. Not only does man speak to God; God speaks to man. The prayer upon human lips is but the reply to the Voice of God spoken in His Word. Something is revealed of God's Will which strikes to the soul of man. This too is a way of worship found everywhere. In many ways man has heard or thought he heard the Divine Oracle through the tempest, the earthquake, the fire, and the still small voice. At all stages of spiritual development man's ear has been open to hear what he thought was the Divine Oracle. Through the lips of the Hebrew prophets the word has been revealed as at other levels in Zoroastrian faith and other religions came the sense of revelation. Within Christianity the oracle thought is very prominent. God's Will is revealed in Holy Scriptures and His Word must needs be proclaimed. Emphasis on God's Word has been the leading trait in the cultus of the Reformed branches of the Church. In obedience to this conception the services of these Churches have been moulded and her devotion has been not so much the lifting up of the heart as the bowing of the soul before the revelation of God's Sovereign Will and Grace.

These three elements belong to the act of public worship—the offering of sacrifice, the vision of the Eternal Drama, and the reception of Divine Truth, and these three elements correspond to the three historic types of human worship.[1] As we have seen, Sacrifice, the Mystery, and the Oracle are not the creation of Christianity, but they have been used by the spirit of Christian worship. Sometimes they have carried with them associations and suggestions that have lowered worship to a pre-Christian level. That does not mean we are to seek to eliminate any of them, but it does warn us that each must be filled with the spirit of Christian worship. Our faith is the religion of the Incarnation. These types were fashioned by man's seeking spirit in God's world under the guidance of Divine Mercy, and as the Word became flesh so must the Spirit enter the world of sense through these three types.

The exclusive use of any one of these types is fraught with peril to the spiritual life. (1) If sacrifice be isolated wholly from the other two types then there is one or other result. (*a*) Either worship becomes legalistic, because man feels that he has satisfied, by his offering, the Will of God and there is the recrudescence of the old superstition in which man seeks to placate the gods by his gift. This is a transaction between two individuals and not the worship of the Infinite Being. Man feels justified by the value of his offering. (*b*) Or worship becomes almost wholly emotional, with little or no moral content, because the bare notion of Divine Sacrifice drowns in contemplative communion all historic revelation and ethical development. Here is a mood, deep and profound, but unrelated to man's place in the world and God's task for man.

(2) If the Divine Drama be exclusively dwelt upon, there results a worship with high imaginative appeal, but it becomes an escape not only from the futility of the temporal but also from the duty of the actual. Such a concentration upon this one type of worship may bring deliverance to the individual soul from thraldom, but it fails to unite men in an enlightened fellowship of service. The jeopardy here is that worship becomes an æsthetic relief and is an escape from life instead of being an interpretation of life.

(3) If there be overmuch emphasis on the reception of Divine Truth, worship becomes intellectualistic or moralistic. To under-

[1] Cf. Will, *Le Culte*, vol. i. pp. 83 f., 117 f., 203 f.

stand the Divine Will is a great thing, but it is not the whole of worship. To comprehend and to adore are not the same thing. Or our worship becomes a means for making us servants of God's Will. That is a noble purpose, but a moralistic acid is prone to remain if the aspiration of mystical devotion and the mood of wondering contemplation be wholly absent. This exaggerated form of worship makes adoration identical with the knowing of theological truth or the willing of ethical tasks.

I would thus argue that we must retain these three types in the Christian service and must endeavour to discern the part each should play. History demonstrates to us how each of these three types has been used by the worshipping spirit. It is part of our aim to discover how they ought to be utilised in the devotion of the coming days. There are those who are impatient of the lessons of history, and who tell us that we have outgrown the past, and perhaps they need to be reminded that we grow out of the past. The only way to transcend the past is to comprehend it. If we are to develop an adequate form of worship, it must be by a spirit sufficiently patient to read the record of God's leading, and humble enough to see its application to the spirit of these days.

III

(1) As well as the historic manifestation of worship we must consider the essential movement of that experience. What, then, are these movements of this experience in which God is present to the soul ? Here I find it necessary to employ spatial terms as a symbolic language. There are two movements, the one upward, the other downward ; there are two moods, a search and a reception.[1] In the first, the soul seeks God. This is the aspiration of worship *sursum corda, Habemus ad Dominum*. This is the ascent of man's spirit, which through the stages of purification and illumination advances to communion. Mystical thought has elaborated this ascending movement, but in its essence it is the seeking heart and the ascending will. There is activity of soul in this movement. However, it is not to be thought that this is man's

[1] Cf. Will, *op. cit.* p. 344 f.

act alone. The initiative is with God. "Seek ye my Face. My heart said unto Thee, Thy Face, Lord, will I seek." Human worship on this ascendant note is in response to the Divine Call. Only that mysticism can be Christian in which the search of the soul is the answer to God's touch upon man. But what we observe here is the emphasis of man's progression to communion with God.

In public worship there is the rhythm of this ascending movement. The confession of sins and the cleansing of the soul through the absolution of Divine Forgiveness is the first reaction to God's presence. The worshipper must purify his soul. Then follows the insight which rejoices in God's wondrous works. The thanksgiving of the soul illumined by the approach of the Divine, the gratitude of the awakened spirit, the offering by the enlightened heart of its desires, its petitions, and its intercessions, the meditation on God's Work and God's Will for us, the declaration of our faith—these all belong to the stage of illumination. The final stage is that of union wherein in adoration before the mystery of God's Being and Grace the will of man becomes one with the Divine Will. Here is the oneness of our little fragmentary life with the marvellous Eternal Life that embraces all lives. The close of this rhythmic movement is when in trust and reverence the soul is passive in adoring awe and blessed peace before God's unspeakable gift. Here I would point out how the movement is from activity to passivity, from seeking to peace, from willing to contemplation.

The external symbols of devotion in public worship are the ladder by which the soul makes its ascent to God. Words, objects, gestures must be of such a nature and arranged in such a sequence that this movement is unbroken. The presence of other worshippers must be so realised that confession is made for the sins of the community, the age, and the world as well as for personal failure. The sins of our time and of our world are confessed as our own sins, for we too have part in them and need cleansing therefrom. The realisation of our union with others makes richer the insight of sympathy in petition and intercession, more living the declaration of our faith, deeper the recognition of our duties, for we are bound with them in the bundle of the living, richer the strain of our thanksgiving, for each of us is but one of God's children, upon all of whom He has poured His mercies. The sense of community also affects our union with the Divine Life in adoration, for we are thereby united also to our fellows in that region wherein differences between lives disappear. Then the Christ in each soul and the Christ Spirit encircling all become one in the union of adoration.

In Public Worship by this ascendant movement the soul of the worshipper is lifted through the sense of community and by means of the ritual employed. This ritual, be it simple or elaborate, consciously or unconsciously utilised, must be present if there is to be the ascent in prayer, praise, and contemplation. There is ever a sequence of word or action corresponding to the ascending mood of the worshipful soul. The liturgy, the words of prayer, the holy image are wholly external things when not in use, but when they are used they become the vehicle of the inner aspirations of the worshipper. Through the concentration of all who are present in devotion upon the external object, be it a material thing like a cross or crucifix, a spoken word of prayer or a passage of Holy Writ, an action like the breaking of bread or the distribution of the sacred elements, a rhythm of sound as the singing of psalm or chant—this external object becomes the symbol and the instrument of worship. It is the symbol of worship, because it represents the inner desires and moods of the worshipper ; it is the instrument of worship, in that it has the power through association of creating and augmenting these moods. The liturgy in use—and by that phrase I mean any form consciously chosen or unconsciously employed—is the embodiment of the worshipful experience. The spirit of corporate worship finds its body and its incarnation in the rite.

(2) The second movement is the descending. This is the mood of reception. The soul is not lifted up to God but bowed down before the face of the Eternal. There is here another starting-point, it is the difference between *sursum corda* and *pax vobiscum*. The descending rhythm begins with " Be still, and know that I am God," or " Behold, I stand at the door and knock." Before the presence of the Eternal Maker and Redeemer of all flesh the soul

lies prostrate in its helplessness before God's majesty. The worshipper's mood is that of passive reception, stilled into silence and awed into a sense of mortal nothingness. The soul does not begin by seeking God, but the tremendous and overwhelming fact that God seeks the soul is the first note struck in worship. As the former movement was that of the soul's ascent to God, this movement is that of God's reaching down to the soul. The passivity of adoration before God's mysterious glory and saving grace, which was the final goal of the ascending movement, appears now as the passive abasement of man's spirit before the Divine Transcendence which is the beginning of the descending movement. Since the starting-point is different, the rhythm in worship must be different. There is first the fact of God's revelation of Himself as creative power and saving grace, which through word of the Bible or in psalm or hymn is set forth. God's Revelation creates the sense of mortal nothingness. The creature is before the Creator, the redeemed in the presence of the mysterious Redeemer. After giving laud and honour to the Eternal the worshipper confesses his worthlessness and humiliates all human works before the Eternal Holiness. Then follows the consequence of God's Immediacy—to seek His purpose and His Will for us in His revealed word, to share in His redeeming work through intercession and through prayer, to meditate on our part in the coming of His kingdom into the life of our world and of our hearts, and finally to make our wills one with His Sovereign Will in furthering His Eternal purposes in mortal life.

Here also as in the first movement the external means of worship must be adapted to the sense of the descending rhythm. Words, objects, actions, and attitudes must be so selected that they convey this movement and do not break or stem its flow. Here too the presence of other worshippers fulfils its function. The unity of the worshippers is the result not of concentration on some object or word that lifts in unison their aspirations, but is the consequence of concentration on some object or word, which reveals God to each, whereby they are united in harmony with God's abiding Will for His world of men. In short, in the ascending scale through human unity men rise to God; here through God's revelation the unity of the worshipper is achieved. At the beginning of this movement, words must be employed that by their august associations and their bare simplicity suggest the Divine Presence, or visible objects such as the uplifted cross or the reserved sacrament which represent God's Presence must be utilised. This movement must be developed by a liturgy and order appropriate to the moods of the worshipper passing from the Awe of the Divine Revelation to the consequences of that revelation.

In this movement, too, we see a relation between the external object and the presence of the worshippers. A text from the Bible such as, "Come unto me all ye that labour and are heavy laden, and I will give you rest," is not a revelation of God without souls to receive it. It is in its use that the words of the Bible become the body of God's Revelation. The consecrated sacrament, apart from the souls of men to whom are given the life and the power within, is not the Body of the Lord. But the sacred elements are the Lord's Body when God's purpose of grace is fulfilled thereby, and the soul of man receives the Presence of his Lord. The sense of God's coming to the soul whether through the power of revelation or through the Blessed Sacrament belongs to every variety of Christian service. The Orthodox Church has an entry of the Word, as well as the Greater Entry of the sacramental elements. We, too, in a Presbyterian service, have the entry of the Word in the setting of the Bible upon the desk. (I could wish that we made this entry more obvious and more marked.) In whatever form the Christian worships the fact of the descending movement is always assumed. Otherwise there would be no communion with the God of Grace Who seeks the souls of men; and this movement must always make use of some word or object. This liturgy is not now, as in the ascending scale, the embodiment of the inner yearnings and spiritual stirrings in worship; it is now the embodiment of God's Spirit coming to men. It is the symbol of God's coming, for it represents in the world of sense God's Presence; but it is not only symbolic, it is also the organ and instrument of His coming, for through these vehicles of sense the Divine enters the soul of the worshipper. The liturgy is thus at once the embodiment of God's Presence and the vehicle of His Power.

These two movements of the ascent of the soul and the descent of the Spirit belong to communion with God. Every service, sacramental or otherwise, bears testimony to this. Often I admit the development of these two movements is broken in the public worship of the Church, and they are not infrequently inextricably confused. One of the problems of public worship is to devise a sequence that does justice to both, for we may not sacrifice the one wholly to the other. They are the two essential movements of the spirit in history whereby the human and the Divine meet. The ascending order rests on the age-long search for that goal wherein man, escaping from the frailty of the flesh and from time's illusion, can become divine. This is the deification of man longed for in many religions and sought in many ways. This weary search finds its fulfilment in Christian worship through selfless adoration. The descending order rests on the precious truth that God becomes man, but the first doctrine is the consequence of the second, for God becomes man in Christ to make man as Christ. To make man at one with God is the work of Christ. This second movement is vital to Christian worship, which is based on God's revelation of His coming. So it is that Divine Communion—the sense of the Eternal in time, the experience of the soul in God—has need of both these movements.

Within Christian worship these two movements bring the two moods of search and of reception; but these two moods are founded on two different aspects of the Divine Life. Söderblom has made the distinction between mystical religion and prophetic religion. The former dwells on the God of mystery, the latter on the God of revelation. Heiler has adopted and even sharpened this antithesis in his treatment of mystical and prophetic prayer. I shall use these words to describe this distinction as they have been adopted by many, though I feel the words are not wholly perfect. In worship God's presence is felt under a double aspect. God clothed in mystery is the Soul of all souls, the Supreme Reality in Whom we live and move and have our being. God is also the God of revelation, who has made known His Will to man. These two concepts—God as Being and God as Will—create two attitudes in worship.

The first attitude worships God concealed from mortal eyes Whose Being is shrouded in wonder and before Whom in awe and veneration we stand. In the sublime there is dread, but also fascination. There is in man a hunger for reality. Man's love of nature and of the manifold creation is witness to this longing, and to the attraction of the real. God as the Ultimate Reality exercises this supreme fascination upon the human spirit, and is sought by man in the height of adoration. God as the home of one man's spirit must be the Absolute, for in naught else can man's restless spirit find peace. Von Hügel has pointed out that the fascination of religion requires emphasis on the unlikeness of God to man, as well as emphasis upon the likeness. In this worshipping attitude the unlikeness of God to man is apparent. The soul seeks oneness with Eternal Being, with God Who is the Perfection of Beatitude. In the super-personal aspect of the Divine there is rest for the soul. This attitude runs the risk of losing the personality of God and falling into a pantheistic absorption. Mysticism has not infrequently done so. Indeed it is only the stress upon the historic in Christianity that rescues mystical piety from pantheistic conceptions. Yet while we acknowledge this peril, none the less we must insist that the attitude of soul developed by mysticism must have its place in Christian worship. Man is drawn to worship by the unfathomable deeps of God. Before the face of God the Source and Goal of all being, man's spirit reacts in two ways in Christian worship. The first is wondering awe before God's unsearchable Glory, the second is adoring gratitude before God's Nature of Love. In Christian worship we worship the God and Father of Our Lord Jesus Christ Who was adored by Jesus, the God Who is beyond His revelation, Whose Being is wider and deeper than His manifestation. The reaction of man's soul to God's unfathomed Mystery and to His revealed Glory is, as we have seen, adoration wherein the sense of self disappears. This attitude belongs to all Christian worship as the atmosphere in and through which we receive God's revelation to us.

The second attitude is the "prophetic" consciousness of Soul. As God draws man to Him in the first attitude, so God visits man in the second. God is here not the *ens realissima* but the Will of holiness and power. Here the personalism of God is put in the foreground. The peril now is that God may be treated as a person, and God's personality, narrowed to our finite personality, may rob the Eternal of wonder. But the notable feature of this attitude is that man is set before the God of Grace Who wills his salvation and Who brings to him salvation. Here the likeness of God to man becomes apparent, for through the act of God's Grace man speaks face to face with his Unseen Lord. This personal attitude is as characteristic of this devotion into which the divine dialogue enters, as is the prayer of unitive desire in the mystical attitude. The personal piety enshrined in the Hebrew Psalter is at one with the intense and personal worship of the early Church and of the evangelical spirit.

In Public Worship the sense of this contact between man's will and God's Holy and redemptive Will must be found. Christian worship can never neglect the fact that its basis is the revelation of God in history. As the worship of the Jew has a fulcrum in God's historic act of redemption, " I am the Lord thy God, Who brought thee out of the land of Egypt," so the worship of the Christian is rooted and grounded on the acts of revelation and redemption whereby the God Who has spoken to us by His Son and Who brought from the dead the Lord Jesus makes known His salvation to man. The response of the Christian to these facts of revelation is through his worship. The God Who has brought deliverance is the God Who answers prayer, and to Whom petitions are made. The common worship must contain the petitions of God's folk, for as contemplative prayer is the feature of " mystical " worship, so petitionary prayer is the mark of " prophetic " devotion. The element of petition is the mark of Christian trust in the God Who has outstretched His saving Arm in Christ Jesus. We never rise above the level in which the soul makes its petition to its Lord. This attitude is an intrinsic part of worship and the Church may not look, as certain mystics have looked, for the time or the stage when this essential attitude will wholly disappear into the attitude of selfless adoration.

These two attitudes of soul are the poles of public worship. Without contemplative devotion whose goal lies in union of soul with God, worship is not offered to the Eternal God, the Source and End of all existence, but to a finite Being, and therefore is less than Christian worship. Without the attitude of petition in which the soul in childlike trust stands before God the Lord, worship becomes a vague and indefinite dreaming unrelated to the world of striving, in which and for which Christ died, and therefore is not Christian worship. Certain communions have made more of the one attitude, other communions have dealt specially with the other. Heiler has driven a deep cleft between the two, and he treats "mystical" worship as the trait of the Roman and the Orthodox Churches, while he regards "prophetic" worship, which he equates with evangelical and Biblical piety, as the feature of the Lutheran and reformed services. I cannot but think that Heiler has overstated the non-mystical character of Protestantism, for he tends to ignore the mystics who have flourished within the pale of the Protestant faith (cf. Boehme, Law, Blake, Fox). But his general contention is roughly correct, that Protestantism has somewhat ignored contemplative worship, and perhaps to-day the Protestant service is apt to sacrifice the sense of mystery to lucidity of expression and clearness of thought. Before the true relation between these two attitudes is determined the question must be raised as to whether worship is primary or secondary in man's life.

Is worship an end in itself or a means to an end? Is it the Church's part to declare that worship is her final aim amd complete duty, or to assert that worship is necessary in order to create and to preserve the spirit of service? The tradition of the earlier centuries is clear as to the primacy of worship. St. Augustine, St. Bernard, St. Thomas Aquinas but state an accepted truth when they teach that the worship of God comes first in life, and that worship is an end in itself. But there has been a reversal of this great tradition.[1] Within Protestant circles the neglect of the attitude of contemplative worship has led to a prevalent view that worship exists for the sake of service. The predominant importance attached to the "prophetic" attitude has had the unforeseen result in the modern world of creating a standard whereby worship is judged by its results. No longer is worship deemed an essential

[1] Cf. *The Vision of God*, K. E. Kirk, p. 428 f.

activity of the human soul, but it is thought of as an action that is only justified by its consequence. So in Roman Catholicism the spread and the influence of the Jesuit mode of prayer form a parallel to the Protestant development. Worship becomes a means of training for life. The Spiritual Exercises are used to equip and arm the Christian warrior for life's contest. The great worth that attaches to Loyola's thought of prayer as a spiritual discipline and gymnastic cannot hide from us the fact that this, too, had as its consequence the subordination of worship to practical ends. Simply because St. Ignatius's emphasis on meditation had such a value for cultivating virtues, the significance of contemplative worship fell into the background. What has happened alike in Protestantism and in the Jesuit practice is the exclusive consideration of the practical fruits of devotion. Let no one deny the intrinsic worth of "prophetic" petition or the precious value of the discipline of meditation, but neither by themselves expresses the communion with God through worship for its own great sake. The eye of the worshipper is not wholly fixed upon the Ineffable Glory of the Infinite God, and, because this is wanting, worship inevitably must be content with a lower place in life than the first place.

To-day there is an awakening of a new spirit. The sense of God's Mystery broods over life. A world which requires the spirit of service in its sore need calls also for service in the spirit of Christ that alone can heal its hurt and comfort its woe. Such a spirit is the spirit of humility, and how can humility be learned save in the school of worship where self is not and God is all in all? Only the overwhelming sense of God can deliver those who seek to serve their fellows from the subtle snare of self-importance. This setting of worship in its true place would provide the escape from the nemesis of salvation by works. Worship, I would argue, is an authentic and absolute attitude of the soul to God. Nothing can take its place. Worship in its essential nature is not simply a means of bringing nearer the kingdom of God, or creating the brotherhood of man. It is the final task and privilege of the Church, for it is the offering of praise and adoration from the creature to the Creator, from children to the Eternal Father. Yet let no one think that worship is an attitude of soul that is partial or leaves out any aspect of life. The idea of service as the fulfilment of God's Will grows out of and belongs to this fundamental attitude. The aim of the Church is to offer the worship of the whole creation and of all souls to God. When we say that worship is the final work of the Church we must ever remember that there is always something lacking in our offering to God if one soul, created by the Eternal Mercy and redeemed by the Eternal Love, lives in ignorance of that pity and grace, and one child of God suffers wrong or oppression. In order to fulfil her aim in worship the Church must strive for the evangelisation of the world, for the creation of human brotherhood, for the destruction of all oppression, for the discovery of all truth and for the creation of all beauty that redeems and makes precious mortal life. So far from worship being simply a means to a higher service, all service is but a means to the highest worship, so that, through the purification of all life from sin and evil, and by the illumination of all life with truth and beauty, there may be offered to God the adoration of the creatures of His Hand, and the Church's worship may be the Christ in man at one with the Christ Who sitteth and reigneth at God's Right Hand. Of this public worship is to be the prophecy, and of this the public service is to be the experience. I claim then for worship this central place in life, for worship is the experience of God in human life, the sense of the Eternal in time.

IV

Certain intellectual conclusions must be drawn if we believe in the primacy of worship. If communion with God through worship be the central fact of our existence, then we must think out the problem of the world from this centre. Those who have experienced the supreme fact of God's wonder and grace must ask for an interpretation of the world that does justice to this fact. Not a few thinkers to-day would dissolve the experience of worship into subjective moods, they would explain by psychological processes the communion with God, they would resolve the aspiration of hope and the certitude of faith into illusion. It is right to explain the process, but to explain away the fact is another matter. When we assert the experience of the Absolute as the Beatitude of adoration, and the experience of the Eternal as Grace revealed in time, we are also demanding a view of God and of the world that not only admits that this experience is possible, but recognises that it is primary. In worship there is at once the experience of God's kinship with man's highest nature, and of the Otherness of God, the experience of the likeness and the unlikeness of the Divine to the human. By no inference can we reach from man's life and from the mysterious processes in nature to the God Whom we worship. There is an immediate experience of the Absolute. Therefore we must start in our thinking not with man but with God. We must live in a world in which it is possible to know God if we take seriously the experience of worship. This is the first intellectual implicate of worship that we must begin from a theo-centric conception and not from an anthropo-centric.

If we would maintain the final worth of worship and the objectivity of God as given in worship, then the idea of God is not a postulate as Kant affirms. The great philosopher of Königsberg treats the idea of God as regulative, and affirms that the moral nature of man demands the postulate of God to make possible that nature. Despite the nobility of the Kantian morality the starting-point is anthropo-centric, and we never reach the objective God of worship. The trail which Kant blazed has been followed by the tradition of religious thought in the nineteenth century. Even the rich thought of Schleiermacher, while acknowledging the idea of God as central by making religion the feeling of absolute dependence upon God, yet treats worship almost exclusively from the human side. It is the expression of man's need and longing for the Divine. So too Ritschl and his followers, in rescuing spiritual life from the clutch of natural law, make use of the value judgment in such a way that God's existence seems to be derived from man's sense of values. It is an intellectual scepticism touched with emotion. Pragmatism has walked the same path. Sufficient justice has not been done to the fact of worship in which God is objectively experienced as the Wholly Other and as personal. Within the Reformed fold Barth and Brunner, and within the

Roman obedience Scheler, have attempted to re-state the communion of God with man from a standpoint that is theo-centric. It is not my task to discuss the work of these theologians, I only mention them to point out that this theo-centric basis is rendered necessary if the worshipful soul really occupies the fundamental attitude to life. We must become pre-Kantian in this respect if our thinking is to be obedient to what is given in worship, and if it is to provide an answer to the indictment that all worship is illusion. Unless worship be accepted as the authentic experience of God in human hearts, man is worshipping the creation of his own imagination, the satisfaction of his spiritual nature, the dream of his poetic fancy. Worship as the fundamental human experience demands a metaphysic which gives this fact central significance in its world view.

The second implication of the primacy of worship is epistemological. In worship there is given knowledge of God. Such is the testimony of the saints, of the great mystics, of the prophets, and of humble worshippers. This is not knowledge of created things and of their relation. It is knowledge intuitive, immediate, and direct. Knowledge it is wherein man is wholly receptive, for it is knowledge given and revealed by God. Man's reason is not creative but receptive of what is given; yet the cognitive side of man's nature has the power, not only of making deductions and passing judgments and forming abstract conceptions, but also of grasping the essence of things. This latter function of knowledge belongs to worship, for in worship man, through adoration, knows the unity and the harmony of all existence. This is not his discovery or his invention, but it is given by God. Only by this idea of the God Who reveals can we explain the experience of the Divine Unity in all kinds of religions and at such various levels of spiritual life. This sense of Divine Union is knowledge of the essence of things given by God to the soul freed from the chains of self. The harmony and union of God, and His creation, behind the fall and ruin of this world of time, is the gift of God to the adoring soul. This experience of worship seems well-nigh as wide as human life, and therefore this gift and revelation of God must be widespread. In this act of adoration the Transcendent God (or perchance the Absolute is conceived under the symbol of many Gods) becomes one with the Immanent God in the life of man. Worship, however, as we saw, has the other pole—God is not only Pure Being, the Home and Resting-place of all existence; God is also the Divine Will of Goodness and the Personal Lord. This is the unique revelation of Judaism which Christianity inherits and perfects. God's Personality is revealed in vivid actuality and arresting power. The Personal Spirit of God makes approach and speaks to man's personal spirit in worship. The God of Grace reveals in Christ the Mediator the path of redemption within this world of history and of time, whereby there is renewed the oneness of God and His fallen children who live in shadows. This is the fulfilment as well as the complement of the unitive experience of adoration. In its cognitive aspect the former experience of mystical adoration is the awareness of the pre-established harmony of all creation with God the Creator, the latter experience of God's Personality is the awareness of that Divine Grace that restores, through His activity in history, this harmony broken and destroyed in the world of time. Worship, if it be a reality, imparts intuitive knowledge, and there are these two intuitions given through the adoration of God's Being and through the sense of God's Grace.

The third implicate that follows from the place I have ascribed to worship concerns the relation between the spiritual and the material. "We never experience," says Professor Kemp Smith, "the Divine sheerly in and by itself; we experience the Divine solely through and in connexion with what is other than the Divine." We only know God through the means by which He reveals Himself. Since the world is God's creation, it is in its essence one in harmony. The confused welter of man's fallen state does not deny the fact of God's omnipotence. God's message of revelation came through the incarnation—the Word made flesh. Through the use of the facts of history and through the medium of things external to our spirits, the Presence of the Divine in worship shatters man's self-sufficiency and redeems human personality. In the sphere of devotion, where knowledge is of essences and not of causes, we may not divide that which God has made one, and we may not make the separation between the inner and the outer, the mental and the physical, the spiritual and the material. "What I have cleansed call not thou that unclean." For God's revelation of His Presence may come through sensible means or material objects or auditory sounds. The sharp antithesis of Descartes has no meaning in this realm. The world in which we live is alive with significance wherein the primrose by a river's brim can be more than a yellow primrose. The world in which we worship is a world incarnate with the Divine Spirit wherein a material thing like bread can be the symbol and the organ of the Divine Presence. If we would possess the freedom and spontaneity in thought that worship demands, we must transcend these distinctions which belong to the life of this day and which shackle the ascending spirit.

Perhaps we can draw a deduction from this third implication about the forms and objects used in worship. These means and methods, actions and gestures, belong not to Christianity but to all religions. Do we, therefore, reject them? Has the long search, wherein man shaped and chose and fashioned material objects and spoken forms for worship, been a bootless quest? Perchance it was not man's unguided impulse that through the long twilight of the coming morn sought these means, but a God-directed instinct that was over all this seeking. May it not be that there are forms, symbols, and actions given to us from the distant past as from the hand of God? May it not be well that the assured modern spirit has to learn the discipline of humility through using in its approach to the Infinite Being that which God has appointed in the course of history?

CHAPTER II

WORSHIP—PSYCHOLOGICAL FACTORS

THE goal of worship, we have seen, is communion of the soul with God. The aim of corporate worship ought to be communion with God through the sense-object, which is at once the expression of the soul's experience and the means whereby through the widening and the heightening of this experience there is community in adoration and in petition, and thereby a collective offering of worship is made. This somewhat psychological definition is our starting-point and it raises two questions which concern us in this lecture. What are the instincts, sentiments, emotions, and ideas that belong to the experience of worship? And what are the influences by means of which common worship widens and heightens individual devotion? Before we can consider the architecture of the Divine Service we must glance at the bricks with which the structure must be built. Man must needs use the things of man in fashioning his meeting-place with the Eternal, and we believe that God approaches man through the powers and faculties of human nature. The Spirit of God uses natural means in its contact with the human spirit. We must therefore direct our attention to the psychological side of our subject. This by no means implies that we accept the decision of the psychologist as to the meaning and the value of our devotion. "Psychology," says Flournoy, "neither rejects nor affirms the transcendental existence of the religious object; it simply ignores that problem as being outside of its field." Unfortunately not all psychologists have been obedient to this wise maxim. Not infrequently the psychologist is prone to magnify his office and to pronounce judgment upon issues which do not fall within his sphere.

Two facts must be borne in mind in all psychological discussions of worship. The first is that nothing is explained by explaining it as something that it is not. Worship like art cannot be explained away by a psychological description of what takes place in the mind of the worshipper or of the artist. The question of an objective experience of God in worship can neither be demonstrated nor disproved by psychological methods. The second is that the origin of a thing does not account for its value. The source of a rite or of a ceremony does not give us its worth and its meaning.

I

Our first query is, What is the content of this experience of worship? In order to know the content we must interrogate the types of the cultus. We must begin, however, by distinguishing between what is worship and what is not worship. What is the difference between the religious rite and the magical spell? In external form they may be alike. The same words or the identical action may be a magical performance or the outpouring of a heart awed before the Mystery of Being. The mood of him who takes part is the differentiating thing. Magic and religion both deal with the supernatural, but they deal differently with it. Magic seeks to manipulate it, religious worship is awed before it. Religion implies a reference to higher beings, magic does not. "I suggest," writes Dr. McDougall,[1] "that the fundamental distinction between religious and magical practices is not, as is sometimes said, that religion conceives the power it envisages as personal powers while magic conceives them as impersonal; but rather that the religious attitude is always that of submission, the magical attitude that of self-assertion, and that the forces which both magical and religious practices are concerned to influence may be conceived in either case as personal or impersonal powers. Hence the savage who at one time bows down before his fetish in supplication and at another seeks to compel its assistance by threats and spells adopts towards the one object alternately the religious and the magical attitude." We cannot derive the religious practice of worship from the magical spell.

In the *Golden Bough* Dr. Frazer propounds the theory that an

[1] *Social Psychology*, McDougall, p. 263.

age of magic precedes the age of religion; because the spells of the magician did not work, men took to supplication. Magic seeks to coerce and constrain the Power, while religion seeks to conciliate and propitiate. "All conciliation implies that the being conciliated is a conscious and personal agent, that his conduct is in some measure uncertain, and that he can be prevailed upon to vary it in the desired direction by a judicious appeal to his interests, his appetites, and his emotions."[1] It is difficult to see how religious worship which rests on the feeling of dependence could ever develop from the baffled effort of the sorcerer. Precisely what is the most characteristic thing in religious worship—the emotion of awe—is missed out. Dr. Marett (*Threshold of Religion*) argues that we have the stage in which there is the indefinite sense of awe, and from this primitive emotion can develop a religious aspiration with its appropriate cultus, or there can result magical fear with its accompanying spells. These both alike deal with "mana," which is the unseen power possessed by certain objects, animals, or persons; and with "tabu," which points out that these objects, endowed with this uncanny power, are perilous to the unwary. The idea of "mana" bears originally the stamp of religious awe, but it can readily deteriorate into magic. Because of this fact Söderblom says that magic implies religion.

Another distinction made between the magical spell and the religious observance is that the former is anti-social and private and the latter is ever the concern of the community and social in aspect.[2] Certain magical practices do come to have an anti-social character, but that is because they are in opposition to an accepted higher standard or outlook. The sorcerer's deed is anti-social whereby he casts the spell of death upon his foe by stabbing his image, but the early drawings which represent creatures of the chase as smitten by arrows are probably a magical charm which certainly cannot be called anti-social, for the clan's supply of food is certainly no private interest. This distinction then, while true of the developed magical rite and of the religious cult, is not the

[1] *Golden Bough*, Frazer, pp. 54–55.

[2] Cf. Robertson Smith, *Religion of Semites*, p. 264; Durkheim, *Elementary Forms of Religious Life*, p. 43 f.

fundamental distinction. None the less it makes us observe a valuable truth that religious worship is in its origin always communal and social.

It is necessary to hold in our mind clearly the distinction between magic and religion. The former is an act with a limited technique which asserts man's power; the latter "has no such simple technique. Its power rests not on the uniformity of its rite but on the function it fulfils."[1] I have emphasised this fundamental distinction between the magical rite and the religious observance, because there are points of contact between magic and religion. They both imply a belief in a realm of unseen powers that are more than human, they both have an attitude of mind that is open to the miraculous, they both employ rites and forms. "Both," writes Dr. Marett,[2] "stir the soul by playing on the life-and-death motif; but whereas the priest seeks to intensify the life-feeling, the sorcerer's object is to intensify the death-feeling."

This contact of magic and religion has provided the channels whereby magical influences can flow into the ritual of worship. These influences are three in number. (1) The first is the assertion of human power. In the Old Testament legend Joshua exercises a magical spell when he bids the sun stay its course. In the belief that the service of the Mass can ensure certain results, or that a multitude of prayers can enforce the Will of God, there is something of the assertion of human power that is the attribute of magic. Some of the expressions we find in Luther's prayers suggest a strange assertiveness that savours of human dictation rather than religious submission. For example, "Grant me my prayer, Thou must grant it." "Do not provoke us to extremes; if Thou move us to anger so that we withhold our reverence tithes, what will become of Thee?" "We must compel God to come; we must force Him to grant our wishes with stern and hostile siege." Such expressions belong not to the sphere of religious devotion.

(2) The second influence is the idolatrous tendency. Material objects are endowed with "mana" or the power of the unseen. The object is thought of not as the vehicle of the invisible power

[1] Malinowski, *Science, Religion, and Reality*, p. 81.
[2] Marett, *Faith, Hope, and Charity in Private Religion*, p. 44.

but as possessing this power like a charm. Then we have the idol. Relics of the saints can become a fetish, the consecrated element is supposed to have the power in itself of working wonders, to carry a Bible is considered a guarantee of safety. Worship has been lowered at times by this downward pull that turns the medium of devotion into an idol and the spoken word into a spell.

(3) The third influence is mechanical in character. Magical rites are performed and no emotion need accompany them. As long as the right things are done the desired results will be obtained. A service may become a mechanical routine, the cultus becomes an *opus operatum*, and it is assumed that it acts automatically for man's benefit without any emotion or thought. Such a superstitious outlook has resulted from the magic that dies slowly in the heart of man.

I would now ask the question—What are the psychological elements at the basis of worship? McDougall [1] mentions these three emotions, admiration, awe, and reverence, and gives this further analysis. Admiration is a complex state and is resolved into two primary emotions, wonder and negative self-feeling, or the emotion of submission. "Wonder is revealed by the impulse to approach and to continue to contemplate the desired object." Negative self-feeling is awareness of the presence of some being superior to us. When fear unites with admiration the result is the emotion of awe, and when the tender feeling blends with awe we have reverence. McDougall denies that there is such a thing as a special religious instinct, and would repudiate Otto's theory of the sense of the Holy as primary. It is not my task to discuss the origin of the religious emotion, but we are concerned with the emotions which are the material of the spirit of worship. Otto certainly gives a more decided place to the overwhelming of the worshipper by awe than McDougall's discussion appears to allow. The tender feeling, fear, wonder (in the sense of the word as given above), and the negative feeling are the instinctive basis of the worshipful mood according to this investigation. We shall note how the tender feeling which is also expressed in the relation between parent and child, or husband and wife, the negative self-

[1] *Social Psychology*, p. 260.

feeling before a greater, wonder which attracts, fear which repels or renders motionless, all come to the surface within the historic forms of religious worship. Such an analysis gives the ingredients of devotion, but by no means their relation to one another; it provides the material of the building but gives no information about its architectural design.

Let us now step further afield in order to observe how the historic types of worship have utilised their psychological basis, and to note the instincts, sentiments, emotions, and ideas which enter into the pattern of each of these worships. This is not, I would observe, an unnecessary pursuit, for if our liturgy of worship is to be full and satisfy it must find room for these instinctive emotions within it, and if the order of our service is to be rich and significant we must arrange them in due subordination to its design. With this psychological aim in mind let us look at the three types of worship we have referred to in an earlier chapter.

(1) The first of these is Sacrifice. This widespread rite belongs to early religion and in its development has taken many forms and expressed diverse meanings. It is not my task to describe the various forms of the sacrificial system, and still less is it my purpose to give a rationale of this institution. All I endeavour is the humbler aim of noting the psychological aspect of this mode of worship. The idea of sacrifice has been the main channel through which the psychology of magic flowed into the current of religious emotion, for the offering of sacrifice admits of a magical as well as of a religious interpretation. In its essence the institution of sacrifice appears to be a means whereby new life or fresh power is given or received. The root idea would appear to be a communion or participation of the worshipper with the unseen powers made possible through this act whereby new energy is created. The sacrificial act can have three results. Firstly, it may give fresh life to the unseen forces that control mortal existence, or secondly a new power may be received by the mortal participants to overcome the hazard of living and the fatality of death and to protect them from evil influences, or thirdly a relation may be created between the worshipper and the Being worshipped wherein there is intercourse between this natural life and supernatural

existence. From this original idea the manifold forms of this rite appear to have developed. Sacrifice as a gift or offering to the lord of the soil comes later, and the sacrifice of expiation is also a later growth from this original root. This element of communion belongs to the early beginning of this rite whether its origin be traced to an analogy with the cult of the dead who desire and need sustenance, or to the flow of mysterious power between the divine and the human through the mediation of the sacrifice offered which possesses "mana." The common meal of the clan at which the flesh of the slaughtered beast is eaten is a sacrificial meal, for through absorbing this mystical substance the life power is renewed and enhanced. Sacrifice thus strengthens the bond between man and the deity, and adumbrates a sense of kinship with the divine.

In the legendary story told us in Genesis about Cain and Abel, two forms of sacrifice are mentioned. Animal sacrifice which involves the shedding of blood is one form. The essential aspect in this, however, is not the slaughter of the creature but the giving of new life. The blood, which is the symbol not of death but of life, is poured forth. The second form is the offering of the fruits of the earth. In its developed forms this can express the sentiment of gratitude and the covenant of loyalty, but in its origin this sacrifice is derived from the fertility motive. This is the sacrifice of the agricultural community whose existence is bound up with the earth's fertility and with animal procreation, as animal sacrifice originates in the stage when man's life was dependent upon hunting. I need not pause to point out after what has been said how easily the institution of the sacrifice can become a vehicle of magic or superstition. But when the spirit of religious worship interprets the sacrificial system in its variegated forms we discern not a few religious instincts, sentiments, and ideas. The mood of communion, the feeling of fellowship and kinship with the unseen, the impulse of thanksgiving, the sense of offering, the emotion of awe hanging like a cloud over the whole act, the expiation of sin of which sacrifice is sometimes the figure and sometimes the instrument, the affirmation of the covenant between the divine and the human, the aspiration of adoration expressed in the longing for new life, these are all voiced through this institution and all are part of Christian worship. It is also true that in the rite of sacrifice are found the slavish desire to placate the jealousy of the gods, the idea that the performance of the sacrifice is a mechanical contrivance for winning the favour of the divine, the feeling that the divine is dependent upon man's action, and the spirit of barter wherein God or the gods make a return to man for his offering; and these magical interpretations have sometimes crept into the worship of the Christian Church.

(2) The second of these types is the Mystery Drama. In origin this is derived from the religious dance, for the mood of religious exaltation demanded expression in action. "My own view," says Dr. Marett, "is that savage religion is not so much something thought out as danced out." The influence of "mana" has effect in this sphere as in that of sacrifice, and this common element can make sacrifice a part of the mystery drama. The origin of the mystery cults goes back to that early age when primitive man represented the mysterious processes of birth, life, and death by ritual acts. In historic times we find the developed cult which with great variety in detail and emphasis repeats on a higher spiritual level the same strain. It would not further our aim to dwell on the distinctions between the Eleusinian Mysteries, the orgiastic Dionysiac Ritual, Orphism, Mithraism, and other Eastern Mysteries. They all make in different degree the same appeal. Firstly, man is lifted out of his helplessness and infused with a new energy by the sense of power which comes through union with the divine hero. The might of death and the menace of life are overcome by the identification of the soul with the god whose power becomes the possession of the worshipper. He who is initiate becomes a "God instead of mortal." "I am a child of Earth and Starry Heaven, but my race is of Heaven" is the language of Orphic devotion.[1] The strength of the immortal belongs to the devotee. This sense of power through worship is a feature Christianity shares with the Mystery Religion.

Secondly, there is the myth which is figured in the ceremonial acts. This is the interpretation of the action; but as Professor Malinowski has remarked, "It is not an explanation in satisfaction

[1] Angus, *The Mystery Religions and Christianity*, p. 110.

of a scientific interest but a narrative resurrection of a primeval reality told in satisfaction of deep religious wants, moral cravings, social submissions, assertions, and even practical requirements." The myth then, as the explanation of the emotional mood, is capable of variety and development whereby even a new meaning may be given and a fresh function attached to the acts performed. This too continues in the worship of the Church. The Christian too has his myth, which is represented in his worship. The Christ Who is the ascended and victorious Lord has tasted death and had communion with mortal weakness, and His experience is recounted in the Eucharistic service. The vital distinction between the pagan myth and the Christian myth is that the former spiritualises the mysterious operations of Nature, the latter interprets historical events.

Thirdly, there is the Vision and the ensuing experience of bliss. The old superstition that no man can see God and live is repudiated. By his initiation there comes to the worshipper directly or indirectly the vision and the state of blessedness. The rapt ecstasy of the devotee may break out in many ways. The mystic of all ages, Christian or otherwise, has kinship with this mood. The emotionalism of the revival meeting is working with the same psychological material as the ancient rites. The identification of the soul with the Deity means the loss of the sense of self; and this escape from self and the note of joy belong to Christian liturgy as they did to the worship of the ancient mystic. "Worship," says Professor A. E. Taylor,[1] "is possible only when one can forget oneself and one's inferiority. It is this which gives its character of free and joyous abandon; all worship is at heart an incipient *jubilus*." The vision of the uplifted Lord is also a psychological fact. "Thou shalt see a youthful god lovely in form with red locks wearing a white tunic and scarlet mantle and holding a bright crown" are words from the so-called liturgy of Mithra.[2] In the Armenian liturgy the Deacon on certain festivals addresses the worshippers in these terms: "Ye who with faith stand before the holy, royal table see the King Christ sitting and surrounded with

[1] *The Faith of a Moralist*, vol. i. p. 310.
[2] Quoted by Angus, *The Mystery Religions and Christianity*, p. 136.

the heavenly hosts."[1] The same psychological experience is referred to in both cases. In this type of worship we find the fourfold appeal to human nature—to its helplessness, to its dramatic sense, to its need of knowledge, and to its yearning for blessedness; and there is the promise that one and all shall be satisfied.

The communion with the Divine which is offered through the institution of sacrifice and the drama of the Divine in human life is reached by external means which are based on three psychological impulses in man. (*a*) The first is communion through blood, the seat of life. Through the sight and touch of the sacred blood the devotee is taken out of his little circumscribed life into a selfless sea of emotion. Each mystery has its characteristic sacrifice, and the axis on which the rite turns is the life-and-death motif. The yearning in man that was satisfied by this mode of seeking communion lives on in evangelical hymn and in the ceremonial of the Eucharist. It has suffered "a sea change into something rich and strange," but it is psychologically the same desire to escape.

(*b*) Secondly, there is communion through the sex instinct. The fertility ritual made use of sexual intercourse as a means of union with the deity. The terminology lives on long after the primitive practice has disappeared. The language of marriage is used of the relation between the soul and God. The mystics of every clime and age have made use of this symbolism. St. Bernard of Clairvaux emphasised this. "Who is the bride? it is the soul thirsting for God." The language of mystical devotion is full of the language of human love. The symbol of marriage is used in the Old Testament, but there is this significant difference that the bride or wife is not the individual soul but the community. St. Paul too applies the figure of marriage to the relation between Christ and His Church. It is not strange that metaphors for spiritual devotion should be borrowed from the fact of marriage. But must we not go further than this? Do we not see here the sublimation of a primitive instinct? Leuba has sought to make the sex instinct the basis of mystical devotion, and has, in my opinion, gravely overstated his case. This much, however, I feel compelled to admit, that in such devotion the energy this instinct

[1] Brightman, *Liturgies, Eastern and Western*, p. 434.

awakens has been turned into the channel not of self-gratification but of spiritual experience.

(*c*) Thirdly, there is communion through the mystical meal. The sacramental banquet plays its part in the mystery, though precisely how the participant was united with the deity is not quite clear. The god is at times the host, at times the guest. "Chæremon invites you to dine at the table of the Lord Serapis to-morrow." Religion makes use of the common meal for the purpose of worship, and the centre of Christian devotion is the common meal that celebrates the Lord's victory. The association of this appetite with a religious ritual is significant and the unitive experience is nourished thereby. "To eat and to be eaten," says Ruysbroeck, "this is union." The association of the act of eating with devotion has not been accidental. We thus see how in these modes of seeking communion there is a religious aspiration which makes use of three primitive instincts. The fear and shudder caused by the sight of blood are made the means of emancipating the soul; the force and warmth of the sex impulse are used as steps by the ascending soul; the hunger instinct symbolises the soul's longing, and the satisfaction of that instinct mirrors the soul's peace.

(3) The third type of worship is the Oracle. Here speech is the medium, the God speaks and man listens. The Voice coming from the crashing storm, or from the wind among the trees, or from some holy place, or sounding within the heart, demands the hearing ear. The auditory sense implies the distinction between the speaker and the hearer. The communion therefore which is the culmination of this type of worship is not the communion wrought through sacrifice—a bond between God and man by means of a material object; nor the communion achieved through the mystery type—a union of God and man through illumination and emotion, so that selfhood disappears; but it is a communion between two persons and between two wills, the divine and the human. Man does not identify himself with God but he hears the voice spoken to him. Speech is the means of human communication, and, when this method is applied to the unseen, God to the believer becomes personal. Before the face of God man stands to hear His voice and do His bidding. Not here is mystical absorption, for man is vividly

conscious of himself as before his Lord and Master. We find fragments of this type in many places and the use of it quite definitely in Zoroastrianism, but its peculiar and characteristic manifestation is in the life of Israel and through the inspiration of her prophets. Amos, Hosea, Isaiah, Jeremiah differ in the accent of their message and in their spiritual temperament, but they are at one in this, that their attitude of religious communion is that of listening to God's word and obediently following it. The psychology of the prophetic spirit is the passive reception of the Divine word whether it be received in trance or in vision or otherwise. The distinction between God and man is kept marked in this worship because it is offered in the sphere of volition. Its culmination is not union of nature but unity of will. Fundamentally this type of worship is volitional rather than emotional. It is, in the phrase of Heiler, personality-affirming. From the psychological point of view we find in this type of worship a sense of submission to the Divine authority which may be the spiritual obedience of a personal will or may degenerate into a legal observance of the letter, an affirmation of personality which may be the consecration of a living soul to the task of God or may be degraded into a self-assertion that makes havoc of humility, a sense of assurance that may be a whole-hearted reliance upon Divine succour or may descend to an individualistic self-centredness. This type of worship has an ego-centric aspect as well as a theo-centric. Its emphasis is on the power and will of God rather than on His nature and being. As the sentiment of desire was characteristic of the Mystery worship, so the sentiment of security pertains to this type. It is obvious how the idea of the word spoken by God and the thought of the listening heart of man are an essential part of the Church's devotion.

II

From what we have seen it is apparent that all sides of man's nature enter into an act of worship. Feeling, will, cognition are all constituents of the historic forms. Worship is an attitude to the Whole which involves the total personality of man and all his faculties are concerned in this experience. Let us see how. Firstly, emotion has been taken by some to be the sole factor in the worshipful act. This mistake is made because the presence of emotion is not only essential to worship but pervasive of the whole consciousness. To worship is something other than to think, and only in an experience emotionally heightened above the converse of the ordinary can there be Divine communion. There is the emotional accompaniment of the " awareness " of the Beyond. Fear, reverence, ardent love may be the emotions concerned. Feeling, however, is not only the response to this awareness ; it can also be the medium of the awareness. Emotion is the effect of contact with the Beyond, but it is also the means through which man knows that he is before the Divine. In the former case we have the process which we termed the descending rhythm of worship ; in the latter the process which was called the ascending rhythm. In the former the sense of God gives rise to the emotions of awe and gratitude ; in the latter through the presence of awe and gratitude which the aspiring mood kindles in the heart of the worshipper there falls upon the soul a realisation of God. The one belongs primarily to " prophetic piety," the other to " mystical devotion." Feeling also is associated with every act in worship. It envelops the beliefs and faith of the worshipping with an emotional atmosphere changing them from abstractions into vital things. Feeling also surrounds the acquiescence of the will and colours its acts with an emotional significance.

Secondly, volition has its place in worship. The will is turned to action in two ways. (1) The directing of the attention to God and setting of the Divine before the mind is not in itself worship, but it is the prelude to it. The Divine must be made present or actual and this can only come to pass through a volitional process. With such a strength does the sense of Divine and Superhuman break into our self-conscious life that the will appears to be overpowered ; yet a closer survey reveals that the mystical experience of flooding power and of all-embracing unity is the result of the will consenting to this Presence. (2) We also find the movement of the will in the activity that is roused. This activity may use some external rite or observance such as sacrifice or the recital of sacred words ; it may express itself in spontaneous prayer or the offering of a vow of consecration. Even in those who would never acknowledge that they had ever consciously bowed their head to the Unseen or knelt before the altar of the Eternal, when the mind is unshackled from the daily round and when there breathes the presence that disturbs with the joy of elevated thoughts, and a sense sublime of something beyond and yet within them overshadows, part of this experience is the activity of will. Wordsworth is a true recorder of the inner life when he relates in the " Prelude " how the still wonder of form and the mystery of existence broke upon his youthful soul. " My heart was full ; I made no vows, but vows were made for me ; bond unknown to me was given that I should be else sinning greatly a dedicated spirit." The will is thus concerned in this experience of worship and the activity of the will will seek its expression in the liturgy of devotion.

Thirdly, there is the activity of thought which reveals itself in two ways. (1) In the sense of Divine awareness there is this activity although the experience is immediate and comes directly without the conscious intervention of the cognitive process. Such intuitive knowledge may be inarticulate, the worshipper being unable to find words in which to convey what he has received. It may seem but a new light on common things, but it belongs to the sphere of cognition. Experts in the sphere of worship like the great mystics have ever insisted on the " noietic " element in their revelations. Not seldom what they tell us about the knowledge they receive seems slight and little worth, but the acquisition of new knowledge though intuitive is to them an assured certainty. This state of awareness may be indefinite in which there is only a vague and veiled Presence, or definite in which there is a firmly conceived Personality, but in worship there must always be an Object of worship whether the image or conception of the Object be shadowy or clear. (2) There is also what the myth stands for. Beliefs, articles of faith, seek to interpret the experience of awareness. The story of God's relation to man is recounted in dramatic form whether as the Immanent God in the processes of Nature or the Transcendent God in touch with human personality in history. The interpretation of humanity's communion with God belongs as a real part to our experience of the Divine.

If worship be the response of man's whole nature to God, we must not only consider the conscious response of the worshipper. For man is not only a conscious mind; he possesses also a subconscious mind. How is the subconscious related to worship? There are those who would discover in the subconscious the whole explanation of worship. Worship would then be a psychological process whose *raison d'être* lay in its usefulness to man. "Mankind," says Jung, "wishes to love in God only their own ideas—that is to say, the ideas which they project into God. By that they wish to love their unconscious, that is, that remnant of ancient humanity and the centuries-old past in all people . . . but in loving their inheritance they love that which is common to all. Thus they turn back to the mother of humanity, that is, to the spirit of the race, and regain in this way something of that connection and of that mysterious and irresistible power which is imparted by the feeling of belonging to the herd." I do not propose to discuss the explanations Freud, Jung, and Adler would give of the experience of worship. I do not feel that any light is cast by them on the question of the communion of God with man in worship, for they deal only with the operations of man's mind. The experience of worship is a revelation in which the objectivity of God is given. On the other hand, value attaches to the work of these psychologists in forcing attention upon the fact of the subconscious and the part it plays in worship. It is true, as Jung says, that individuals differ widely in the content of their consciousness, but in their unconscious they are closely alike. A power does work in the unconscious that moulds and at times sways the conscious. "God is to be considered as the representative of a certain sum of energy," is one of Jung's dicta. If we take seriously the belief in the immanence of God and if the Incarnation be one of the main doctrines of the faith, could we not reverse Jung's statement and say a certain sum of energy is to be interpreted as the action of God? We believe that man lives and has his being in God, and therefore God has relation to man's unconscious life as well as to his conscious.

We have thus to reckon with the unconscious in the make-up of the worshipper. There are three fundamental mechanisms of the psychosis whose influence has to be noted in this sphere. These are transference, introversion, and equivalence. Transference is the means of escape from the complex to reality. By this our subconscious minds are freed from bondage and are delivered from a state " cabined, cribbed, confined," into the open spaces of the soul. Introversion is the " means of detaching oneself from reality through the complex." Our subconscious is lifted up out of the grip of the actual and rescued from the domain of mortal things by means of the " emotionally tinged ideas repressed partially or entirely, which is called a complex." Equivalence means that the activity of the unconscious tends to balance the activity of the conscious. What is thrust out of consciousness is found in the unconscious, but even more significant for us is the fact that whatever is found in consciousness has its opposite in the subconscious as an equivalent or counterpoise. Note what happens if the subconscious be ignored. It becomes restless in its dissatisfaction and dominates consciousness. These mental conditions cannot be neglected in a scheme of worship.

Let me give three illustrations. (1) Worship has been called simply auto-erotic—a falling in love with oneself. This has been termed the Narcissus state. Such of course is not worship at all, but it may look very like it. A person has this complex of self-love and the sphere of worship may be the sphere in which this complex works. He displays himself spiritually and feels the assurance of being a special favourite of the Divine Grace. He imagines that he is worshipping but all the while he is simply regarding himself with interest and with devotion. It is the task of true worship to break down this complex, and very definite means must be provided so as to allow the Spirit of God to do so. The self must be brought into the experience of worship, and either the sense of its own importance eliminated before the awful presence of Eternal God, or it must be so identified with Christ as its own reality that the distinction which St. Paul felt between Christ in me and the weak human self is recognised.

(2) Again, it has been asserted that the acts and attitudes of worship are simply the exercises of the infantile mind. So it may be if worship be misused. Undoubtedly the attitude of man to God in devotion ought to be that of a trustful child; it is the

prerogative of a religious service to make men feel this great fact. But worship may be so misapplied that an infantile outlook towards life is created. Some worshippers make worship not an escape from the limitations of their circumstances in order to find strength, but an escape from the difficulties and duties of life in order to live in a world of fancy. This introversion must be checked by the sense of God's reality and His relation to life. One of the functions of the Christian service is to prevent this infantile attitude and to correct it if it should exist.

(3) Thirdly, there may be involved in worship a father complex. The statement of the new psychology that God is a father complex is so far true that most of our ideas of God are gathered from our fathers. But something that our fathers could not give, worship gives in the present reality of God. This father complex, however, which is the morbid fear living on in the subconscious, can have two consequences. The first is a neurotic outlook which the act of worship has to correct. If we recall the law of equivalence, then we see that the emphasis upon the awe and the mystery of God in the conscious will cause in the subconscious its equivalent, and destroy the power of the hidden fear. Or secondly, the father complex can cause in the conscious the projection of buried fears and the God Who is worshipped becomes a being of dread. Here the remedy lies in escape from this gripping complex of fear through transference into the real experience of God that is in Christ.

Of what does this subconscious consist ? There are three constituents. (1) What is not attended to. The concentration of living pushes out of the focus of consciousness much of man's life. Ambitious effort, moral striving, the search for purity, the task of winning one's daily bread, sympathy with the tears of humanity, the ascent of the Hill Beautiful and the winning of joy's crown, drive below the surface their opposites. " Clearly," says Professor Hocking, " whatever tightens the strain of conscious attention will increase the burden of the unconscious. To live strenuously means to create in the subconscious the equivalent." (2) What is repressed. All that our conscious and ethical outlook has outgrown is huddled beneath the surface. The ancient memories of the race, the impulses from primeval days, the lust of blood, the call of sex, are repressed by the moral censor. So in the affairs of every day we are ever thrusting down feelings of jealousy and of envy, impulses of passion and of anger; the primitive bodily instincts that conscience and convention banish from the light of day live on in this dark cavern. (3) What is growing but not grown. All the new buddings of thought and the bright dreams of the ideal that have not yet blossomed in the conscious life are inhabitants of this underworld of instinct. The unborn aims and the unformed ideals lie concealed from sight in this womb.

Now if worship is to "minister to a mind diseased, pluck from the memory a rooted sorrow," it must provide the appropriate relief to the subconscious so as to cleanse it of "that perilous stuff that weighs upon the heart." The relief must be of such a nature that it appeals to conscious and subconscious alike, and provides a common object in which both may rest. As there are three elements in the subconscious, so there are three ways of relief.

(1) In our natural life there is the relief of sleep, "nature's kind nurse," that rests the conscious from concentrated attention and frees the subconscious from tension. So worship must give the spiritual equivalent of physical sleep. The mystics knew this in their "sleep of the powers" or the "prayer of union" (St. Theresa), and in the elevation of St. Catherine of Genoa. But repose of spirit is not a prerogative of highly developed mysticism; it belongs to the devotion of ordinary folk. The striving of the soul is at an end and the spirit rests in God. As this delivers the mind from its anxieties and gives repose to the attention stretched like a bow through concentration, so it frees the subconscious from enforced inactivity, restless discontent, and strained tension, and leaves it open to the suggestion of the Divine Presence. We need to provide in worship through silence and through symbolism an opportunity for this repose of spirit that refreshes the conscious and frees the subconscious. Psychologically stated, the cure for concentration is relaxation, and by this lowering of pressure the sense of the Infinite can be experienced. "To sleep," says Bergson, "is to be disinterested." The quality of disinterestedness pertains to the repose of the worshipful spirit. The aims and goals of our striving fall away and the peace of the eternal is ours. In our

natural life sleep does not destroy consciousness but it brings us into a state whereby the conscious and the subconscious are concerned with the same object. For in the state of sleep the individual self and all the outer world whose claims and duties separate the conscious from the subconscious are excluded. So by the rest of the spirit in worship our consciousness is not abolished, but it is divorced from the distraction of self and the world's concern. The conscious and the subconscious are turned to the same object—the presence of God ; and because we no longer seek to control our mind and heart by conscious effort, the subconscious is also freed and able to be directed by the Divine Presence.

(2) The second relief is for what is repressed. This means of relief consists in heightened feeling and increased activity. The natural remedy for repression is expression, and in our earthly life recreation and play, the joys and the emotions of the arts, are the remedy through which the repressed instinct finds rest for itself. In worship also the repressed must find utterance. The imprisoned energy escapes the prison-house. This energy may have physical associations of savage instinct and of sex passion, but in its captivity it awaits liberation. When I recite the great words of the Creed " descended into hell," I feel that the experience of worship casts a new meaning on this phrase. Within man pent up and writhing are powers and impulses awaiting a deliverer. They are rightly imprisoned by the law of the ethical and conscious life. It is the experience of worship that furnishes the deliverance. They do not escape as lawless madness which no man can tame, but their energy is freed in the outpouring of Christian devotion. This energy of illicit passion and primitive savagery is made use of by the spirit of God in Christ. In the language of psychology this is termed sublimation. In the experience of worship this is known as communion. Here too the conscious and the subconscious must find a common object that stimulates and inspires. No object or interest is there in this natural life that can unite the ethical conscious with the primitive subconscious. It must be an object from beyond the bourne of time and space. Such an object is the Divine Presence revealed to the conscious as God in Christ and felt by the subconscious as the immanent power which is the

source of all existence. I would therefore criticise our modern church service as being far too tame and decorous. Sufficient opportunity is not given either in the kind of exultant praise or in the dramatic use of symbol for that heightened activity and intense feeling which are the occasion of the deliverance of the subconscious from its bonds. Not thus did the early Church offer her worship tingling with emotion and glowing with spiritual colour. We go to worship afraid of being moved and taken out of ourselves and we miss the exultation when the chains are loosed and all the hidden forces of man's life are redeemed in the pæan of praise or in the exuberance of emotional symbolism. "Unless," says Hocking,[1] "the characteristic of pleasure that is of wholly spontaneous and original conviction of worth enters into worship . . . worship is to that extent a failure."

(3) The subconscious also contains, as we saw, the undeveloped dreams and ideals that have not yet emerged into consciousness. Much in the ordinary churchgoer exists in this ghostly state and has not yet been born to life. These fragmentary ideals and this fleeting vision of the common man are ofttimes at war with his accepted code and conventional moral standard. Sometimes in the subconscious life lie concealed richer values and a more precious heritage than he is consciously aware of. The remedy for this is found when the discovery of what is there is made. Then "like some watcher of the skies when a new planet swims into his ken" there comes the thrill of a new truth born into the soul. This happens in the life of the artist when the gropings of his spirit find expression in a fresh vision and a new creation of beauty. So also in the experience of falling in love the sleeping dreams and dormant desires which nestled in the subconscious bound into the light of day. In the same way in worship there needs to be a remedy for this separation between the conscious and the subconscious. The unformed thought that gropes in the dark, the veiled desire, the unconscious longing for purity and peace, the hidden hunger for God and the unrecognised passion for reality surge into consciousness beneath the quickening experience of worship, for they find in this realm a power which gives them birth and in which their

[1] *The Meaning of God in Human Experience*, p. 422.

goal is fulfilled. Here too worship ministers to the subconscious, and a service must be so planned that by the use of word, symbol, action, and silence opportunity is provided for the emergence into conscious reality of the immature dreams within the subconscious. It is the Presence of God in Christ that satisfies and fulfils these hidden desires, and so the presence of Christ ought to be recognised by action and attitude as well as by visible form and speech.

(4) There is one other remedy for the disharmony between the conscious and the subconscious. Conscious control is sometimes possible, and then the remedy is not along the line of instinct but of conscious thought and will. " A timely utterance gave my heart relief." The submerged thing may be brought into consciousness just as it is. This can happen when an idea at once attracts and masters the conscious and the subconscious. The experience of confession is an example of this. The hidden sin is tracked to its lair and acknowledged by the conscious mind. The sin has been so neglected by consciousness that it is forgotten. Confession before the Judge of all flesh when a penetrative sincerity opens the eyes to see the concealed sin and strengthens the will to hold it in the light of conscience, is the remedy for this disharmony in the life of man. This insight is the gift only of the soul bowed before the Eternal Spirit, and the sense of man's creatureliness precedes the discovery of what he has to acknowledge. The sense of Divine forgiveness it is that restores to unity the life thus divided, and the pardon of God makes the fragmentary, split consciousness a whole. This involves that a service must provide opportunity for the silent discovery of what there is to confess, and also, I think, points to the spoken declaration of God's forgiveness in a formula of absolution.

III

The subject of the unconscious leads us to the second question—What are the influences through which public worship widens and heightens individual devotion ? We have seen that there is a greater likeness between the subconscious of people than there is between the conscious. Differences of taste, outlook, culture, mental power, art sense, and ethical insight are prominent in the conscious, but the subconscious in which race memory survives and primitive instincts abide is much more homogeneous. What therefore appeals to the subconscious and sublimates its energy creates an instinctive basis of unity. Since there is a likeness between the subconscious mind of all the worshippers, and since there is even an identity between the instincts that are hidden in the minds of all, there is the foundation for a common emotional experience. Contact in worship with others is felt by some as a quite positive thing drawing them out of the reticence of convention and creating a common temper. But whether felt or not, this influence of others is there. For example, the elevation of the host in the Mass gives a more overwhelming sense of the stupendous mystery because others are responding with their subconscious mind as well as with their conscious to this psychologically wonderful piece of ceremony. The evidence of revival meetings demonstrates that the influence of others working in the region of the subconscious is very real. Psychology recognises the existence of the group mind, and a company of worshippers is certainly a group.

Let us glance at the group mind, and to do so let us begin with the simplest form of group. A crowd is a group brought together by the accident of time and of space. Its temper is not the temper of the individuals who compose it. A crowd can be far more emotional than any member of it. It can do deeds of cruelty of which no single person in the crowd would approve, and it can have impulses of generosity that transcend the generosity of any of its members. The qualities of the crowd are not then the sum of the qualities of the individuals who compose it. "What really takes place," writes Le Bon,[1] "is a combination followed by the creation of new characteristics." The creation of new characteristics through human contact has significance for communal worship. There is an overplus. "I have sometimes wondered whether if we were able to think this out we might find here some solution of what we call the special Presence of our Lord Jesus Christ with His people in their higher acts of worship."[2] This is a valuable suggestion, and I think here we find the psychological explanation

[1] *The Crowd*, p. 6.

[2] R. S. Simpson, *Ideas in Corporate Worship*, p. 49.

of Our Lord's phrase, " Where two or three are met together in my name, there am I in the midst."

Let us pursue this inquiry. What in a crowd gives rise to these new characteristics ? These may be summarised as two. (1) The individual " loses in some degree his self-consciousness." [1] He is no longer as aware of himself, and this may lead to emotional outbursts, for as his vivid sense of self-consciousness is blurred so also his sense of personal responsibility disappears. He is no longer subject to the restraints of self-criticism. When we apply this to a company met together for worship, is not the capacity for escaping from the consciousness of self extremely important ? How can we realise God's Presence except by abandoning the attitude of self-consciousness in which we are the centre of life ? I know that this escape from the control of personal criticism may be a descent into a riot of emotionalism or a debauchery of sentimentality. The story of how religious crowds have acted is sad proof of this. However, if the escape be not into unlicensed indulgence but into the presence of the God of righteousness, is not this escape of the highest spiritual value ? Indeed, is there not here a psychic condition which aids the soul in its flight to God ?

(2) The second trait of the crowd is its great suggestibility. Very readily a crowd will adopt suggestions. This is caused by the fact that the individual feels himself swamped by the power of the crowd, " its unknown capacities, its unlimited and mysterious possibilities. These are the attributes that excite in us the instinct of subjection and so throw us into the receptive suggestible attitude." [2] Now this instinct of subjection is one of the instincts that finds its place in worship. The soul has to feel its total and utter dependence upon God, and already the presence of others has aroused that instinct. Intellectually the crowd is suggestible that is prepared readily to accept propositions without adequate proof or authority, and this is accounted a symptom of low intelligence. So it is if we are dealing with the intercourse of human life, but when the soul is seeking God's Presence and His Word it is of vital import that the soul be quick to hear. The temper of " proof " has no

[1] McDougall, *Group Mind*, p. 40.
[2] *Ibid.* p. 41.

part in the temple ; it is the spirit ready to receive that hears the voice. In short, the fact of suggestibility heightens the possibilities in worship.

However, a church at worship is not simply a crowd. It is not a chance gathering, but a highly organised group with a purpose in view. Dr. McDougall argues that five conditions are necessary for the more developed group mind. (1) The first and basal condition is that there be continuity of the existence of the group. The Church with her long record of devotion throughout the centuries fulfils this. She stands surrounded by a great cloud of witnesses and is obedient to a great tradition in the act of worship. This consciousness which a church group possesses increases the solidarity of the group feeling. (2) It is of importance that in the mind of each member there should be some adequate idea of the group, its nature and functions. The Church at worship is alive to the reason of her being and keenly conscious of the function she has to fulfil. (3) The third condition is the interaction between the group and other groups usually in the form of rivalry. Worshippers come to worship, conscious that they bear witness in a world throned by other and hostile interests. The worshipper is aware that he with his fellows possesses an experience which belongs only to the Christian fold. (4) Traditions, customs, and habits, which are in the minds of the members, link them to the group. The Divine Service is no new invention to which men come to see what it is like. It carries out agelong customs and fulfils established practices in obedience to a great tradition. There is thus given to the Church as a group a sense of stability through following the order and the ordinance of the past. (5) A group possesses an order and organisation which consist in the differentiation and specialisation of its functions among its members. The Church, as the instrument of worship is organised, possesses an order which attaches certain functions to her ministry. This is not a fortuitous arrangement, but it goes back to the call and injunction of the Lord Who set certain apart for their tasks. Every branch of the Church Catholic acknowledges the existence of an order appointed from above to serve her interests and further her ends.

We have seen how the Church at worship fulfils in a special

way the conditions of a highly organised group, and we must now ask what are the traits of the organised group? There are two marks of the group spirit to which I would call attention. (1) The first is a sense of responsibility towards the group. We saw that responsibility was weakened through contact in the crowd, and that diminution in self-consciousness had its value as a condition of worship. Here the sense of responsibility returns, but it is no longer an individual and isolating sense of responsibility. As members of the group men have responsibilities, and the group spirit creates this responsibility. Now if the Church be thought of simply as an institution guided and governed by presbyteries or bishops, then this idea has little or no effect on acts of worship; but if the Church be conceived as the instrument of God, the Body of the Lord Jesus Christ, then our sense of responsibility as those "called to be saints," as members of this mystical community of whom are the heroes of the faith and our own blessed departed—then our sense of responsibility before the Face of the Most High God becomes a conscious assistance to our devotion, helps to awake the spirit of worship, and widens our spiritual grasp.

(2) The group spirit gives rise to a sense of confidence and satisfaction. This is not the individual's satisfaction with himself, but satisfaction with the group. In our case the group is the Church Invisible—the home of God's Spirit that is represented by the gathering of worshippers. Now this satisfaction has two elements: (*a*) It springs from a sense of power and security. No longer isolated and alone is the worshipper, and his hesitations and shortcomings do not debar him from the sense of security. This security is not self-sufficiency but security in God. The trust which belongs to the complete dependence upon the Eternal Father and Saviour is ministered to because the sense of security has been awakened by the group spirit. I stress the point that security is only security in God's Grace whose symbol is the communion of saints. Any sense of security apart from this would be founded upon human pride. (*b*) The gregarious impulse is more satisfied when like associates with like than when there is little resemblance between the members of the group. How does the sense of likeness aid the mood of worship? Are we not conscious of the unlikeness

of man to man, the dissimilarity of endowment, the difference of culture, the variety of temperament ? But does not that unlikeness make all the more vital the resemblance, the common loyalty to a common Lord and a common experience of God's Wonder and Grace. The sense of our oneness in aspiration and in experience generates a joy which makes the sense of God's Wondrous Love more poignantly felt. Yet, further, we can trace this resemblance between the worshippers. There is the mystical likeness of soul to soul. The Christ Who lighteth every man that cometh into the world, the Christ in each, the indwelling Christ Who is the Life within the lives of all, this Christ in the Blessed Sacrament is unfolded in His Wonder and Grace. Upon the Holy Table rest the symbols of His Presence and He is in us and we are in Him. Thus we experience our likeness as we experience Christ the Redeemer, and our individual devotion is raised to a new height and widened by the sweep of this twin experience.

Two deductions I draw from these considerations. (1) The first is that in the architecture and the content of a service we may not omit the fact that man's bodily life, and his contact with physical things must be given a place. Whether consciously present to the mind or not, what we call material and physical must enter into this mood of worship. "Worship," says Hocking,[1] "is too spiritual a process to dispense with the material. It is only by the enlistment of the body in some fashion that the body can be held in leash during the difficult flight of the soul." Material symbolism has a place, the gesture and the attitude of the body have a function. A study of the psychology of mysticism makes apparent the physical accompaniment of spiritual devotion. It is not, however, only to the mystical temperament that this principle applies. No one could call the religion of Sir Walter Scott mystical in nature, and yet in his diary he tells us, "I have been always careful to place my mind in the most tranquil position which it can assume during my private devotions." This tranquillity of mind is in part the consequence of a physical attitude, and our modern service ignores too much the reaction of bodily posture upon mind and mood. So also this principle bids us take notice of the unconscious influence

[1] *Meaning of God in Human Experience*, p. 372.

of spatial form upon the mental state. The character of a building in which worship is offered can be an aid or a hindrance to devotion. The time of the offering of worship also has an influence, for the hour of the day and the season of the year have a subconscious effect upon the emotional mood of the worshipper, and with this the service must reckon.

This principle applies more generally, then, to the subconscious effect of material objects and physical attitudes. In accord with the fact of the Incarnation ethical ideas must be given form and spiritual aspirations must be embodied. Here we touch upon the kinship of worship with art. An æsthetic impulse exists only in the limbo of uncreated things until it has gained the definition of form. So the vague moods in communal worship need to gain concentration and definition. If a pastoral scene and lone figure in Corot can express the pity of human existence and the pathos of mortal striving, and Michael Angelo's figure of a man in his creation of Adam can utter the inarticulate sense of man's destiny broken by evil and crowned with glory, shall not the image and the picture have potency to represent man's needs in worship and God's abounding ministry to His children and creatures ?

(2) The second deduction is the social character of all worship. Historically worship began as a collective exercise and this social aspect is inherent in it. "Worship is imperfect," says Hocking, "unless when I worship I am joining the race in worship." For this reason the Church has made her worship public in order to impress this essential reference. I do not, of course, mean that individual worship has not been potent in religious history. In hours of solitude great souls have greatly worshipped, and in every faith the path to the mountain-top has been trodden alone. It was necessary that the individual mind become self-conscious and the personal relation of the soul to God be vividly realised. Therefore in the history of worship we see the movement from communal celebration to personal and individual devotion. "When thou prayest, enter into thy chamber and shut thy door," said the Lord Jesus. The solitude of the mystic, the consecrated privacy of the individual prayer, personal communion with God belong to the higher religions and are characteristic of our faith. But this does

not negate the social character of worship or rob it of its reference to others as members of the family of God. The solitary place has been the altar whereon has been experienced God's relation to mankind. The existence of other lives is felt most sharply when we are detached from them by circumstance. Yet this individual spiritual life with its poignant sense of other lives has to fulfil itself in a common devotion else otherwise it is incomplete.

We can accept as an axiom that no human activity can reach its goal in isolation. In its essence knowledge implies the relation and intercourse of other minds. Willing involves a society of wills through which the consciousness of our own will has been created. Feeling is affected by the contact of others and is partly called into being by their reactions. Worshipping, which embraces these three activities of human nature, finds its completion and fulfilment in unity with the race and with our fellows. Thus consciously we must aim at providing in our Church service this sense and realisation of spiritual communion, not on the lower level where man is not conscious of the difference of his inner life from his fellows, but on the higher in a synthesis where individual distinctions are transcended through a common and personal bond. Public Worship is not, then, the sum of the worship of the individuals who compose the congregation. Something is created—a social medium—a fellowship before God and the Creator Saviour in which the individual experience of each worshipper is fulfilled. The service of the Church is not, then, the gathering of a number of individuals to worship. The social aspect of worship insists that there be a reference to the race and to our fellows, and this involves that worshippers are representative at that time and in that place of the family of God. That is to say, the service ought to be the worship of the Catholic Church, and in accord with this social reference implicit in all worship our public service must be framed.

We may, then, define worship from this psychological standpoint as the attitude of the total personality of man to the Whole of existence—to the Absolute. Worship is, then, an inevitable attitude if the soul is to be freed from the trammels of this earthly existence. Worship is not the whole of life; it is but one aspect of life and exists alongside other aspects—work, recreation, art, health, love, social service, and moral standards. It is, however, an attitude to the whole of life which is harmonised in the sense of God. In human life there is a rhythm which alternates between the attitude to the Whole and the attitude to the part and fragment. The aspect of the Whole is worship; the aspect of the various parts is that rich medley and "God's plenty" which we call human activity.

IV

I would conclude this chapter by mentioning the functions that worship fulfils in the psychological experience of the worshipper in accordance with the definition given above. (1) First, Worship renews the life force spent in the distractions of conflicting interests and exhausted in the multiplicity of mortal tasks and duties. The brightness of the first dawn fades into the light of the common day. "There has passed away a glory from the earth." The joys of life in friendship, in work, in beauty, and in moral duties lose their lustre. "Pleasures are like poppies spread," and "change and decay in all around I see." Worship restores these ruined dreams, brings back the worth of living, recaptures the joy and zest of life. Life is renewed because the soul reaches towards and is touched by the Power that holds all the values of existence. Sometimes, as we have seen in unlovely forms, this renewal is shown in the worship of the lower religions; but in the noblest and ethical mysticism there is a retreat from the fragments of existence in order to recover the sense of life as a whole and to find anew that vigour and valiancy which give meaning to the joys and values of our little day. This recovery is found in communion with the Power that we as Christians have learned to know as the God and Father of our Lord Jesus Christ.

(2) Worship fulfils the function also of being the security for the rest of life. Worship is not the repudiation but the affirmation of existence. The fiercest asceticism in its most rigid worship does not deny the value of life though it may repudiate the worth of its possessions and the validity of its pleasures. Even the contemplative adoration of the Buddhist who denies the worth of all existence finds bliss in the Nirvana, and thereby affirms the value

of the unconscious which is present there and now in this present life. Above all, in historic Christianity we find a worship that is the assertion of all life's values and within which the partial loyalties of man's battered heart can find their meaning and their fulfilment. Beneath the shadow and the shelter of the Worship of God through Christ there nestle human loyalties and mortal loves to hearth and home, to country and to duty, that divorced from this worship would be but the irrational product of an unconscious force. To us, then, the worship of God is the bulwark because it is the consecration of all life.

(3) In the third place, the function of worship is creative. Höffding has defined religion as " the conservation of all values." Such a definition is inadequate because it leaves out the creative power of worship. It is the spirit of worship that creates new values. There are in worship two impulses—the current of tradition and the original fountains of immediate inspiration. The former is the tide that bears upon its waters the precious freight of past experience. Tradition can lie " heavy as frost and deep almost as life," but it can also be the ladder of freedom to the individual soul, for it can free the soul from spending its efforts in seeking what has been already won. The revelation of God is given, and has not to be sought by mortal activity but accepted by human faith. Our worship is not something we have to invent or to discover but something we have to receive and use. We are free to advance to new truths and to fresh experiences in this modern world because the fact of worship and our standard in worship are given. Otherwise we spend our days in making and manufacturing what is already ours, and we do not advance but stand still. Tradition enters into worship through inherited belief and the accepted cultus and becomes directive. It ought to be expressed in worship in such a way that it wakes the worshipper to the riches and the width of God's Grace.

The other element is the personal experience of the worshipper, and this is the spring of the authentic waters of the Spirit. It is the union of these two elements in worship that renders it a creative power. Then the personal experience of the worshipper acting along the line of tradition creates fresh values in the world of to-day and in the hopes of the future. The creative energy of worship, as in the prophets of old, lights the past with meaning and illumines to-day and the coming days; it makes the familiar gleam with fresh intent. From Pentecost until to-day this has been proved truth, for the creative power is not of man but of God. The Spirit moves upon the waters. Where but in worship are men made humble for the entrance of new life and made powerful by the entrance of life? Sometimes, it is true, worship has created a temper in man that flung him headlong to disaster. For the greatest things are the most perilous, and worship that lifts man out of himself can lift him out of custom and beyond safe mooring and set him upon the restless and inexorable ocean. When the Divine and human meet, mighty are the possibilities, and therefore it behoves us to offer our worship to that Eternal Spirit Who has unveiled to us His Will in the face of Jesus Christ. Then worship which we share with our fellows will be a Divine Communion in which the Spirit of God speaks and through which are unlocked new powers and fresh forces.

CHAPTER III

WORSHIP IN THE NEW TESTAMENT AND ITS DEVELOPMENT

I. The Jewish Background

In the following chapters I would trace the development of Christian worship and glance at the diverse forms it has taken; in this chapter I would briefly sketch the fount and origin of our public devotion. I begin at the beginning, which is New Testament times, for within the pages of the New Testament there is a standard which the Church must ever remember in her divine service, and a norm of revelation which she must ever apply. Christianity sprang from Judaism, and our Lord lived the life of a Jewish teacher. The first believers belonged to the household of Israel. The background to our faith is Judaism, and the worship of the early disciples is rooted in the worship of their nation. Although the followers of Jesus first appear as a sect in Judaism, the little church felt that it was the true Israel and that the great promises of the Old Testament belonged to it. The new faith in the Risen Lord came to those who had been trained in forms of piety and to whom ways of worship were familiar. Therefore if we would grasp the worship in New Testament times and in the early Church, we must look at the background. Jewish worship at the beginning of the Christian era was of two kinds, the temple worship and the synagogue worship.

(1) The temple worship was primarily the offering of sacrifice, and the thoughts contained in sacrificial worship sooner or later influenced the outlook and the liturgical form of Christian worship. I would therefore pause to mention the ideas enshrined in this Hebrew type of worship. Whatever may have been the origin of sacrifice, there were present in Hebrew sacrifices the two ideas,

the gift idea through which could be expressed the sentiments of gratitude and praise, and the communion idea through which could be represented kinship with the Divine and human fellowship. The post-exilic development of sacrifice emphasised certain elements. The idea of praise became more definite. The burnt offering made twice daily became the centre of the temple cultus, and the incense offering is perhaps also linked to this idea of praise and thanksgiving. There is also an increased emphasis on the idea of atonement for sin. Both the sin offering and the trespass offering suggest the idea of expiation.[1] This need for reconciliation with God and His holy law is a basic thought revealed also in the Day of Atonement. In this connection the old sacrificial idea of the gift is made prominent and its scope extended. The gift that is well pleasing to the deity becomes the gift that reconciles. Also we must not forget the other idea of communion, where the worshipper, the priest, and the deity share in the sacrifice —for example, the peace offering.[2] This communion thought of the sacrificial meal is very clear in the Passover. The religious meal is an institution in Judaism which doubtless springs from this old sacrificial idea. At the beginning of the Christian era such religious meals apart from the great festivals were not uncommon.

Apart from sacrifice there was also in the temple worship the liturgical use of the psalter. "During the daily sacrifices—burnt-offering, sin and trespass offering, peace offering and drink offering —the psalm for the day was sung; each day of the week had its special psalm." [3] The Hallel was used at the great festivals. Obviously some of the psalms were in origin individualistic and for special purposes, but in the psalms of praise the communal aspect is apparent. This wedding of the sacrificial act to the words of devotion is significant. Rabbinical tradition tells us that the Shema' (Deut. vi. 4–9, xi. 13–21; Num. xv. 37–41), with its eighteen benedictions, and the Decalogue were in use in the temple worship. Whether or not this statement be wholly accurate it points to the use of prayer and the word of the Law in the temple ceremonial.

[1] Cf. Oesterley and Robinson, *Hebrew Religion*.
[2] Lev. vii. 29 f.
[3] Oesterley, *Liturgy and Worship*, p. 55.

In addition, there were also ritualistic acts such as ablution and benediction.

(2) The second kind of Jewish worship was that of the synagogue. In its inception the synagogue was a place of instruction wherein the law was heard, and its worship gathered round the oracle or word of God. During the Exile a substitute had to be found for the temple sacrifice, and here is the beginning of the liturgy of the Oracle. With the recognition of the Word comes the sense of history, and the great festivals are linked to historic events. In synagogue worship we have congregational worship, which consisted of readings from Scripture, a homily, prayer, and the use of the psalter. Unfortunately we do not know the synagogue liturgy before the year 70 A.D. Our sources of information do not extend as far back as that, and the Rabbinical writers of the early Christian centuries show a tendency to antedate liturgical usages and forms. Indeed, the scanty information in St. Luke (iv. 15–21) is our only contemporary evidence. We may, however, regard it as extremely probable that in the time of Jesus there was a fixed liturgy, and it is most likely that some of the liturgical material we have goes back to before the destruction of the temple. The two traits which the synagogue prayer seems to possess were its scriptural form and its congregational character. As the psalter was the book of the temple cult, so the prayers that accompanied the Law and the Prophets in the synagogue service would be steeped in the same fountain of devotion. In the synagogue we find a new type of worship with its congregational basis, and this is the Oracle type. In all probability the worship would consist of an elaborate service of prayer in which the Shema' was enshrined, followed by a reading from the Pentateuch and then the prophetic lesson.

II. New Testament Times

From the New Testament we learn that the early followers of Jesus followed the example of their Master and took part in the traditional worship of their people. After the Ascension the disciples continued this worship.[1] "Now Peter and John were

[1] St. Luke xxiv. 52–53.

going up into the temple at the hour of prayer."[1] "They were all with one accord in Solomon's porch."[2]

Had this worship any relation to the worship of the Christian community? The answer of Duchesne[3] is quite definite—that it had no influence on the Christian liturgy. Certainly this great liturgical scholar is right in saying that we cannot take seriously the connections that mediæval ingenuity has found between the Pentateuch and the Christian liturgy. But surely his statement is too absolute. In subsequent years we find the shadow of the Jewish system cast upon the Christian rite, the thought of Christ's sacrificial death derived from ideas innate in this worship and the influence of the liturgical use of the psalter. Perhaps also enough weight has not been attached to the fact which the author of Acts mentions, "and a great company of the priests were obedient to the faith."[4] Yet notwithstanding this reservation it is not in this sphere that any direct and immediate influence is found. The Book of Acts, however, gives abundant evidence of the close relation between St. Paul's work and the synagogue,[5] and from the same book we gather that the Palestinian Christians regarded themselves as belonging to the faith of Abraham. The influence of the synagogue is direct and obvious. The Christian Church took from it the reading of Old Testament Scripture, the practice of prayer and the homily, and this formed what a later age called the liturgy of the catechumens.

Two other forms of worship the early believers took part in. (1) There were meetings chiefly for prayer that were informal in character.[6] Here in these meetings of the Jerusalem church the atmosphere would tingle with Christian feeling, but the expression of their devotion could not but be influenced and moulded by the prayer form which they had learned in the synagogue worship. When under the leadership of St. Paul Christianity moved out into the Hellenic world there was the definite need of missionary preaching and instruction. The breach with Judaism made it necessary

[1] Acts iii. 1.
[2] Acts v. 12.
[3] *Christian Worship*, p. 46.
[4] Acts vi. 7.
[5] Acts ix. 20, xiii. 5, 14–15, xiv. 1, xvii. 1–2, 10, 17, xviii. 4, 19, xix. 8.
[6] Acts i. 12–14, iv. 23–31, xii. 12.

for the Apostle to exercise his function of preaching, and instruction outside the precincts of the synagogue.[1] Here we see the sermon or exposition which is a feature taken from the synagogue. Probably in the Gentile world meetings were held whose aim, like the original purpose of the synagogue, was instruction, and doubtless this exposition of truth would be accompanied by prayer of some kind. But we gather from the Book of Acts [2] that preaching was associated with another form of meeting. (2) This other form of worship was the meeting to break bread or the Lord's Supper. This is the specificially Christian service and is the original contribution which the new faith makes to the forms of worship. All else that enters into the Christian liturgy may be said to have a Jewish ancestry, but here we touch something that has no equivalent in the worship of Israel. These meetings for the breaking of bread appear originally to have been held in private houses ; but perhaps St. Paul's remark, "Have ye not houses to eat and drink in, or despise ye the church of God ? " [3] and the statement "there were many lights in the upper chamber " [4] suggest that already a larger meeting-place was required. Into the services of the little community entered praise through the singing of hymns and psalms.[5] We can find fragments at least of the spiritual songs embedded in the New Testament. A hymn on the Advent (Rom. xiii. 11, 12), a hymn of spiritual awakening (Eph. v. 14), a fragment on Christ the Lord and Judge (2 Tim. ii. 11–13), a confessional chant (1 Tim. iii.16 ; Phil. ii. 6–11), and hymns of adoration (Rev. v. 9–10, 12–13, xi. 17, xv. 3–4). At the outset of her career the lips of the Church were opened to praise her Lord with thanksgiving. The trite observation that a creed should be sung and not said is proved truth here, for confessional statement is touched with the breath of adoration and in rhythmic speech and hieratic language the Church sings her confession of faith. The fact that St. Paul begins all his letters with a benediction suggests that these were taken from the liturgical use of the blessing at the beginning of the service. The doxology that follows the Lord's Prayer in St. Matthew's Gospel seems to point to a liturgical use. The Bible of

[1] Acts xix. 9, 10. [2] Acts xx. 7, 11. [3] 1 Cor. xi. 22.
[4] Acts xx. 8. [5] 1 Cor. xix. 26 ; Eph. v. 19 ; Col. iii. 16.

the Jewish faith the Christian Church had made her own and in time set beside it the writings of the New Testament; the psalter of the Hebrew Temple became the praise book of the brethren. He would greatly err who would seek in the worship of the New Testament Church precise definition and regulated forms. Within this worship lie the seeds which the centuries will develop; but the forms are in process of being evolved. When people talk of the modern Church imitating the forms of New Testament times, they are apt to forget that the new spirit had to seek its own means of expression. As long as the Jewish believers stood within the confines of Judaism, their worship was semi-Jewish and semi-Christian in form, and a part of their worship was expressed through the institutions of the ancient revelation. After the final separation the Church had to fashion for herself modes and methods for voicing that part of worship which the temple and the synagogue had expressed. There was not in the Palestinian Church a specifically Christian form that contained the whole orbit of the soul's devotion. In the Pauline Church, on the other hand, we are in touch with a missionary movement which has not as yet had time to frame its modes of worship. The New Testament Church gives the standard for the spirit of worship, but the forms are yet indefinite and undeveloped.

But as yet we have only looked at the outside of the cup. What are the characteristics of this new spirit of worship which sought expression in the ways we have mentioned? The first is the Sense of the Risen Lord. For, as Deissmann has truly said, Christianity did not triumph because, like many another religion, it was a religion of redemption, but because it was the cult of a Redeemer Who had lived and died and risen and was present to His followers. The Sense of Christ throbbed in their worship, filling it with joy and gladness, for, however dark this mortal life of theirs, was not their Lord Who had overcome the sharpness of death with them in His power? Because of this, their worship glowed with hope and with confidence. This feeling that the Lord was with them found utterance in the worship associated with the breaking of the bread. This Sense of the Lord showed itself also in another way that seemed almost contradictory. There was the assured certainty that the Lord would come. With yearning and with hope the Church prayed, "Come, Lord Jesus." The mood of expectancy that awaited His immediate coming passes, but it disappears only to change its form. The Lord comes—this finds its medium of witness in that Supper of the Lord Who comes to have fellowship with His own, bringing the foretaste of the Messianic Banquet.

(2) Secondly, there is the sense of the Spirit, through Whose agency alone prayer could be offered and the confession made that Jesus is the Lord. The enthusiastic devotion of prophetic souls was the work of the Spirit and the rapt ecstasy the sign of the Spirit's presence. It was the heart aflame with the Spirit that broke forth into prophetic moods of prayer and of speech. "Suffer the prophets to give thanks as much as they will," says the *Didaché*.[1] Perhaps the custom of extempore prayer was an inheritance from the synagogue for "there was always an aversion among the Rabbis to making prayer a matter of fixed formulæ."[2] The prophetic ministry was active, and traces survive in the later liturgies of this early practice; the spontaneous response of the worshipper quickened by the Spirit is seen in the assent of the Amen.[3] This is the outward sign of a worship that had been free and untrammelled. The prayer which a succeeding age called the "epiclesis" lives in the liturgy as a testimony to this Spirit-filled devotion, for in its earliest form this prayer invokes the Spirit "upon us and upon these gifts." This spirit which kindles the heart and quickens life is no empty ecstasy of excited feeling; it has content, for it is the Spirit whose fruit is goodness and righteousness and truth.[4] Where the Spirit is there is liberty; freedom and spontaneity are features in the worship of these great days.

(3) Thirdly, there is the fellowship of the believers. All the brethren are knit to one another because they possess the same spirit and are obedient to the same exalted Lord. It was a fellowship of religious fervour shot through with warm humanity and brotherly love. In the Jerusalem church the noble attempt was made to practise communism, and in the Gentile churches at the one table the richer shared their food with the poorer. The offering

[1] *Didaché*, x. [2] *Liturgy of Worship*, Leverloff, p. 73.
[3] Justin Martyr, 1*st Apology*, lxv. 3; lxvii. 5. [4] Eph. v. 9.

was made in the Pauline churches for the saints that were in Jerusalem. So the fellowship was not simply an enthusiastic neighbourliness, it was the recognition that all who belonged to the household of faith were united in a great allegiance and a living sympathy with one another. This fellowship found its religious expression in a social meal.

As we would expect, the three characteristics of the Christian Church point to that institution which was uniquely Christian. It is a significant fact that the genius of this new religion is expressed in the Lord's Supper or Breaking of Bread, and that public worship has this for its core and centre. The Synoptic Gospels and St. Paul give an account of the institution of this sacred meal at the Last Supper when Jesus met with His disciples on the night on which He was betrayed. It was for long assumed that this final meal of which Jesus partook with His followers was the Passover feast. The Synoptic writers did so consider it. Yet there are difficulties in the way of this identification, for while it is spoken of as the Passover no reference is made to any of the special traits of Passover observance. For example, nothing is said of the roasted Paschal lamb, and the bread is termed *ἄρτος* and not *ἄζυμα* as the unleavened cake would most naturally be called. Further, the meal is partaken of before the blessing of the cup and bread while in the Passover the meal follows the blessing. One cup only seems to be used from which all drink, whereas at the Passover each would use his own cup. There is also the discrepancy between the Synoptic writers and the Fourth Gospel as to the date. The fact too has to be remembered that if the Last Supper were the Passover meal, then the feast had commenced before the betrayal, and all the circumstances attendant on the arrest and the crucifixion would involve a breach of the law. It has therefore been suggested in view of such considerations that in the Last Supper we have not the Passover meal but the Kiddush or Sanctification for the Sabbath.[1] The Kiddush was a religious ceremony which frequently terminated the household meal. It was a Jewish custom for friends to be partakers of a religious meal

[1] Oesterley, *The Jewish Background*, p. 156 f.; Macgregor, *Eucharistic Origins*, p. 37 f.

as a symbol of their friendship. If this suggestion be correct, then Jesus with His disciples partook of a meal which was the last of His customary meals with them. Perhaps the stories of the feeding of the multitude carry in them the hint that such religious meals took place, for the same words are used in these stories for blessing and the same procedure followed as at the Last Supper. If this be the true interpretation that the institution took place at the Kiddush—then we would understand why it was that in the early Church the Eucharist was celebrated weekly as was the Kiddush, and not yearly as was the Passover. The opinion of most scholars inclines to the view that this explanation is the true one.

There are four accounts of the institution in the New Testament (St. Matt. xxvi. 26–30 ; St. Mark xiv. 22–25 ; St. Luke xxii. 15–20 ; 1 Cor. xi. 23–26). The variations between St. Matthew and St. Mark are unimportant. The narrative of St. Matthew is a somewhat fuller statement in more rhythmic prose (perhaps the result of liturgical use). The likenesses are such that they point to a single source. St. Luke's account links with that of St. Paul. While there is a general similarity between them, there are noteworthy differences which are not easily explained. Perhaps the simplest explanation is that the differences represent different uses in the various churches from which these Gospels sprang.

In St. Matthew and St. Mark the injunction, "This do in remembrance of me," is wanting. In St. Luke's account there are two cups (ver. 17 and ver. 20). The first giving of the cup is thus related: "With desire I have desired to eat this Passover with you before I suffer. For I say unto you I will not any more eat thereof until it be fulfilled in the Kingdom of God. And he took the cup and gave thanks, and said, Take this and divide it among yourselves. For I say unto you I will not drink of the fruit of the vine until the Kingdom of God shall come." The words spoken before and after the taking and the blessing of the cup have an indubitable eschatological meaning. They point to the Kingdom that is to come and to a day that is not yet. The second cup, ver. 20, "This cup is the new testament in my blood, which is shed for you," relates to the redemptive death of Christ, and in this is at one with St. Paul. But there is a further difficulty with regard to the text. There are two texts—the longer, the Alexandrian, is what is given above; the shorter or Western omits ver. 19*b* and ver. 20. This leaves the cup with the eschatological reference, the blessing and the breaking of bread and the wonderful saying "This is my body." This order of distribution (cup-bread) corresponds to what is found in 1 Cor. x. 16 and in the *Didaché*, ix. This shortened account throws a marked emphasis on the bread; indeed even the first cup is omitted in one later text. The shorter or D text is accepted as authentic by some scholars.[1] The interest of this for us is that it suggests that there may have been a primitive use of eucharistic worship with the order of distribution cup-bread. The text which omits the first cup and leaves only the bread links with the references to the breaking of bread in Acts,[2] where nothing is said about the wine and with the other Lucan passage.[3] Perhaps there was a usage in which only bread was partaken of, and the tradition of this use would be preserved in later times among gnostic circles.[4] Other scholars [5] prefer the Alexandrian text. This text gives us: the first cup with its eschatological reference, the second cup with its reference to the covenant, the injunction to repeat the ordinance and a Paschal reference.

Let us compare this with the other accounts. In the Markan record we have a word spoken concerning the bread and a word spoken concerning the wine and a definite eschatological reference. St. Mark's description is that of a Jewish meal of fellowship. After the words of blessing over the bread, "Blessed art thou, O Lord, Ruler of the Universe, the One who causeth bread to spring forth from the earth," [6] Jesus brake and gave it to them and said, "Take,

[1] Westcott and Hort put ver. 19*b* and ver. 20 in the margin of their text.

[2] Acts ii. 42, 46.

[3] St. Luke xxii. 30, 35.

[4] Acts of St. John, 106–110; Acts of St. Thomas, 27, 29, 49–50, 133. In one case (Acts of St. Thomas, 121: "He brake bread and took a cup of water and made her a partaker in the Body of Christ, and the cup of the Son of God") we observe the practice of using water instead of wine, perhaps owing to the poverty of the early Christians. This suggests that Bread was the essential element.

[5] Goguel, *L'Eucharistie*, pp. 112–116; Macgregor, *Eucharistic Origins*, p. 54 f.

[6] The Kiddush Blessing, taken from a later source.

eat, this is my body." Over the cup He again gives thanks: "Blessed art thou, O Lord, Ruler of the Universe, He Who createth the fruit of the vine."[1] The account simply says that the disciples drank of it but no injunction to do so is given. Here we find the identification of the bread with His Body, the covenant cup, and an eschatological saying which points to the Messianic Banquet. St. Matthew's account, as we said, is modelled on St. Mark's, and the differences are slight. "Drink ye all of it" is added.

We now turn to the account given by St. Paul. The apostle uses the phrase "for I have received of the Lord that which I also delivered unto you." Loisy and many other scholars interpret the phrase "received from the Lord" to mean received in a vision, and from this they deduce that there is no relation between the Corinthian eucharistic feast and the supper in the upper room. The more extreme statement of this position which involves that St. Paul borrowed nothing from the tradition of the Church can be set aside, for it is hard to see how the regulations for a ceremonial observance could be received in a vision. This theory, however, has been stated in a more attractive form. What St. Paul received in a vision was the interpretation of the Last Supper. This interpretation was the reference to the death of the Lord. Such a view implies that as was likely the Last Supper was but the final meeting of Jesus with His disciples. This habit of Jesus, which was consonant with Jewish custom, continued in the Church. This breaking of bread, probably without wine, would be a feast of religious fellowship. Perhaps as the Emmaus story suggests there came to those gathered at such a meal the vivid and overwhelming sense of Christ's presence, for we must note that in this story the two disciples do not appear to have been present at the Last Supper. That this type of religious meal did exist in the early Church there is every reason to believe. Yet I cannot persuade myself that this interpretation of the Apostle's words is correct. I admit that one would have expected the phrase "the Lord Jesus" instead of "the Lord" if St. Paul referred to information which he had received indirectly through others as to what Jesus did at the Last Supper, but the solemn and authoritative way in which the Apostle expresses

[1] The Kiddush Blessing, taken from a later source.

himself, and also the parallelism between what and how he " received " and what and how he " delivered " compel me to hold that St. Paul is here building upon the verdict of history and the consent of tradition.

The Pauline account of the institution is given to the Corinthians in order to prevent abuses which were present at the table of the Lord. St. Paul is seeking to regulate their conduct and practice at a congregational meal during which what we would term the Eucharist proper was celebrated. He points to the fact that their method is similar to that of the Last Supper, where the institution followed upon a meal. In his account he stresses the reference to the Lord's death and its Paschal signification, he emphasises the covenant cup, he introduces the eschatological thought by the phrase " till He come," but he does not mention the Messianic Banquet, and finally he gives the injunction that the rite is to be repeated. We see how the eschatological meaning of the cup has vanished, and the apostle only adds in his own words an eschatological note. But most significant of all is the dominical institution. It certainly is strange that if Jesus spoke these words, " Do this in remembrance of Me," the Markan account omits them. From the standpoint of historical criticism it is hard to understand how if they were used they could be omitted from the account of the institution. It appears likely that St. Luke borrowed from the Pauline version the dominical institution. Perhaps we may be forced to admit that these words never fell from the lips of Jesus. Gore's remark is, however, quite relevant that the Markan account implies the repetition of the Last Supper, but this, while a true interpretation of the Church's attitude, does not throw any light on the words spoken. St. Paul may have altered the emphasis of the rite by bringing into greater prominence the significance of Christ's death and by revealing its abiding quality. " St. Paul," says Dr. Rawlinson, " did not invent the Last Supper, but it is just possible that he was indeed the first Christian to see what it meant. Its permanence in the Church is one of its essential meanings."

However the differences in the accounts of the supper are to be explained we must insist that the meaning of the institution of the Eucharist must not be cut away from the interpretation of

Christian experience. We cannot explain what the Eucharist meant by ignoring all the rich development of its meaning. It is difficult, perhaps impossible, to choose between the forms of words and to say exactly what the lips of the Master spoke. I question if the most careful scrutiny can take us beyond probability with regard to the details. The words of Jesus were spoken at a time when they would make an undying impression upon the hearts of His disciples, and the events that followed with the startling experience of joy that befell them would for ever make their meeting in the upper room memorable ; but it is not when men are most impressed they recall with greatest accuracy the precise words they have heard. What moved them was burnt into their souls, but the very depth of their emotion would blur the memory of meticulous details. It is perilous to speak of this high subject as though we were drawing up the minute of a meeting. We cannot explain the Eucharist by seeking to discover what the Supper meant to those who partook on that far-off night in an Eastern city. They were not in a position to comprehend its import. When Jesus spoke of the Messianic kingdom that lay beyond, crude and swift expectations would crowd into the minds of His hearers ; but the Jesus of the Gospel narrative did not think the thoughts of His contemporaries without a difference. Again He would be with them, He does not explain how ; perhaps He could not, for that lay in the Hands of His Father. After His dark Passion He would be with them, how could they comprehend ? But in the light of the resurrection faith and the coming of the Spirit has not the believing heart found true the Lord's prophecy and promise ? " If the Kingdom of God is the Christian Church and Faith, what else can the Messianic Banquet be than the Eucharist ? "[1]

Nor can I feel that the attempt to determine what this supper meant to Jesus can supply the answer to the question, What is the Eucharist ? Even if it were possible to know all that was in the mind of Our Incarnate Lord when He took the bread and blessed it, would that in itself give us all that we require ? " This is my body," said Jesus. It was a moment of creative activity ; at such times the great genius cannot explain to us what he is

[1] Williams, *Essays Catholic and Critical*, p. 405.

doing. In the throes of creation Shakespeare could not express to us what he meant by Hamlet, for he is the creator and not the expositor, nor—and I speak with all reverence—could we find in the mind of Jesus all that in the providence of God would flow from this act. Jesus is here, like the supreme artist of the spiritual, creating something that He knows to be of infinite value. It will take the whole spiritual experience of mankind to grasp that value. In a certain sense this Last Supper must be a kind of prophetic Eucharist, for it interprets His death, makes His presence abiding, and creates His Body in the fellowship of His followers.

The dissimilarity of the accounts of the institution bears witness not only to a variety of ritual but also to a difference in emphasis and meaning. The rich content of this Last Supper is too great for any one interpretation, and its full breadth is given not in any one of these forms but in their united testimony to the width and depth of meaning that the early believers found in this worship. Every type of eucharistic worship goes back to Jesus ; His memory is enshrined in it ; His Personality dominates it, His Presence is vouchsafed by it, and His Coming is looked for through it. Very readily may we accept the distinction made so definitely by Lietzmann between two types of eucharistic observance in the first times : the one deriving from the common meal of friends is the breaking of bread together in the glad expectation of Christ's coming in power and with the immediate sense of His Presence ; and the other or Pauline type is the eating and drinking in communion before the fact of Christ's redemptive death, whereby the individual believer has union with the Glorified Lord (1 Cor. x. 16). We can accept this distinction between a rite practised in Jerusalem and the observance of the Pauline churches. But the Markan account, with the dependent one of St. Matthew, reveals the fact that the sacrificial aspect of the Eucharist belongs not only to its Pauline form, for the phrase " this is my body," uttered at the time and in the circumstances, carries within it the assertion that here our Lord makes a deliberate act of self-dedication to sacrifice.

For our purpose it is sufficient to note that by means of these differing forms the varied aspects of eucharistic worship are expressed. The two main thoughts in the New Testament records are those of the Messianic Banquet and the Sacrifice; yet in the early Eucharist many notes are sounded—the expectation of this Heavenly Feast, the Memorial of the Lord's Passion and Sacrificial Death, the corporate fellowship in and through the Lord's Presence, the practice of social intercourse and communal feeling that continues the custom of Jesus, the reception of new power, and the strengthening of life by participation in His Life and Power. The spirit of the club-meal is part of this rite as well as the remembrance of the Sacrificial Death and the hope of that glorious expectation that lay behind the curtain of man's little day. From this source there flows all the development of the coming days and of the long centuries.

The Love-feast or Agape was in its origin linked to the Eucharist. Together the Agape and the Eucharist represented the circumstances of the Last Supper, the Presence of Christ, thanksgiving, the sacrifice of His death. Later the social side of the meal is separated from the side of worship and in course of time the Agape was abandoned by the growing Church. Perhaps the Love-feast had served its purpose by emphasising the fellowship of believers which is in the Holy Communion, and which might have been missed by a rite less definitely rooted in human contact. Perhaps, on the other hand, there will be always something lacking in our celebration of Christ's Presence and Victory until we recapture the first note of Christian rapture, when all things were shared and held in common before the gleaming vision of Christ's presence. It may be that until social conditions and economic circumstances are bent to the service of fellowship the note of gladness will be thinner than it ought to be in this celebration of God's most sacred Presence. It is well, therefore, to observe the atmosphere and the associations of the primitive celebration.

In addition to these two aspects of the Supper—the Agape, or congregational supper, and the Eucharist proper—I have already suggested that there were two types—the Breaking of Bread, enshrining Christian fellowship around the Person of the Risen Lord but with no explicit relation to the Last Supper, and the Lord's Supper in which the believer has communion with Christ through His redemptive Death. In part corresponding to these two types, we find two outlooks. The first rests on the idea of the Messianic Banquet and nourishes the mood of expectancy. "Come, Lord Jesus" (Rev. xxii. 12) is the prayer of this temper. "Come and communicate with us in this eucharist which we celebrate in Thy name," says the apostle in the heretical Acts of Thomas. The future will develop this mood along lines unfamiliar to Jewish religion. The second outlook is not fundamentally eschatological, but is rooted in the sacrifice made by Christ. It looks back to what has been accomplished by the sacrificial death. This too will undergo a definite development.

Within the pages of the New Testament there is a difference of approach to this sacrament. The first is the Johannine with its distinctive atmosphere. "The Holy Eucharist ever appears . . . attached to the scene of the multiplication of the breads—a feast of joy and of life with Christ at the zenith of His earthly hope and power. For not 'a shewing of the death' in the eating of this bread is dwelt on by St. John, but we have: 'I am the living Bread.'"[1] In the sixth chapter St. John, speaking of the Bread, lays emphasis on the need of faith, and in the fifteenth chapter, speaking of the Vine,[2] he urges the necessity of oneness, and by the two thoughts of faith and unity shows kinship with St. Paul's thinking. None the less it is true, as Von Hügel adds, that this type of eucharistic thinking dwells more on the individual aspect of the rite of communion[3] than the Pauline does with its markedly social emphasis. Another feature is that the future becomes present. It is not "till He come" but it is the present eternal fact of the Divine Immanence. We are shown what Christ is rather than what He does. The parallel to the Eucharist is more the mystery of the Incarnation than the sacrifice of the Passion. This line runs into the future. Irenæus and Origen walk this path. "We eat the bread that has been offered and has become by prayer a certain holy Body which sanctifies those who partake of it with

[1] Von Hügel, *Mystical Element of Religion,* vol. ii. p. 88.

[2] Cf. *Didaché,* ix.: "First for the chalice: We thank Thee, Our Father, for the Holy Vine of David, Thy servant"; and Ignatius—*Trall.* viii.: "Faith which is the flesh of the Lord and love which is the blood of Jesus Christ."

[3] Cf. the use of the singular in St. John vi.

right intention." [1] This type of thinking and its expression in the liturgy ever runs the risk of becoming materialistic ; yet one great richness of this approach is that it sets the Eucharist at the very centre of all things. Holy Communion does not deal with an isolated event of God's Grace but with the whole working of Divine Providence. It is an authentic approach and we can trace its progress through the subsequent liturgies.

The second approach is the Synoptic or Pauline approach which is tied to the direct memory of the Last Supper, the Passion, and the Death.[2] The weight of emphasis falls on what Christ does —the redemption He offers, the life He imparts, and the Power He bestows. The social side of communion is very pronounced, for is not the Church in St. Paul's thinking the Body of the Lord ? The idea of the redemptive sacrifice predominates, and one development of this thought is found expressed in Tertullian : [3] " the bread which He took and distributed to the disciples He made His body, saying, ' This is my body '—that is, a figure of my body." Further, there is in this approach a more personal and historic sense of Christ's presence, as seen in the concentration on the Death of the Lord shown forth in the rite, and on the appropriation by the faithful of the merits of the Redeemer. This too will have its Western evolution alike in the Roman Mass which unites the sacrificial Death of the Personal Redeemer with its more impersonal thought of the elements as the means of receiving this redemption, and in the Protestant setting forth of the Lord's death in sacrament and sermon. In the account that Justin gives we see these two thoughts of the Incarnation and of the Sacrifice undivided—" the bread which Christ commanded us to use in remembrance of His incarnation for the salvation of those who believe in Him, for whose sake He endured His passion, and the cup which He bade us drink in thanksgiving in remembrance of His blood." [4] " Perhaps," says Dr. Brilioth,[5] " it is no mere accidental connection which he here makes of the bread with the Incarnation and the chalice with

[1] Origen, *Contra Celsum*, viii. 33.
[2] Von Hügel, *The Mystical Element of Religion*, p. 87.
[3] *Adv. Marcion*, bk. iv. ch. xi.
[4] Justin Martyr, *Dialogue with Trypho* (chap. 70).
[5] *Eucharistic Faith and Practice*, p. 36.

the Passion." Certainly it is interesting that Justin seeks to hold together these two thoughts—the Incarnation with its wide and rich suggestiveness, and the Passion with its intense and poignant appeal.

Three attitudes to the Presence in the sacrament are adumbrated in the New Testament. (1) Christ is the host, or the guest. St. Paul speaks of the table of the Lord, and St. Luke in the Emmaus story represents the Lord as the guest of the disciples. In both cases in this attitude the emphasis is on the fact that we receive a gift from the Lord. Christ is the priest at His own table. (2) Christ is the bread of life, and He is received in this symbol or form by the believer.[1] St. John in his chapters on the Eucharist dwells on this aspect of Christ's presence. (3) There is the Presence of the Spirit. Pentecost was the experience of the Spirit in the hearts of the believers—an enlightening, life-giving, and emotional experience. In the thought of St. Paul the Church as the Body of the Lord is the abode of the Spirit, and this general thought of the Presence belongs to the Eucharist. In the Christian fellowship—the Body of the Lord—His Spirit is present. These three attitudes have each a different orientation, but they are one and all contained in the New Testament.

Of the three religious types, Sacrifice, the Oracle, and the Mystery, it is apparent that within the New Testament two have a place. The idea of Sacrifice in Christ's Death and the worship which heard the oracles of God are manifestly there. But does the Mystery type have any influence? That the mood of the Mystery had an effect on the growth of the Christian liturgy I think no one can doubt; but does it enter into the precincts of New Testament Worship? The popularity of the theory that derives the Christian Sacrament from a supposed Mystery cult has faded and the theory has lost its lustre. There are resemblances between Christianity and the Mystery religions. The early apologists saw the likeness, and they argued that the demons had imitated the sacred rites. Certain modern scholars also see the likeness, and argue that the Christian Sacrament is derived from pagan sources. This explanation is unnecessary, ignores history, and can offer no evidence of a contemporary pagan mystery from

[1] St. John vi. 55, 56. Cf. 1 Cor. x. 3, 4.

which the Christian rite could be borrowed. Wetter[1] has ably argued that during the first two centuries of our era the eucharistic celebration was a true mystery—a cult of Jesus "who was dead and is alive again." He denies the historical memorial, and thinks that the thought of sacrifice was a later addition. There is truth in this point of view in so far as it brings into prominence the mystery side of the Eucharist. But to accept the conclusions of Wetter would involve certain disastrous consequences. He is compelled to argue that the institution is not part of the original rite, and seeks to displace its firmly established place in the liturgies. Only in the Nestorian liturgy of Addai and Mari are the words of the institution wanting; in all other liturgies they are present. How they came to be inserted at this later date if tradition did not associate them with the service is hard to comprehend. So apart from other difficulties with regard to the New Testament accounts his theory must be set aside.

None the less, the likeness between the Mystery cult and the Christian Sacrament is not wholly accidental, and Wetter has made it evident that there is such a thing as a Christian mystery. It is not a question of the dependence of the Christian mystery upon the pagan mystery; it is rather a matter of mood. The Christian story and the ritual of the upper room are planted in the world which produced the Mystery cults. The converts in that world brought to the interpretation of this rite their own temper and mood. The apostle of the Gentiles does not hesitate to compare the table of the Lord to the table of demons. The element which the Mystery type contributed was nothing but an atmosphere. This interpretation added nothing to the historical, nor did it take the place of the sacrificial aspect of the Eucharist, but it did, I believe, discover spiritual moods and a spiritual power in the Eucharist that might have been missed. The joy of the Eucharist might have been swallowed up in the mood of Holy Thursday or Good Friday, and the triumphant note of Easter lessened if the Mystery interpretation had not applied these glorious truths. St. Paul's conception of the union with the Glorified Lord is the mystery mood within the sphere of Christianity.

[1] *Altchristliche Liturgien.*

The Christian Mystery has not the same attitude to its myth as the pagan mystery to its myth, for the Christian myth has its basis in history; it seeks to make eternal an event in time, and to make a present Union with the Eternal Christ unlimited in space and unfettered by time. Pliny[1] describes the early Christian as singing a hymn to Christ as to a god, and in that he mentions a definite trait in Christian worship—the exaltation of Christ. Christian worship was not a mood of recollection but of immediate inspiration. This quality the Mystery interpretation nourished. Jewish phrases were diffused with a new light. "Blessed is He that cometh in the name of the Lord becomes to a later age an experience in the Eucharist. The prayer of the veil[2] suggests the opening of the heavens. There is the vision of Christ crowned as King. This is the dwelling of the spirit of adoration on the facts of history, illuminating them with a new light and making them part of experience. The later liturgies preserve the glowing worship of the early ardour. "O Thou Power of the Father," says the Testament of Our Lord, "the Grace of the nations, Knowledge, true Wisdom, the Exaltation of the Meek, the Medicine of the Soul, the Confidence of us who believe, for Thou art the Strength of the righteous, the Hope of the persecuted, the Haven of those who are buffeted, the Illuminator of the perfect, the Son of the Living God, make to arise on us out of Thy gift which cannot be searched into, courage, might, reliance, wisdom, strength, unlapsing faith." The sense of a victorious Lord dominates the adoration. "O ye that have been invited by a great purpose to the living feast of the banquet of the King of those in Heaven and those on earth," says the Nestorian liturgy.[3] The sense of eternity destroys the distinction between the seen and the unseen, and death is swallowed up in victory. The Mystery interpretation in its original application did not mean the introduction of alien elements. Surely the early Church did not err in applying this temper of adoration; already in the Fourth Gospel as in St. Paul's mysticism the path is opened. It is because our faith is deep as the anguish of death

[1] "Christo carmen quasi deo dicere secum invicem."

[2] Syrian Jacobite Rite.

[3] Brightman, *Eastern and Western Liturgies*, p. 257.

wide as life's immortal pageant, high as the soul's dream, that the Mystery mood as well as the sacrificial thought and the revealed word is necessary to unfold its meaning. I am aware that in later times a darkened understanding and a dimmed conscience have allowed to enter the sacred domain of revelation alien impulses and unhallowed desires; but the Glory of God's revelation had to be adorned by man's worship, and had to find a home in man's heart. It was this impulse that made essential the Mystery interpretation which helped to hand on to duller and less inspired ages the rapture and the wonder of the first splendour when God's Grace broke upon the souls of men. My contention is that the seed of this impulse is found in the New Testament itself and within the worship of the early days.

Within the New Testament there is but little mention of Sunday as the day of worship,[1] but "from a very early period the Christians adopted the Sunday,"[2] although "the idea of importing into the Sunday the solemnity of the Sabbath with all its exigencies was an entirely foreign one to the primitive Christians."[2] Perhaps in their enthusiastic faith there was little distinction between the week-day and the Sunday Worship, for daily would the believers assemble together. Within the New Testament we see the shaping of this Sunday service where all the worship was built round the peculiarly Christian element—the common meal with the Eucharist. Here was a worship free and spontaneous and with an intense sense of brotherly fellowship. Within the ambit of the New Testament we find an observance—the Kiss of Peace[3]—expressive of that strange new brotherhood which made the Christians stand together sharing one another's burdens in the joy of the Lord. Shortly afterwards this observance is associated with the Eucharist. Perhaps the word of Jesus about being reconciled to our brother ere we bring our gift to the altar suggested the place of the Pax in the liturgy. Though in its origin it has no liturgical significance, the fact that the apostle speaks of a holy kiss shows that it is not simply the Eastern salutation.

[1] 1 Cor. xvi. 2; Rev. i. 10; Acts xx. 7.
[2] Duchesne, *Christian Worship*, p. 47.
[3] Rom. xvi. 16; 1 Cor. xvi. 20; 2 Cor. xiii. 12; 1 Thess. v. 26; 1 Pet. v. 14.

III. The Development of Worship to Fourth Century

In the New Testament we saw that eucharistic worship was the distinctively Christian form of worship, and associated with it there are elements taken from the Jewish synagogue. In Justin Martyr [1] we have the form and order of a Christian service in the middle of the second century. This is his description: "On the day of the Sun all who live in towns or in the country gather together to one place, and the memoirs of the apostles or the writings of the prophets are read as long as time permits. Then when the reading has ceased, the president verbally instructs and exhorts to the imitation of the good examples cited. Then all rise together and prayers are offered. At length, as we have already described, prayer being ended, bread and wine and water are brought, and the president offers prayer and thanksgiving to the best of his ability, and the people consent by saying Amen; and the distribution is made to each one of his share of the elements which have been blessed, and to those who are not present it is sent by the ministry of deacons." [2]

In this there are taken from the Jewish synagogue, reading of Scripture, the sermon, and prayer at which the attitude is standing. Water is mingled with the wine in accordance with the Jewish practice; the eucharistic prayer has the response Amen. In another passage [3] Justin adds that the kiss of peace was given after the offering of prayer and before the sacred feast. The note of fellowship is sounded in the fact that the elements that have been blessed are carried to the absent. In the same apology Justin points out that the Eucharist is only to be given to the baptized believer, but from his free account of the service there appears to be as yet no *disciplina arcani*.[4] Immediately before the passage quoted Justin explains the Eucharist "not as common bread and common drink do we receive these," [5] but "the food which is blessed by the prayer of the Word [6] from him, and from which

[1] Justin, *Apol.* i. 67.
[2] Duchesne, *Christian Worship*, p. 50.
[3] Justin, *Apol.* i. 65.
[4] Fortescue, *The Mass*, p. 21.
[5] Justin, *Apology*, i. 66, quoted.
[6] The phrase is: *τὴν δι' εὐχῆς λόγον τοῦ παρ' αὐτοῦ εὐχαριστηθεῖσαν τροφήν*. It is also translated "by a word of prayer which comes from him."

our blood and flesh are nourished by change, is the flesh and blood of that Jesus who was made flesh." In his description of the Eucharist after baptism Justin mentions that prayers are made "for him who has been enlightened and for ourselves that we, having learned true things, may be worthy to be found good workers in deed and keepers of the commands." The statements of Justin imply two senses of the offering of the gifts. The first is that gifts are offered to God and blessed, and then are used in a common meal or distributed to those who are absent. The second sense is that gifts are offered to God and become the body and blood of Christ.

From the description Justin gives we can see that the service is assuming a fixed order and has this scheme : (*a*) Readings from the Bible "as long as time allows," read by the reader ; (*b*) a sermon by the president ; (*c*) prayer, including thanksgiving and petition and intercession ; (*d*) the Kiss of Peace ; (*e*) offertory, consisting of gifts for orphans, widows, and the needy, and the elements for the Eucharist ; (*f*) the Eucharistic Prayer which gives "praise and glory to the Father of the Universe through the name of the Son and of the Holy Ghost, and gives thanks at length because we are counted worthy of these things," and includes the prayer of the Word (or word) ; (*g*) communion in both kinds which is taken by the deacons to those absent. Justin while he gives us the order does not give us any specimen of prayer.

To get an example of prayer we turn to Clement of Rome, who gives such an illustration at the close of his letters to the Corinthians. The prayer seems to arise out of an uttered wish : "May the sealed number of the elect in the whole world be preserved intact by the Creator of all things through His well-beloved Son, Jesus Christ, by Whom He has called us from darkness to light" ; and begins with the note of adoration, "Thou hast opened the eyes of our hearts that they may know Thee, Thou the sole Highest among the highest, the Holy One in the midst of the holy, Thou who bring'st low the pride of the haughty and who bring'st to naught the imaginings of the people, Who exaltest the lowly and puttest down the mighty, Thou who givest riches and poverty and bestow'st death and life," etc. The next note is that of intercession, "Take pity on the lowly, raise up them that fall, reveal

Thyself to those in need," and so the intercession continues for the hungry, the sick, the faint-hearted, and those in prison, "that all people may know that Thou art the only God and that Jesus Christ is Thy servant [1] and we are Thy people and the sheep of Thy pasture." Then follows an extolling of God's power, wisdom, and mercy which is the prelude to confession and petition: "Make Thy face to shine upon us in peace for our good, that we may be sheltered by Thy right hand and delivered from every sin by Thine outstretched arm." Thereafter there is intercession for rulers, and finally the prayer closes: "O Thou who alone art able to do these things and things more exceeding good than these, we praise Thee through the High Priest and Guardian of our souls, Jesus Christ, through Whom be the glory and the majesty."

In this prayer we see the influence of Scripture which is the legacy the Christian Church inherited from Judaism. We note too that it is worship offered to God through Christ who is termed the servant and High Priest and Guardian; prayer is not made to Christ; the Pauline tradition is followed. It is a prayer which strikes the solemn note of liturgical devotion; it is purified from exaggeration and restrained by reverent awe; it is wide in its vision and penetrating in its insight.

We find a very different ethos in the *Didaché*. Here too the influence of Jewish prayer is strong and its eucharistic devotion is formed on a Jewish model. "First give thanks over the cup. We thank Thee, our Father, for the Holy Vine of David Thy servant, which Thou hast made known to us through Jesus Christ Thy servant [1] to Thee be glory for ever." Then at the breaking of the bread. "We thank Thee, our Father, for the life and knowledge which Thou hast made known to us through Jesus Christ Thy servant,[1] to Thee be glory for ever. As this broken bread scattered on the mountains was gathered together and became one, so let Thy Church be gathered from the ends of the earth into Thy Kingdom, for Thine is the glory and the power, through Jesus Christ for ever." There is a resemblance in this scheme to the arrangement of the passover Kiddush, and the thought of Christ as Vine and Bread lies close to the Jewish thanksgiving "for the

[1] παῖς.

fruit of the vine" and "for the bread brought forth from the earth." The prayer for the unity of the Church has echoes in the tenth Benediction of the Shemôneh Esreh. "Sound the great horn for our freedom, and lift up the ensign to gather our exiles and gather us from the far corners of the earth. Blessed art Thou, O Lord, that gatherest the outcasts of Israel."[1] The Jewish skeleton shows through. "Let no one eat or drink of your eucharist save those who are baptized in the name of the Lord. For concerning this the Lord said, Give not that which is holy unto the dogs." Here we see the origin of the phrase "holy things unto the holy" in the liturgy; it is an adaptation of Christ's word. After partaking, thanksgiving is made and an intercession for the Church, concluding with the aspiration, "May grace come and the world pass away." The Aramaic phrase "Maran atha" is used after the communion and seems to have a double signification, a reference as in Rev. xxii. 20 to the Second Coming, and the recognition that in the sacramental presence Christ has come.

The prophetic ministry is in the *Didaché* still present and the mood of expectancy is expressed. It is a service different in tone from that described by Justin and unlike in temper to the prayer of Clement. Here then we have the descendant of the Breaking of Bread Service with no definite relation to the death of Christ. The Jewish feeling for order is here, but an opening is left for the outpouring of Christian enthusiasm. The note of thanksgiving dominates throughout. "Hosanna to the Son of David" sounds for the first time in the liturgical service, and carries with it the longing and the yearning for the great consummation. The Messianic Banquet is the background of this rite and not the sacrificial death. Its width of sympathy reaches out to include the whole Church. In the *Didaché* we first meet with the word "sacrifice"[2] applied to the Eucharist; it does not occur in the celebration but in the exhortation to confession, and is an echo of a Biblical phrase, "that your sacrifice be pure."[3]

Pliny tells in his report to the Emperor that the Christian had two hours of meeting on a stated day (*statodie*) which would mean

[1] Quoted Oesterley, *The Jewish Background*, p. 131.
[2] *θυσία*.
[3] Cf. Mal. i. 11.

Sunday. At the first gathering before daybreak they sang hymns to Christ as a god; at the later meeting they came together again in order to eat food (this would be the Agape or Eucharist). This adds little information save that it emphasises the adoration of Christ in praise which St. Ignatius also speaks of—to "sing to Jesus Christ in unity and loving concord." This is enough to indicate that in the praise of the Christians devotion was offered freely to Christ. In Origen we touch the distinction between the service of the catechumen and the service of the faithful. The *disciplina arcani* is developing by means of which the mysteries of the Eucharist are only for the faithful, and catechumens and penitents retire. In Origen also we have an indication that the Sanctus (Isa. vi. 3) is part of the liturgical service.[1] There is a growth and expansion of the liturgy, but we cannot in detail follow its development, since in this period owing to the *disciplina arcani* the rite of the Eucharist is not freely described.

Let us see the result that has been reached as the second book of the Apostolic Constitutions reveals it. (1) Lessons from the Old Testament two in number. (2) "Then let another sing hymns of David and the people sing in reply the ends of the verses."[2] (3) Reading from Acts and epistle. (4) Gospel reading, all stand. (5) Sermons preached by presbyters, and lastly the "bishop as becomes the captain of the ship." (6) Dismissal of Catechumens and penitents. This is the liturgy of the Catechumens.

Then follows the liturgy of the Faithful. (1) Prayers of the faithful facing the East. (2) Deacon brings the offering. (3) Kiss of Peace. (4) Deacon's prayer for the Church and the world, for the fruits of the earth, for the priests and rulers, for the bishop, for the emperor and for universal peace. Thereafter the bishop blesses the people and prays, "Save thy people, O Lord, and bless Thine inheritance which Thou hast obtained and purchased by the precious blood of Thy Christ, and hast called it a royal priesthood, a holy people." (5) Then the sacrifice is made, all standing and praying silently. (6) Communion in both kinds.

[1] Cf. Fortescue, *Mass*, p. 31.
[2] Translated by Cresswell, *Eighth Book of the Apostolic Constitutions*, p. 74.

The doors are watched that no pagan or catechumen may enter. One is struck with how little is said about the Eucharistic prayer.

If we turn to the Apostolic Tradition of Hippolytus, which represents a primitive document,[1] we find the contents of the eucharistic prayer. These are : (1) Thanksgiving for the incarnation and redemption. (2) Narrative of institution. (3) Memorial and oblation—" being mindful then of His death and resurrection, we offer to Thee the bread and cup, giving thanks unto Thee that Thou hast deemed us worthy to stand before Thee." (4) Invocation—" we beseech Thee to send Thy Holy Spirit upon the sacrifice of Thy Church." (5) Intercession—" give to all the saints who partake the fulfilment of the Holy Spirit unto the strengthening of faith in truth that we may praise and glorify Thee." (6) Doxology —" through Thy servant Jesus Christ, through Whom unto Thee be glory and honour—to the Father and the Son with the Holy Spirit in Thy Holy Church now and for ever." This prayer is steeped in the idea of sacrifice, for in the Invocation the power of God is thought of as descending upon the sacrifice on the altar. " All of the thoughts," says Lietzmann,[2] " here apparently devolve from the conception of sacrifice, and have no possible origin in the words of the institution." Here in embryo is the Roman thought, and here most markedly is this sacrificial idea asserted in its naked austerity. The Sanctus, that hymn of adoring praise, is absent.

Doctrinal tendencies, as I have hinted, reveal themselves in the worship, and these are the expression of moods and of outlook. In the early *Didaché* the same word [3] is applied to Jesus as to King David. What a world of feeling lies between that and the late prayers of Serapion, where the word " only begotten " is constantly used of Jesus. Differences of atmosphere can be felt. In the Clementine liturgy there is a Jewish strain which probably points to an early inheritance, for it dwells upon God's activity in nature and upon the working of His power in Old Testament

[1] Gavin, *Liturgy and Worship*, p. 97.
[2] Quoted, *Liturgy and Worship*, p. 100.
[3] παῦς:

history. Here is a full rich praise ; it gives the Tersanctus, " Holy, holy, holy is the Lord of hosts ; Heaven and earth are full of His glory ; Blessed is He for ever." The bishop administers the oblation saying, " the Body of Christ " ; the deacon administering the wine says, " the blood of Christ, the cup of life." In the Apostolic Tradition of Hippolytus there is, as we saw, a marked concentration on the idea of redemption. " We give thanks unto Thee, O God, through Thy beloved servant Jesus Christ, Whom in the last times Thou didst send unto us to be a Saviour, Redeemer, and Messenger of Thy Will, Who is Thine inseparable Word through Whom Thou hast made all things and Who was well-pleasing unto Thee. Him Thou didst send from Heaven into the womb of the Virgin, being borne in her womb was incarnate and shown to be Thy Son born of the Holy Spirit and the Virgin. He in fulfilment of Thy will and preparing for Thee an holy people stretched out His hands when He was suffering that He might deliver from suffering those who believed in Thee." The note of thanksgiving is not prominent ; the wider horizon of creation is but little urged in comparison with other liturgies. Contrast this with the devotional language of Serapion at the same point in the service. " We praise Thee, O uncreated God, Who art unsearchable, ineffable, and incomprehensible by any created substance. We praise Thee Who art known by Thy Son the only begotten, Who through Him art spoken of, interpreted, and made known to created nature. We praise Thee Who knowest the Son, and revealed to the saints the glories that are about Him. . . . We praise Thee, O Unseen Father, Provider of immortality, Thou art the fount of life, the fount of light, the fount of all grace and all truth, O Lover of men, O Lover of the poor Who reconcilest Thyself to all and drawest all to Thyself through the advent of Thy beloved Son. We beseech Thee make us living men. Give us the spirit of light that we may know Thee the true (God) and Him Whom Thou didst send, Jesus Christ. Give us the spirit of holiness that we may be able to tell forth and proclaim Thine unspeakable mysteries. May the Lord Jesus speak in us and the Holy Spirit and hymn Thee through us. For Thou art far above all rule and authority and power and dominion and every name that is named not only in this world but also in that which is to come. Beside Thee stand thousand thousands and myriad myriads of angels, archangels, thrones, dominions, principalities, powers; by Thee stand the two most glorious six-winged seraphim with two wings covering the face, and with two the feet, and with two flying and crying, Holy, with whom receive also our cry of Holy as we cry Holy, holy, holy, Lord God of Sabaoth, full is the heaven and earth of Thy Glory." This accumulation of adoration rings out in the preface, breaking down the wall between the seen and the unseen. Yet, despite their different tone, both prayers reflect truly Christian moods.

Differences of temperament, of race, of environment, were at work to bring forth these varieties of accent. Yet at the beginning of the fourth century we discover a framework within which the various tendencies and moods find their place, and it is on that framework the great liturgies are built. The more or less fluid liturgy of the third century passes into definite form. Local distinctions, customs, personal traits of great teachers, differences of race and tradition, have caused certain divergences in public worship, and the complementary factor, the drawing together of those who are associated in circumstance and who are dependent on the life of some great central community, creates within certain areas a similarity in the form of their service. "We may," says Duchesne,[1] "refer the liturgies with which we are acquainted to four principal types—the Syrian, the Alexandrian, the Roman, and the Gallican." Others, as Mr. E. Bishop, have sought to reduce the number of parent rites. As Duchesne himself suggests, there is an interdependence between them, but we shall accept the fourfold division. Two are Eastern, the Syrian which has its origin in Antioch, the Alexandrian which springs from Alexandria; two are Western, the Roman named after the "Eternal City," and the Gallican or perhaps better named the non-Roman, whose origin is hid in the mist of uncertainty and in the clouds of controversy. In the Eastern rite we shall find the accent on the Mystery and its basis the Incarnation; in the Western the emphasis falls on the idea of Sacrifice and it builds on the Atonement. From these parent stems there are many offsprings, and we must distinguish

[1] *Christian Worship*, p. 55.

between the rites that are merely interesting as liturgical documents, and those that are used by our fellow-Christians in worship.

Yet, despite the variation in these rites, there is a common element that far outweighs any difference. There is a framework that belongs to all and an order which in general each preserves. They all give the weekly Public Worship on the Lord's Day, although in some cases the rite was or is used daily ; but in every case it is the celebration of the Holy Supper, for all these liturgies are faithful to the practice of New Testament times in that respect. Our aim is to see what in these rites unfolds the truth and principles of worship, and crowns the Glory and Grace of God with man's devotion and praise. For I must repeat that to no one communion has it been given by God to preserve and to adorn the high splendour and deep mystery that make the full harmony of the Church's devotion. The seamless robe of adoration and of obeisance has been torn and divided between the followers of St. Peter, St. John, and St. Paul. It therefore concerns us to note what is the common heritage of all. There is the distinction between the service of instruction in the word and of prayer whose note is revelation, and the service of prayer and eucharistic offering where the note is redemption—the liturgy of the catechumens and the liturgy of the faithful. There is in the liturgy of the faithful the eucharistic prayer whose boundaries are fixed. Thanksgiving is made for (1) God's Glory, the creation of the world and of man, the guidance and control of Providence ; (2) for the gift of salvation and redemption, the incarnation of the Word in human life, the institution of the sacrament by Christ, the Passion, Death, Victory of the Lord which is expressed in the oblation ; (3) the reference to the Spirit which is explicit or implicit, the thanksgiving, and the doxology.

Before we speak of the characteristics of the rites it is well to enumerate them. I. Those of Antioch. (*a*) The Clementine liturgy, to which we have referred, and which probably was a model rather than a live liturgy. (*b*) The liturgy of St. James, once used in Jerusalem, now in Greek, is only used once a year at Zakynthos on 23rd October (St. James's Day) and at Jerusalem on the Sunday after Christmas ;[1] but in Syria it is used by the Syrian Jacobites

[1] Fortescue, *The Orthodox Eastern Church*, p. 345.

and by the Uniates who are in communion with Rome. The former Monothelite community of Lebanon now use it in a Romanised form which is called the Maronic liturgy.[1] (*c*) The Chaldean Rite,[2] used by the Nestorians and the Chaldean Uniate Church who have returned to the Roman obedience and also in a Romanised version by the Malabar Uniates.[3] (*d*) The Byzantine Rite of St. Basil and of St. Chrysostom, which is the rite of the Orthodox and which is used in many languages. It is also used by Melkite and Byzantine Uniates. (*e*) The Armenian Rite used both by the Armenian Church and also by the Armenian Uniates. II. The Alexandrian Rite, which is the parent of (*a*) St. Mark in Greek, no longer a living rite, and also of the Coptic St. Cyril (an adapted translation of St. Mark) which is used once a year in the Egyptian Church on the Friday before Palm Sunday. There are two other Coptic rites which derive ultimately also from the Alexandrian source. These are the Rite of St. Basil, which is in regular use on every occasion save four, and the Rite of St. Gregory, which is used for the Midnight liturgies of Christmas, Epiphany, and Easter. The only difference between the three Coptic rites is in the anaphora.[4] III. The Roman Rite in its original form is not in use. The present Mass is a composite form of the original rite with many Gallican variations. It is used by the whole Roman obedience in the West. There are various derived monastic rites such as Carthusian, Carmelite, Dominican, and the Lyon Rite, and the Rite of Braga. These rites were allowed to remain in 1570 when the Missal was reformed, because they "could prove a usage of at least two hundred years."[5] Uses like that of Sarum and York are no longer used in worship. IV. Non-Roman consists of (1) The Gallican Proper, which is "a family of Liturgies"[6] once used in Gaul and in Spain, in Great Britain and in our Celtic Church. It gradually disappeared. (2) The Mozarabic, which still is the form in which the Mass is celebrated at Toledo. (3) The Ambrosian, which is now in use at Milan.

[1] Fortescue, *The Mass*, p. 84.
[2] *Ibid.* p. 108.
[3] Fortescue, *The Uniate Eastern Churches*, p. 9.
[4] Duchesne, *Christian Worship*, p. 80.
[5] King, *Note on Catholic Liturgies*, p. 614.
[6] Fortescue, *The Mass*, p. 109.

During this long period from the New Testament times to the great liturgies one would naturally look for the origin of the Divine Office. Formerly these offices were thought to derive from the practice of the apostles and the early believers who were wont to observe the Jewish hours. The *Didaché* inculcates the repetition of the Lord's Prayer thrice daily, and scattered through the works of the patristic fathers there are allusions to the hours of prayer. Yet when this evidence is examined it proves faulty. These all refer to private devotion, and the Divine Office is a Church Service. Indeed apart from the liturgy we know but little of public worship throughout this period. Meetings for instruction appear to have been held but they seem to be of the nature of an instruction class. The view that the Divine Office was a public service which the laity abandoned through lukewarmness to the "religious" cannot therefore be maintained because there appears to have been no public worship of this nature. Duchesne suggests that it was the monastic movement that changed the private prayers in the Hours.

Doubtless as the enthusiasm waned the practice of private prayer would be neglected, and quite early we find the duty of prayer pointed out and recommended. In the Apostolic Tradition of Hippolytus, however, there is no longer the note simply of commendation but of injunction. "Every Christian is commanded to pray on rising in the morning; at the third and sixth hours because of their association with our Lord's Passion; at the ninth hour; on going to bed; and in the middle of the night, on account of Matt. xxv. 6 and 13." [1] This may of course have been applicable only to a limited group, but we recognise the beginning of a movement. The ascetics carried out this programme, and the consequence was that the hours of private devotion became the Office of the Hours, a public service which belonged to the duty of the religious. In time the full-orbed office—Vespers, Compline, Midnight Service, Matins, Prime, Terce, Sext, and None is completed.

One cannot ignore the influence of the ascetic spirit upon worship. One may not admit the fact that a sense of discipline as well as the spontaneous instinct to worship appears in the Church's life. An element of Jewish legalism doubtless leaked into the Church, for

[1] E. C. Ratcliff, *Liturgy and Worship*, p. 256.

wherever there is institutional religion the shadow of the Law is cast, and yet man cannot continue to worship without the institutional element in religion. When the day comes—as come it must—and the vision is dimmed, then discipline is the safeguard of what enthusiastic faith has given. The use made of the psalter in later days is a symptom of the darkening shadow of formalism. Yet there is a real sense in which discipline enters worship. The law of the spiritual life is not the superstition that merit is acquired, but the recognition that in the realm of the spiritual only through discipline is there cleansing. "The emergence of monasticism," says Dr. Kirk,[1] "finds no explanation except in the genius of Christianity itself," for since early days the Church had purified her worship by discipline. Fasting is a New Testament ordinance. The *Didaché*[2] enjoins it; the *Shepherd of Hermas*[3] discusses fasting, dwelling on its spiritual side as well as its charitable application. Fasting was practised before baptism,[4] and to this Justin Martyr and Tertullian and Hippolytus bear witness. Easter was the usual time for baptism, so this fast would coincide with the pre-Easter fast, originally only of two days' duration. The one factor in Christian worship to which the ascetic spirit testifies is the transcendence of God before Whom man is a thing of nought and in Whose presence with awe and humility he must worship. This is far from being the whole Christian thought of God, but it is an essential part. Perhaps the Church is lacking in her Public Worship of that profound and piercing sense of the Awfulness of God, because the ascetic aspect of the Christian life has fallen somewhat into the background.

Within the Ante-Nicene Church there develops the keeping of the Christian Year. From Judaism Christianity took over the custom of keeping certain festivals; but it would appear that this practice of keeping the Church Year was developed just as was the singing of hymns in Gnostic circles. Most obviously Easter is kept as the day which celebrates Christ's Victory, and Pentecost—the season which commemorates the Spirit's outpouring. To begin with, Pentecost included all the days of rejoicing after Easter, and only later came to be confined to the day which concluded

[1] *The Vision of God*, p. 470.
[2] *Didaché*, 7 f.
[3] *Similitudes*, v. 1 and 111.
[4] Acts ix. 9, 18 f.

the Easter season. Epiphany was a day early kept in the East where it celebrated the birth of Jesus, His baptism, the coming of the Magi, and the first Miracle. Baptism as a rite of initiation and of illumination was associated with the revelation to the Gentiles (the coming of the Magi) and the showing forth of His Glory (the miracle of changing water into wine). Perhaps the association of initiation and illumination in the Mystery Cults helped to link together these two thoughts in the life of the Church. Ascension Day as a festival comes later than Pentecost, for there seems doubt in the mind of the Church when this event or experience should be celebrated. Ascension appears at one time to have been commemorated together with the descent of the Holy Ghost at Pentecost,[1] and, on the other hand, in the Epistle of Barnabas [2] the phrase "when He had appeared, He ascended to Heaven," seems to mean that the ascension took place on the resurrection day. The seed of the Christian Year is thus found at an early time with certain hesitations as to the date of commemoration. The Roman Calendar goes back to the fourth century.[3] Martyrology also traces its roots to this time. It springs from the sense of the great cloud of witnesses which was a vital thought in the Eucharist. The martyr who had drunk the cup of the Lord was thought of as going straight into the presence of his Master, and his memory was inevitably connected with the remembrance of God's saints in that Public Worship which spoke of Christ's death. What does this tendency mean? Its first meaning is the sense of the historical. It stresses the events in the life of the historical Jesus, Who was born, lived this mortal life, suffered, and died; it celebrates the great experience of the Church and the acts of Divine Power; it commemorates the great figures in the Scriptures of the Church and in the Church's own history. In this the Church expresses her thankfulness to God for His gifts of great human personalities and also recognises the great saints and warriors of the faith as belonging to God's purpose. To see God's spirit and power in human lives creates the humility and gratitude of heart which the thanksgiving to God requires.

[1] Maclean, *Ancient Church Orders*, p. 129. [2] Barnabas, xv.
[3] Duchesne, *Christian Worship*, p. 289.

CHAPTER IV

WORSHIP IN THE EASTERN CHURCH, OR THE CHRISTIAN MYSTERY

THE worship of the Eastern Church possesses definite characteristics and a quality all its own. In the liturgies of the East there are enshrined many devotional practices and prayers which go back to primitive times. No form of worship has preserved so many traits of the primitive Church. There is in it also a racial characteristic. "As the Greek when he sacrificed raised his eyes to heaven, so the Roman veiled his head, for the prayer of the former was contemplation, that of the latter reflection." Mommsen's remark applies to this worship, for the height of its prayer is union with the divine, and its goal a selfless adoration. Very obvious in Eastern worship is the presence of that aspiration and mystical mood which in an earlier chapter I termed the *ascending movement*. In this worship also the deep truths embedded in the Fourth Gospel come to their fruition. Its atmosphere is that of mysterious wonder as it contemplates the course of the Divine salvation. Its centre is a Divine process rather than a Divine event; its core the Incarnation rather than the Atonement; its emphasis is the Divine Being and Nature rather than the Divine action or word. In short, it is a Christian mystery, and it gives to us the fruit of that development which under the dominant direction of the mystery mood interpreted and experienced the great Christian verities. Here we find the growth of Christian worship under one of the three historic forms of religion.

I have mentioned in the previous chapter that the expression of this spirit of devotion took two liturgical forms, the Rites of Antioch and the Rites of Alexandria. Let us take note of some of the liturgical features that are revealed to us in these rites. These rites are not subject, as are the Western Rites, to the influence of the calendar. With the exception of the lessons, they remain almost unaltered throughout the Christian Year. This does not seem to my mind to be an accidental mark in the Eastern service of the altar. The liturgy is unchanging because it contains within itself all the differences marked by the Christian Year. It is the whole drama of the Divine coming, and not simply the celebration of one act of the Divine grace. Another feature is that the responses of the people are much more evident in the East than in the West. It may be that the changing prayers of the Western Rite made more difficult the people's part in the service, and therefore it tends to disappear, or, as is more likely, the elimination of the people's part may be the "true genuine Roman tendency and spirit."[1] For example, in the Greek Liturgy of St. James[2] the people make as a response in the eucharistic prayer the words of the Sanctus and Benedictus, "Holy, Holy, Holy, Lord of Hosts, Heaven and Earth are full of Thy Glory. Hosanna in the Highest, Blessed is He that cometh in the name of the Lord. Hosanna in the Highest." In the same liturgy, after the institution spoken by the priest, the deacons say, "We believe and confess," and the people say, "We proclaim, O Lord, Thy Death and confess Thy Resurrection."[3] In the Syrian St. James,[4] after the oblation and deprecation, there are two responses, "Have mercy upon us, O Lord, the Father Almighty," and the response of adoration, "We glorify Thee, we bless Thee, we worship Thee, we believe in Thee, we beseech Thee be propitious and have mercy and hear us." This trait is more apparent in Eastern liturgies when we remember the place which the deacon has. His part is very prominent, and he is the spokesman and representative of the people, and thereby bears witness to the significant part the people had in the original service.

I have observed that the framework of the Mystery is a pronounced Eastern feature. While, of course, in eucharistic celebration the death of Christ is emphasised, it is the death that is a prelude to the Resurrection. "For as often as ye eat this bread

[1] E. Bishop, *Liturgica Historica*, p. 122.
[2] Brightman, *Eastern Liturgies*, p. 30.
[3] Brightman, p. 52. [4] *Ibid.* p. 88.

and drink this cup, ye do proclaim the death of the Son of Man and confess His Resurrection until He comes," so a Syrian rite bends to its instinctive mood the word of Scripture. "Blessed is He that came and cometh in the name of the Lord," is how the Rite of St. James modifies the established Benedictus, and links the historical coming of the Lord with His coming in the Eucharist. The Coptic Anaphora of St. Gregory is addressed to the Son, and in many places adoration is given to Christ as God. "O Lord Christ, God, King of the ages and maker of all men, I thank Thee for all the good things which Thou hast bestowed upon us, and for this communion of Thy most pure and life-giving Mysteries," are words from a prayer of St. Basil in the Divine Liturgy. At a blessing of an offering of grain in the Armenian Rite, the prayer concludes with these words, "For Thou art our resurrection and life, O Christ God, and to Thee with Father and Holy Spirit are due glory, rule, and honour." The juxtaposition of the grain offering and Christ as our resurrection is noteworthy, and the primacy given to Christ in this Doxology is significant. The Trisagion in the Armenian Rite is addressed to the Second Person of the Trinity. "Holy God, Holy and Mighty, Holy and Immortal, Thou that wast crucified for us." Alike in the Orthodox Church and in other communities we find that the whole Eucharistic service in the dramatic commemoration of Christ's incarnation, life, death, and resurrection is the forthtelling of the Christian mystery. The service sets forth in symbol and word the activity of Christ, and the worshipper is the spectator of this great drama. This approach to Christ in prayer seems to my mind to be the interpretation of the Christian faith through the cloud of the Mystery. Here is the God-man whom the worshipper adores. I do not suggest for one moment that this is not Christian worship, but it is certainly not the temper of Hebrew Christianity. It is the survival of the life-enhancing joy of the primitive Church preserved through the Mystery interpretation. In the Armenian rite of baptism there is this prayer, "Thou who hast enlightened this thy creature (*i.e.* water), Christ God darting the light of Godhead into this thy servant (the baptized person) hast freed him and cleansed him and justified him and bestowed adoption, graciously grant him equal participation of life; vouchsafe to him perpetual incorruptibility."[1] These words sound the note of the Mystery Drama. Such a quotation as the following, from a hymn at the ninth hour on Great Friday, "When the thief beheld the Author of life hanging upon the Cross, he said, 'If Thou who art crucified with us wast not God incarnate, the sun would not have hidden its rays, neither would the earth have quaked with trembling, but do thou who sufferest all things remember me in thy Kingdom, O Lord.'" creates the same impression. Far off this world of thought may be to these our modern days, but we catch in it the echoes of something that sounded also in the great mediæval mystics. It is one way, certainly not the only way, of experiencing our religion; it is the ascending spirit of worship which adores God Immanent and Eternal above and yet within all life.

I would not be blind to the fact that in the Eastern rites strange things have survived and into them certain pagan traits have entered. We find a blessing of crops, and even in the ancient Armenian Ritual prayers in connection with animal sacrifice.[2] This latter Jewish relic, like other fragments of pagan origin, is retained by the intensely conservative spirit of the East. We can say of many practices, which tended to superstition and became in the popular mind magical, that dimly shadowed behind these crude superstitions was the living sense that worship must touch all life. We have learned to live and think departmentally, but I do not think we have yet learned how to apply the spirit of our religion enshrined in the Blessed Sacrament to the economic sphere or to international relations. Perhaps even the crude paganism, which lifted its head within Christianity, has a message for our worshipful mood, since it at least felt that somehow this great wonder must make a difference to the external circumstances of man's life.

Certain differences show themselves between the Antiochene and Alexandrian liturgies, and these distinctions are most significant in the Eucharist. There is a difference as to the place of the intercession in the eucharistic prayer. Both types of liturgy link intercession to this prayer. This is not of course the only intercession in the service, for intercessory prayers are offered in the

[1] *Rituale Armenorum*, p. 95. [2] *Ibid.* pp. 55, 413.

earlier part alike in the liturgy of the catechumen and at the beginning of the liturgy of the faithful. I do not think we can dismiss this fact as simply a technical question in liturgies. In some way the Divine Presence in the Eucharist is conceived as not quite similar to the sense of God in the story of revelation; or others might put it thus, that in the eucharistic prayer our spiritual attention is concentrated on a special relation of God to man. Before this mystical Presence, or in this atmosphere, the soul must utter its desires and aspirations for the world, the Church, and God's work. Since communion is more than an individual experience of mystical union, we may not forget in the soul's ascent to God the place and portion we are assigned in this life. Therefore it is that a note of intercession must be struck. *Where* is the question.

A salient characteristic of the Antiochene eucharistic prayer is that the intercession comes after the invocation of the Spirit. This means that the intercession comes towards the close of the prayer, but the significant thing is that it comes after the consecration. This seems appropriate, for in the presence of the bread and wine, consecrated for their wondrous purpose, the remembrance of God's world and Church and of others' needs comes to the soul. This intercessory note is perhaps the outcome of prayer for those who are about to communicate, which widens out into prayer for all souls. The Alexandrian Rite, on the other hand, sets the intercession amid the thanksgiving and glory offered to God the Father. This position is probably not the original place for such petitions, as they do not fit into the context. Yet I suppose this position must have met a spiritual want or this intercessory note would never have been found in this place. Amid the contemplation of God's glory and wondrous works we remember the needs of man, into the contemplative adoration of God's nature and work comes the poignant sense that man wears the garment of mortality. Such a position is, as I have said, probably not primitive, but we must beware of that temper which speaks of a liturgical arrangement as though there were a definite right and wrong as in a mathematical conundrum. Such a liturgical assumption forgets that there is no one and exclusive way, and that liturgical differences may be the sign of different spiritual apprehensions.

Another difference is that the Alexandrian has not, as the Antiochene has, a reference to the Incarnation and the Redemption after the Sanctus. For example, the Alexandrian St. Mark reads: "Holy, Holy, Holy, Lord of Hosts, Heaven and earth are full of Thy Holy Glory. Full, in very truth, is the Heaven and earth of Thy holy glory through the manifestation of our Lord and God and Saviour Jesus Christ. Fill also, O God, this sacrifice with the blessing which is from Thee, by the descent upon it of Thy All-Holy Spirit. For our Lord and our God and Universal King, Jesus Christ, in the night wherein He surrendered Himself for our sins and suffered death in the flesh for all, sitting down at supper with His holy disciples and apostles, took bread."[1] Compare this with the Antiochene Rite of St. Chrysostom: "Holy, Holy, Lord of Hosts. Heaven and earth are full of Thy glory. Hosanna in the Highest. Blessed is He that cometh in the name of the Lord. Hosanna in the Highest. We also with the blessed powers, O Master, Lover of men, cry aloud and say, 'Holy art Thou and all Holy, Thou and Thine only begotten Son and Thine Holy Spirit, Holy art Thou and All Holy, and great is the majesty of Thy Glory, Who did so love the world as to give Thine only begotten Son that whosoever believeth in Him might not perish but have everlasting life, Who having come, and having fulfilled for us all the dispensation, in the night wherein He was given up, or rather gave Himself up, for the life of the world, took bread.'"[2] The reference in St. Chrysostom to the coming and work of Christ is very brief and very much shorter than in other liturgies of this family, but it is there. The Antiochene liturgies give the commemoration of creation and providence and of Christ's coming and life in an unbroken sequence and in a historical order from the glory of the Sanctus to the grace of the Last Supper; the Alexandrian passes with swift haste from the resounding adoration of the Sanctus to the words of the institution and carries into the upper room the glory of the Eternal hymned by the celestial choir.

Sometimes also in the Antiochene liturgies, which go back to Jerusalem (St. James and Syrian St. James), we find that they

[1] Linton, *Twenty-five Consecration Prayers*, p. 89.
[2] Linton, *op. cit.* pp. 56, 57.

have a deprecation or confession of unworthiness before the invocation of the Holy Spirit or the Epiklesis, we " offer to Thee this awesome and bloodless sacrifice, beseeching Thee that Thou wouldst not deal with us after our sins nor reward us according to our iniquities, but according to Thy gentle and unspeakable love toward men passing by and blotting out the handwriting that is against us Thy suppliants." This bears testimony to the fact that a sense of human weakness and of mortal sin is apt to break into the mood of adoring praise. Here again we may argue that this is not the occasion for this mood; but ere " the awesome and bloodless sacrifice " is offered when about to call to God for His Holy Spirit " upon us and upon the Holy gifts," it is surely natural that before this numinous fact man is conscious of his frailty and his sore need. These differences in the East take us back to real spiritual apprehensions. In the Embolismos (the expansion of the last two clauses of the Lord's Prayer) as it is given in certain rites, there is an authentic echo of the spontaneous utterance in primitive days. " Yea we beseech, O Lord our God, lead none of us into temptation which we are not able to bear by reason of our frailty, but with the temptation give us also the way of escape, that we may be able to quench all the fiery kindled darts of the enemy and deliver us from the evil one and his works." [1] Do we not feel that the origin of this lay in the outcry of some troubled soul who, ere he makes his communion, remembers the perils and snares of life? In all Eastern liturgies there is the Epiklesis or invocation of the Holy Spirit upon the worshippers and the offering in the eucharistic prayer, for to the East the words of the institution and this prayer of invocation constitute the consecration. Such prayers vary in expression, but they all point to the thought that the service is a movement, for through the coming of the Spirit there comes something new and original. They are a testimony to the Spirit's Power and reach back to the glad fervour when the Spirit-possessed found all things new. The invocation asks for power and life on God's creation, for the souls who offer and the bread and wine they offer are His creatures.

I may not linger longer on these considerations, but I would

[1] Liturgy of the Coptic Jacobites.

plead that these liturgic remains be treated with the reverence that is owed to the fabric through which the deep within man cried to the Deep in God. Here surely is holy ground, for through these words souls have been strengthened and hearts made brave. Much there may be that is foreign to our thinking and unfamiliar to our mood, but more there is that keeps alive the haunting sense of the soul's strange pilgrimage. Certainly there is in these liturgies what may seem to some minds a localised sense of the Divine Presence, but behind what to the *Zeitgeist* of to-day may seem something not far removed from the modes of magic, are shadowed the form and features of Him Who was and is the Light of the world. Let us neither treat with indifference these ways of worship because they are unlike ours, nor regard them as formulæ to be slavishly imitated. To understand how others worshipped is an exceeding help to worship. What a noble opening of a service is that of the Coptic Offering of the Morning Incense usually offered just before the Divine Liturgy: "We worship Thee, O Christ, with Thy Good Father and the Holy Ghost, saying Thou hast come, Thou hast saved us. Amen Alleluia. Lord, have mercy; Lord, have mercy; Lord, have mercy." Perhaps it belongs not to this generation (yet perchance it does) but there is something moving in the swift and direct approach to Christ without Whom the Good Father is shadowed by uncertainty and the Spirit's power dimmed by doubt. What a soul-reassuring opening is the anarxis or preliminary service, "Sir, give a blessing," and the priest responds, "Blessed be the Kingdom of the Father and the Son and the Holy Ghost, now and ever and world without end, Amen." At once a note is struck that makes worship no circumscribed thing but wide and deep and unending in its range. Is there not something that touches all Christian hearts in the distinctions made in the Coptic Offices? These are two absolutions—the absolution of the Son and the absolution of the Father. The latter begins, "Lord God Almighty, Healer of our Souls and our bodies and our spirits," speaks of Peter and the power of the Keys, and prays for pardon, "for Thou art a merciful God and pitiful, Thou art long-suffering, great in Thy mercy, and true though we sin against Thee. Pardon us, forgive us, as the Gracious One and lover of men." The other

—the absolution of the Son—begins, " Lord Jesus Christ, the only begotten Son and Word of God the Father Who hast broken every bond of our sins through Thy saving, life-giving sufferings," speaks of the receiving of the Holy Spirit whereby sins are remitted and seeks pardon, " dispense unto them (our fathers and brethren) and unto us Thy mercy and break all bonds of our sins, whether we have sinned against Thee in knowledge or in ignorance or in fearfulness of heart or in word or in deed or in faint-heartedness ; Thou, O Master, knowest the weakness of men." The distinction between the Divine as merciful and pitiful God and as the Master Who knoweth, having lived this mortal life, a distinction which can be so unreal a thing in theology, is very real in devotion. A true nuance is given here. Over the Eastern worship broods the spirit of mystery, whether the worshipper direct his gaze as in the Coptic service to the altar open and visible whereon the mystery is wrought, or as in the Byzantine Rite where the altar is veiled behind whose screen the worshipper knows the priest beseeches the mysterious coming. The hidden things of the spirit are told in ritual.

Orthodox Worship : Its Traits and Values

Let us now turn our attention to the living worship of the Orthodox Church that we may seek the meaning of this type of service and learn its value for us. To do so we shall look at the worship offered through the great Byzantine Rite which is now more widespread than any other rite save the Roman. The Orthodox Church has three liturgies—the Liturgy of St. Basil, the Liturgy of St. Chrysostom, and the Liturgy of the Pre-Sanctified (sometimes, though mistakenly, called the Liturgy of St. Gregory). The first two liturgies do not differ greatly ; the variations are only in certain prayers said in secret by the priest, one hymn and several phrases in the course of the service. The Liturgy of St. Chrysostom is a later and shortened version of that of St. Basil, and it is the liturgy that is now in common use. St. Basil's Liturgy is used only on Lenten Sundays (except Palm Sunday), Maundy Thursday, Easter Eve, and the vigils of Christmas and Epiphany, and St. Basil's Day (1st Jan.). The Liturgy of the Pre-Sanctified, which is a service where there is no consecration, is used on the weekdays of Lent except Saturdays.

There is no uniformity of language in the Orthodox communion; more than fourteen languages are permitted. The liturgical language for the patriarchate of Constantinople is Greek (not modern), Old Slavonic for the Russian Church, Roumanian for the autonomous Church of Roumania. There is even a service book published in English for the use of the Orthodox in Alaska. While therefore there is no one liturgical language it is not as a rule the speech of every day that is used. Old Slavonic, for example, is not modern Russian. Yet the use of these varied languages is the surviving evidence that the worship once was offered everywhere in a speech "understanded of" the worshippers. The Divine Liturgy is not offered daily, but on Sundays and on the greater festivals. Each church has only one altar on which the offering of the liturgy is made once a day only.

The form of the Church shares in that symbolism which is so obvious a trait of this type of worship and plays a distinctive part in the ceremonial of the service. The Church is usually built in the form of a cross or of a ship, and it has three divisions which perpetuate the early distinction between the catechumen, the energumen, and the penitent, the faithful, and those who officiate. The narthex or western porch, corresponding to the Court of the Gentiles in the Jewish Temple, was for the catechumens, energumens, and penitents, but this is now reserved for other purposes, such as baptisms and prayers for the departed. The nave is for the faithful, and corresponds to the Court of the Jews. The sanctuary, which corresponds to the Holy of holies, is behind the iconostasis or screen—the most striking feature in an Orthodox church. On the people's side of the iconostasis are the choir and the place from which the deacon directs the service. The sanctuary behind the iconostasis in which the priest offers his prayers in secret contains the Holy Table on which lie the Gospels or the Word of God to denote the Presence of the Lord, a cross signifying where the sacrifice is offered, the Reserved Sacrament and the Holy Gifts which declare the presence of redemption. The Altar [1] represents

[1] That is, the whole space behind the screen and not simply the Holy Table.

the Throne of God and also the Tomb of Christ. On the northern side behind the iconostasis is the Table of Oblation or Credence—the table whereon the bread and wine are prepared. The iconostasis has three doors; the middle door is the Royal Door. The opening and the shutting of this door have symbolic value in the various services. Sometimes the opening typifies the opening of the gates of Paradise, sometimes the opening means that entrance into the Kingdom of God has been opened to men. "The entrances and the exits through it," says a modern Orthodox service book,[1] "of the clergy symbolise the progress to and from those places where the Saviour of the world abode, since the priest at different points represents the Saviour Himself or the Angel of God proclaiming the Resurrection of Christ, while the deacon represents the Angel of the Lord or John the Baptist the forerunner." Icons of Christ and the Holy Mother are on either side of this Royal Door, and on the door itself there is a representation of the Annunciation. The door on one side is the deacon's door and on the other is the server's, used for the two processions—the Little and Great Entrance. When the curtain which hangs behind the Royal Door is withdrawn, the worshipper can look over the door and see the Holy Table. This curtain is drawn and withdrawn at fixed times during the service, and these actions have a symbolic meaning.

The Divine Liturgy is really two services going on simultaneously. The priest's actions and prayers are almost entirely behind the iconostasis and with the exception of a few exclamations his prayers are in secret. The deacon is the visible and audible figure in the service; he leads the devotions of the people. The service begins with the prothesis, which is the preparation of the bread and wine. This highly elaborate ceremonial takes the place of what was originally the offering of bread and wine made by the people. This preparation is made by the priest at the Credence Table out of sight of the congregation. Five small loaves of leavened bread (which typify the five loaves of Christ's miracle) are as a rule used. While the priest and the deacon make the preparation for the wondrous mystery, the reader goes through

[1] *Service Book of the Holy Orthodox-Catholic Apostolic Church*, p. xxxii.

the service of the Hours in front of the iconostasis. The prayer of the censer, "Unto Thee, O Christ our God, we offer incense, the symbol of spiritual fragrance; be pleased to accept it upon Thy heavenly Altar and in its stead vouchsafe to us the grace of Thy Holy Spirit," and the prayer made as the priest covers the paten and chalice, "Cover us with the shelter of Thy wings and drive away from us every foe and adversary; order our lives in peace, O Lord, have mercy upon us and upon Thy world, and save our souls for Thou only art good and lovest mankind," are illustrations of the prayers spoken in secret by the priest; but it is evident that in their origin these prayers were meant to be shared in by all.

The liturgy of the Cathechumens, which is the service of prayer, psalm, and scripture, begins with the blessing of the priest, who bestows it crosswise with the Book of the Gospels from the Holy Table. The litanies now commence; the deacon comes into the choir to read the prayers. The doors of the Iconostasis are opened because the heavens were opened at the baptism of Jesus. The litany, whose response is Kyrie eleison (Lord have mercy), is very beautiful. "In peace let us make our supplication to the Lord, ℟.[1] For the peace that is from above and for the salvation of our souls let us make our supplication unto the Lord, ℟. For the peace of the whole world, the welfare of God's Holy Church, for the unity of all, ℟. For this holy house, for those that in faith, devotion, and fear of God do enter therein, ℟. . . . For this city, for this holy church, for every city and land, and for those who in faith dwell therein, ℟. For healthful seasons, for abundance of the earth's fruits, and for peaceful days, ℟. For those who travel by sea or by land, for the sick and the suffering, for those that are in bonds and their safety, ℟. That we may be preserved from all tribulation, wrath, and necessity, ℟. Assist, preserve, pity and keep us, O God by Thy grace, ℟. Calling to mind our all holy, undefiled, most blessed and glorious Lady, the Mother of God and Ever Virgin Mary, with all the saints let us commend ourselves and each other and all our lives unto Christ our God, ℟. To Thee, O Lord." The priest (*aloud*): "For unto Thee are due all glory,

[1] ℟ Lord have mercy.

honour, and worship, to the Father, to the Son, and to the Holy Spirit, now and ever and unto all ages." This lengthy quotation illustrates certain qualities of the whole liturgy, the beauty of its prayers, the high veneration paid to the Blessed Mother, the sense of the presence of the saints, the double worship that is offered—the deacon and the choir aloud and the secret prayers of the priest, who at stated times speaks aloud as above.

At the Little Entrance the deacon, bearing the Gospel, and the priest come from the sanctuary in procession, preceded by the reader with a lighted taper. This is the symbol of Christ's entrance on His work of preaching and His approach to men. The taper teaches that Christ is the light of the world, and its bearer represents the Baptist. After this dramatic procession follows the reading of Epistle and of Gospel, which is surrounded with ceremonial. Before these readings the choir sings hymns, including the Trisagion, and the priest in secret offers prayers. Here there is an example of a characteristic trait in the service—the dialogue between the deacon and the priest. "*Deacon:* Command, Master. *Priest:* Blessed is He that cometh in the name of the Lord. *Deacon:* Bless, Master, the seat on high. *Priest:* Blessed art thou on the throne of glory of the kingdom, who sittest on the cherubim for ever and ever." Then follows the litany of the catechumens, after which they are dismissed by the deacon. In this litany the catechumens are prayed for by the faithful while the priest also prays for them in secret. This is the survival of the ancient custom. One notes that the homily has almost disappeared from this part of the liturgy. It is a characteristically Eastern omission, for the teaching ministry has been sacrificed to the dramatic presentation of the Christ Mystery.

The liturgy of the faithful is the third division of the service. After the prayers of the faithful the hymn of the Cherubim is sung, during which the Great Entrance takes place. The Royal Door which was closed before the litany of the catechumens is now opened. In this solemn procession the deacon carrying the diskos or paten with the veiled bread, and the priest bearing the chalice with its veil, preceded by the bearers carrying tapers, come from the server's door and proceed through the Royal Door to the altar.

This is the apex of the service, for this represents Christ's going to His passion and death. It is, therefore, the custom to do homage to the elements although they are not yet consecrated. The following is the hymn of the Cherubim—" Let us who represent mystically the Cherubim sing unto the life-giving Trinity a holy chant and lay aside all earthly cares (here the Great Entrance takes place) that we may receive the King of Glory escorted by the invisible company of His Heavenly Host." After prayers of intercession and prayers said by the priest and the deacon for each other, the deacon gives the warning cry, " The doors, the doors ! " and the doors of the Iconostasis are shut. The Nicene Creed is sung, " Christ is in our midst " says the priest, to whom the deacon responds, " He is and shall be."

The Trinitarian Benediction introduces the Anaphora, " Let us lift up our hearts." The preface does not alter in the Byzantine Rite, then comes the Sanctus, followed by the adoration of God and thanksgiving for His Revelation and for the Redemption of man, the words of the Institution, the Anamnesis, the Epiklesis. The doors are thrown open before, and shut after, the commemoration of the living and the dead ; " Give them rest " the priest prays for the departed, " Where they may rejoice in the light of Thy countenance . . . furthermore we offer unto Thee this our reasonable service on behalf of the whole world of the Holy Catholic and Apostolic Church . . . remember, O Lord, those who in Thy Holy Church bear fruit and are rich in good works and forget not the poor." Such are some of the petitions from this lengthy intercession. The Lord's Prayer is said. During this part of the service a dialogue between the deacon and the priest takes place. " Bless, Master, the Holy Bread," " Bless, Master, the Holy Cup," " Master, give a blessing." To all the requests of the deacon, the priest responds ; it belongs to the genius of the whole service that the priest answers the petition of the deacon. At the elevation the priest says, " Holy things to the Holy," and as he breaks the Host says in secret, " The Lamb of God, son of the Father, is broken and distributed, divided but not diminished, distributed but not consumed, sanctifying those who partake," and as he places a portion of the Holy Bread in the chalice says, " the Fulness of the

Holy Spirit." The priest communicates and thereafter the deacon, who then in secret says, " In that we have beheld the Resurrection of Christ let us bow down before the Holy Lord Jesus, Who alone is sinless. We adore Thy Cross, O Christ, and glorify and praise Thy Holy Resurrection, for Thou art our God and we know none but Thee. We call upon Thy Name, O come all ye faithful, let us acclaim Christ's Holy Resurrection, for He has endured the Cross and by death conquered death. Rejoice, O New Jerusalem, for the Glory of God sheds lustre upon thee ; lift up your voice, O Zion, and be glad. And do thou, O pure Mother of God, rejoice in the resurrection of Him whom thou hast borne. O Christ, great and most holy Passover, Wisdom, Word, and Power of God, vouchsafe that we may more perfectly partake of Thee in the eternal days of Thy Kingdom." While each person is communicated, the choir sings, " Receive ye the body of Christ, taste ye the fountain of life." In the Eastern Church adults and infants may communicate, and a child under seven communicates without the sacrament of confession. Before the communion of the faithful the Royal Door is opened so that the worshipper may see within. Prayers of thanksgiving, that God has most " graciously bestowed upon us Thy terrible and life-giving sacrament for the blessing and sanctification of our souls and our bodies " ; and prayers for continuance of joy, " assist, preserve, pity, and keep us, O God, that the whole day may be perfect, holy, peaceful, and without sin," " so that this life ended in hope of life eternal I may come into that everlasting rest where the voices of those who keep high festival shall never cease, and where the beatitude of those who behold the ineffable beauty of thy countenance is infinite." The service then concludes with the dismissal.

This hasty sketch of the liturgy is perhaps enough to show the dominant mood of Eastern worship. Here we see the representation of the drama of salvation. This dramatic quality is not confined to the Divine Liturgy, but is also paramount in every service. For example, in the service of Great Vespers symbolism is apparent. The service begins with the aspiration of worship, " O come let us worship God our King, O come let us worship and fall down before Christ our King and our God, O come let us worship and fall down before the Very Christ our King and our God, O come let us worship and fall down before Him." The priest censes the church, and this now symbolises the Spirit that moved upon the face of the waters at Creation. Then the Holy Door is shut as the entrance to Paradise was lost by man's sin in Adam, and the priest before the shut door prays in secret the prayers of light which are petitions for guidance, enlightenment, God's succour, and the presence of His Grace. In Matins after the Great Litany, "God is the Lord and hath revealed Himself unto us; Blessed is he that cometh in the name of the Lord," exclaims the deacon, and the choir sings the words four times. This is the reception of Christ. I labour this point for I wish to insist on the dramatic element. In consequence the ceremonial is of the highest import in the rite. Of course the other types of worship, Sacrifice and the Word, have a place in the service, but they are subordinate to the overmastering movement of the Mystery. In the Divine Liturgy there is the expression of man's seeking and God's coming. It belongs despite the great and rich profusion of its intercessions to the sphere of adoration rather than to that of petition. Its emphasis is on the mystical approach to God rather than on the prophetic.

In the Divine Liturgy of the modern Eastern Church we are aware of an atmosphere very unlike that in which we think and move. We feel that we are not far from the thought-world of Nicæa. Harnack has spoken of the East as static in contrast to the movement and development of the West, and in the sphere of worship this conservative instinct is shown. Right back to the far-off days of the ancient Syrian liturgy and behind it to the patristic Church and the early Church we can trace this mode of worship, and embedded like fossils in the orthodox ritual are the spontaneous cry and eager outburst of thanksgiving that were characteristic of the first beginnings. These are now embalmed in the fixed ritual. No type of worship has been so faithful to the words of devotion that were once upon the lips of bygone worshippers; but let us not dismiss this simply as a blind conservatism that has cherished the word and denied the spirit. There is a sense in which there must always be something unchanging in worship. Before the Eternal the distinctions of time are swept away; something in worship is given and is not the product of the mind and mood of the present generation. We may criticise this worship as being quite out of touch with modern thought and the outlook of a scientific age; yet we must surely admit that this worship bears testimony to the fact—so important for public devotion—that, however created, there must be the sense of the Eternal changeless and beyond time. The Eastern Church makes the Divine Liturgy itself a means by which this sense is created. The liturgy is no creation of man, but the gift of God. "We thank Thee also for this liturgy," says the form of St. Chrysostom, "which Thou hast deigned to accept at our hands, although there stand about Thee thousands of Archangels and myriads of angels, the Cherubim and the six-winged Seraphim of many eyes soaring on high, borne on the wings of worship." It is through the liturgy that man's praise becomes part of the great hymn of creation. To the Eastern, the ceremonial acts and the recited words are modes of God's Presence. To the Western and modern mind, the ritual is holy because of what it means or on account of the deep feelings it utters or evokes; to the thought of the East, the liturgy is holy in itself. It is the *Divine* Liturgy; it is the incarnation of the Spirit. The drama depicts the Incarnate God Who is present, and the liturgy is the garb which He wears. From this there results the supreme importance of public worship and a new significance is attached to united adoration and praise. It is a liturgy, a religious duty that must be fulfilled.

As in the early Church there is in the Divine Liturgy a wealth of expression; the tendency [1] which made the early believer apply to Christ titles of adoration culled from varied sources is alive. Its appeal is not intellectual but emotional. Devotion is searching for words that "half conceal and half reveal" the mystery and the wonder of the Divine. There echo in this liturgy a width and freedom of expression that belonged to the creative age of Christian faith. Christ is the fulfilment of the law and the prophets, and the Son and Agent of the Creator God. So it is not unnatural that the thought of the creation and the history of the chosen people [2] are mentioned in the high act of Eucharistic devotion, and that prayers for the crops and the weather are brought into the sacra-

[1] Cf. Deissmann, *Light from the East*, p. 388. [2] Liturgy of St. Basil.

mental service. The East also retains—perhaps some would say embalms—the spirit of joy and of festival that was the primitive atmosphere. Not exclusively with the forgiveness of sins and the sacrifice of the Cross is her great service linked.

One finds also in the Liturgy of St. Chrysostom a sense of awe, even of terror, before the holy Presence, and the mysteries are hid from the gaze of the onlooker, for the "holy sacrifice was not merely a mystery of faith, the unspeakable mystery that must be withdrawn from the eye of the unbeliever, but a mystery so dread that upon it not even the Christian himself might gaze."[1] In the Greek liturgy there is in the prayers of the priest a note of concern lest he be unworthy to perform this sacrifice.[2] This makes emphatic at once the individualistic aspect of this preparation and also the sense of fear, awe, and dread. This sense of dread is not primitive; it does not sound in the Liturgy of the Apostolic Constitution, which is indicative of the attitude of the Church of Antioch, nor in the Liturgy of Serapion, which gives the tone of Egyptian devotion. This dread aspect is probably the fruit of St. Chrysostom's spirit whereby the sense of dread interfuses and shadows the glad and joyous mood.

If we put alongside the Divine Liturgy the Western Mass we feel the contrast. (1) The Liturgy moves, as we have seen, around the presence of God in the Incarnation, the Mass turns on the Redemption at Calvary. The most impressive moment in the Liturgy is the Great Entrance, where the worshipper adores the Lamb that is to be pierced as He goes to His death and resurrection; in the Mass the moment of greatest psychological power is the elevation of the Host, where the worshipper bows before the sacrifice made for man's sin. (2) The Consecration in the Liturgy is associated with the invocation of the Spirit, but it is not definitely fixed to one point in time. This corresponds to the sense of God Immanent in the Liturgy. In the Mass the repetition of Christ's word, "This is my body," transformed the offered bread into the consecrated Host through the power of the transcendent Lord. (3) There is a difference in language corresponding perhaps to

[1] Edmund Bishop, *Lithurgica Historica*, p. 11.

[2] Edmund Bishop, *op. cit.* p. 23.

racial inheritance. The Eastern prayers are richer and more suggestive; they amplify and circle round their subject. The Roman Rite is pregnant, terse, and even at times precise and legal. Let me give one illustration. At the priest's communion in the Roman Mass, just before he receives the Host he prays, "Lord, I am not worthy that Thou shouldest enter under my roof, say but the word and my soul shall be healed," offering the simple words of the centurion. In the Liturgy the priest prays, "O Son of God, receive me as a partaker of Thy Mystical Supper. For not as a secret enemy do I approach, not with the kiss of Judas but as the thief will I confess Thee. Remember me, O Lord, in Thy Kingdom. I am not worthy, Lord, that Thou shouldest come unto me, but as Thou wast content to lodge in the stall of brute beasts and in the house of Simon the leper, and didst receive the harlot a sinner like unto me, vouchsafe in like manner to enter into the stable of my brutish soul, my defiled body dead in sin and spiritually leprous, and as Thou didst not disdain the mouth of the harlot when she kissed Thine unpolluted feet, disdain not me a sinner, O Lord my God, but make me worthy to partake of Thy most Holy Body and Blood." The Eastern gives the poetry of devotion which may at times expand to what is florid; the Roman has the directness and power of simple speech which can descend to the business-like. (4) While in the Roman use there are many ceremonies that are patent of an allegorising interpretation and are so explained by the devout imagination,[1] the essence of the Mass is not representation but the assertion of a definite result. The whole Eastern Rite, on the other hand, is not simply in all its details transfused with symbolism, but in its essence it is a dramatic movement. It is perhaps symptomatic of this that despite the display of gorgeous colour and of splendid adornment in the East, there is, as Dr. Fortescue has said, "no idea of definite liturgical colour at all."

From the standpoint of the Roman and Western outlook the Eastern Liturgies have been criticised as suffering from "arrested development."[2] (1) There is a criticism of style; the language

[1] *Way of Hearing Mass*, commended by Cardinal Vaughan, p. 9. The priest going to the altar is Jesus entering the garden of Olivet.

[2] Phrase of Dr. Fortescue.

is at times too florid and too figurative. (2) There is a criticism of content, " Apocryphal and dubious matter, spurious Gospels and legends appearing in the liturgies side by side with the authentic and true."[1] There are also surviving Jewish customs, *e.g.* Saturday is treated as having a quasi-festal character. (3) There is the practical criticism. The Liturgy is unduly lengthy and cumbrous.

In addition to these, from the Western and Reformed standpoint there are the following criticisms passed. (1) Instruction is largely ignored in worship; the sermon has often disappeared altogether and at least has a subordinate place. The ministry of the Word which originally belonged to the Liturgy of the Catechumens is not now adequately maintained. (2) There is an excess of ceremonial and ritual acts, *e.g.* the elaborate partition of the Holy Bread. (3) The adoration offered to the Holy Mother, " Meet is it in very truth to bless thee, O Birth-giver of God, ever blessed and all undefiled one and the Mother of Our God, O Most Holy Birth-giver of God, save us " ;[2] and the prayer in the Byzantine Office of the ἀποδειπνον μικρόν (Compline) : " O spotless, undefiled, immaculate, chaste Virgin lowly, espoused to God, Thou who didst by thy marvellous travail unite God the Word to mankind," are perhaps more suggestive of Isis than of the maid of Galilee and the mother of Jesus. The statement when at the preparation of the bread the priest taking one portion says, " In honour and commemoration of our most blessed Lady Mary, mother of God, ever virgin, through whose intercessions, etc.," does not recall to us the Apostolic outlook and is suggestive of other associations than of the New Testament. Let us admit there is truth in the sentence of Hatch written many years ago : " In the splendid ceremonial of Eastern (and Western) worship, in the blaze of lights, in the separation of the central point of the Rite from common view, in the procession of torch-bearers chanting their sacred hymns, there is a survival and in some cases the galvanised survival of what I cannot find it in my heart to call a Pagan ceremonial because, though it was the expression of a less enlightened faith, yet it was offered to God from a heart that was not

[1] King, *Notes on Catholic Liturgies*, p. 346 f.
[2] From the Hours.

less earnest in its search after God and in its effort after holiness than our own." [1]

Having acknowledged the presence of these tendences that are not New Testament, let us estimate the worth of this worship for us.

I. In the first place, I think there is found the sense of a Presence. Here is the *Mysterium tremendum.* In this worship the worshipper not only hears the words of God spoken by the deacon, and knows that within the sanctuary the priest makes supplication that will bring the Divine near, he also sees the pictures and the actions that show in symbol the approach of God. The sense of the " Otherness " is not a vague mysticism but God incarnate is present. If, however, the sense of mystery be missed, the whole service is but play-acting. Of course, a drama that confines itself to words and thoughts more than a thousand years old may fail in its appeal to-day. Yet it is an interesting and valuable idea which is exhibited in the Liturgy—the dramatic representation of God. Perhaps the future may give further development to this method whereby the sense of the Mysterious Presence is made central through the appeal to the dramatic sense. This need not mean that worship would be moulded only by the attempt to represent the Divine as has been done by icons and images or pictures or through acting religious plays. Such is the representational art of worship. There is also action as there is ceremonial that, while it does not represent to the eye and mind, presents the Divine Life. We would not then need to be told in word that God was present or see His Presence depicted to the eye, but we would be made to feel that God was in this place. This is the presentational side of worship. This Orthodox service uses the presentational side of worship through the influence of space, the soaring dome, the vision of the Holy Place framed by the open door, through the impenetrability of the closed door to the eye, through the light and colour, the gesture and action which are in the rite. It is not what any one of these may be supposed to signify; it is the cumulative effect that presents the Mystery. Of course, this worship freely uses the representational side also—

[1] Hatch, *Hibbert Lectures*, 1888.

pictures and icons—and it bids the open-eyed worshipper see. However this dramatic instinct be used in the future of worship—and it lies with the vision and vigour of youth to discover the methods—the East exhibits its use by evoking through symbol and ceremonial the sense of God's Mysterious Presence.

II. The Mystery is the Mystery of the Incarnation, as we saw the theme of the Liturgy is the Incarnation. This is no isolated act of the Divine. God's humility, His atoning sacrifice, and His triumphant conquest of death are the eternal verities of mysticism. They are all represented in the service. "He was transfigured before them, and His face did shine as the sun, and His raiment was white as the light."[1] This happens again; the flesh is transfigured and hence there is need of colour and action and light, for these are the raiment of the Present Lord. God becomes flesh again, and so to the worshipper these symbols are not simply objects in this world with an allegoric meaning; they belong also to that other world of God's Mysterious Life. In Christ Present mortality is glorified and becomes immortal. The worship is Christo-centric, but it is not adoration of Jesus of Nazareth but of God Incarnate. In the Byzantine Offices there are clear indications of the place Christ takes in devotion. The cosmic significance of Christ is seen in such words, "Thou didst rise as God from the tomb in Glory, and didst raise the world with Thee." Christ who brings God's Immortality into the world of created things is adored in this ode "Being true life, O Christ, Thou as a God of compassion didst garb Thyself with my corrupt nature, and didst descend into the dust of death, O Master, and didst rend mortality asunder, and rising on the third day didst clothe dead bodies with incorruption." It is noteworthy how many prayers are addressed to Christ. "O Lord Christ God, King of the ages and Creator of mankind." Christ is not so much the mediator of God; Christ is God, for the Blessed Trinity Father, Son, and Spirit is ever conceived to be present. There can therefore be no mortal mediator in this service. The priest is not prophet or leader, for it is the deacon who directs the devotion of the worshipper and gives the bidding prayer. The priest does not mediate through his personality

[1] St. Matt. xvii. 2.

God's truth, as in the Protestant faith. He is the instrument through which God acts. He is an actor in the eternal drama of the creative and redemptive power of God whose visible and outward sign is the Divine Liturgy.

III. The sense of something objective is most apparent in this service. What is heard is not vital. It is what is shadowed forth that is important. What is accomplished is the receiving and enhancing of life which comes through contact with the Divine Drama. Most clearly in this service the Holy Spirit the Lord and Giver of Life is worshipped. There is something quite outside of and apart from the feelings of the worshipper, and this prevents that subjectivity of mood which renders some forms of worship only an intercourse with the worshipper's own aspirations. Because of this emphasis it is of little matter that the secret prayers are unheard; the worshipper knows what is happening; something he does not see, something he does not hear is going on, and this unseen and unheard worship of the priest will accomplish the mysterious miracle. The fixity of the liturgy also supports this objective sense, for the liturgy has been handed down unchanged from generation to generation. This objective expression of worship makes possible the practice of contemplative prayer and the discipline of silent worship. The worshipper in the presence of this God-inspired liturgy is free to seek his own individual experience of mystical union and to follow the promptings of his own nature.

IV. There is an orderly movement which guides the devout spirit. This order has four stages: (1) In the first place, the sense of God's glory awakens the sense of human need. "O King of Heaven" recites the deacon at the opening of the Office of Oblation, "Comforter, Spirit of Truth, who art in all places and fillest all things, Fountain of all Good and Giver of Life, abide in us and cleanse us from every stain; save our soul O Beneficent One." This order—adoration and the resultant sense of weakness and unworthiness—recurs again and again. At the moment of the Trisagion, "Holy God, Holy and Almighty, Holy and Immortal," there follows this prayer in the Armenian Liturgy: "O God, who art Holy and dost rest in the Holy of holies, Who art praised by the song of the seraphim and glorified by the cherubim and adored by all heavenly powers, Who didst create all things out of nothing and didst make man after Thine own image and didst adorn him with all graces, Thou Who givest to him that seeketh wisdom and understanding, and passest not by the sinner but doth give him repentance unto salvation, Thou Who hast vouchsafed that we Thy worthless and humble servants should stand even at this time before the Glory of Thy Holy Altar . . ." From adoration to the sense of mortal need and weakness is a definite line of spiritual movement. This is evident in all Eastern worship, and the Divine Liturgy makes quite definite this first stage.

(2) Secondly, there is the sense of an equality of need. It is not private but public worship. The barriers of individuality are breaking down, and the common need of the creature before the creator is felt. This is what public worship should create, and if it fail to do so it is not corporate worship. There is in the Liturgy prayer for one another. The catechumens, as we saw, are prayed for, and there is the frequent request of the deacon for a blessing and for prayer on his behalf. For example, "Pray for me, Master," says the deacon. "May the Holy Ghost," responds the priest, "come upon thee and the power of the Most High overshadow thee." Again the priest, giving the censer to the deacon, says, "Remember me, O brother and fellow-minister," and the deacon replies, "May the Lord God remember thy priesthood in His Kingdom." Then the priest bows to the deacon and to the people, and says, "Forgive me, father and brethren." The initiative in the service belongs to the deacon who in making his request voices all the worshippers. "Bless the Holy Entrance." "Break, Master, the Holy Bread," "Fill, Master, the Holy Cup." The common request for the acts of devotion springs from the need of all. This is the overcoming of the wall of separation between individuals. This is a common worship arising from a common need. So too the presence of the departed and of the angelic hosts breaks down the barriers of individual and private exclusiveness. Confession also is made before all, for all have an equality of need. "I confess," says the priest in the Armenian Rite, turning to the

people, " before God and the Mother of God and before all Saints, and before you all the sins I have committed." Here is preserved the idea of public confession. In the modern movement termed the Oxford Group, one recognises the feeling after this sense of the equality of need in group confession. In the Divine Liturgy the presence of the unseen servants and saints of God makes the need of all felt as a common need.

(3) The worshipper gains the sense of his own place in the order of God's creation. In the Liturgy there is the acknowledgment of spiritual ranks in this great kingdom, the Divine Mother, the Holy Apostles, the Great Forerunner and Chiefest of Saints the Baptist, the Prophets and the Blessed Saints, the Blessed Dead are a spiritual order in the unseen of those who have lived the life of mortality. The Seraphim, the Cherubim, and the Angelic Host are a spiritual hierarchy of the world that is beyond sense. So the Bishop, the Priest, the Deacon, the Reader, and Servers are ranks of the Church Militant belonging to the hierarchy of this temporal world. In this corporate celebration the personal confession of each is made in face of this ordered spiritual universe of God, wherein each of God's creatures finds and fulfils his appointed vocation. Before this hierarchy the soul of the worshipper finds its own rank and station. He is no isolated soul nor individual life shut off from his fellow-creatures, be they his mortal companions or the glorified saints or God's wondrous Powers. The worshipper worships as one belonging to a great hierarchy. The discovery of his spiritual vocation and place in God's system is the worshipper's discovery of himself ; for our real self is found in the fellowship of others, when they, like us, are before the face of the Eternal, before the vision of God's Creation and Redemption, and in contact with the marshalled hosts of the unseen. The only path to true humility lies along this road of corporate communion. Otherwise we find our spiritual life without the sense of our indebtedness to others and we seek humility before God our personal Lord, forgetting that humility only is ours when we accept our spiritual place in God's hierarchy of life. In the ornate service of the East this sense of order in the spirit realm is given to us, and we learn our spiritual place. The constant evangelic appeal that is incarnate, though

sometimes hidden, in the ritual enforces this finding of our true life in the solitude of our souls as the priest unseen prays and the drama of the Divine is before our eyes.

(4) The fourth effect that belongs to this corporate worship is that the individual soul, being conscious of its own vocation and station, is united with others in an organic unity. The worshippers are made one in Christ Jesus. This is not alone a unity of feeling and of aspiration; it is the vision of a spiritual reality. "Unite us all who partake of this one bread and one cup in communion of the Holy Spirit," says St. Basil. This unity takes place not in a meeting to satisfy spiritual needs nor in a congregation of devout spirits, but in a creation of God's, the Holy Church, and His Divine Liturgy. "Let us commit ourselves and one another unto the Lord Almighty God . . . let us say with one accord, Lord have mercy," is the aspiration of the Armenian Liturgy. The fulfilment is uttered in the choir's song, "Christ is sacrificed and distributed among us, Alleluia," while the priest, breaking the consecrated bread, puts it into the chalice saying, "the Fulness of the Holy Ghost." The individual becomes part of an organic whole, and there is a common spirit which only belongs to those who having felt their common need discover their vocation; this common spirit is the spirit of holiness.

This spiritual sequence—adoration of God, the sense of unworthiness, the discovery of our spiritual place and station in the fellowship of others, and the possession of a common spirit—is the spiritual order that lies within the liturgy. The final experience of worship whereby the soul along with other souls becomes part of what is greater and more real than any soul is the great fruit of corporate worship. How it is to be expressed may leave room for debate. We moderns may attempt to analyse this experience and explain it in psychological terms, but its full expression with the sequence that leads to it is embedded in the Eastern Rite.

V. Finally, there are two traits in the Eastern Liturgies that I would mention: (1) A definite method is used to create the impression of the Presence. It is given to a few spiritual teachers by the gift of spiritual dramatic power to make the sense of Christ so actual that we feel we could touch and handle Him. This gift of imagination which belongs to a few souls is present in the liturgy. We observe the insistence on being concrete. A definite scene or incident is made use of to fix the floating aspiration to some pictorial image and thereby give the feeling of actuality. This is but the expression in words of that symbolic spirit which delights to adorn itself in ceremonial, procession, action and gesture, sensible form and lighted radiance. It may be called a psychological device or an artistic method; yet it is not ineffective. The priest setting the holy chalice on the table says, "The noble Joseph took from the cross Thine undefiled body and wrapt it in a fine linen with spices and laid it in a new sepulchre with due regard. As God Thy body was in the grave, Thy soul was in Hades, in Paradise with the thief Thou wast on the throne, O Christ." This trait of being specific is a mark of all Eastern Liturgies and Offices. In the Abyssinian Jacobite Liturgy it is exemplified by the use of Scriptural names, and in the Nestorian after Communion such phrases occur: the priest says, "the disciples wondered when the cloud received Him from them"; the people respond, "Thou hast fed us, O my Lord, with Thy body and blood"; the priest, "the doors are opened and the multitude is celebrating Thee, and the Father crieth Come, enter, My Beloved"; the people, "Thou hast fed us."[1] Or in the prayer before the Midnight service in the Byzantine Office: "Receive, O Lord, the voice of my supplication as well as that of the Holy and Wise Powers, and graciously grant that in a pure heart and spirit of humility the praise of mine unclean lips be brought before Thee, that even I may be a companion of the Wise Virgins in the brightness of my soul and may glorify Thee, the Word glorified as Father and Spirit." Allied to this illustrative trait is the way in which posture and gesture are employed to heighten spiritual feeling. "Holy Ghost, which art the fountain of life and the spring of mercy, have mercy on this people which, bowed down, adore Thy Godhead. Keep them whole and stamp upon their hearts the posture of their bodies for the inheritance and possession of good things to come." This is the prayer in secret of the priest as he and the people bow down.

(2) There is a richness of imaginative insight along with the

[1] Brightman, p. 299.

brooding of a poetic spirit. Proof of this is shown in the prayers the great Eastern services have given to other communions. To illustrate this beauty would require a volume; but I note one characteristic which may be called spiritual appropriateness. There is that most fair and very ancient poem sung at the lighting of the lamp in Great Vespers which Keble has translated.[1] At the Midnight Service one of the odes in the canon is, "O Christ, Who hast enlightened the ends of the earth by the illumination of Thy Presence and hast cleansed them by Thy Cross, enlighten with the light of Thy Knowledge of God the hearts of the faithful who sing praises unto Thee." How could the aspiration and the desire of the soul in public worship have a better expression than this bidding? "The angel of peace to guard our souls let us ask of the Lord, the expiation and forgiveness of our sins let us ask of the Lord, the great and powerful strength of Thy Holy Cross for the help of our lives let us ask of the Lord." Does not this prayer from the Nestorian Liturgy voice in its fulness and rich completeness the devotion of the Universal Church? "O Christ, the peace of those above and the tranquillity of those below, grant, O my Lord, that Thy tranquillity and peace may abide in the four corners of the world and especially with Thy Holy Catholic Church, and grant peace to the priesthood within the realm, and make wars to cease in all the world, and scatter the divided peoples that delight in war, that we may lead a quiet and peaceable life in all sobriety and godliness."[2] Time would fail me to describe the great adoring praise of the Eastern spirit. It has been vouchsafed to the Eastern Liturgies to offer the highest pæan of human adoration to the Eternal. The service of the Orthodox Church is a very splendid and majestic act of praise, instinct with poetic feeling and adorning with glowing colour and beauty the Glory of God. Because her sole aim is adoration and not a search for beauty or an effort to touch the emotions, from her ritual flow a haunting and rich beauty and a deep and glad emotion.

[1] *Church Hymnary*, 281. [2] Cf. Brightman, p. 288.

CHAPTER V

WORSHIP IN THE ROMAN CHURCH, OR THE IDEA OF SACRIFICE

IN the West there are two liturgies, the Roman and the non-Roman or Gallican which consists of the Gallican properly so called, the Mozarabic, and the Ambrosian. These Western Rites have two marks in common. The first is that certain sections of the Mass vary according to the calendar ; the second is that they use in the eucharistic prayer, " Qui pridie quam peteretur " (" Who the day before He suffered "), instead of the usual Eastern phrase, " On the night in which He was betrayed." The non-Roman Rites have in other respects a strong affinity with the Eastern Liturgies and undoubtedly they have borrowed features from the East, particularly in the sixth and seventh centuries. So pronounced is this likeness that Duchesne [1] has asserted that " the Gallican Liturgy is an Oriental liturgy introduced into the West towards the middle of the fourth century."

There are three theories as to the origin of the Gallican Rite. The first [2] is that this Liturgy came from the East by means of Lyons and thence spread throughout Gaul. This view was strongly advocated by a former generation of Anglicans, but it is now largely discarded along with its unproved assumption that there was an Ephesian Rite.[3] The second view is that Milan was the point of contact with the East. The great importance of Milan at the beginning of the fifth century may account for certain traits in the Gallican that suggest an Oriental origin, but it can hardly explain the existence of a rite spread all over the West that was different from the rite which was used in Rome, the great and inspiring capital of Western civilisation. The third view, advocated by

[1] *Op. cit.* p. 93.
[2] J. M. Neale and G. H. Forbes and F. E. Warren. [3] Duchesne.

Abbot Cabrol and Don Cagin, is that the Gallican Liturgy is the oldest form of the Western Rite, and that it is the basis from which the Roman has grown. This is the view I adopt without entering into the intricacies of this liturgical question. This opinion, however, in no way closes the door to Eastern influence upon Western liturgy, for such is undoubted ; but it does not dissociate the two Western Rites from one another. Originally the Roman Rite was confined to the Imperial City, but finally it superseded the other rites which had been used in Gaul, Spain, Britain, Northern Italy, and perhaps Africa.

In its attitude Western worship is orientated to the expiation of Christ's death as the East is towards the Incarnation. In its atmosphere Western worship aims at a certain end and specific purpose ; definite in statement and purposeful in action, it seeks to achieve an object, while the East is shadowed with mystery and vague with wonder. In its aspiration Western worship possesses a profound desire for release from bondage in the present, and the Mass declares an accomplished fact, while the East has a restless longing for what is beyond and the Liturgy gives nourishment unto eternal life, "the medicine of immortality." The Roman Mass is concentrated on the sacrifice in the Death of Christ and begins in this way a great Western tradition which is alive to-day. Barth quotes with approval the saying, "Blood is the basal colour in the portrait of the Redeemer," and the late Dr. Forsyth, who was far from being a mediævalist, points out how the Roman Mass with its Agnus Dei at Communion stresses the thought of Christ as Redeemer rather than the conception of Our Lord as the spiritual food of the soul, and is "in closest connection with the sacrifice of Christ and the virtues of His Cross."[1] And the leader of the French Neo Catholics[2] echoes the same great tradition in his noble utterance, "Christ crucified draws to Himself everything there is in man ; all things are reconciled but at the height of his heart."

The sacrificial thought is rooted in the New Testament and grounded in St. Paul. But why is the particular application made of this thought by the Roman Rite, and why is the Eucharist

[1] Forsyth, *The Church and the Sacraments*, pp. 239, 275.

[2] Jacques Maritain, *Art and Scholasticism*, p. 139.

exclusively interpreted by the category of sacrifice? The word "sacrifice" was early applied to the offering of praise and prayer.[1] Owing perhaps to Old Testament thoughts the word came to be used of the material offering rather than of the prayer offering of thanksgiving. Perhaps after the defeat of the ultra-Paulinist Marcion, and when his outlook was repudiated as heretical, there was an inevitable reaction in Rome to the Old Testament which the heretic had scouted, and a door was opened for the entrance of Hebrew sacrificial ideas as applicable to the Eucharistic offering. St. Cyprian makes first the distinction "between the oblation offered by the faithful and the sacrificium hallowed by the operation of the Holy Spirit."[2] The two great minds that influenced Western development most markedly along the line of sacrificial interpretation were St. Ambrose and St. Augustine. To St. Ambrose the Great High Priest Himself is manifest among us as the offerer, since it is His holy word that hallows the sacrifice that is offered,[3] but he also links this thought of Christ's offering to the elements which by means of the holy prayer are transformed (*transfigurantur*) into flesh and blood."[4] St. Augustine unites the idea of sacrifice to the thought of the Church's communion. "The whole redeemed city, that is the congregation or society of the saints, is offered as a universal sacrifice to God by the High Priest Who offered nothing less than Himself in suffering for us so that we might become the body of so glorious a head in that form of a servant (our human nature) which He had taken. For it was this that He offered, in this that He was offered, as it is in virtue of this (His humanity) that He is mediator, priest, and sacrifice."[5] Also Augustine's teaching on irresistible grace intertwines with his thought of communion in the Eucharist and strengthens the impulse to attach a mystical virtue to the sacred elements themselves. The expressions of the great Ambrose helped to make definite the thought of transformation; and the influence of the profound and many-sided Augustine resounds through the coming centuries. The effect of both these great leaders was to intensify the thought of sacrifice

[1] *Didaché*. [2] Brillioth, *op. cit.* p. 46. [3] Quoted Brillioth, p. 64.
[4] St. Ambrose, *De Fide*, iv. 10, 124, quoted Stone, *Holy Communion*, p. 291.
[5] *City of God*, quoted Gore, *Body of Christ*, p. 207.

as linked to the Eucharist. The sense of sin calling for expiation and the dread and peril of living which sought safety built on these basal thoughts the temple of worship.

Let us look at the Roman Mass of to-day. There is a distinction between the ordinary of the Mass which is said at every celebration and the proper, which is proper to the special day or season. There are invariable elements and variable in the Mass. The following is its order: *Prayers at the foot of the Altar*, *Introit*, *Kyrie eleison*, *Gloria in excelsis*, Collect, Commemoration (if any), Epistle, Gradual, Tract, Sequence, Gospel, *Creed*. That is the Mass of the Catechumens, and there follows the Mass of the Faithful, although the old distinction is now obliterated; Offertory, *Oblation Prayers*, *Lavabo*, Secret, *Preface*, *Sanctus*, *Canon of the Mass*, Communion, Post-Communion, *Last Gospel*.[1] The Canon which is the oldest part of the Mass is its core and centre. "In the Canon," writes Abbot Cabrol, "we find the whole doctrine of sacrifice, and of the four ends—latrentic, propitiatory, impetratory, and eucharistic—for which it is offered." The Canon, which is said silently, originally included the Preface and Sanctus; but now it begins with the prayer Te igitur, "which asks God to accept and bless the offering," and "then abruptly begins the intercession."[2] Thereafter the following is the order: the commemoration of the living, the commemoration of the saints (Communicantes, which is variable), another prayer of oblation, the prayer of consecration and the first elevation which is at the words "Hoc est enim Corpus meum" and "is a late mediæval ceremony,"[3] the anamnesis or "commemoration of the principal mysteries of the life of our Lord,"[4] the two prayers, Supra quae and Supplices Te, break the sequence of ideas and point to dislocation—the former asks God to receive this sacrifice as He received the sacrifices of the Old Testament, the latter that the sacrifice be borne to the altar on high; then the commemoration of the dead with no connection with what has preceded, then a prayer Nobis quoque, asking that we may come to the blessed fellowship of the saints, a final doxology with the

[1] Italics give the ordinary of the Mass; the rest is the variable proper of the Mass.

[2] Fortescue, *Mass*. p. 329. [3] Fortescue, *op cit.* p. 338. [4] Cabrol.

second elevation, which corresponds to the ancient elevation before communion. The Canon originally ended here, but the Lord's Prayer and embolismos have been added. The fraction follows the embolismos. Before the priests' communion there is the Pax or Kiss of Peace, and during communion at High Mass the Agnus Dei is sung by the choir. When we examine the Mass we learn that it is not a perfect unity but, like a great cathedral, parts belong to different periods. Here and there we find gaps; and the evidence that the additions do not always fit perfectly with the ancient structure. As it stands it is the survivor of many rites that once were the living vehicle of man's devotion.

There are certain peculiarities in the Roman Rite which separate it from all other Christian liturgies. Chief of these is the absence of the prayer of invocation or epiclesis, but also there is wanting the litany of intercession said by the deacon. The Kiss of Peace comes just before communion and not as in other rites at the opening of the Mass of the Faithful ; the Great Intercession in the Eucharistic Prayer is broken up in the present Mass, part comes after the Sanctus and the rest after the consecration. In the time of St. Justin Martyr, as far as we can gather, these Roman traits did not exist, but by the time of the Gelasian Sacramentary the Mass had acquired these characteristics. This is not only a question of great interest to liturgists ; it is also, as we shall see, symptomatic of the genius of the rite.

Let us glance at the origins of the Mass of to-day. Apparently what was first written down for the service was the diptychs (twice folded) [1]—the names of the living and of the dead who were mentioned in the prayers. Next the lessons appear to have been noted down. However, we do not gain a sure footing in the swamp of uncertainty until we reach the three sacramentaries, the Leonine, the Gelasian, and the Gregorian, whose dates have been much discussed and whose authors are not the names attributed to them.

(1) The Leonine Sacramentary is the oldest and is purely Roman ; but unfortunately it is very far from being complete. It does not contain the canon nor the ordinary of the Mass. Duchesne dates it about 538, but it must contain much earlier material.

[1] δίπτυχα.

Yet from it we can gain some indication of what was the temper of the Roman spirit in worship. "We beseech Thee, O God, propitiously to sanctify these gifts, and accepting the oblation of their spiritual sacrifice to make us ourselves an eternal offering to Thee" is a prayer in the Leonine. In its directness of expression it is Roman, and in its thought of sacrifice and communion it is truly Augustinian.

(2) The Gelasian Sacramentary is a Roman production with Gallican additions and insertions which have been fused with the Roman. Unlike the Leonine this is an ordered collection giving a continuous missal, masses for saints' days and votive masses, other offices and miscellaneous prayers.[1] Most plainly do we see the legalistic idea that the saying of a Mass has intrinsic value. The idea of sacrifice is detached from the idea of communion in the Eucharist. "By the term Gelasian," says Duchesne,[2] "we understand a Roman liturgical collection introduced into France some time before Adrian I. and certainly subsequent to St. Gregory."

(3) The Gregorian Sacramentary, as it is called, is a composite book. Charles the Great, desirous to unite the worship of his kingdom, asked Adrian I. for a copy of the Roman Sacramentary. Adrian seems to have sent a most inadequate book culled from an earlier sacramentary with post-Gregorian additions, but lacking in much essential material. To this a supplement was added, probably by Alcuin, and when these supplements had been fused into the original, we have the book called Gregorian, from which many of the prayers in the later missals are taken. Rome thus gave to Gaul the framework of her liturgy, and received back eventually into her own service these Gallican additions, which radiate another devotional spirit than her own. There is another type of sacramentary made up of a mixture of the Gelasian and Gregorian with certain additions,[3] which is the source of many prayers called Gelasian.

What then is the temper of the original or native Roman Mass? When we set aside the mediæval additions and the earlier adoption

[1] Cf. Fortescue, *Mass*, p. 120, and Bishop, *Historica Liturgica*, p. 39 f.
[2] *Christian Origins*, p. 129.
[3] Cf. F. E. Brightman, *Liturgy and Worship*, p. 133.

of Eastern forms and the Gallican elements, we are left with a ritual that is simple and almost puritanic.[1] It is without the ornate mystery of Mediævalism and the fervour of expression that echoes the East in many later devotions. The genius of Old Rome, dignified, sober, and practical, broods over the early expression of Christian Worship.[1] In his able essay on the Genius of the Roman Rite, Mr. E. Bishop points out its simplicity of ritual and ceremonial. "It is the Mass reduced to its least possible expression." "The singing of a psalm, the introit by the choir at the beginning on the entry of the clergy; a prayer or a collect said by the celebrant followed by readings from the Bible, separated by a psalm sung by the choir, which was called the gradual. After the collection of the offering of bread and wine from the people, during which the choir sing another psalm, our offertory, the celebrant reads another collect having reference to the offered gifts, which collect we call the secret. Next comes as an introduction to the great action of the sacrifice what we call the preface said by the celebrant and followed by a solemn chant or choral song of praise to God, the Sanctus. Then follows the great act of sacrifice itself embodying the consecration, namely, the prayer called the canon. As a preparation for the communion of the priest and people the celebrant says the Lord's Prayer, adding a few words. Then comes the communion of the people, during which a psalm is sung by the choir, which we call communion. Finally the celebrant says a third collect, our post-communion, and the assembly is dismissed."

In the ceremonial, our author adds, "we find the same character of simplicity. Ritual pomp is confined to the entry of the celebrant into the church and to the altar, and in connection with the singing of the Gospel." All the elaborate ceremonial that clusters round the elevation is wanting. We are in the presence of a type of service that is simple and restrained and makes no emotional appeal to mystery. Of the two points marked by ceremonial pomp the one is at the beginning of worship which preserves the thought that worship is the meeting-place with the Eternal, but it also marks the coming of the celebrant because he is the priest of the sacrifice.

[1] E. Bishop, *Historica Liturgica*, p. 19 f.

Something is to be done and the entry of the official who alone is empowered to offer the sacrifice is emphasised. The second element of ceremonial lays emphasis on the Gospel as the message of redemption, but this is not, as in the East, symbolic of Christ's coming, nor is it simply honour paid to God's word ; the particular emphasis is on the Gospel as the authority and warrant for this sacrifice, since it is the Gospel that narrates the story of redemption. There is here not only the absence of elaborate expressiveness, of the appeal to sensuous ornateness, there is not that moment of psychological intensity—the elevation of the Host. This mediæval addition of the elevation changes the poise of the service, for it gives a fresh apex. No longer now are the beginning of the soul's worship and the coming of the priest and the revealed word as the warrant for the sacrifice the twin foci of worship ; the moment now is the miraculous and localised Presence. It does not belong to the native Roman genius to offer the sacrifice in emotional intensity or to envelop it in mystery. What we find in it is sobriety of feeling, a restraint of expression that can seem chill, and a definiteness of purpose which can appear practical and prosaic. The mind that as in the Canon can express itself about the supreme offering of devotion in these words, " This oblation do Thou, O God, vouchsafe in all things to make blessed, consecrated, approved, reasonable, and acceptable, that it may become unto us the body and blood of Thy most dearly beloved son Jesus Christ," is a mind that loves precision and accuracy more than mystical devotion and spiritual imagination. It is a spirit that is set on accomplishing something, that is heedful to use the correct word or expression. To some minds this may savour of the external and its spirit appear legalistic. I admit there is here what belongs to the offering of the sacrifice from earliest time—the sense that the right word be used ; but I would also point out that there is a real objectivity of spirit. Worship is not simply the expression of our feelings. Something is done apart from what we are feeling, and this belief gives authority and power to the rite.

The same conclusion is reached by considering the special creation of the Roman spirit. This is the Latin collect restrained, almost impersonal, directed to one end, almost invariably addressed to

God the Father. This collect form will not prove suited to the Jesus-Mysticism of mediævalism so dominant in St. Bernard, or adapted to the warmer devotion of the younger nations ; but there is a terseness and dignity about the Latin collect that make it a permanent element in public worship. The Roman genius which in the sphere of worship as elsewhere is characteristically receptive rather than creative has here at least been touched by the creative spirit. The collect has the stability and strength of stone carving. It is a testimony to the temper of the devotional spirit in the native rite.

Mr. Edmund Bishop has illustrated from the Missal of to-day the different qualities of emotional mood by contrasting two sets of prayers which seek to voice the same spiritual desire and thought. The first, which is original Roman, is taken from the Mass for the dead on All Souls' Day, and is as follows : " O God, the creator and redeemer of all the faithful, grant to the souls of Thy servants departed the remission of all their sins that through pious supplications they may obtain the pardon which they have desired," and the secret : " Mercifully look down, O Lord, we beseech Thee, upon this sacrifice which we offer to Thee for the souls of Thy servants, that to those to whom Thou didst grant the merit of Christian faith Thou mayest also grant its reward." The second set, which is Gallican in source, comes from the Commemoration said during Lent, and is as follows : " O Almighty and Eternal God, Who hast dominion over the living and the dead and art merciful to all whom Thou foreknowest shall be Thine by faith and good works, we humbly beseech Thee that they for whom we have determined to offer up our prayers, whether the present world still detains them in the flesh or the future world hath already received them out of the body, may by the intercession of all Thy saints and the clemency of Thy pity attain pardon of all their sins," and the secret : " O God, Who alone knowest the number of the elect who are to be placed in supernal felicity, grant, we beseech Thee, that by the intercession of all Thy saints the names of all those who have been commended to our prayers and of all the faithful may be kept in that book of blessed predestination." There is a change of atmosphere in passing from the one to the other as there is also a difference of expression.

The former is more concise and simpler ; it is almost matter-of-fact in its baldness. The latter is vague and figurative as the phrase, the " book of predestination," more theological in tone, " those whom the future world hath already received out of the body."[1] This indicates within the Roman Missal the presence of two devotional moods. The rich sense of fulness that the Roman Liturgy gives is largely the result of the fact that it is not culled from one source but blends diverse emotional moods within the compass of one over-reaching aim.

The bareness of the original Roman Mass corresponds to its stark assertion of the sacrificial memorial of Christ's death. Man needs forgiveness, and this is mediated only in one way. This first emphasis continues throughout all its changes. This may seem narrow compared with the wide vista of the Greek Rites, but this concentration gives a piercing poignancy and a commanding power. Of course sacrifice as a type of worship is fraught with jeopardy. So easily can the soul of man slip back into that twilight of the spirit wherein the ghosts of magic dwell. In the Mass there is clear statement of its sacrificial intention ; in the prayer " Te igitur "—" Wherefore, O most merciful Father, we humbly pray and beseech Thee through Jesus Christ Thy son our Lord that Thou wouldst vouchsafe to receive and bless these gifts, these offerings, this holy and unblemished sacrifice which in the first place we offer Thee for Thy holy Catholic Church, that it may please Thee to grant her peace " ; or Suscipe Sancte Pater from the Offertory, " this spotless host which I thine unworthy servant do offer " ; or Unde et Memora of the Canon, we " do offer unto Thy most excellent Majesty of Thine own gifts bestowed on us." This thought of offering a sacrifice is everywhere dominant in the Missal, and it is capable of interpretation through the profound thought of St. Augustine which linked sacrifice and communion. " We can hardly turn a page of the Missal," says Abbot Cabrol, " without being struck by the evident and continued desire of the Church for the active co-operation of the faithful in the celebration of the Holy Sacrifice." The ceremonial of the Roman Mass may at times disguise this fact to which the ritual witnesses. The

[1] E. Bishop, *Historica Liturgica*, p. 3 f.

earlier prayers in particular underline the fact that the act of sacrifice is an act of the whole people. Later mediæval prayers, such as Suscipe Sancte Pater or the Placet tibi (" grant that the sacrifice which I though unworthy have offered in the light of Thy Majesty may be acceptable to Thee) at the end of the Mass which is not found in the earlier Orders and is really the private prayer of the priest, may refer only to the priest, but these are not typical. We find in " Hanc igitur " *our* bounden duty, in " Supplices Te " *we* beseech Thee, at the offertory " *we* offer unto Thee, O Lord, this chalice of salvation." " It may in fact be said," says the learned Abbot we have quoted, " that the presence of the singular number in any prayer in the Missal is an almost certain sign of later origin." Sacrifice and the sense of communion are blended.

The additions and the alterations in the Liturgy bear witness to this mastering thought. The Roman Rite has no epiclesis though probably originally the invocation was there; but the sacrifice idea does not call for this invocation of the Spirit which belongs to the Mystery circle of ideas. The validity of the sacrifice depends on its warrant and authority, and this is found in the Word of the Lord. The consecration is not dependent on the supplication of the Holy Spirit; it is wrought by the power of the Word. It is the fashion to-day to belittle the practice in the Roman Rite and to insist on the necessity of the epiclesis. I agree with this view that this invocation is spiritually appropriate and in accord with the tradition of Christian worship, but I cannot regard the thought expressed in the Roman Rite as aught but noble and austere. The wondrous miracle that brings upon the altar the Body of the Lord, this act of consecration that renews the sacrifice of Calvary before the eyes of men, is wrought by the Word of Christ spoken by His appointed servant. It is a great confession of Christ's power, but it is also a way of stating Christ's presence that accords and only accords with the sacrifice type of worship. The prayer in the Missal which takes the place of the epiclesis is the strange and difficult prayer Supplices Te, " We most humbly beseech Thee, Almighty God, to command that these things be borne by the hands of Thy holy angel to Thine altar on high in the sight of Thy divine Majesty, that as many of us as at this altar shall partake of and receive the most Holy Body and Blood of Thy Son may be filled with every heavenly blessing and grace." The thought of an altar in heaven is a familiar one in the liturgies, and Irenæus long ago spoke of "an altar in heaven to which our prayers and offerings are directed"; but the idea of Christ's Body being borne to the heavenly altar is admittedly difficult. The thought, however, is much more akin to sacrifice than the thought of the Spirit's Coming upon the elements. The Deity receives the gift and in return confers the benefit.

So of the other characteristics. The Kiss of Peace is found in other rites at the beginning of the liturgy of the faithful, and is then the sign of fellowship and unity among those who are about to join in the highest act of common worship; in the Roman the Pax comes after consecration and before communion, and it now testifies to the special communion through the sacrifice offered. The additions to the primitive Mass, while they introduce a new ethos and atmosphere, are obedient to its fundamental thought. The Agnus Dei which was added by Pope Sergius is sung at the fraction and emphasises the root thought. So too when the breath of a different spirit blew upon the Roman Rite, and when mystical feeling found entrance, the marvel was not the sweeping movement of the Orthodox Drama, it was the miracle of the sacrifice wrapt in the dark cloud of mystery. In the Canon, which is the most explicitly sacrificial part of the Mass, we find the significant addition to the words of Scripture, "This is the chalice of my blood, of the new and *eternal* testament, the mystery of faith."

I have said enough to indicate the paramount importance of the sacrificial offering in the Mass, and I have suggested the presence of other moods. In addition to the development of the mystery of the offering there are indications of the mystery mood. The Collect of the Midnight Mass at Christmas, "O God, Who hast made this most sacred night to shine forth with the brightness of the true light, grant, we beseech Thee, that we who have known the mystery of His light upon earth may enjoy also His happiness in heaven Who livest and reignest," might in sentiment have come from a celebration of the birth of Mithra; and the post-communion at the third Mass on Christmas Day, "Grant, we beseech Thee,

Almighty God, that as the new-born Saviour of the world is the author of our divine generation so He may also Himself be the giver of immortality," sees Christ as the giver of new life as well as the Saviour from sin. And Aufer a nobis, a collect from the Gelasian and Gregorian sacramentaries, "Take away from us our iniquities, we beseech Thee, O Lord, that we may be worthy to enter with pure minds into the Holy of holies," has the movement of the mystery within it.

These other thoughts and notes enrich the worship of the Mass. The Gloria in excelsis—the noble Western counterpart to the Eastern *μονογενής*—"Glory be to God on high, and on earth peace to men of good will. We praise Thee, we bless Thee, we adore Thee, we glorify Thee, we give Thee thanks for Thy great glory, O Lord God, heavenly King, God the Father Almighty; O Lord Jesus Christ, the only begotten Son, O Lord God, Lamb of God, Son of the Father, Who takest away the sins of the world, have mercy upon us; Who takest away the sins of the world, receive our prayers; Who sittest at the right hand of the Father, have mercy upon us. For Thou only art holy; Thou only art Lord; Thou only, O Jesus Christ, art most high together with the Holy Spirit in the Glory of God the Father," entered the Roman Rite from the East [1] where it is in the Byzantine morning office (Orthros). At first it was used only for Christmas, but like some other additions introduced for special occasions it has become part of the rite (save only Advent and Lent). The song of the angelic host awakens the adoring response of the Church on earth which hails the incarnation of the Divine with rapt ardour. Thus here is marked the high note of mystical adoration. It is one of the great triumphs of Rome that she, unlike the Eastern and the Gallican Rites, continues this noble and soul-satisfying song in her liturgy. Another addition with the flavour of the East [2] in it is the Kyrie. In the East this was the response of the congregation in a litany where it has a dramatic significance; but Rome has lost the litany and preserves only the cry for mercy in obedience to her spirit. She also says Kyrie eleison, Christe eleison, Kyrie eleison, changing the second

[1] Cabrol thinks it is pre-Gelasian.

[2] Introduced about 500; Fortescue.

petition to make a definite appeal to Christ the Redeemer. This great prayer, " O God, Who in creating human nature didst marvellously ennoble it, and hast still more marvellously renewed it, grant that by the mystery of this water and this wine we may be made partakers of His divinity Who vouchsafed to become partaker of our humanity, Jesus Christ Thy Son our Lord," has in its place at the blessing of the water a mystical significance. The Sanctus gives the note of the unseen worshippers, and the Hosannas and the Benedictus both lend themselves to the interpretation of the Coming of Christ to the soul in the Sacrament. The mediæval additions, like the elevation, bring the spirit of adoration into the heart of the rite. In one of the later communion prayers (Perceptio Corporis) the Ignatian thought of heavenly food is present, " through Thy loving-kindness may it avail me for a safeguard and remedy both of soul and body." This mystical mood supplements the sacrificial idea and throws over the Mass the sense of a Great Presence like the shadow of a cloud upon the face of the waters.

The Mass also bears witness to the mood of communion in the type and nature of the prayers. There are vestiges [1] of bidding prayers in the Mass, and in the prayers said in the Good Friday service which retains many old usages there is a definite example. Perhaps the collect was the summary and conclusion of the people's devotion.[2] " The liturgy," says Guardini, " is not celebrated by the individual but by the body of the faithful " ; it is not the assembled congregation " for within its embrace it includes all the faithful on earth, and it reaches out to those for whom time is not and who exist in Eternity." There is the presence of the unseen witnesses in the Confiteor, and there is mystical fellowship with apostles and saints in Nobis quoque, " to us sinners also thy servants, hoping in the multitude of thy mercies, vouchsafe to grant some part and fellowship with thy holy apostles and martyrs, with John, Stephen, . . . and with all saints into whose company we pray Thee admit us, not considering our merit but of Thine own free pardon." This is the petition to share the felicity of the blessed,

[1] " Oremus, orate fratres."

[2] Cf. Duchesne, *Christian Worship,* p. 107 ; and Frere, *Some Principles of Liturgical Reform,* p. 141.

but the communion of saints has other aspects. In the Commemoration of the Dead these words occur: "to these, O Lord, and to all that rest in Christ, we beseech Thee grant a place of refreshment, light, and peace." Here the liturgy reaches beyond the curtain of time in its desire, and makes intercession for those who have passed out of this life. Finally, here is an explicit reference to the intercession of saints "by the intercession of the blessed and glorious Mary, ever virgin, Mother of God (*Dei genetrice*), together with Thy blessed apostles Peter and Paul and Andrew and all saints, mercifully grant peace in our days."[1] This contrast shows how the seemingly inflexible Canon has been moulded by the changing thoughts of the generations. The quite simple ideas of the remembrance of the saints and their goodness and of commending the departed to God's Grace have moved into the petition for their aid. These different approaches to the sense of unseen communion enrich the liturgy.

In the liturgy the true function of corporate worship is fulfilled. The barriers of the individual self are transcended and spiritual isolation is forbidden by the use of the external and objective rite; and yet there is a wise restraint which guards the sacred intimacies of the soul. "The individual is, it is true, a member of the whole —but he is only a member; he is not merged in it, he is added to it in such a way that he throughout remains an entity."[2] This the liturgy accomplishes, for it calls men not simply to express their own desires and feelings, but to pray for what does not directly concern them, and to take part in exercises which do not always answer to their need. Through this educative discipline a fellowship reticent and yet impressive is created.

The Missal has not escaped criticism or at least tentative suggestion for improvement from Roman Catholic writers and other Catholics[3] who are not Roman. (1) Low Mass which in most country churches has become the normal service involves the saying of Mass almost entirely by the priest. The consequence of this is that the Mass tends to become a quite inaudible service. High Mass is really the true norm of the service, and Low Mass is

[1] *Libera nos.* [2] Guardini, *The Spirit of the Liturgy*, p. 47.
[3] Cf. Legg, *Essays Liturgical and Historical*, p. 22.

but an adaptation to meet the needs of local conditions where there is but a single priest. While the unheard service may leave room for personal petition and for mystical adoration, it interferes with the congregational element and tends to obscure the fellowship of corporate worship. The efforts which are made to meet this difficulty by the introduction of appropriate and popular hymns during the progress of the service are fraught with the risk which is present in the Eastern Liturgy, that two services go on at the same time whereby, if there be not dislocation, there is at least a distraction of attention. (2) The Canon is not audible, but the fact that certain prayers are called secret makes us aware that originally all the prayers of the Canon were not said in secret. (3) There is a departure in the Roman Rite from early tradition by the omission of the Epiclesis.[1] This certainly is a liturgical weakness. (4) The Missal shows signs of disorder. The prayers of intercession have been divided, the relation of one prayer to the following is not always plain, even the grammar reveals dislocation.[2] (5) A tenacious if not blind tradition maintains certain errors in the liturgy, for example, " Through the intercession of the Blessed Michael the Archangel," where apparently the angel St. Gabriel[3] is meant. This obvious correction has not been permitted, and this is perhaps typical of the spirit that refuses any change in the Mass, although the liturgy itself is the product of development. I grant that it is possible to justify certain obsolete phrases and thoughts on the ground that Cabrol brings forward. " What we may call the archaisms of the Missal are the expression of the faith of our fathers which it is our duty to watch over and to hand on to posterity." While admitting that the liturgy has greatness simply because it is not the creation of this age and that this historic continuity has real value in worship, none the less I think it unfortunate that, without sacrificing her testimony to the faith of past days, Rome does not admit of a less unbending attitude to the traditional element in her devotions. (6) The closing of the Canon has meant the loss of many noble utterances of liturgical devotion

[1] Duchesne finds the Epiclesis in Supra quæ and Supplices te. So Fortescue; but E. Bishop and W. C. Bishop find it in Quam oblationem.

[2] Who could parse " communicantes '

[3] St. Luke i. 11–19.

contained in the rites which were superseded by the Roman. (7) To these criticisms we may add that the element of common devotion has been somewhat neglected owing to the one-sided emphasis on the Miracle of the Sacrifice. (8) The importance attached to the action of elevation detracts in a measure from the thought of revelation in the Word, and obscures partially the essential ideas and order of the service—offertory, consecration, communion. (9) To minds nurtured in the Reformed branch of the Church there is an attitude to the Holy Mother, a mediævalism of theological expression, a use of the names of unknown saints, the application of the sense of mystery which at times to untutored minds approaches perilously near the magical, and a type of ceremonial which despite its impressiveness is little calculated to enlighten the mind with spiritual insight. Yet when all these criticisms have been passed, the Roman Liturgy remains a monument of liturgical power, the most moving rite and noblest liturgy in Christendom, and a most potent means of leading the soul to the sense of God.

Let us seek to evaluate some of the features in this liturgy. We shall begin with what is more external. I. There is the use of a liturgical language. To-day the Roman Rite is always said in Latin, with two exceptions—Slavonic [1] is used on the Eastern shores of the Adriatic, and occasionally Greek [2] in Papal Masses. The drawback to this practice is very apparent, for it may mean to many a service that is incomprehensible. Manifestly the use of a tongue that is not spoken by the worshippers encourages the pagan superstition hid in every heart which Tennyson speaks of in the Northern Farmer,

> "And I hallus coom'd to's chooch afoor moy Sally wur dead,
> An' 'eard 'um abummin' awaay, loike a buzzard-clock ower my 'ead,
> An' I niver knaw'd whot a mean'd, but I thowt a' ad summat to saay,
> And I thowt a said what a owt to 'a said and I coom'd awaay."

A special speech for religious purposes was not of course an original custom in Rome, for if she had been ever against the use of the vernacular, Latin would never have taken the place of Greek in the Imperial city. Latin, which appears first to have been used in

[1] Cf. King, *Notes on Catholic Liturgies*, p. 12 f. [2] Cf. King, *op. cit.* p. 13.

worship in North Africa, drove out Greek not because it was a hieratic language, but because it was the speech of ordinary life. Yet there seems to be a tendency in religious practice to employ a liturgical language. Liturgies tend to be adapted to the permanent needs of the children of men. The vague yearnings, the aspiration for assurance, the search for purity, the remembrance of the past seen in the light of a golden sunset, the gleam of the dawning future, need for their utterance words with associations removed from the commonplace. Owing to this men set aside a hieratic language for the purpose of public worship as they set aside a special building for the same end. This custom expresses not only veneration for the past but also a sense of unity in the present. The oneness of the Church takes the external form of uniformity in language. In the ears of the devout Roman Catholic, though he stand in an alien land, the same great words sound, and this fact has a certain spiritual significance.

In addition to this we must notice the power of a liturgical language to create the sense of the mysterious. The mystery of the unseen is reflected in the foreignness of the sounds. The repetition of words whose use is confined to worship, *e.g.* the triple Kyrie, the triple Agnus Dei, and Dominus vobiscum (fifteen times) has the effect of inducing a special mood.

II. Our second point is the distinctive feature of the Western Rite, namely, its Proper is governed by the calendar, so that the service is altered to "fit the feast, fast, or Saint's day." The Western Church has built its unity out of its yearly observance. The anticipation of Advent, the celebration of the Incarnation, the discipline of Lent, the passion of Holy Week, the joy of Easter, the mystery of Ascension, the gift of the Spirit, these and the remembrance of Saints give variety. The Ordinary of the Mass which gives the idea of sacrifice in the Canon is unaltered, but the Proper varies, giving its atmosphere and colour to the sacrificial offering. This variety is not an original trait of the Latin Rite, but after the fixing of the ecclesiastical year [1] ceremonial and ritual, colour and lights, interpret the appropriate mood of each season. By this adoption of the ecclesiastical year a stage is provided for

[1] Second half of fourth century.

dramatising Christian experience.[1] The effect of this is twofold, (*a*) To the mind half-awakened to spiritual truth there is exhibited the mysterious and dramatic life of Christ in its prophecy, in its sacrifice, in its victory, and in its fulfilment. This gathers into it the old feelings which in the dawn of life found expression in the birth and dying of the year. Through the pageant of the Divine Life the glories of the year's processional mysteries, the twilight secrecies of nature, find expression which stirs if it does not enlighten man's heart. This expression is fraught with peril if it be dissociated from the insight of an ethical conscience and from the light of history's revelation.

(*b*) The second effect consists in the spiritual interpretation of this dramatic portrayal. The soul finds within an echoing chord and the rhythm of human experience is one with the rhythm of the Church Year. The birth of hope, the appeal of truth, the bleak tragedy of defeat, the triumph over disaster, the opening of the unseen, and the inspiration of the Spirit's presence are inner experiences ; and the events in the life of Christ and the whole drama of Divine Redemption as presented to the eye and ear unfold the hidden drama of the inner life. If one reads the variable portions of the Missal from this point of view, we see this weaving together of the world of redemption and the story of the soul. " To Thee, O Lord, have I lifted up my soul," is the opening of the introit for the first Sunday in Advent. " Stir up our hearts, O Lord, to make ready the ways of Thine Only-begotten Son that through His coming we may be worthy to serve Thee with purified mind," is the Advent Collect. May " we who are bathed in the new light of Thine Incarnate Word show forth in our works what by faith shines in our minds " is the aspiration of the Christmas Collect, which declares the vision of new truth and its consequences. The result of this revelation is to make known our true nature. " He restored us by the new light of His Own Immortality." [2] We can trace this rhythm through the purgation of Lent, " Who by the fasting of the body dost curb our vices, dost lift up our minds, dost give us strength and reward " ; [3] the strange fact of experience that redemption

[1] Cf. Heiler, *Der Catholismus*, p. 386.
[2] Preface to Epiphany. [3] Preface to Lent.

comes out of defeat, "Who didst set the salvation of mankind upon the tree of the Cross, so that whence came death thence also life might rise again, and He that overcame by the tree on the same tree also might be overcome";[1] the appeal and the redemption of Good Friday declared in the Reproaches; the victory of Easter, "Who by dying hath overcome our death and by rising again hath restored our life";[2] the Ascension whereby the temporal becomes eternal, "On which Thine Only-begotten Son, Our Lord, set at the right hand of Thy Glory the substance of our frail human nature which He had taken to Himself";[3] to the joy and unity of Whitsuntide, "The Spirit of the Lord hath filled the whole earth."[4] Throughout the season after Pentecost the ritual echoes the Pentecostal theme in different moods, the unity and glory of the Trinity, the hidden presence and blessed joy of Corpus Christi, and the Proper of each Sunday expresses the variety of this supernatural experience. Through the yearly circuit there is presented the panorama of the soul's redemption with the cleansing and illumination which spring from the contemplation of the blessed in the festival of saints. The outward sequence points to the stages of the soul's pilgrim path. Sometimes to the face of a world buoyant with this world's hope and smiling with the fresh life of Spring the Church Year speaks the stern discipline of Lent and unveils the piercing tragedy of the Passion; sometimes the tidings of Easter are echoed through the vigour and freshness of the earth's new life.

III. There is a uniformity in the Roman Rite. The Roman obedience in the West, with the exception of the Ambrosian Rite at Milan and the Mozarabic at Toledo and at Salamanca,[5] is uniform. It is only right, however, to remember that in the East eighteen different rites are now used by the Uniates who are subject to the Roman obedience. Uniformity, however, is a real feature in this worship and fulfils a definite function. It is not to be regarded as the relic of a legalistic outlook. As we look across the centuries we see that something was at stake when Rome insisted on a uniformity of rule and of rite, for this uniformity was a means of creating unity.

[1] Preface at the Passion. [2] Preface at Eastertide.
[3] Communicantes at Ascension. [4] Introit for Whit-Sunday.
[5] Cf. King, *Notes on Catholic Liturgies*, p. 251.

Nothing can be more life-destroying than the heavy foot of a blind mechanism trampling everything into sameness ; but uniformity may mean something quite other than dead tradition. Unity without uniformity has been accepted by many as the ideal of religious worship. Perhaps these advocates do not always allow for the facts of human life and the way in which human nature works. If uniformity meant the crushing of individuality few would be found to speak a word in its favour. But is it so ? Our behaviour is not always the result of knowledge. We do not walk because we know how to walk, we learn how to walk because we can walk. Generous actions are the fruit of generous feeling, but also by doing kind deeds the feeling and motive of kindness may be induced. There is in human nature the double relation—our knowledge prescribes and shapes for us our deed, but our behaviour also creates and brings to consciousness our knowledge. To no sphere does this apply more than to worship. Our knowledge of God and our sense of the Unseen give rise to certain acts of worship ; but our acts of worship awaken the sense of the Unseen and bring to awareness our knowledge of God. Corporate worship can be the outward sign of a real unity and fellowship, but corporate worship can also be a means of creating and stimulating this sense of unity. As long as the methods of worship are the choice of an eclectic taste it will evoke unity only among the select who share that taste. Uniformity of worship will not make men alike, but it can help to make men united. To this truth testimony is borne in the rigidity of the Roman ritual. Something is needed to create the sense of Christian unity amid the sharp cleavages of racial feeling and national spirit, and the bitter chasm of economic distinctions. The Roman worship at least tries to fashion a rite which will unite men of all races and of every temper. Her method is the uniformity that seeks to create a unity through common associations with the same rite and ceremonial. Those of us who are old enough to remember the tragic weakness of national churches at the outbreak of the Great War and the pitiful incompetence of their spiritual leaders ought to recognise that the unity of Christian feeling may be promoted through a common behaviour in worship. I am not advocating that we adopt the uniformity of the Roman Rite but I do suggest that unity without some form of uniformity is apt not to exist at all, and that we must seek to express the common Christian feeling through common acts and to create by these same acts of worship this feeling of unity. Since to-day we see the ship of the Christian faith exposed to wreckage on the waves of racial feeling and by storms of national discords, it is supremely important for the welfare of the Church Catholic and for the peace of the world, not simply to discuss the differences between the Churches, but to make a definite and bold attempt to find identical acts and words of worship in which the members of different communions could share.

IV. A unique feature in the Mass is the power and the method with which the Sense of the Presence is given. The sacrifice which man offers becomes by supernatural power the Body and Blood of our Lord. This is the blending of the sacrifice idea with the mood of mystery. The renewal of the sacrifice of Calvary is made before the eyes of the worshippers, and the miracle of Christ in the Host is present to their awed feelings. In the finding of the Council of Trent on the Eucharist it is explicitly taught that the Body and the Blood as also the Soul and Divinity of the Lord Christ are "truly, really, and substantially in the sacrament of the Holy Eucharist," and the faithful are required to believe "the change of the whole substance of the bread into the Body and the whole substance of the wine into the Blood, only the appearance of bread and wine remaining." The doctrine of the Roman Church has become associated with outworn philosophical phrases and for its interpretation we require a fresh vocabulary. What we notice about the mediæval doctrine of Transubstantiation is that it follows the footsteps of popular devotion which was often crude and unenlightened in its thought. St. Thomas Aquinas accepts as a fact the physical miracle and seeks to explain that fact spiritually. The substance, *i.e.* the essence which is beyond the reach of the senses, becomes after consecration the Body of Christ. This belief we must admit is a singularly impressive method whereby the sense of the Divine Presence is mediated to man. Obviously this worship has in it the sense of mystery, and the feeling of mystery supplies the life-blood to the sentiment of reverence. Further, this form of worship uses the aid of the senses to make actual to the soul the fact of the Divine Presence. Sight and sound are employed, and through the use of incense the sense—whose associative power is strongest—of smell is utilised. The primal sensations that circled round man's earliest worship are summoned in the liturgy to the aid of Christian worship. I do not stay to consider the adequacy or inadequacy of the doctrines implicit in this method of worship, I only point out that it does succeed in creating the sense of a mysterious presence and in making the sacrifice of Calvary an eternal verity and a direct experience.

V. The Worship of the Mass has both a personal and an impersonal aspect.

(1) I take in the first place the latter aspect, the impersonalness of this Worship. The feeling that something is being done outside the emotions and the thoughts of the worshipper is clearly present in this rite. Let us analyse this impersonalness of worship. We see it revealed in two ways, (*a*) as a method, (*b*) as a mood.

(*a*) The parallel between worship as an art and other forms of art is obvious here.[1] This Latin rite is restrained and unemotional in its original form, and because of that might be said not to have a personal appeal. That, however, is not the main point here. There is in this type of worship a deliberate veiling of personality. Most obvious is this in the action of the priest. He is divested of personal attributes and is garbed in clothing that cloaks his individuality in his office as celebrant of the sacrifice. Many of the prayers are unheard and no trace of personality vibrates through the service. But the rite is impersonal in a deeper sense than that. A more subtle method is used than simply cancelling the personality of the celebrant. In the rite are voiced not the reactions of the worshipper—his emotions, his feelings, his spiritual interpretations—but the simple and austere facts of the spiritual life. This might be called the classical spirit of worship. In classical art an artist does not depict his impressions. If he would make us feel as he felt then he must leave out his own feelings and must not delineate the impressions that the object made on him. He must reduce to its essential features the object and give it to us refracted through his personality as a mirror. This is what happens

[1] Cf. Berenson, *Central Italian Painters*, p. 70 f.

in the worship of the liturgy. The salient facts of redemption are set forth, the essential motif of the spirit is mentioned in confession, adoration, thanksgiving, and intercession. The method used is impersonal in that it is not a vivid and moving description of how these great religious verities affect men. Something of what we find in nature is here. "The silence of the starry skies" and "the peace that is among the lonely hills" echo the same majestic power beyond our life. In the type of prayer offered, in the way in which the prayer is offered, in the processional movement of the service there is active this impersonal method. The worshippers make their own reactions, feel their own personal impressions before Something that goes on with the certainty of a law of nature and with the marvel of God's supernatural Presence. I am not discussing the truth or falsity of the ideas involved; what I do wish to point out is that this method of worship, owing to its impersonal aspect, can have great impressiveness.

(*b*) Impersonalness is not only a method but a mood. The mood springs from a quality that the rite possesses. There is something impassive here, something lifted up and outwith all human experience. It may seem strange to use the word "impassive" about the cultus of the Church that has so dwelt on the bleeding wounds and pierced heart of Jesus, so magnified the dolours and the suffering of Our Lady, and so clung to her human sympathy and mother heart, so brought near the warm fellowship of immortal saints in bliss and invoked by tender appeal their aid. Most clearly is all this romanticism of sentiment written in history and stamped upon the forehead of this cult. None the less, there is something impassive enshrined at the heart of this worship—the inexpressible God beyond our imaginings, the Deity that tabernacles in things mortal and hides beneath the appearance of bread and wine, a Being thinking not our thoughts nor subject to what influences us. Indeed the very presence of these other romantic and sympathetic traits is a proof how carefully guarded is the mystery of the innermost. Behind all the moving appeals there is a remote mystery. Perhaps the cult of the Virgin and the appeal to the Saints are but symptoms of how God's impassivity is enshrined in the liturgy. For a distinction in doctrine is drawn between supreme worship (*latria*) which can be offered to God alone, and the veneration (*dulia*) which is rendered to saints and angels, and the worship (*hyperdulia*) which is given to the Virgin. These latter are but the outworks of this Infinite—the tribute mortal weakness pays to the Eternal and Changeless. This may or may not be akin to Aristotle's Unmoved. It is not conscious thought but a worship form with which we have to do. For this reason I find that the quality of impassivity in the liturgy creates the mood which I have called impersonal. A solemn stillness lies behind the movement of the priest and the whispered prayer and the soaring anthem—something hieratic, majestic, lone. There is a spell in this akin to the spell of towering crag or starlit sky.[1]

In the liturgy of the Mass I find this mood not only in the mystery of the twilight but also in the communion of the saints. The saints like us have lived their mortal lives but they are now in glory. They are not simply remembered but named. Certainly the approach to them may be made through the memory of what they once were, but they too have gained a certain impassivity in the halo of their glory. The rite is little concerned with what we know about their mortal doings. Some of the saints exist only as names; their mortal lives are swallowed up in the night of forgetfulness. But they are in the rite because they are in glory. Now the saints are impassive in the sense that they are not moved by what moves us; they do not react as we do to the fears that dismay and the dreads that overwhelm, to the dreams that dazzle and the hopes that inspire. This too contributes to the impersonal mood.

The strength of this impersonal appeal in the Liturgy rests on two things. (*a*) Where there is no personal expressiveness, no emotional likeness to oneself, where it is not possible to be in communion with one's own moods, that is the situation most conducive to the mood of mystery so strongly attractive in its self-oblivion. (*b*) Just as in certain moods we are ardently drawn to those who share our thoughts and yearnings, so in other moods we are equally attracted by those whose lives are unlike ours—who do not react as we do and whose inner life is hid from us. The latter seem to move through what perplexes and entangles us in

[1] Cf. Guardini, *The Spirit of the Liturgy*, p. 149.

calm and sovereign indifference. This chord sounds in the liturgy. The vision of an existence undismayed by what dismays us and untouched by what makes us afraid ministers strength and solace. Whether this be through the sense of a Divine existence beyond our imagining, or by the communion with the departed in bliss whose life is not shadowed like ours, there is in this experience a strengthening. Not alone in sympathetic understanding is there comfort, but also to the strangely endowed soul of man in the life beyond his reach there is succour. The aspect of God Who is unlike us, the Infinite and the Eternal, the Otherness of the Supreme, the aspect of Christ Who is unlike us, the strange and mysterious Figure Who has attained through His Own Power and who can veil Himself in hidden guise, the aspect of the saints in glory who breathe a clearer air than ours and live a life veiled from our knowing—these are all vital to this rite and give this feature of impersonalness.

(2) Yet there is another side to the shield. In two respects the liturgy is personal in its appeal and in the sequence of its order. (*a*) We have seen that the liturgy resembled a great work of art or the mighty powers of Nature in possessing an impersonal character which has great and emancipating meanings, though we cannot say what its purpose is. But within this framework there is set a purpose definite and personal. The purpose is salvation, to free the burdened soul, to cleanse the guilt by making anew the sacrifice which will bring peace and content of spirit. This aim is ever showing itself and making a personal claim on the worshipper. Into the lonely recesses of the soul the worshipper is led as he is brought before the stupendous fact of God's saving Presence. The appeal comes in concrete form so as to arouse the imagination and to strike the conscience. In books of devotion we find a detailed correspondence between the events of the Gospel story and the acts performed and the words spoken. Thrice is the Kyrie sung, three times did Peter deny his Lord. The going to the altar recalls how Jesus and His disciples entered the Garden before the Great Sacrifice ; and the movement from the Epistle side of the Church to the Gospel side figures the taking of the Lord from Pilate's court to Herod. The lifting of the veil mirrors Christ stripped of

His garments. These explanations may seem very artificial, and are quite heedless of the origin of the ritual act or ceremony; but they are evidence of how the liturgy is used in worship, and they reveal the concentrated purpose of the whole service.

(*b*) There is also a personal interpretation of the sequence or movement in the Mass. The preparation of the priest (Psalm 42, the Confiteor and the versicles, which since the tenth century are part of the Mass) gives the disposition in which to approach the dread mystery of God's Sacrifice—" humility, love, desire, contrition, and confidence." [1] The confession before God and His saints and those present (Confiteor), the appeal of the Kyrie and the adoration of the Gloria, the revelation of the Word (Epistle and Gospel), the answer of faith (the Creed), these belong to the preparation. Then the offertory—formerly the material offering of the people, now the offering of bread and wine and prayer, is the first stage in the sacrifice. The offering of poor human nature is to be made supernatural by God's Power, for God has created life and redeemed it. (" O God, who in creating human nature didst marvellously ennoble it and hast still more marvellously renewed it.") In the nearer approach to the Divine there comes the note of renewed humility (In spiritu humilitatis) and the cleansing of the soul figured in the lavabo or washing. The offering is made before the remembrance of Christ's Passion and Resurrection and of the saints whom He hath redeemed (Suscipe sancta Trinitas). The high duty of thanksgiving (Vere dignum et iustum) declares the wonder and glory of the Eternal who is besought to accept this offering (Te igitur). Now as we are nearing this supreme moment our fellow-creatures are remembered,[2] for in union with them this offering is made and consecrated and the saints are commemorated [3] with whom in this high act the worshippers are associated. God's blessing is asked [4] that the offering may become the Body and Blood of Our Lord,[5] and the historical narrative of the Last Supper is made part of the prayer.[6] The historical Jesus is the Christ of devotion; the Anamnesis or commemoration of the Lord's Victory and Death, " Wherefore, O Lord, we Thy servants as also Thy

[1] Cabrol. [2] Memento domine. [3] Communicantes.
[4] Hanc igitur. [5] Quam oblationem. [6] Qui pridie.

holy people, calling to mind the Blessed Passion of the same Christ Thy Son Our Lord, and also His Rising up from hell and His Glorious Ascension into heaven, do offer unto Thy Most Excellent Majesty of Thine Own gifts bestowed upon us a pure victim, a holy victim, a spotless victim, the holy Bread of eternal life and the Chalice of everlasting salvation," is followed by the symbolic prayer (Supplices Te) which is the petition for the ascension of the mortal to the Eternal. The limits of this life are transcended and the worshipper is reaching to that heavenly reality where abide the departed (Memento etiam). Into this high fellowship [1] he too would enter through Christ the present Redeemer [2] and the broken Bread,[3] in Whose words he prays [4] and Whose Grace is implored in the Agnus Dei. The prayer to Christ for a true [5] and fruitful [6] communion is offered. The high resolve to take the Bread of the Lord gives rise to the sudden stab of unworthiness (Lord, I am not worthy). Then is the reception of God's wondrous Presence given through the sacrifice, which is followed by the thanksgiving of the Post-communion, and the blessing of dismissal. This is the old end of the "Missa," but now the priest's prayer that the sacrifice he has offered be blessed, and the first chapter of St. John, "In the beginning was the Word . . ." have become part of the Mass, so that the rite ends on the note of the Incarnation of Him Who was made the Sacrifice and is the Redeemer of man. The horizon of Eternity is the final landscape which is given by this sacrificial worship.

This is the liturgy of life. From the resolve of the Will, through penitence and praise, by the wonder of God's Grace and Sacrifice new life is created and a new spirit comes. Interwoven in the movement are moods of humility and exaltation, of vision and of self-immolation, of the Divine Presence and of human friendship. So the mystical spirit has read this service in which we recognise a great work of art not created by one mind but by the slow fashioning of human need. It is along these lines that we find the liturgy

[1] Nobis quoque.

[2] The uncovering of the Chalice and the making of the sign of the Cross with the Blessed Bread.

[3] The fraction.

[4] Pater noster.

[5] Domine Jesu Christe.

[6] Perceptio corporis.

used in a teaching ministry. Its prayers are explained, the spiritual reasons why they are in the Mass are given, sequence of mood is demonstrated from it, and the desires which ought to be in worship are illustrated by it. One must acknowledge there is a real advantage for the purpose of teaching in a liturgy with an historical development which is a compendium of theological thought. It is far more effective than any creed or catechism, because its teaching is part of the practice of devotion. Yet all attempts that have been made thus far to adapt to the needs of other communions and of another theological outlook the great Roman Rite have within them the seed of failure. The Roman system is one and the Missal has its supreme place because it affirms hierarchical rule and the uniformity and the discipline of worship. It is a great work of art which cannot be cut to pieces, and illustrates a vital type of worship whose essential traits must belong to the ideal liturgy of the universal and catholic Church.

CHAPTER VI

NON-ROMAN WESTERN RITES

While certainly the Roman Mass received additions such as the Kyrie and the Gloria from Eastern source, the Non-Roman Western Rites are in all respects but one much nearer the Eastern forms in order and in contents. The one point of outstanding difference between these Non-Roman Rites and the invariable liturgies of the East is that they contain much greater variety than even the Roman Mass. The resemblances, however, between the Western Non-Roman and the Eastern Liturgies are far more significant than their differences. The "Eucharistic Mystery"—the recital of the drama of Redemption—which is characteristic of the East and was lacking in the original or native Roman Rite is present in these liturgies. They retain the traditional order of the East, they originally possessed an invocation of the Spirit, they contain prayers redolent of Eastern phrase and Oriental thoughts. Yet we cannot see in them any definite theological difference from Rome, or any fundamental opposition between their type of worship and that of Rome. The distinction between the Roman and the Gallican is real in the sphere of liturgical usage and expression, but this does not point to an essential difference in the outlook upon worship. The sacrifice idea is expressed in the Columban Book of Deer, "Here give the sacrifice to Him."[1] The phrase "valid Eucharist"[2] found in the Missal of Reichenau[3] as in the Mozarabic Rite is akin to the Sacrifice-offering circle of ideas, for it suggests that the Eucharist must be duly performed in order to be a means of grace. The Gallican contribution to worship does not consist in a new conception of sacrifice, but rather in a mode of expression that is moulded by racial temperament and national feeling.

[1] Warren, *The Liturgy and Ritual of the Celtic Church*, p. 164.

[2] *Legitima eucharistica.* [3] Neale and Forbes, *Gallican Liturgies*, p. 4.

Varieties of religious temperament colour the type of worship and give it a special emphasis and a fresh tone.

Let us first glance at the living Ambrosian Rite which in its present form has been largely Romanised. Some liturgical scholars, *e.g.* Fortescue and Duchesne, regard it as being Gallican, while others, *e.g.* Edmund Bishop, treat it as being a variation of the Roman Rite. Into this intriguing but difficult question I shall not enter. If we call it Gallican and trace its sources to Antioch, we must admit that it has been Romanised in a remarkable way; or if we say that it is Roman in origin, we must needs recognise in it features that are specifically Oriental and do not belong to the historic Roman Rite. It is enough for our purpose to note that while it possesses something of the Roman terseness of form there are also present Oriental usages and non-Roman modes of feeling. For example, the following ingressa or introit for Quinquagesima Sunday, "Pleasant is this present life, and it passeth away; terrible is Thy judgment, O Christ, and it endureth. Let us therefore abandon a love not firmly established, and reflect upon the boundless terror, crying aloud, O Christ, have mercy upon us"[1] points to an Eastern origin. Whether or not this rite was deliberately adapted from an Antiochene source there is no question that the Orient has cast its shadow upon it. Whether or not Milan was the gateway for Eastern influence to pass into the West, there is no doubt that Byzantine and Palestinian resemblances are a striking feature of all Gallican Rites. Whatever we call the Ambrosian Rite it is in many respects Gallican in tone. Take as an illustration this prayer from the Ambrosian Breviary: "O God, Who by the leadership of Thy servant Moses didst vouchsafe to deliver Thy heavily oppressed people from the Egypt of darkness, grant that we also Thy servants being freed from the darkness of this world may enter into the rest promised to the fathers."[2] This collect is obviously Roman in form and in expression, and yet it is suggestive of two Gallican traits—the one is a love for scriptural references, the other is the thought of rest. The same trait is

[1] Quoted Atchley, *Ambrosian Liturgy*, p. ix.

[2] Lauds Secret Collect, quoted W. C. Bishop, *Mozarabic and Ambrosian Rites*, p. 102.

found in the commemoration of the departed, "Thou, Who didst raise Lazarus after he had been dead four days, give rest to them and a place of indulgence," with the response, "Eternal rest give to them, O Lord, and let perpetual light shine upon them. Give unto them rest and a place of indulgence."

We find some interesting survivals. Alone of all rites has this rite of Milan retained in the ceremony of the Vecchioni the primitive offering of the people when they brought bread and wine. In the original Milanese liturgy there was not only an epiclesis, but there is preserved in the Missal on Maundy Thursday a logos epiclesis [1] which reaches back to the far-off prayer of Serapion. Ambrosian Vespers [2] seem to be the continuation of the little post-agape service which Tertullian describes. There are in this rite one or two liturgical variations all its own.[3] Neale [4] has set this liturgy below the Mozarabic as lacking its richness, and beneath the Roman as without its pointed brevity; but I cannot but feel that there is a nobility in this rite. What prayer could be finer in expression and mood than "O God, the true light of the faithful; O God, the everlasting Glory of the just, Whose light goeth not out, Whose splendour knows no end; grant that we may live in Thy glory and may enter into the light of Thine eternity, so that as Thou hast made light to dawn upon us after the night, Thou mayest cause us to attain to that blessed and eternal day." [5]

Duchesne [6] in his description of the Gallican Rite uses the Mozarabic or Spanish to supply the omissions that are found in the extant Gallican Liturgies. Thereby he acknowledges the essential likeness between the liturgical worship of Spain, Gaul, and Britain. Unquestionably the Mozarabic and the Gallican testify to a common source, and there are "Spanish Symptoms" [7] in the devotion and practice of the Irish Church. The precise point in history may be difficult to determine, but there is a definite relation between the Mozarabic worship and the Celtic rite and prayers. Let us turn for a little to the ancient rite of Spain that

[1] King, *op. cit.* p. 244.
[2] W. C. Bishop, *op. cit.* p. 130.
[3] For example, the peculiarity of the phrase "Dominus Jesus" at the beginning of the liturgical Gospel goes back perhaps to St. Ambrose.
[4] *Essays on Liturgiology*, p. 197.
[5] Lenten Collect at Lauds.
[6] *Op. cit.* p. 189.
[7] Edmund Bishop, *op. cit.* p. 165.

still has liturgical life. In the Mozarabic Liturgy there is a rich profusion and an imaginative fluency. As in the Byzantine we find in this rite a love of scriptural reference and quotation and the desire to adorn prayers with Biblical analogies. There is a glow of colour and a wealth of expression and a spontaneity of feeling about these Spanish devotions. In the illatio, which is equivalent to the Greek anaphora, for Easter Monday, we find " it is meet and right that we should render thanks to Thee Almighty Father and to Thine only Son, our Lord Jesus Christ, Who descending from heaven ceased not to humble Himself until He found the fugitive servant whom He was seeking, not that having found He might destroy him, but setting him free from the chains of diabolic damnation that He might re-create him as His own possession. . . . He arose alive from the dead because He was not obnoxious to destruction Who was free from sin. Nor could death hold him captive Who was not buried by the death of transgression. He arose alive from the dead Who visited the place of death by the right of the Redeemer, not through the wickedness of a sinner. Death stood aghast at the advent of the Almighty—fearing his own death," etc.[1] This quotation shows the frequent practice of turning a prayer into a meditation and also the characteristic quality of reiteration and redundance of thought. This quality can be at times effective when it is shot through with the hues of imagination and at other times it may lead to wearisome repetition and irrelevant detail. Mr. Edmund Bishop [2] has pointed out that the preface for Pentecost in the Roman Rite consists of eight lines, while in the Mozarabic it extends to eighty. This illatio dwells on the coming of the Spirit, points out that the unity of the faith is not destroyed by variety of languages, and meanders on to give mystical meanings to the fifty days of Eastertide, and finally concludes, " O flame that in burning confers fruitfulness, whom every intellectual creature, vivified by it, confesses to be the Lord Omnipotent." Such emotional expansiveness may become prolix but it is an authentic note in certain religious temperaments. Even in the Gloria Patri the Mozarabic shows this tendency : " Gloria et honor Patri et Filio et Spiritui Sancto." This religious nature

[1] Neale, *op. cit.* p. 61. [2] *Op. cit.* p. 4.

can never be quite satisfied with any expression and its devotional feeling makes it add fresh words. In the case of the Gloria Patri "gloria" signifies splendour and "honor" denotes excellence.[1]

Another trait of this rite is the passionate devotion to the Holy Mother. The celebrant's first prayer is Ave Maria, and at the festival of the Assumption the Post Pridie, which is the prayer asking for a blessing, is directly addressed to the Virgin. This indicates how this fervid devotion may lead to what Neale [2] has called "the wildest excesses of Mariolatry." In the prayers of this rite we see a most valuable tendency to make the prayers into doublets. The first is in the form of a bidding, which may even take the fashion of an exhortation, and the second is a collect or prayer that sums up the people's devotion. The place of the people as in the East is more recognised in devotion. The Lord's Prayer is not now said by the people as in the East, but after each clause the response Amen is said, save after the petition, "Give us this day our daily bread," when the reply is "because Thou art God." As we would expect, the emotional character of the people called for hymns and chants, and at the Council of Toledo, 633, "it was determined that hymns composed in the Divine honour can no more be condemned than prayers."

In this Spanish Rite there was evidently originally an invocation of the Holy Spirit, for in fourteen Masses we either find a definite epiclesis or evidence that such an invocation once was there. "Remembering therefore and obeying the precept of Thy only begotten Son, we beseech Thee, Almighty Father, to pour Thy sanctifying Spirit upon these creatures set forth upon Thine altar." [3] But no further must I wander among the detail of this rite. I trust I have not spoken unsympathetically of this liturgy, for there is a graciousness in the devotion expressed in this fair worship. "We are sick, Thou art the physician; we are pitiable, Thou are pitiful; therefore by this atoning sacrifice do Thou heal us who do not hide from Thee our wounds" are the moving words from the Post Pridie. In the text of the Mozarabic Missal there are found words which though they do not belong to the primitive rite

[1] King, *op. cit.* p. 277. [2] Neale, *op. cit.* p. 127.
[3] W. C. Bishop, *op. cit.* p. 52.

are the token of a fine spiritual insight: "Be Thou present, O Jesu the good Priest, be Thou present in our midst as Thou wast in the midst of Thy disciples; bless this oblation, that we may partake of holy things through the hands of Thy holy angel, O Holy Lord and Eternal Redeemer." Great ingenuity and at times searching spiritual power are shown in the variety of prayers that are composed on the same subject. For example, the prayer Ad pacem catches the note of the Scripture lesson and repeats with constant change the same theme. This is one illustration: "Saviour of the world, Word of the Eternal Father, Who after receiving the faith of the woman didst abide with the Samaritans two days at their request, that under the type of those two days might mystically be commended the number of the two precepts, love to God and love to our neighbour, cleanse our hearts from all crime and from all blindness of ignorance, that we, preparing for Thee a most poor mansion in our souls, may obtain from Thee as they obtained, and retain in very deed the love of our neighbour, whereby we may be able to come to Thee and to know in every way Thy love with which we may attain to the joy of life everlasting." This is founded on the Gospel lesson which was that of the woman of Samaria. Could there be a more fitting close for prayers for the departed than that with which the Mozarabic always concludes, "Because Thou art the Life of the living, the Health of the sick, and the Rest of all the faithful departed for eternal ages"?

From these rites which still have a limited use we turn to those Gallican remains which are preserved as fragments in liturgies that have been more or less Romanised. These so-called Gallican Rites were the local variants of the fluid liturgy which was widespread in the West before the Roman form, by accepting much from them, became the predominant liturgy of the West. Although we have no Gallican Liturgy extant in its original purity we have enough preserved to allow us to recognise its temper and atmosphere and to enable us to conjecture its order.

The emotional atmosphere and devotional temper give rise to certain marked traits. As I earlier mentioned, there is an effusiveness about the Gallican prayers and the tendency to dwell on a subject and to linger over its association is apparent. There is no feeling for orderliness and for relevance, but emotional colour and tone are found. Phrase is piled upon phrase, ejaculations of praise or apostrophes of wonder are interjected in the prayers. Emotional warmth expresses itself in prodigal speech. Connected with this there is also a vagueness in the devotional expression of theological truths. "Words when touched by emotion necessarily lose their sharpness of definition."[1] Prayers are addressed to Christ which from the standpoint of theological appropriateness would more fitly be addressed to the Father. For example, a prayer is addressed to the Son through the Holy Spirit.[2] The word, "majesty," usually confined to the Godhead and the Trinity is used of the Passion. "We believe, O Lord, we believe that we are redeemed in this breaking of the body and pouring forth of Thy blood," says one Gallican Missal, ascribing redemption to the present act of sacrifice rather than to the Sacrifice of Calvary. A term like "sacrificial bread" is employed, revealing a pictorial imagination rather than intellectual apprehension. There is also a certain poetic quality which breaks out in the recognition of the Divine Power in Nature;[3] and one feels that a mysterious awe like a cloud at times broods upon these devotions.

Into the outpouring of the soul there enter racial characteristics. The thirst for life, the longing for stability amid the changeful and passing days, the yearning for rest and security are voiced in the Gallican approach to the Divine. By this craving for life and rest the thought of the Hereafter is moulded. An elaborate analysis has been made by Mr. Edmund Bishop[4] of the words used in regard to the state of the departed (quies, requies, refrigerium, pax et lux) and he finds that "quies" and "requies" are distinctly Gallican. In the familiar prayer which begins the introit of the masses for the dead, "*Requiem* aeternam dona eis Domine et *lux* perpetua luceat eis," the first phrase gives "the aspiration of the mind and soul of the Goth," while the second expresses the Roman attitude. This is not merely a question of the use of terms; it is

[1] Dowden, *Scottish Communion Service*, p. 3.
[2] Neale and Forbes, *Ancient Gallican Liturgies*, p. 154.
[3] Neale and Forbes, *op. cit.* p. 25.
[4] *Book of Cerne*, edited by Kuypers, p. 267.

symptomatic of an inner mood. This difference of temperament belongs to all Western devotion and shapes the characteristic types of Western mysticism. "St. Gregory's favourite symbol," says Dom Cuthbert Butler,[1] "to which he returns again and again in describing contemplation, is light"; "St. Bernard likens contemplation to the sleep of the soul in the arms of God, but it is a deep sleep, alive and watchful—a sleep which dulls not the senses."[2] Thus there emerges in the sphere of mystical contemplation the same distinction as we find in liturgical devotion between the Roman and Gallican temper.

One most atractive quality we find in these devotions is the expression of a warm human affection. In the bidding prayer we find such phrases as, "fratres carissimi,"[3] "fratres amantissimi," "fratres dilectissimi." This affectionate disposition is shown in Mozarabic as in Gallican, but it is a Gallican feature to use the words "cari nostri" about the dead. This tenderness reveals itself in the frequent Gallican prayer that "our dear ones" may rest in the seats of the blessed and be admitted to the joys of the first resurrection. Human affection follows with tender yearning those who have passed into the Unseen, and the feeling of these prayers is similar to the mood expressed in Virgil's matchless line, "tendebantque manus ripæ ulterioris amore." The constant use of the petition that the names of those we remember may be written in the book of life[4] illustrates also that the Gallican soul longs that life be the portion of its dear ones. The bond of mortal affection draws the worshippers near to the Unseen. Prayer for the departed is made as in all ancient forms of worship, and the intercession of the saints is not always distinguished from the power of their example.[5] In its tender feeling for those within the veil the Gallican spirit makes a real contribution to worship. From these qualities we can deduce the obvious fact that a place must be found in the liturgy of the Church for the expression of special traits and racial characteristics.

The contents and the order of the Gallican Service are akin to Eastern usage rather than Roman practice. The general scheme of

[1] *Western Mysticism*, p. 110.
[2] Butler, *op. cit.* p. 154.
[3] Neale and Forbes, *op. cit.* p. 5.
[4] Neale and Forbes, *op. cit.* p. 79.
[5] Neale and Forbes, *op. cit.* p. 305.

the service was [1]: the greeting of the celebrant and the people, the Trisagion is sung in Greek and Latin, the Kyrie and the Benedictus; a collect is followed by the readings, Old Testament, Epistle, and Gospel; after the Trisagion has been sung again in honour of the Gospel, there is the sermon followed by intercessions, in which the deacon leads. This with a prayer for the catechumens concludes the first part of the service. The order of the Mass of the Faithful is as follows: the offerings are made by the people, and there is a procession similar in character to the Great Entrance in the East; the offerings are veiled while a prayer is said; the diptychs or the names of those to be remembered in prayer are read, and then the Kiss of Peace. After the Sursum corda the Eucharistic prayer, which in Gaul was called "contestatio," [2] or "immolatio"; the Sanctus is sung by the people; a few words introduce the account of the Last Supper and the words of institution; then come two prayers: the first is the commemoration of Our Lord or the anamnesis, the second is the epiclesis or invocation. The Fraction is an elaborate ceremony—the bread being divided into nine portions, seven of which form a cross, the other two are called Gloria and Regnum. Thereafter a prayer leads into the Lord's Prayer, which, as in the East, is said by the congregation. Then after a blessing the communion follows and the service is finished with thanksgiving. This general scheme, however, embraced within it much variety, for the number and the difference of the prayers are Gallican features. The sermon seems to have occupied a more important place in the Gallican service than in the Roman.

Despite, however, the qualities of emotional tone and the kinship to the Eastern sequence the service belongs to the sacrifice type and is centred round the mysterious offering. I would trace these differences a few steps further as they are exhibited in the worship of our Celtic forefathers. This I would do not only because there are elements of interest worthy of our attention, but also to remind ourselves that we inherit a tradition older than Calvin and wider than Rome. The specific quality of Celtic piety is shown in the spontaneous outpouring of individual devotion rather than

[1] Cf. Duchesne, *op. cit.* pp. 189–229; Fortescue, pp. 102–103.
[2] Equivalent to Roman Preface.

in the liturgical texts. The loricæ, the petitions of their litanies, the prayers ascribed to St. Patrick and other saints exhibit not only a fluent rhetoric and a fertile imagination, but also a surrender of heart, a keen feeling of penitence, and an intimate sense of God's grace.[1] The prayer that " the blessed Jesus, the Dear Friend, the Morning Star, the Hidden Sun of the day " may deliver from the peril of the evil ones at the entrance of the world to come, from the fire of hell and judgment, from the dangers of this world, the prayer that cries with eager passion for help from on high, has a sincerity and spontaneity, a distrust of self and a trust in God which have the special flavour of the Celtic spirit.[2] While it is true that in Celtic liturgical remains we do not find in its full fragrance the essence of Celtic piety, yet its tenderness, its freedom, its humility, and its poetic touches leave traces upon liturgical worship. We are not surprised, therefore, to find in the Stowe Missal the litany form of prayer, for this " ejaculatory, litanic, asyndetic type of prayer is peculiarly suited to the Irish genius." [3] Nor when we bear in mind the lengthy and meticulous prayers of the Irish monks is it an astonishing thing to discover the great number of collects contained in the liturgy.

The liturgical remains of the Irish Church are mixed in character, *i.e.* they contain Celtic elements with a Roman background.[4] Chief of these is the book just mentioned, the Stowe Missal, which contains an ordinary of the Mass, certain Mass prayers, an order of baptism, an order for visiting the sick, a treatise in Irish on the Eucharist, and three Irish charms. In this Missal we find the blending of sections from the Mozarabic, Gallican, and Ambrosian Rites as well as the Roman Canon. From it we can discover the order of the service, which does not materially differ from the scheme I have given of the Gallican Liturgy. Confession is the note first struck in the service, followed by a litany of saints, and the following points are perhaps worthy of mention. The readings are two—Epistle [5] and Gospel [6]—which are fixed. Perhaps the

[1] Cf. Gougand, *Christianity in Celtic Lands*, p. 335.
[2] From so-called Prayer of Colin ; Gougand, *op. cit.* p. 336.
[3] Edmund Bishop, *op. cit.* p. 148.
[4] Duchesne, *op. cit.* p. 156 f.
[5] 1 Cor. xi. 26–31.
[6] St. John vi. 51–56.

traditional use of these passages at the Lord's Supper in the reformed communions has an anticipation here. After the Epistle there is an intercession which is of the nature of a bidding prayer. This prayer, called Deprecatio, is modelled on the Oriental type of prayer.[1] The rubric in the vernacular, " a holy uncovering," appears to mean that one of the two cloths which veiled the chalice and the bread of offering was removed. The significance of this before the Gospel is perhaps the thought that Christ was manifestly foretold in the law, but only fully revealed in the incarnation.[2] Such an interpretation suggests that an Old Testament lesson has slipped out of this Missal. The full uncovering which with an elevation takes place later, after the Gospel and creed and sermon, commemorates Christ's birth and glory. The diptychs are couched in the affectionate language which we saw was characteristic of the Gallican usage. During the consecration the strictest silence was maintained. The perilous prayer [3] was from the words " accepit Jesus panem " to the end of the consecration. " The people prostrated themselves and lay in profound silence. Not a sound was to disturb the celebrant during the solemn moments of consecration." [4] A mistake in this prayer was fraught with danger, for the words were sacrosanct. Here we recognise the haunting sense of mysterious dread that in Celtic piety hung over the offering of the sacrifice. The prayer which commemorates the dead changes in an odd fashion into a liturgy of the saints. It is impossible to say whether this is a scribe's blunder or another indication of the Irish spirit subject to emotional association rather than obedient to order. An interesting declaration of belief follows the Fraction, " We believe, O Lord, we believe that in this breaking of Thy Body and this pouring forth of Thy Blood we are redeemed, and we trust that strengthened by the reception of this sacrament what we now possess in hope we shall enjoy in truth enduringly in the heavenly Kingdom." The Stowe Missal shows by its monastic traits that it has a Celtic outlook, for the basis of the Celtic Church was the monastery.

The Antiphonary of Bangor is an Irish liturgical book composed

[1] Duchesne, *op. cit.* p. 200.
[2] Warren, *op. cit.* p. 255, note 29.
[3] Periculosa oratio.
[4] Ryan, *op. cit.* p. 348.

mainly of hymns and prayers from the Offices. The version of the creed given varies from the Nicene-Constantinople symbol in some interesting details which seem to indicate a Celtic mood. The addition of the word " invisible " to the first article, " I believe in God the Father Almighty *Invisible* " and the addition to the second article, " I believe in Jesus Christ His only Son, our Lord *God Almighty*," as also to the third, " I believe in the Holy Ghost God Almighty," and the statement, " I believe in life after death and eternal life in the glory of Christ," distinguish this creed from all other known forms. These differences have no theological significance, but they point to the Celtic love of change. There is also a eucharistic hymn [1] which has been translated " Draw nigh and take the body of the Lord." [2] It seems unfortunate that the Church of Scotland does not use this, the most ancient communion hymn of the Celtic Church. In the Book of Deer, a Scottish fragment containing part of the service of communion for the sick, we find evidence that we are dealing with the Sacrifice type of worship, for the word " sacrificium " is used for " sacramentum." In the other Irish books of Dimma, Mulling, and Armagh, and in the manuscript of St. Gall,[3] the fragmentary remains show kinship with Mozarabic and Gallican Rites, and reveal a likeness to Oriental forms.

The service of the Mass was called by many names in Celtic writings and its character thereby is shown. It is termed Communion, Eucharist, the Offering, and the Sacrifice. Adamnan speaks of " making the sacred mysteries of the Eucharist " and of " making the Body of Christ " and of " breaking the bread." Phrases like " offering the sacrifice " and " being joined to the altar " are used of the celebration. So we may not read into the Celtic service any other meaning than we have already found in the Roman idea of offering the sacrifice. The Mass seems to have been celebrated on Sunday and on feast days, and communion was received on these days. The sermon was a frequent accompaniment of the Mass service. The service of Mass lasted, says Dr.

[1] Sung during communion. [2] *Ancient and Modern*, No. 313.

[3] A list of Celtic liturgical remains is given in Warren's *Liturgy and Ritual*, p. 153 f.

Ryan, about two hours, and the habitual attitude of the worshipper was standing save where during the consecration prayer he prostrated himself. "We do not know," says the same author, "whether the people as in Gaul brought rugs and couches to sit upon during the sermon, or whether, like the Gauls, they clapped, waved handkerchiefs, and shouted themselves to hoarseness when the preacher was particularly eloquent." Music then must have been used in the service, as the references to hymns and chants imply. "As in Gaul, so in Ireland it was extremely difficult to prevail upon the people to abandon servile work on Sunday."[1] Rules of a puritanic nature were laid down to overcome this unwillingness. Saturday was apparently regarded as having the character of a semi-festival,[2] and probably here is the influence of the ancient practice in the East.

In the Offices we find great importance attached to prayer, for the Celtic monk abounded in the exercise of praying. Celtic prayer, as we saw, might have the character of spontaneous utterance, free and unrestrained, and also the quality of a meticulous confession or detailed praise, but in addition there was involved the idea of discipline. Prayer is made in the day hours for forgiveness of our sins, and intercession offered for the whole Christian people, for priests, for those who bestow alms, for peace, and for enemies.[3] This prevalence of prayer alike as fervent devotion and as a discipline betokens the sense of a need for succour in this troublous life, and the intercession for others is mingled with the aspiration for the worshipper's own salvation. The desire of the Celt reached out into the dim hereafter, and he intercedes for the spirits who are hid in the Unseen. "The monks at Iona were enjoined to display fervour in singing the offices for the dead as if every dead person were a particular friend of theirs."[4] The Reserved Sacrament was carried by the devout monk as he went abroad, not for the purpose of administering communion nor for adoration, but as a kind of spiritual charm to guard his life from evil. Akin to this was the practice of making the sign of the cross. This was not confined to its liturgical use; the sacred sign was made on many

[1] Ryan, *op. cit.* p. 349.
[2] Gougand, *op. cit.* p. 323.
[3] Ryan, *op. cit.* p. 340.
[4] Warren, *op. cit.* p. 105.

occasions and over all sorts of things—over a tool before using it, over bread and water. This may spring from superstition or from childlike faith ; but it is evidence of a nature unspeculative, endowed with an emotional temperament whose creed is symbolism.

The Celtic Church had five emblems of vital import—the staff, the relics, the Cross, the bell, and the Book of the Gospels.[1] Perhaps in this we find a parable of Celtic Worship and of its lesson for us to-day.

(1) The staff was the symbol of office, and authority was a felt need. " Life on earth would never be comfortable or even tolerable if man had no way of grappling with its mysteries and its terrors." [2] By her authority the Church provided a way through which man found salvation and escaped from the clamour and fear of his own restless heart. Behind the exuberance and freedom of Celtic devotion lay the sense of God's authority made known through His Church.

(2) The relics are the precious remembrance of the saints in bliss. Whatever the saints had touched was stamped by their virtue. The heroes of the faith had left an example and an influence. Certainly the use of sacred objects can be but blind superstition playing with magic, but to treat relics simply as that is to miss the religious aspirations they expressed. They were the remembrancers of the great and noble, and they were a confession of faith that the virtues of those with God had not left this earth. With this belief it is not surprising that in their hard-pressed and hazardous lives the ancient Church of the Celt cried for the prayers of the saints. " May Patrick the bishop pray for us all, that the sins of which we are guilty may forthwith be remitted." [3] In the Stowe Missal there is a prayer asking that the Virgin, St. Peter, St. Paul, the apostles, and the evangelists, come to the help of all who are present. It is the working of the same instinct that cherished relics. Man seeks the aid of those who have triumphed.

(3) The Cross is the perennial symbol of man's salvation. The Celtic Church turned its eyes to the Cross and found there the ground of hope. The feeling of human helplessness, and the sense

[1] Ryan, *op. cit.* p. 359. [2] Powicke, *Legacy of the Middle Ages,* p. 33.
[3] Antiphonary of Bangor.

of this life's peril, which are so manifest in her devotions, anchored the Celtic Church on this image of God's Help.

(4) The bell was the tongue which reminded man, amid his duties and life's labours and all his varied activity, of the supreme duty he owed to God; it was the call which summoned the worshipper. I do not think we of to-day can afford to scoff at this symbol of warning and of summons.

(5) Finally, the Book of the Gospels was the record of Christ's doings. True it is that the Jesus of history was largely concealed from the eye and the imagination of the ancient worshippers; but the book was the story of His Passion and Victory, and that story was as a succouring hand to needy souls. This book was the charter of the Church's faith, the warrant for the offering she made. The Church of the Orient had found a place for the Book of the Gospels upon the holy altar; the Celt also made it an essential attribute of a church.

CHAPTER VII

LUTHERAN WORSHIP, OR THE WORD IN HUMAN EXPERIENCE

THE Oracle, the third historic type of worship, has entered into the service of the Church. The great religious movement of the sixteenth century brought into prominence the idea of God's Word, and made that idea directive in the sphere of worship. The conception of the Word is rooted and grounded in the fact of revelation. God speaks and man responds to what is spoken. God's revelation has been regarded as enunciated in a sacred book like the Jewish Law, and the holy books of all religions have been treated as the record of divine oracles. Along this line the Christian Scriptures have been interpreted, and then the Bible becomes the Word of God in an almost legal sense. It is the objective statement of God's will and nature. Or God's revelation may be viewed from the effect it produces in human experience, and then authority and validity will belong to the written word because it recounts the authentic experience of God in time. In this case the approach is more personal and subjective. It is the Word revealed in human experience which is the Lutheran outlook, just as the Word revealed as sovereign will is the Calvinistic approach. In either case the supremely important thing is God's revelation which is related to historical happenings. At certain times God has spoken and revealed what was beyond man's search.

The fact of revelation implies certain things. The first is about the nature of God and His relation to man. God can reveal Himself and man can receive that revelation. The Word has been spoken and man has heard. The second implication is that man's relation to God is something personal and intimate. God and the soul are the two realities, and by His Word God has created a new relation of the soul to Him. In the third place, man responds to

God's revelation in his experience, and this response is the prayer of faith and self-surrender through which man utters his thanks and vows his obedience. In this experience the consciousness of God does not swallow up the sense of self, but makes man supremely conscious that he is the creature and child of God to Whom he owes the utter obedience of his will.

These characteristics of revelation have certain consequences in the idea of public worship. The first is that the message of God must needs be proclaimed. Therefore there is a concentration on Holy Scripture as the record of His Revelation and a high place must be given to preaching as the exposition of the Divine Will. In addition to the declaration of God's message there is also the human response to it. This experience of God needs to be expressed in worship and the soul has to utter what is within. Also before this revelation man has to express his need in confession and supplication, to voice his thanksgiving, and to subject his will to the will of God for the service of His kingdom which is the prayer of intercession. This type of worship makes a primary appeal to the hearing ear and to the understanding heart.

It is not our task to discuss the causes and conditions that were the precursor of the sixteenth-century Reformation. This great spiritual awakening is fundamentally a reaction from a paganised outlook and a spiritual protest which seeks to strike back to the early days of eager belief and to mould itself upon the primitive Christian practices of worship. With the Bible in its hand as the open Word of God this movement of the spirit opposes the errors of blind superstition and the paganism of an unawakened life. Yet this movement does not deal with a *tabula rasa*; it accepts an inheritance even though it makes its conscious protest against it. We must allow for the fact that not only was all the thinking of the reformers done in a reaction, but also that the forms of worship they developed were the product of this same spiritual reaction. We ought not therefore to look for anything quite new in the forms of worship which emanate from the heart of the Reformation. The interest was not essentially in the form of worship, but in the spiritual experience that was to be expressed. This experience gathered itself around the idea of God's Word as opposed to tradition, dwelt on God's touch upon the soul in opposition to the acceptance of ecclesiastical authority.

The personal experience of Luther influenced in no small way the character of Lutheran worship. The monk who had inherited the profound teaching of St. Augustine found in St. Paul's experience the echo of his own, and turned to the early days of the Christian faith to find how the authentic Christian experience expressed itself. Luther, however, was a child of mediævalism in this, that the fear and menace of judgment had lain like a dark shadow across his soul. To him the forgiveness of sin bulks as the one supremely significant thing in all spiritual life. This colours and even moulds the service of Holy Communion, and it does so in accordance with the great Western tradition of penance. This tradition, which goes back to the early Church, had a twofold aspect. Only for the holy was the holy mystery, and therefore there was developed the sacrament of penance with its four elements—contrition, confession, satisfaction, and absolution. It is in accordance with this that the Lutheran Eucharist strikes the note of penitential devotion, but there was also the other side of the tradition whereby forgiveness is received through the Mass which in itself is a cleansing and a renewing of life. Luther fixes upon this element in the tradition and makes the communion the receiving of forgiveness by the individual worshipper. The result of this is that the Lutheran Sacrament dwells too exclusively upon the one note. The atmosphere of Good Friday rests upon it. To Luther the idea of a sacrificial offering in the Mass was abhorrent, and the Canon was to him "abominable." Therefore in framing his communion service he simply cut out those portions of the Mass which to his mind were filled with this superstitious thought. Unfortunately Luther does not appear to have been acquainted with any other form of service than the Roman, and so he had to construct a new liturgy by the process of excision. In concentrating on the personal experience of forgiveness he limited the scope of this service, which is lacking in the buoyant note of praise so characteristic of Eastern worship, and in rejecting totally the thought of sacrifice in the Mass he missed out the idea of the Church's oblation which was a valuable element in the Roman

Mass. It so came about that owing to Luther's mighty personality Holy Communion has acquired its distinctive atmosphere and its individualistic interpretation.

Another personal idiosyncrasy of the reformer has affected the idea of the eucharistic service. He accepts the literal interpretation of the words " This is my body," and he develops his theory of the ubiquity of the Body of Christ in order to conserve the religious value of the sacrament and to preserve its wondrous mystery. Too deeply religious was he and too embued with mystical feeling to be impressed with the lucid but somewhat shallow teaching of Zwingli. Whatever criticism may be passed on Luther's doctrine of consubstantiation the theory is at least a brave though unsuccessful attempt to assert the horizon of the Eucharist. By his endeavour to link the thought of the sacramental Presence to the idea of the creative Word he may have localised the Body of Christ in the elements, but at least he escaped the more disastrous conception of Calvin, who localised the Body of Christ in heaven. This sense of mystery has also been a legacy of Luther to his church.

The great discovery which Luther made in this sphere was the idea of fellowship. During the later Middle Ages more and more the Mass service had become a commemoration of Christ's sacrifice upon Calvary by a renewal of His sacrifice in the consecration, and the idea as well as the custom of communion had fallen into the background. Upon the idea of fellowship Luther's mind fastened, and he turned the Memorial of the Mass into a Communion service. " To eat this sacrament in Bread and Wine," he says, " is nought else than to receive a sign of this fellowship and incorporation with Christ and all His saints." One cannot but feel that in so doing Luther left out some elements of great spiritual value which had been present in the Mass, but he was reviving a neglected factor in the sacrament.

In connection with the idea of fellowship there is a great contribution which Luther made to the liturgy by his introduction of German hymns. Hymns had been used in the Mass and in the Offices of the Hours, but their number was limited and their import was hidden by a foreign tongue. These great vernacular hymns of Luther were the expression of fellowship in worship. We have seen how in the liturgies of non-Roman lands there was the instinctive feeling after something in worship which was distinctively racial and even national. This tendency Luther furthered, and by his hymns the Teutonic soul found utterance in worship. This was all to the good, since worship must be acclimatised to the hour and place of its offering, but none the less there is a seed of danger in expressing the sense of fellowship mainly by those elements in worship which are characteristically racial. Worship which ought to be the uniting force in the life of Christendom can become a disruptive element when the sense of fellowship which ought to express the unity of the faith is couched mainly in terms which are less than universal.

Luther in reacting from the Roman Liturgy, and in shaping it to suit the expression of his own experience was reacting from more than a Roman Rite; he was reacting from the growth of an ordered worship which in East and West alike sought to grasp and to delineate the manifold wonders of revelation and redemption. Let us put alongside the Roman Mass the service which Luther fashioned. In 1523 Luther prepared a Latin Mass in which he eliminated from the service all that savoured of sacrifice but otherwise retained as much as possible. Luther was not afraid of ceremonial, nor did he object on principle to the use of Latin in the service, but this Latin Mass was merely a stage to the German Mass which he brought out later. I shall contrast this later service with the Roman. In the Mass of the Catechumens Luther adheres somewhat closely to his Roman model. I put in brackets the German elements that correspond to the Roman. Introit (Hymn or Psalm in German), Kyrie 9 times (Kyrie 3 times), Gloria in Excelsis (the Gloria disappears [1]), Collect (Collect), Epistle (Epistle), Gradual and Alleluia (a German hymn), Gospel (Gospel), Nicene Creed (a metrical version). Here is the sermon in the German Mass, and here too, if any, would be the sermon in the mediæval [2] Mass. One notices that the alterations are not great, and that the symmetry of the service is preserved. Then follows the Mass of the Faithful:

[1] It was, however, in use at Wittenberg in 1536. Brillioth, *Eucharistic Faith and Practice*, p. 126.

[2] Fortescue, *The Mass*, p. 285.

Offertory, Antiphon, *i.e.* singing of verses from the Psalter. Offertory Prayers (what correspond to these are a paraphrase of the Lord's Prayer and an exhortation to communion), Anaphora, Salutation, Sursum Corda, Preface, Sanctus with Hosanna and Benedictus, Canon of the Mass with its prayer for the Church and its Prayer for Communion with the Saints and the Prayer of Oblation, the narrative of the Institution (all we have in the German is the narrative of the Institution), Commemoration of Christ's work, Prayer for the acceptance of the Oblation, Prayer for Heavenly Blessing, Commemoration of the Dead, Prayer for fellowship with the Saints, Our Father (here we have Sanctus and Hosanna in a German form; it is a real weakness that the historic form has been paraphrased), Fraction and Agnus Dei, Kiss of Peace, Prayers at the Priest's Communion, Communion Antiphon, Prayer of Thanksgiving, and Dismissal (during communion Agnus Dei in a German version may be sung, followed by Prayer and Aaronic Benediction). One sees from this synopsis that the whole structure of the latter part of the service is broken and altered; and that these omissions are largely guided by Luther's insistence that the idea of an offering in the Mass must be expurgated. One notes also the somewhat unhappy change that is made in the place of the Sanctus. Its new place at communion has little appropriateness and robs it of its adoring praise. Many and diverse were the liturgies framed on the basis of this German Mass. The ordinary Sunday service was a Eucharistic service with sermon, although from the beginning there was a service drawn up for use if there should be no communicants. This sketch shows that there were two moods in the Lutheran service which at times were unrelated if not antagonistic. These two moods are the effect of Luther's own personality. We find a heart throbbing with evangelical passion, but also instincts and habits which were the inheritance of the pious monk of Erfurt.

Luther's favourite idea of the priesthood of all believers brings a new accent into public worship. Worship becomes now the utterance and expression of what has been experienced. Thus, although the Lutheran form retains certain elements of the mediæval Mass it wholly alters their significance. Beneath his use of mediæval customs and ceremonies lay his thought of congregational worship. He did not discard the Elevation, but it is not now for the purpose of adoration ; when it is made at the singing of the Sanctus its meaning is according to Luther that " Christ has commanded us to remember Him." [1] He did not depart from the idea of the Christian Year though he limited its extent. The Gloria, the Sanctus, and the Agnus Dei were sung at times in Latin. His one principle was that whatever did not conflict with this new experience might remain.

Two mistakes can be made in estimating the Lutheran forms of worship. They may be looked upon as merely a mutilated version of the Mass. Certainly the Lutheran liturgy is but a torso of what was once a complete work of art if we judge from a merely liturgical standpoint and fail to recognise the directing power of a fresh experience in this worship. It is true that the order is misplaced at times and omissions are made of what is essential to the movement of the service, but we must needs acknowledge that an evangelic experience is seeking to find expression through these forms. Sin and grace were the master thoughts of this experience. The Grace of God spoken in Word and in Sacrament is the impelling motive of worship. Too rich a nature was Luther's to confine the proclamation of God's Word to one act. The Word speaks through Scripture and preaching, but also in sacrament and rite. It is by this standard the Lutheran forms are to be judged. They were found fitting in the sixteenth century for the proclamation of the word of salvation. These forms do not make a unity unless we see what unites the various parts, and that is the experience of salvation in the soul of man. The unity in the Roman Mass consists in its objective power to call forth contrition, to awaken gratitude, and to arouse adoration before the Mysterious Presence. Lutheran worship was a romantic expression of living Christian experience. The subjective element is not now the accompaniment of the presentation, it creates the unity of the service.

The other mistake in estimating Lutheran worship is to regard the liturgy as a unity in itself. History tells us how arid this worship could become when it was cut off from the power and passion that

[1] Quoted by Brilioth, *op. cit.* p. 123.

called it into being. John Wesley in 1738 was present at a communion service in the Lutheran Church at Meissen and to his mind it was but a formal observance. "Alas, alas, what a *reformed* country is this."[1] It is easy to see why the charge of formal dullness could be brought against Lutheran worship of a later day. The form of the Mass had been broken and the Lutheran service could not arouse the same emotions as the Roman Mass, for the psychological movement of the service had been changed and its emotional impressiveness had been lost. To the age which poured into it the living experience of redemption this Lutheran service had a real appeal and a most potent power, but it did not inevitably awaken the moods and emotions which engender that experience. In short, as a liturgy it was expressive but it lacked creative power. That the Lutheran ritual did become formal is a proof that the reconciliation of the various elements which the sixteenth century achieved belongs only to that age. It was not a reconciliation for other times.

Let us look at the seed ideas that are inherent in this Lutheran worship. The first is the emergence of the sense of truth. The revelation of the Word rests on an historic fact. As long as the Word is something assured, definite, and admitted, the response is immediate. The proclamation of the Word does what the Mass accomplished, for the Word has not merely to give light to the mind and spiritual insight, it has also to make God's Presence, His Grace, and His standards real to the soul. The mediæval Mass achieved this end by the use of symbolic appeal, impressive ceremony, and an emotional atmosphere by means of which the worshipper believed and felt that something was done and a mysterious communion effected. By different methods thus far the two types of service are seeking to achieve the same purpose, but here a difference emerges. The difference is connected with the sense of truth. To a certain extent it might be said that the worship of the Mass, like a work of imaginative art, does not depend on the conscious reference to the standard of historical truth. The dramatic power of Shakespeare's *Macbeth* is not dependent on its truthfulness to the facts of history. The dramatist creates a new world of imagination and to the truth of

[1] *Journal* of Wesley, vol. i. p. 113.

that world only must his characters conform. It matters little if they ever existed apart from his presentation. So in the mood of worship in the Mass there is given a world of experience into which the sense of truth as historical fact scarcely enters. I do not mean that the truthfulness of the historical facts is denied or that belief in them is not held, but for the time this fidelity to fact is irrelevant. Here to the devout Roman is present a world of mystery and of power. Thus to the mystical soul there is given a communion of soul with the Eternal, for the mystic finds this world of the unknown to be the real world; or again to the unenlightened multitude heavy with the burdens of mortality there are vouchsafed a sense of vague mystery and a warmth of union. This mood may remain unlit with insight and its ethical effects may be only indirectly seen in a heightening of hope and a bestowal of peace. But what this type of worship cannot give is the unity of a conscious purpose. There need not be here the consciousness of the self-same experience which gives rise to common aims and conscious ideals. That can only be given by the sense of possessing a common truth. This aspect of worship the Lutheran form brings into the foreground. The Word of God is the testimony of God's Power and Grace, and calls for a response from all. The ideal of the Lutheran service is that all have a similar experience of God's Power and Grace, and therefore a common response is possible. We see how this type of service in order to be effective is bound up with the existence of a common mind. It is not sufficient to possess a common mood or disposition. There ought to be a community in spiritual knowledge. This is given by the proclamation of the Word in sermon, Scripture, and Sacrament. There is of course the peril of intellectualism in this emphasis on the importance of preaching, but because of the dangers that surround we must not ignore the factor that is here made emphatic. The presentation of God's Power and Presence in speech means a conscious reference to the standard of truth, and the end that is achieved, a common response, implies the conviction that this Power is an actual and historic fact. The aspect of worship which Lutheranism here underlines cannot be ignored by the modern world. The worship that is gathered round the Revelation of the Word must have a conscious reference to history. Nor can we set aside this aim of creating a common mind in spiritual experience because it is difficult. Certainly to an age that no longer vibrates to the master thoughts of the sixteenth century it is no easy task to create this unity, and to a culture that no longer finds the Word confined within the compass of a book the proclamation of the Word must be a very difficult thing.

We find also in Luther's conception of a service the idea of the community of all the worshippers. He speaks of the priesthood of all believers. This thought of Luther doubtless needs restatement, but the underlying idea must not be allowed to slip out of worship. To the declaration of the Word there is the reply of the common mind in worship, and that reply links together the two thoughts—the one God's Glory and Mercy, the other man's fellowship and community in a personal experience of forgiving Grace. How is this response made in the Lutheran service? When we ask that question we are forced to admit that the rich religious nature of Luther cherished spiritual values that his mind could not make consistent with each other. At times one might think that this response was made in the communion before the presence of the Word made manifest. A section in the Lutheran Church has caught the echo of his thought and has maintained a high sacramental position. By emphasising the Catholic element in Luther they make the Eucharist the supreme act of worship. Another section in Lutheranism, attentive to other aspects of his thought, has stressed the place and the function of the sermon, and found in that the apex of the service. Others, like Karl Voll, impressed with yet another side in Luther, have made much of congregational praise and sought in that act the highest expression of man's glad response to God. Others, like Otto, touched by Luther's sense of the Mysterious, have endeavoured to build a service round a united act of adoration in silence. They are all the spiritual descendants of Luther, for he set a problem which he did not solve, but to Luther at least it was given to feel the many-sidedness of worship. It is evidence of the bigness of his nature that his spiritual appreciation outstripped his intellectual consistency.

I see then in Luther two approaches to worship which he did

not harmonise. The one side of Luther was feeling after a service whose elements were the word of revelation, the experience of that revelation and the response to it. This would require some liturgy that gave first the declaration of the Word, secondly the outpouring of the congregation's praise, and thirdly the prayer of intercession and of obedience that seeks the place and the task appointed in the world. But there is also the other side of Luther, alive to the greatness of an ordered liturgy and sensitive to the appeal of traditional forms. Throughout, however, his directing thought is the Word that speaks in human experience, and that creates this fellowship. He makes the Eucharistic service central and finds in it both the communion of believers and the mystery of the real Presence. Yet we must note that it is the Word as revealed in Scripture that is the mystery. The narrative of the institution is given a singular prominence. This is in keeping with the value he attaches to Holy Writ as the revelation of God, and a literal interpretation of the phrase "Hoc est corpus meum" follows from his conception of the Word. Here again an inner disharmony is seen in his treatment, for I do not think he has united the sense of Mystery with the sense of fellowship in worship. Here too we find a parting of the ways between those who bear Luther's name. The High Church party seek to put a new interpretation on the canon of the Mass which deals with the sacrifice and the offering. By this spiritual interpretation they are faithful to the profound teaching of St. Augustine and perhaps to Luther's own spirit had his eyes been cleansed from controversy. This movement leans to the side of Rome. There are also others who, influenced by the thought of Schleiermacher, react from the Lutheran communion shadowed by the mood of Good Friday and of penitential grief, and would revive the other aspect of the Supper as a feast of gladness foreshadowing in joyous fellowship the Messianic banquet. Both movements could find their predominant thoughts, the mystery of fellowship and the joy of fellowship, adumbrated in Lutheran thought, though he would violently have disagreed with both.

Criticisms have been passed on the Lutheran form of worship. It has been condemned as lacking in variety. There is a measure of truth in such a statement, but sameness is not inherent in its genius. It could escape from the sense of sameness by adopting more extensively the practice of the Christian Year. It has been called subjective in tone. Although the service did preserve some of the traditional elements of worship it has not avoided a too exclusive emphasis on experience. The liturgy is the response of the worshipper and the expression of his devotion, but the service as God's instrument whereby He draws nigh to the worshipper is not stressed. The neglect of the idea of the offering in the Sacrament dulls in the Lutheran service the thought of the Church's offering herself in obedience to God's Will, and limits the horizon of the Eucharist to the individual soul. The disarrangement of the traditional Christian service robs the liturgy of dramatic appeal, for the form of worship no longer delineates the story of redemption. Finally, Luther's dread of the sacrifice in the Mass made him tend to ignore that in worship something is done. At times, as the consequence of this, Luther seems to view the divine service mainly as a means of instruction, and because of this the position of worship as an end in itself is imperilled.

On the other hand, the Lutheran service has one outstanding merit. It is a Christian service. " To have a God means that I trust Him with my whole heart," Luther once said. The God of Lutheran worship is the God revealed in Christ Who pardons. Other aspects of the Divine Being that belong also to worship may fail to receive full recognition, but the centre and the core of the Christian experience find expression in the worship of God in this service. There is also a richness and a warmth in this worship that are sometimes lacking in the worship of other reformed Churches.

Let us finally look at a Lutheran Rite in order to illustrate the ideas I have suggested. I choose a liturgy that shows that the Lutheran form and spirit are not simply a German trait. The Swedish Rite is Lutheran in origin and shows the beauty and greatness of this form of service as well as its limitations and one-sidedness. In Sweden the morning Sunday service is eucharistic in character, and is called the Divine Service of High Mass. This may or may not be a celebration of communion. This depends on the presence of communicants, so that in some parishes communion is much more frequent than in others.

The service begins with the singing of a verse or verses suitable to the particular Sunday. Thus the character of the service is announced at the beginning through the singing of the congregation. A call to worship is given by the priest also couched in a form adapted to the time and season of the Christian Year. Thereafter follows the confession. "I, a poor sinful man who was born in sin and ever afterward have offended against Thee in manifold ways all the days of my life, heartily confess before Thee, O Holy and Righteous God, Father of our Lord, that I have not loved Thee above all else, nor my neighbour as myself. Against Thee and Thy holy commandments have I sinned in thoughts, words, and deeds, and know that I am therefore worthy of everlasting condemnation, if Thou shouldst judge me as Thy justice requireth and my sins have deserved. But now hast Thou promised, Dear Heavenly Father, to embrace with tenderness and mercy all penitent sinners who turn towards Thee, and with a lively faith seek refuge in Thy Fatherly Kindness and the merits of the Saviour Jesus Christ. For unto such wilt Thou grant remission of all sins against Thee, nor wilt Thou at any time impute unto them their transgressions. In this I, miserable sinner, put my faith and pray Thee trustfully that Thou wilt according to Thy promise vouchsafe to be merciful and gracious unto me and forgive me all my sins, to the praise and honour of Thy Holy name." This "prayer of Olaus Petri," says Heiler,[1] "is perhaps the most profoundly penitential prayer in any of the Christian liturgies." Alike in its personalness and its trustful assurance one recognises the mood of Lutheranism. Then follows the absolution in the form of a petition, "May the Almighty Eternal God after His great and unfathomable mercy forgive us all our sins for Jesus Christ our Saviour's sake, and give us grace to amend our ways and with Him attain everlasting life." Then the congregation sing the Kyrie, and the priest says "Glory be to God on High, and on earth peace and goodwill towards men." Thus the act of confession culminates in glorifying God for His forgiveness. Then comes a hymn which is

[1] *Spirit of Worship*, p. 87.

usually[1] the ancient hymn of adoring praise, Gloria in excelsis. This is the exultation of the soul in God's pardon. A collect follows, and the two lessons are read with a hymn between them. The Apostles' Creed is recited, beginning " We believe " or on the greater festivals the Nicene Creed beginning " I believe." It seems odd that there should be a difference between the creeds in the use of singular and plural. Owing to the influence of a mistaken reformed tradition the Apostles' Creed finds its place in a service that is eucharistic. Or is it because this part of the service is instructional that the creed of baptism is used ? The sermon follows, and the notices.

At this point the service varies according as there is or there is not a celebration of Communion. In the former case the prayers of intercession are made, as this is the time of the offertory in the Mass. The Sursum Corda follows, but instead of the accustomed response we have " God lift up our hearts." This is a trace of the Lutheran mood, wherein even the resolution of man " We have lifted them up unto the Lord " is set aside. The change from the traditional response ignores the fact that at this point in the service there ought to be the expression of the soul's desire to ascend. There is a preface which consists of thanksgiving for Christ's sacrifice for us but is characteristically lacking in any wider reference and curiously thin in tone. There is no prayer of consecration and no prayer of offering and no sense of the communion of the saints. Thereafter is read the narrative and the Lord's Prayer is recited. It would appear that the consecration is effected by the Lord's Prayer said " with special intention." This marks the apex of the communion service. Then the Sanctus is sung, continuing Luther's liturgical error. Since Luther did not care to sing the Benedictus before consecration, the Sanctus and Benedictus were placed here. The Agnus Dei is sung, and communion, during which hymns are sung, is followed by a prayer of thanksgiving and the dismissal on the note of gladness, " Thanks and praise be unto the Lord. Alleluia." The Aaronic blessing is given, which is another liturgical blunder of the reformers, for surely after the celebration of the specifically Christian service the benediction

[1] All festivals and any special occasion.

should be of a New Testament character. Luther, who could always find a reason for what he did, asserts that he uses this benediction because Christ used it at the Last Supper. Happily this Swedish Rite adds to it the Trinitarian blessing. When there is no celebration there are the same prayers of intercession, Our Father, and the dismissal, which is the same as in the other form.

It is, I think, strange how meagre is the thanksgiving that is gathered round the consecration and how limited its extent. There is also a lack of emphasis on the mystery aspect of the sacrament. The value of the service is not in its ordered sequence nor in its fulness. Its worth is not in its portraiture of the soul's ascent nor in its picture of the redemptive drama. Its import is not in the offering of the Church's oblation and the consecration of her life in the sacrament. All those things are lacking. Its significance rests in its experimental and psychological aspect. There are certain motifs strung together on a thread, certain notes are sounded. The depth of penitence, the shout of praise (Gloria), the reception of the Word in the confession of faith, the intercession as a spiritual offering, the Lord's Prayer as an act of consecration, or as (in the service without a celebration) the final prayer, the glad note of thanksgiving on which the service ends—these form a service which is the expression of Christian emotion and the utterance of Christian feeling. So far it fulfils one of the functions of worship, but I think it is somewhat lacking in another. It is not an instrument for awakening the spirit of worship ; it is not figurative of what worship means ; it has not that objectivity which we find in the historic liturgies. It is the response of the soul to the Word experienced within. So far it is great and noble, rich in feeling and in meaning, but it does not fulfil the whole function of worship.

CHAPTER VIII

REFORMED WORSHIP, OR THE WORD AS GOD'S WILL

We now turn to that form of worship which of all Church rituals seems to depart most definitely from mediævalism—the Reformed or Calvinistic service. Like the Lutheran Rite, this ritual is based upon the two thoughts—the supremacy of the Word and the repudiation of the mediæval doctrine of the Mass. There is, however, a distinction between the Lutheran and the Reformed attitudes to the Word. In the case of the Lutheran service we have seen how worship tends to become the expression of that experience which the Word engenders. In the Reformed worship, on the other hand, more exclusive prominence is given to the declaration of God's Will and the announcement of an eternal purpose in the Word. Both services are gathered round the idea of the Word but the atmosphere is different and the accent not quite the same. The atmosphere of the Lutheran service is that of glad thankfulness for God's gracious forgiveness ; the atmosphere of the Reformed type is that of reverential awe before the Sovereign Will of Grace. The accent in the Reformed service falls more exclusively than in the Lutheran upon the transcendent nature of God. In the Reformed rite the sense of creatureliness is very marked ; man bows before the inscrutable Will of glory and of grace. The sovereignty of God dominates this worship ; and the service proclaims and seeks the revealed Will. In its idea or essence this worship stresses the objective character of that Word which reveals the Eternal Will. The Oracle of God is presented here in a more absolute and abstract character ; and the Reformed service is the most consistent and most logical development of worship around the proclamation of the Word. The first duty of man was to know this Divine Will and to be obedient to it. Therefore it was inevitable that the function of preaching should, in this worship, be supremely important. "The central place," says Dr. Mitchell Hunter,[1] "occupied by the Mass in the services of the Roman Church was taken by the sermon, in those of the Reformed, teaching was the preacher's great business; the service was indeed often called the preaching or the sermon."

This distinction between Lutheran and Reformed worship to which I have referred is reflected also in their different attitude to Holy Scripture. To Luther the Bible is the Word of God in which he finds the fountain and the corroboration of a spiritual experience. To Calvinism the Bible is the declaration of God's Will and in its entirety has authority. Both accepted the authority of the Bible instead of the authority of tradition, and based their worship on this authority. Yet the authority of the Bible is for Luther ultimately interpreted by experience, while the Calvinistic position finds in all Scripture the infallible rule of an external norm. By this view Calvinism accepted much that was pre-Christian and sub-Christian, and to the modern mind the standpoint of Luther is at once more historical and more religious. Yet Calvinism was the more consistent application of the principle of Scriptural authority; and it gained thereby an absolute standard, for in every part of the Bible there was a revelation which it was man's duty to find and to apply. The Bible was therefore to the Calvinist the norm for worship, and only what Scripture sanctioned was admitted into the Church service. But further, since Calvinism did more rigorously apply than Lutheranism the authority of Scripture, it gained a greater objectivity in worship. The sermon becomes an objective element in worship for it is the announcement and exposition of a Will declared in every part of the sacred writings. To-day we are prone to regard the sermon as the subjective expression of the preacher's thoughts and experience, and prayer as the more objective element in the service. To the Reformers, however, it was the sermon, the statement of the Word, which had the objective character, while prayer, which was the response to the Word, possessed more the subjective quality. Calvinism provided through its view of Scripture a stable foundation for this interpretation of preaching.

[1] *Teaching of Calvin*, p. 205.

Another difference between Lutherism and Calvinism emerges. Both alike repudiated the doctrine which the Mass contained. Luther's mind while violently rejecting this doctrine was open to the appeal of the mediæval service; he had been a priest, and doubtless religious impressions and associations clustered round the age-worn words of devotion. He therefore was willing to admit into the Lutheran service what did not contradict the truth as he found it in Scripture. Calvin looked with the eye of a hostile outsider upon the structure of the ancient rite as well as with dislike and abhorrence upon the thoughts enshrined in mediæval ceremonial. Thus it is that the Calvinistic Rite, which is the distinctive Reformed Rite, is barer and bleaker than the Lutheran Liturgy. The latter had retained many elements of the ancient ritual and preserved something of the framework of the Mass; but the Calvinistic Rite is shorn of the ancient prayers of devotion, deprived of all ceremonial, wanting in colour and in form. It has been said of the Lutheran service, that only the torso of the Mass remained; but here the whole structure seems smashed, the most precious expressions of devotion scorned, the noblest aspirations of the human spirit in worship neglected or parodied by being paraphrased. A gaunt skeleton alone remains.

What then did the Calvinistic service contribute to the idea of worship? What had it that could make amends for all it had not and its peers possessed? Lacking in stately ceremonial, without the glory of the mighty utterances which the spirit of worship had fashioned, divested of impressive ritual and without the dramatic movement of the soul's ascent, without the poetry of devotion—such it had not, and its limitations crowd thick upon our minds. It makes its appeal exclusively to the hearing ear, it forgets that human nature is more than conscious mind, its temper is apt to be intellectual rather than devotional, its range is narrow, its language too often pedestrian and commonplace—these things it had. But one thing it was—the clearest illustration of the type of worship founded exclusively on the idea of Revelation. It drives home with concentrated energy the abiding truth of the Revelation of God. God has spoken, and man, the creature and child of the Most High, can learn the Eternal Purpose. It has not the warmth and splendour of a picture with the glow and glory of colour, but it has the sharp distinctness of an etching with clear-cut line. Abstract in character it is without dramatic impressiveness, but it possesses the two qualities of abstract art,[1] it has sincerity and dignity—a sincerity symbolised in its bareness, and a dignity which springs from the overwhelming sense of God high and lifted up beyond all mortal striving. The God of Calvinism is the God man can never apprehend save through His revelation. It is the service which most exclusively exhibits what I called earlier the descending movement in worship. God speaks and man responds. The service with which it contrasts most is the service which exhibits the same spirit of utter consistency. As the native Roman service was built around the idea of making a sacrifice, so this service is founded upon the thought of hearing the Word. As the Roman service through the sacrifice offered experienced the miracle of God's presence in the world of space, so this service through the ministry of hearing knows the Revelation of God in the world of time. Because these two services were true to type, each has the consistency of an underlying principle. They are both direct and purposive, and they both have an ethos that distinguishes them from the mediæval service which was the product of Gallican infusion. Neither in the original Roman nor the Calvinistic service is there anything vague or indefinite. The Roman service possesses the definiteness of an action as compared with the vague mood of the East; and the Calvinistic service has the precision of a Word spoken in the light of truth as compared with the dim twilight of the mediæval mood.

The Reformed service was an attempt to escape from what these Reformers thought were mediæval perversions and to return to the primitive purity of worship. To-day a more accurate historical knowledge informs us that the attempt to reproduce the worship of the primitive days was not wholly successful because certain elements in the early Church's worship were not recognised by the Reformers. But the Reformers believed they were instituting a form of worship which was a return to the primitive practice. Thus in accordance with the norm of Scripture they framed a form

[1] Konody.

of worship in which the worshipper hears and responds to the Word of God. All that was secret or hidden or allusive in mediæval worship is abandoned, for everything must be understanded of the worshipper. Hence the secret and hushed prayer of the priest in a hieratic language is abandoned and the use of the vernacular is essential. Public Worship becomes an open thing. The worshipper from being a spectator becomes a hearer.

There was a double aspect of the Reformed tradition which had its effect on the form of worship. It is the difference between the standpoint of Zwingli and the outlook of Calvin. There is a distinction between the Zürich Rite and the Genevan. On the surface we notice that Zwingli is less impervious to the appeal of the old devotion and admits more of its historic expressions. While thus on the surface the Calvinistic Rite is barer than the Zürich form, there is a deeper distinction in spirit. This reveals itself in the sacramental service most clearly.

The Zwinglian service of the Lord's Supper seems to find its norm in the "breaking of bread" as recounted in the Acts of the Apostles. The service is a congregational meal declaring fellowship and communion and expressing praise and gratitude; but in it there is lacking the note of mystery. It is a memorial of the past rather than an experience of communion with the Present Lord. Indeed the celebration of Holy Communion is an illustration in symbol of the power of the Word. It adds nothing to the proclamation of the Word and is not in itself a means of grace. It is an acted sermon. This view follows from the idea of God which lies at the basis of Zwingli's thought. God is wholly transcendent and like a chill shadow there falls on the service Zwingli's unfortunate thought that the Body of Christ is localised in Heaven. His clear emphasis that only through faith can Christ be received undoubtedly delivers his service from the menace of superstition; but we feel there is something in the Sacrament that the Zwinglian service omits. From his thought of the Sacrament we trace the origin of the view that holds unnecessary frequent communion. If the communion service is only a repetition in another form of the proclamation of the Word, then there is no vital need that this communion be observed very often. Four times a year would be sufficient for this special service that in a symbolic fashion preached the same great tidings of Christ's passion and victory. This infrequency of communion is the inevitable outcome of limiting the service to a service of remembrance. It is probably from this side of the Reformed tradition that the Scots custom of infrequent communion is derived. On the other hand, the observance of the sacrament in the Zürich Rite repeats a true New Testament note in two respects. It is a service of fellowship—a corporate act of communion; it is also a service of thanksgiving and gratitude.

This is the framework of the service. Communion follows the preaching of the Word. A prayer for grace to give worthy thanks in obedience to Christ's command and in memory of the Lord's death begins the service. It is an act of obedience, declaring God's wondrous deed, which the faithful fulfil rather than an act of communion that feeds the souls of the needy. A Scripture reading of 1 Cor. xi. 20–29 precedes the Gloria in Excelsis, recited by the officiating minister and people. A second Scripture lesson, St. John vi. 47–53, is read; thereafter the Apostles' Creed is repeated, and an exhortation is given calling to thanksgiving and warning against the guilt of eating unworthily, and concluding with the Lord's Prayer; a prayer for a worthy reception follows. Then the account of the Institution is read and there is the distribution and communion. After this, a psalm of praise is read, and the thanksgiving (" We thank Thee, O Lord, for all Thy gifts and Thy goodness, Who livest and reignest God for ever and ever ") is made, and the dismissal, " Go in peace," is given.[1] There was no singing throughout this service; the Psalm was recited antiphonally.

Such a type of service is admirably fitted to bring out the ideas that Zwingli desired to emphasise. It is a coherent appeal to faith, and the eye of faith is turned to commemorate the one great historical event, the death of Christ. The service is not wholly denuded of the ancient forms found in the Mass. It contains, for example, the Gloria, and a dim shadow of the order of the Mass remains. Yet it has sacrificed more of the traditional worship than the Lutheran service, and the feeling for the Church Year

[1] Cf. Brillioth, *op. cit.* pp. 159–164. Pullan, *Christian Tradition*, pp. 150–151.

disappears from it. One observes here the beginning of that movement which separates the Communion service from the weekly service which proclaims the Word. The Eucharistic service becomes an occasional and not the normal service of the Church. The cause of this is perhaps to be found in the special emphasis Zwingli gives to the aspect of congregational fellowship. At the time of the Reformation, although the Mass was a Eucharistic service, the communion of the people was infrequent. The Zwinglian service seeks to increase the frequency of communicating and this purpose is achieved. No service could express more clearly than the Zürich Rite this aspect of fellowship. The worshippers are seated, and there is reproduced the aspect and atmosphere of the religious meal which in the New Testament is called the Breaking of Bread. Here Zwingli does emphasise a feature neglected in the mediæval Church ; but the other elements in the service of the Mass found their equivalents in the Zwinglian thought of the preaching of the Word, and therefore if the Word was preached the purpose of the mediæval Mass was fulfilled.

When we contrast the clear and definite service of the Zürich Rite with the Calvinistic service of the Genevan Rite we find a profound difference. This difference betokens another approach to the thought of communion, and is the second stream of the Reformed tradition. Calvin's theory of the Sacrament makes the service not simply a memorial feast as Zwingli's view tended to do, but a spiritual communion with the Risen Lord. While Calvin denies the physical miracle of the mediæval Mass he is alive to the truth mirrored in the thought of a supernatural change. To him the Sacrament has the efficiency of the Word. The two thoughts present in his view of the Sacrament are the power of the Word, which is expressed in the service through the reading of the Institution and the presence of the Spirit, whereby there is a real and objective presence given to faith. He does not hold Luther's metaphysical view of the ubiquity of the Risen Body of the Lord, for to Calvin the Body of Christ is localised in heaven. Yet though to Calvin the Body of Christ is in heaven, its Power which is its substance or essence is given to the elect by the Holy Spirit through faith. We must interpret the bare form of the Calvinistic service by the great thoughts implicit in it. If we do so, then the ineffable mystery remains, but it has been stripped of all appeal save to the conscious mind.

As I have suggested, this form is barer and bleaker than the Zwinglian type. The Apostles' Creed remains, but the Gloria has vanished. The concentration on the commemoration of Christ's death is marked. The place of liturgical prayer is not prominent, but exhortation bulks largely in the rite. *La Manière de célébrer la Cêne* consists of a prayer for the Church along with a prayer for worthy partaking, a paraphrase of the Lord's Prayer, the saying of the Apostles' Creed, a Prayer which corresponds to the "Consecration Prayer," the reading of the Institution as the warrant for the celebration, an exhortation ("Let us lift up our spirits and our hearts to heaven where Jesus Christ is in His Father's Glory") which is slightly reminiscent of the Preface to the Mass. Thereafter is the Fraction followed by the distribution, while a Psalm is sung or sentences read during the act of communion. Then a Prayer of thanksgiving which is the post-communion. Bootless it is to seek here for liturgical richness for only the bare skeleton of the ancient order remains. What, however, this service does possess is a sense of mystery in the act of communion, for, though Calvin's unfortunate theory that Christ's Body is localised in heaven makes it difficult for him to express adequately the Presence of the Lord, the spirit of mystery broods over this service. This quality of Calvinistic Worship was imported into Scotland and has ever been a mark of the Reformed Communion there. Unfortunately, however, Calvin's own view for which he could not find support in Geneva that the complete service of the Reformed Church required the "Liturgy of the Upper Room" as well as the "Liturgy of the Word"[1] was not transplanted into the practice of the Scots Kirk.

An unsympathetic eye can read in the Calvinistic Rite the massacre of the ancient ritual and the destruction of its fairest elements. What, for example, could be more atrocious than a paraphrase of the Lord's Prayer? This evil tendency to translate into their own speech the great historic utterances of the faith is

[1] Maxwell, *Knox's Genevan Service*, p. 51.

shown also in the so-called Liturgy of John Knox, wherein his confession of faith is a somewhat wordy exposition of the traditional symbol—the Creed. Yet even this vile practice has its root in a spiritual purpose, for its aim is to make the service intelligible and sincere. The same spirit of liturgical restlessness lies behind this Reformed practice as lay behind Gallican expansiveness and the mediæval habit of farcing. The same motive is present, but in the Reformed custom the meaning is emphasised and in the mediæval practice the impressiveness. This absorption in meaning is of course caused by the root idea in the Reformed Rite that there should be a true knowledge of God and His Will. None the less, it reveals a total lack of true liturgical feeling and a meddling disposition that sins against the devotional mood. For poetry loses its soul in a paraphrase however exact and careful. A paraphrase may be an exercise in teaching us to understand what is said, but to paraphrase the great spiritual creations such as the Lord's Prayer, the Gloria, the Creed, the Preface, and many of the Collects, which like poetry have a value in themselves as the expression of spiritual reality, is to parody them. There is no liturgical harvest to be gleaned from the Calvinistic service save the warning of terrible mistakes.

On the other hand, we must acknowledge what is there. M. Doumergue has pointed out that Calvin alone of all the reformers has rejected the division of the service into two parts, one liturgical and the other entirely at the discretion of the officiant. Calvinistic worship is a unity. This is illustrated in the idea that the Communion service and the morning Sunday service of preaching belong together. Calvin was unable to have a weekly communion and so his morning Sunday service is a service without a visible partaking, but all the elements that belong to sacramental worship in his view are given in this service. Calvin's order of service is as follows: First the invocation, "Our help is in the name of the Lord," the exhortation, "Brethren, let each one present himself before the Lord," the general confession, the singing of a Psalm or metrical version of the Decalogue, another prayer, in which the minister "prayeth for the assistance of God's Holy Spirit," another Psalm, Scripture, and the sermon, the great prayer of intercession for "the whole estate of the Christian Church," concluding with the Lord's Prayer, the recital of the Creed or the singing of it in a metrical form, and finally the Blessing in the Aaronic form, which is Lutheran in origin, or the Trinitarian Benediction. "Calvin's customary benediction," says Dr. Mitchell Hunter,[1] was—"The Grace of God the Father, and the Peace of Our Lord Jesus Christ, through the fellowship of the Holy Spirit, dwell with us for ever." Here doubtless are all the elements of Christian Worship, but it is a gaunt skeleton which has to be clothed with flesh and made alive by the faith of the worshipper rather than a living liturgy that awakens faith. Unfortunately a fear of superstition dogged the steps of the reformer and the dread of superstition became itself a superstition in reformed circles, as, for example, the Westminster Directory reveals in the prohibition of prayer at funerals lest prayer be thought to be offered for the dead.

One is sometimes surprised at the scanty place given to adoration and thanksgiving in the prayers of the Calvinistic Rite. Two things have to be remembered. The first is that the Calvinist service included the singing of psalms and in the congregational praise the note of thanksgiving found voice. The exclusive use of the Psalter is derived from its conception of revelation. This deprived the service of the great Christian hymns, yet there is within the compass of the Psalter a wide range of praise. The other thing to be noted is that the genius of this service did not have the unitive experience of adoration as its goal. The service belongs to what we have already called the descending movement in worship. Indeed we might say that this service tends to lop off everything that is not consonant with this movement. In far more radical fashion than the Lutheran service it exhibits the revelation of the Word and the response of man. Its characteristic note is the bowing down of the spirit of man before the glory and power of the Eternal. We must distinguish between the awe and veneration which is such a characteristic mood of this service, and the mood of adoration which is the climax of the mystical service belonging to the ascending movement. In the awe of the Calvinistic Rite there is a sense of creatureliness and the feeling that man is nothing in the sight of God. There is,

[1] *Calvin*, p. 215.

however, in this sentiment of awe no obliteration of the self. Man knows himself as worthless and unworthy, full of sin and stricken with mortal frailty. He is conscious, vividly conscious, of his soul as distinct from the Eternal God. The mood of adoration, on the other hand, reaches its apex when the soul loses all sense of self in union with the Divine. This latter mood does not belong to the spiritual movement of the Calvinistic service, which begins with the mood of self-abasement before God, proceeds through confession, petition, praise, and the hearing of the Word, to seek in intercession unity of will with God's will. The aim therefore of this service is not the loss of the sense of self in adoring contemplation of God's nature, but it is the heightening of the sense of self through the recognition of worthlessness, which results in the self finding its place and purpose in obedience to the Divine will. Because this is its aim the declaratory side of worship is foremost, and we miss its value if we estimate it by standards which do not belong to it.

There is in this service in the main a repudiation of all symbolism which appeals to the eye. Its appeal, as is obvious, is almost exclusively addressed to the ear. Two things result from this: the first is the peril that the service may become intellectualistic or moralistic and the sense of worship be reduced to a vanishing point. Yet even when this danger is averted because of its intellectual character the range of the service is limited. It makes its appeal too exclusively to one side of human nature. The second limitation is that by ignoring the symbolic it sacrifices a dramatic appeal. It has no movement that can be appreciated and felt by those who do not possess conscious faith. It therefore tends to lack the power which the dramatic liturgies have of inducing the spirit of worship. Yet it is not wholly lacking in the dramatic sense. In the service of Holy Communion the attempt is made to reproduce and to represent the circumstances and the situation of the first Supper. The Roman priest at no point of the service is anything but the offerer of the sacrifice; in the Calvinistic service the presbyter at certain points represents and personifies our Lord Himself. Something of the mystery drama is here.

As we saw, both types of the reformed communion service were based on the proclamation of the Word through the Sacrament.

We must not, however, compare the Reformed Communion with the consecration of the offering in the Mass, and the reformed sermon with the Roman sermon. The reformed sermon, as I said, seeks to do not only what the Roman sermon did, but also what the Roman offering effected. As the Mass brought God near to man's need, so the sermon fulfils a similar function. To estimate the service aright we must recognise its original intention. The same circle of spiritual emotions belongs to both. Taken by itself the Reformed Communion is lacking in much that the Mass has, but we must remember that it is not the substitute for the Mass. On the other hand, the fact that the sermon has to do what the Mass offering did means that the centre of worship is receiving and not offering, and therefore throughout its history there has been in this service a want of emphasis on devotional offering.

When the influence of the Reformation came to the Scots Church it came wearing the garb of Calvinistic thought and expression. The Church in Scotland had experienced its Celtic phase and had known its Roman phase during which, among others, the Sarum use had been employed in worship; in reformed days her liturgical life was influenced by the Prayer Book of 1552. But in the Book of Common Order the outlook of Calvin is mediated through the spirit of John Knox. It was given to Scotland to have as the man who most deeply stamped her religious life at this time one whose greatness lay in other spheres than that of liturgical and devotional feeling. The impulse to spread light and knowledge interfered with the expression of devotion, for the instructional element which had been so largely neglected in the Middle Ages bulked predominantly in the service. Since men in the eyes of the reformer had to be taught the true aim of worship and had to learn the practice of prayer the development is away from beauty of expression and the sense of order. Yet in this book Knox, like Calvin, conserved the framework of the ancient service though it is reduced to its baldest elements. The liturgical genealogy of this Book of Common Order or Forms of Prayer has been demonstrated by Dr. Maxwell.[1] Its descent is traced through Calvin's Strasburg service, whose foundation was the service of Bucer to the German

[1] *John Knox's Genevan Service Book*, p. 17 f.

Mass of Schwarz and hence to the Mediæval Mass itself. However, though this descent is real, the reformers were not conscious of it. In this two points are of note. The first is that all unknown to themselves the reformers could not escape from the power of a liturgic tradition. So inevitable had been the order of the ancient service, so impressive its mood and so massive its appeal, that even the attempt to abolish the Mass acknowledges the Liturgical necessity of the historic order and framework. The second is that the Sunday morning service in Scotland is the substitute for the service of the Mass. It is not derived from Matins nor is its origin to be found in the mediæval vernacular service called Prone. This latter service consisted of a general confession, the Creed, the Lord's Prayer, the Decalogue, and the Homily. I think there is little doubt that this service of Prone influenced the Calvinistic service, for Prone was largely a teaching service and it would therefore be congruous to the reformed insistence on the preaching of the word. Certain of its contents are found in the reformed service; perhaps it was through the influence of Prone that the Apostles' Creed was used in the Scots communion instead of the Nicene Creed. Yet while admitting this influence we must definitely hold that our morning service is derived from and fulfils the purpose of the Mass.

The communions that have been influenced by Calvinistic teaching and practice have in a special way cultivated free and spontaneous prayer in public worship. Yet in neither Calvin nor in Knox do we find the repudiation of read prayers which became such a marked feature in the worship of a later day in Scotland. In the mind of the early reformers there was no objection to the use of a liturgy or form of prayer. In the records of its history Scots devotion under the ægis of Presbyterianism recognised not only the place of liturgical prayer but even the use of collects. We find the existence of collects based on the psalms which evidently were used as the response to the Word spoken in the psalm.[1] We may have grave doubts as to the quality of these prayers, but their existence proves that this form of short prayer was not wholly outside the limits of the Scots practice. It must, however, be admitted that the germinal idea of worship propounded by Calvin

[1] McCrie, *Public Worship of Presbyterian Scotland*, p. 138 f. and p. 390 f.

and his follower Knox had its logical outcome in free prayer. This at times led to dire results in a communion which had turned its back upon the classical expressions of human devotions. The spoken prayer at times lost its spontaneity and became hackneyed, the distinction between individual devotion and public worship was blurred, and at times the devotions were such as to justify Hudibras's criticism of those "who made prayers, not so like petitions as overtures and propositions." I confess that to my mind the Church has little or nothing to learn from Knox about liturgical prayer. His public devotions appear to me to lack range of sympathy and sweep of spirit, and in poignancy of appeal they are far surpassed by Lutheran devotion.

The section in the Book of Common Order which shows the highest expression of devotional feeling is the administration of the Lord's Supper, and yet it is also the part which leaves us with the greatest sense of bareness. We miss the high notes that peal in the great liturgies, and we do not find the sweep and the beauty of ancient devotion. Yet when we examine this rite, bleak and bare as it is, we see that its baldness is the baldness of the mountain-top. Too rarefied an atmosphere perhaps for man to live in, but not without health-giving qualities to the climber of the peak.

Let us look more closely at this service of the Supper. A monthly communion is contemplated, and there is thus a definite departure from the weekly celebration of the early Church. Yet it must be borne in mind that the provision of a monthly communion for the laity was an attempt to increase and not to diminish the frequency of partaking. At this service the Institution of the Sacrament is read from Corinthians, but there is a note to the reader: "As for the wordes of the Lord's Supper we rehearse them not because they should change the substance of the bread and wine, or that the repetition thereof with the intent of sacrifice should make the sacrament (as the Papistes falsely believe), but they are rede and pronounced to teach us how to behave ourselves in that action that Christ might witness unto our faith as it were with his own mouth that he hath ordained these signs to our spiritual use and comfort." Quite obviously the transformation of the Mass is explicitly denied, but we see also the attempt to do what the Mass seeks to do—to present Christ to the worshipper. In the Mass it is a Presence seen in the form of bread and wine, here it is a Presence heard in the words Christ spoke " as it were with his own mouth." Perhaps the fact that the pictorial sense is more native to the dwellers in Southern Europe and the auditive sense the accustomed form of expression to the northern and Nordic races has something to do with this difference. The reading of the Warrant is followed by an exhortation in which are echoes of the English Prayer Book. The benefit of spiritually eating the flesh of Christ is pointed out and the peril of unworthy partaking is set forth. The excommunication of the unworthy from the Table is declared. This practice—however much we may criticise it—implies the belief in an objective Presence however it be explained. The Sacrament is not simply a commemoration of a past event nor a dramatic reacting of the Last Supper, but it is " a singular medicine for all poor sick creatures." Here is the age-old thought which permeates the ancient rites that Holy Communion is a food. One wonders why this conception which ought to imply frequent communion so faded in the practice of Presbyterian Scotland until recent times. Was it perchance the unconscious instinct to retain the sense of mystery in the observance ? The rite had been stripped of all that awakened the sense of wonder save words, and language which is not liturgical loses through familiarity the power of kindling the feeling of the mysterious. Was the result of the Calvinistic destruction of the symbolic this dilemma that only by infrequent celebration could the Communion keep its aspect of mystery ?

Traces there are in this austere service that echo the ampler movement of a richer worship. There is the most interesting statement, " The only waye to dispose our soules to receive nourishment, reliefs, and quickening of His substance is to lift up our mindes by fayth above all things worldlye and sensible, and thereby to enter into heaven that we may finde and receive Christ." This is not only a repetition of Calvin's idea of Christ's Body in heaven, it is also reminiscent of the Mass prayer Te supplices. In the prayer of thanksgiving which is offered at the Sacrament there are three notes which suggest the liturgical usage of the universal Church. (1) There is the reference to the Incarnation, the Passion of Christ, His Resurrection and His bringing of life. This note, sounded in all liturgies, is particularly the feature of the Christian Mystery in the East. (2) The offering of ourselves. "Yet neverthe-less at the commandment of Jesus Christ our Lord we present ourselves to His table to declare and witness before the world that by Him alone we have received libertie and life." This corresponds to the ancient offertory, but the thought visibly expressed in the bread and wine as a sacrifice is abandoned, and the idea of presenting ourselves at the table as a way of declaring God's Gracious Word of life is substituted. (3) There is the reference to the Holy Spirit, "We Thy congregation moved by Thy Holy Spirit render Thee all thanks." This is what is left of the prayer of invocation. "The service," says an Anglican writer, "contains no consecration of the elements at all." This statement is technically correct, and fortunately in the Westminster Directory and in the later practice of the Church this grievous defect was remedied. Frankly I admit that Knox's service is singularly inadequate and no Communion rite is open to greater criticism, since it is lacking in many of the precious aspects of the celebration in the early Church. Yet I think a con-secration is implied. It was from one angle that the somewhat narrow mind of Knox drew up his service, and that was the avoidance of certain abuses. Knox is so afraid of idolatry coming to man through the eye that he is ever seeking to lift the eyes of men from the visible elements lest they worship material things. He was no mystic, and his rather insensitive nature had little or no under-standing of how the visible can speak of the invisible. But I do not think we can accuse him of deliberately leaving out the consecra-tion. He takes it for granted. He is seeking to react the first Supper and by the Spirit Christ is present to faith. In that Presence lies the consecration. It is certainly a one-sided description of the Eucharist, but it was drawn up in a mood that is explicit in its disagreements but implicitly assumes that with which it agrees.

In obedience to its dominant idea of the proclamation of the Word this type of worship tended to make the value of the Sacra-ment as an act of worship rest in its character as a declaratory symbol. So in its weekly service the tendency was ever to stress the place of the sermon as the exposition of Divine Revelation.

Valuable undoubtedly was the teaching trait in Scots worship. The reader's service, which is probably matins adapted to the reformed idea of worship, had for its content prayer and the reading of Scripture and was preliminary to the service of the preaching of the Word. The value of teaching and the spirit of prophecy are real aspects of worship which were rescued by the reformed tradition from desuetude. But this type of service was partly the result of a reaction from abuses. It is a form of worship that emphasises the prophetic office of the Church rather than its priestly vocation. And while the priestly office of the Church without the light and inspiration of the prophetic impulse becomes vague, indefinite, and clouded with floating yearnings which may darken into superstition, the prophetic office of the Church without the priestly can become exhortation and intellectual exposition, which readily falls into the teacher's snare of explaining away the Inexplicable. The positive aspect of the Service of the Word was the insistence that the worshipper should know and receive the Word and the Will of the Eternal Lord, and this prophetic testimony assuredly belongs to worship. But unfortunately the positive aspect carried with it a negative side. In the first Book of Discipline there is the suggestion that the Sacrament be observed on the first Sundays of March, June, September, and December. These dates are chosen to avoid the Holy Days which belonged to the keeping of the Christian Year. This seed of negation which the reformers sowed in their protest against abuses develops, and the protest becomes a tradition. The negative attitude which was originally the result of reaction becomes a standard.

This negative attitude developed its own peculiar spirit which deeply affected the form of worship in Scotland and that spirit was the spirit of Puritanism. This spirit seeks to escape from obedience to all liturgical order which seems to it a bondage, feels free only by repudiating as outworn what has been practised, finds its sincerity by discarding any expression but its own. Over against this is the other spirit that seeks to incarnate its desires in hallowed forms, finds its relief in ordered expression, and plants its liberty in an authority beyond itself. This is the catholic spirit.

They belong both to the realm of the Spirit. The winds of those two spirits blew across the devotion and worship of the Church in Scotland. Unfortunately this ebb and flow of the Spirit was complicated by another issue. Worship became the arena in which was fought a great question and wherein a spiritual issue was raised which had nothing to do with worship itself. This issue was freedom, and since in Scotland the assertion of freedom was linked with political aspirations toward liberty, the historic structure of worship was sacrificed on the altar of liberty. The noblest devotions of the past were neglected and even the use of the Lord's Prayer became suspect. From the standpoint of liturgical worship and the beauty of holiness it was a night of darkness. Other vital issues were at stake, but worship as an art was demolished. Yet apart from these distorting causes, these two spirits in their nobler aspects are but the ebb and flow of the same spirit. The current runs in opposite ways, but it is the same sweeping tide that makes the different eddies. It is our old distinction between the two movements in worship—the ascending movement and the descending. At the Reformation there came into Scotland with the force of a creative spirit a form of worship whose centre was the idea of revelation and the proclamation of the Word, and in her subsequent history around this centre of spiritual gravity the two tendencies, the inclusive or catholic and the exclusive or puritanic, have played. Surely and certainly the Church in Scotland is returning to the historic forms and the catholic expression of the truth, but the conception of the Word uttered is inherent in all the enrichment and the widening of the original reformed rite.

CHAPTER IX

THE ANGLICAN *VIA MEDIA*

In the worship of the Church of England there is no one dominant idea. This is by no means a weakness, for in this rite are found the idea of Sacrifice, the influence of the Mystery Drama, and the Oracle type of devotion. A reconciliation is attempted between the claims of these three forms. This fact by itself would make the Book of Common Prayer an interesting liturgical document. Yet there is a further significance here. The Upward or ascending movement of worship, which is associated with mystical piety, and the Downward or descending movement, which is the trait of prophetic devotion, are both present in this Prayer Book. The framers of this beautiful liturgy were not of course conscious of the opposites which they brought together. The circumstances of the time stated the problem, and the sources from which Cranmer and his coadjutors derived their rite blended these forms and movements of Christian worship.

To estimate aright the Anglican form and its derivative branches and to evaluate the reconciliation achieved we must bear in mind the wells from which the water has been drawn. These sources are four in number.

(1) There is the mediæval practice in England. There were several varieties of Divine Service. The Prayer Book speaks of five kinds—those of Salisbury, Hereford, Bangor, York, and Lincoln. Of these the Sarum use, as the practice of Salisbury was called, is much the most important as it was by far the most widespread. These "Uses" are not different rites, but are variants of the Roman Rite, from which they vary only in matters of detail. Certainly in the Sarum use there are traces of Gallican and Celtic influences, but in structure and in intention the use is identical with the Roman Rite. In one or two slight ways the Prayer Book

bears the mark of special Sarum variants. For example, Sundays are reckoned after the octave of Trinity as in the Sarum use, and not after the octave of Pentecost as in the Roman Rite.[1] The existence of this source has had two effects. The first result is that something of the restraint and dignity which enshrines the idea of Sacrifice enters this rite. The second consequence is that through the Sarum use there flows into the Prayer Book a portion of the great devotional riches contained in the collects of the Leonine, Gelasian, and Gregorian sacramentaries.

(2) The second source is the Breviary of Cardinal Quignon (1535). Quignon's effort was directed to the reform of the Breviary by omission and rearrangement. His aim was to make the reading of Holy Scripture more coherent and the order of the service more intelligible. Any influence of the Breviary can only be in Morning Prayer and Evensong, since Morning Prayer is compiled from Matins, Laud, and Prime, and Evensong from Vespers and Compline.[2] The direct influence of Quignon is little, but the aim which he expresses in his preface appears to have been at work in the mind of Cranmer.

(3) The third source is that of other ancient liturgies. Cardinal Gasquet has demonstrated that the supposed influence of the Mozarabic Rite is unproved. But certainly Cranmer had not been unaware of the Eastern Liturgies. The so-called prayer of St. Chrysostom appointed for Morning and Evening Prayer reveals the fact that the Eastern Liturgies were not without their effect. The Litany also perhaps shows evidence of Greek influence.

(4) The fourth source is continental rituals. At first from

[1] The feast of the Trinity is not ancient. "It was at first kept only in certain private churches" (Cabrol). In 1334 Pope John XXII. made the festival universal. The Carmelite Rite and the Dominican agree with the Sarum in numbering the Sundays after the octave of Trinity. It seems unfortunate that the Anglican Prayer Book should conform to this reckoning which emphasises Trinity, the Sunday of Orthodoxy, rather than Pentecost, the Sunday of Inspiration. Here the practice of Rome is at once more primitive and more evangelic than that of Canterbury.

[2] This is a rough statement of the fact. New matter was added. In general, however, Matins gives the line to Morning Prayer from the beginning (which was in 1549 the Lord's Prayer) to the Te Deum, and from the second lesson to the third collect with which the service ended, the line of Lauds is followed.

Wittenberg and then from Geneva the winds of reformation swept into the thoughts of those who fashioned the Prayer Book. We can trace the spirit of Luther, the expression of Melanchthon, the mind of Calvin, and even the hand of Knox in this Anglican rite. The presence of Bucer in England cast its shadow. Cranmer's own thought of Holy Communion is more than tinged with Calvinism, while Latimer sometimes leans to a Zwinglian mode of speech. Most definitely, however, we can find the influence of a German book published in 1543 upon the first Prayer Book of Edward VI. This German book was produced by Hermann, Archbishop of Cologne, with the assistance of Bucer and Melanchthon. In the service of Holy Communion the invitation, confession, and absolution, as also the Comfortable Words, are derived from the work of Hermann. So also in the Sacrament of Baptism there is evident the same influence. I need not spend further words in proving that it was from a wide area of Christian devotion that this Anglican book drew the waters of its devotion.

The Book though culled from many fields is no mere compilation. It has an atmosphere all its own and possesses a dignity and a unity worthy of high praise. Neither in Lutheranism nor in the Reformed communion can there be found so rich and so varied a store of liturgical devotion. That the Book has been patient of many and even opposing interpretations is far from being a discredit. The changing thought of men has not simply called forth different interpretations : it has also left its impress on the Book itself.

Its Development—the Prayer Book of 1549 is obedient to five regulating ideas which are akin to Lutheran practice and to the thought of Quignon. (*a*) The substitution of the vernacular for Latin was made. This change had been partly anticipated by the use of the vernacular in the private devotions of the laity as the primers issued by the authority of the Church show. Yet the use in public worship of the spoken tongue was a momentous step. (*b*) The elimination of the legendary material that had strayed into the Breviary, and the arrangement for the orderly reading of Holy Scripture and the full use of the Psalter was effected. (*c*) The ceremonies and forms were greatly simplified. This affected especially the Daily Offices, but in 1552 the same principles were applied to the

Liturgy Proper. (*d*) There was the endeavour to recognise the place of the people in worship. Thus the Daily Offices aim at reviving the supposed primitive custom whereby the office is the daily offering of the people's prayer. (*e*) Uniformity is sought through the kingdom in all the public worship of the Church " after the use of the Church of England." These ideas govern the adaptation of the mediæval service to the requirements of the new age.

Let us glance at how these ideas operated. Two sections of the Prayer Book alone concern us here. (1) The first is the section which deals with Matins and Evensong. The same basis is found in both these offices. They begin with the Lord's Prayer, which is not now said secretly as a preparation for common worship, but repeated aloud by the officiant. The reformers' suspicion of all silent worship is evinced here and the special purpose of the prayer is rendered null. Thereafter the service follows this order—psalms, lesson, canticle, lesson, canticle, preces, and three collects. Material taken from the mediæval offices is skilfully adapted and adjusted. Morning Prayer derives Psalm 95 and Te Deum from Matins, the collect for the day and Benedictus from Lauds, the Creed and the third collect from Prime, Preces from Lauds and Prime, and the second collect from Lauds of the Blessed Virgin. Evensong derives Magnificat, Preces, and collect of the day from Vespers, Nunc Dimittis, the Creed, and the third collect from Compline, and the second collect from Vespers of the Blessed Virgin.[1] There are thus preserved the ancient springs of piety, and with these well-worn forms of praise and prayer there is associated the reformed emphasis on the Word revealed in Holy Writ. In the second Prayer Book of 1552 an introduction is added consisting of exhortation, confession, and absolution. Whoever was the author of these, the spirit of the continental Reformation echoes in them, and again there is witness that the old and the new are joined together in the service of the sanctuary. Perhaps in these additions the uniformity and fixity of the Anglican rite meet with a difficulty. Constant repetition does not detract from those liturgical expressions which, sifted by time, have become the

[1] *Liturgy of Worship*, p. 156.

classic utterance of mortal need and aspiration. But the too frequent use of devotional language and thought which owe their birth to a particular movement of the human spirit—no matter how great that movement be—does lose its freshness and tends to become formal simply because it can only convey the mood that gave it birth. Further, while the selection made by Cranmer shows liturgical genius, the price exacted by the idea of uniformity was that great and priceless spiritual treasures were left outside the narrow limit of the prescribed service.

The book of 1552 makes but little difference in this section though the flow of its tendency is strongly in the Puritanic direction. The names of the offices are altered to Morning and Evening Prayer, but even this change points to something distinctive in the Anglican form. Unlike the reformed liturgies the place and discipline of prayer are never sacrificed to the preaching of the Word. For the Prayer Book, though hospitable to much Lutheran and Calvanistic influence, decisively declares that it is at once a necessity and a duty to offer public prayer.

(2) When we turn to the second section, which deals with "The Supper of the Lord, and the Holy Communion commonly called the Mass, the departure from mediæval ritual and thought is much more manifest. As Luther had repudiated the sacrificial idea of the Mass, so Cranmer's steps seem to walk in the same path. What Luther called "the abominable canon," which is the core of the Mass, is so altered by Cranmer that it really becomes a new prayer and is divested of its former character. Cranmer explains the phrase "to accept this our sacrifice of praise and thanksgiving" by pointing out that, "another kind of sacrifice there is, which does not reconcile us to God but is made of them that be reconciled by Christ to testify our duties unto God and to show ourselves thankful unto him, and therefore they be called sacrifices of laud, praise, and thanksgiving." It is perhaps characteristic of the Prayer Book that however they be interpreted the words "offer" and "sacrifice" do occur in the prayer which corresponds to the Roman Canon.

If we look at the eucharistic rite in greater detail, we observe that it corresponds in general to the order of the mediæval Mass.

The Prayer Book of 1549 gives the following sequence: Introit has become a whole psalm, as was the original custom. Then in accordance with the opening of the Sarum Mass, the Lord's Prayer is said, and the collect of cleansing follows. The service, apart from ceremonial, now corresponds to the order of the old Mass, Kyrie, Gloria, the collect for the day with an added collect for the King, Epistle, Gospel, the Nicene Creed. The Gradual between the Epistle and the Gospel is omitted and the sermon is after the Creed. Here the three exhortations found in the Order of Communion (1548) may be used. These exhortations are a mark of the Reformation period and are meant to supply oral instruction. The collection is now taken at the place of the old offertory. Now follows Sursum Corda, the Preface (of which there are five), and the Sanctus. Thereafter there is a long prayer which takes the place of the Canon. This prayer is composed of (*a*) the Intercession representing Te igitur and Memento of the Canon, a thanksgiving for the saints which takes the place of Communicantes, and a remembrance of the departed which corresponds to Memento etiam. (*b*) The Prayer of Consecration which contains an epiclesis in these words, "Hear us, we beseech Thee, and with Thy Holy Spirit and word vouchsafe to bless and sanctify these Thy gifts." This reveals the influence of the Eastern Liturgies. (*c*) The Prayer of Oblation in which are the words, "And here we offer and present unto Thee ourselves, our souls and bodies, to be a reasonable holy and lively sacrifice unto Thee," and which contains the petition for a true union with Christ. Finally there is this request, "Command these prayers and supplications by the ministry of Thy holy angels to be brought unto Thy Holy Tabernacle." [1] Now comes the Lord's Prayer without the embolismus, the Pax, an invitation compiled from the Epistles which is a new feature. "From this point," says Gasquet, "to the conclusion of the service, the Book of 1549 practically leaves the Missal entirely and adopts the Order of Communion of 1548." This Order issued by Cranmer goes back in part to mediæval sources and in part to the *Simplex et pia deliberatio,* a document published by Hermann of Cologne, and written

[1] Cf. Supplices Te. The idea of the worshipper being lifted into the presence of the Lord is a favourite Calvinistic thought.

by Melanchthon and Bucer. The sequence is this; invitation (Ye that do truly), confession, absolution, comfortable words, prayer of humble access. The Agnus Dei is sung during the communion, and the service concludes with a prayer of thanksgiving, and with the blessing (The Peace of God).

This sketch of the service of Holy Communion reveals a liturgy well balanced which does not ignore the thought of the Church's oblation, the ministry of the word, and the historic development of the eucharistic drama. Mediæval and reformed piety are linked together. As it stands, catholic interpretation may be given to its expressions or protestant meaning attached to its language. Gasquet has shown how the whole service is capable of a purely protestant interpretation and how in its type it lies close to the Lutheran form. Yet the developments that have taken place within the Anglican communion demonstrate how a truly catholic kind of thought and of piety can be nurtured upon and within the language of the Prayer Book. However, the Book of 1549 did not remain intact. In 1552 a new Prayer Book was issued which swings to the side of Protestantism and breaks the symmetry achieved by the 1549 Book. In the revised Book of 1552 little of the sequence of the Mass is left but the collect, Epistle, Gospel, Creed. The changes made are drastic. The altar becomes the table, the vestments of the Mass are forbidden, only communicants are now present at the celebration. The place of the Lord's Supper as the chief service of the Church is put in jeopardy by the regulation that the sermon is not a necessary accompaniment. This injunction at that time meant that the eucharistic service was no longer counted as the primary and the normal service of the Church. In the rite itself the main alterations are these: The introit is omitted. The Kyrie no longer occupies its true place as a cry for mercy. It is set within the ten commandments. This farcing of the Kyrie is probably due to Lutheran influence. The Gloria in excelsis is removed from its proper place and placed after the communion. This was a most unhappy change, for it not only defied the tradition of worship, it also introduced at the post-communion a note of adoration that belongs to the soul's preparation for the feast. The exhortations which had stood after the Creed in lieu of a homily are placed after the offertory sentences, where they interrupt the movement of the service. The preparation for communion which was found in the 1549 Book just before the act of communion is now set before the preface. The most disastrous alteration was the treatment of the canon, which is broken up in such a way that the movement from the Sanctus to the act of communion no longer appears as one continuous act of memorial. The prayer for the Church shorn of all reference to the saints and to the departed is made to follow the almsgiving. Most inappropriately the prayer "We do not presume" divides the Sanctus—itself altered—from the prayer of consecration and thereby obliterates the vital connection between these two expressions of worship. Communion immediately follows consecration. The later part of the canon with the oblation of ourselves now follows communion, and oddly enough is the alternative to a prayer of thanksgiving. This curious result is caused, I believe, by the unconscious confusion between the offering of ourselves in the two movements of worship. In mystical devotion the offering of self is in order to receive and to experience the sense of Divine Communion. The Service of Holy Communion belongs to this order and demands the oblation of self before the act of communion. This prayer in the 1549 Book is the true oblation of self in the mystical movement. But in the movement of prophetic piety the offering of self is made in order to be of service for the Kingdom. It is an offering in order to fulfil the Divine Will rather than an offering in order to experience the Divine Union. Fittingly this offering of the self belongs to the end of the service; but as we read this prayer we perceive that the purpose of this oblation is to experience this union in worship. Therefore the meaning of this prayer is largely destroyed through the place now assigned to it.

Other significant omissions are the invocation of the Holy Spirit in the prayer of consecration, the Pax Domini and the Agnus Dei. The Lord's Prayer is also misplaced, being said after communion instead of before. Some of these blemishes were rectified at a later date, but unhappily the Anglican rite still suffers from this misguided zeal which mutilated the proportion of the early Book. This revision of the Prayer Book was, as we saw, in the puritanic direction. Few changes were made in the issue of 1559, but those that were made had a conservative tendency. It was at a later date that a new interpretation was put upon the Prayer Book.

The devotional thinker whose mind coloured this High Church interpretation was Lancelot Andrewes. His thought was largely moulded by the Greek Fathers, and the Johannine attitude to the Incarnation overshadows his sacramental thought. To him the sacramental Presence is explained by the analogy of the Incarnation. Andrewes tells us that Christ gives us two things, "remembering" and "receiving," which are mentioned by St. Paul also, though he uses other words, "showing forth" and "communicating." The "remembering" and the "showing forth" refer to the consecration, and the "receiving" and the "communicating" to the partaking.[1] The sacrificial aspect of the Eucharist is recognised by Andrewes as well as the fellowship side. To him the words "altar" and "table" are both appropriate, as the one points to the sacrificial aspect of the Eucharist and the other to the fellowship aspect. This new insistence that the Eucharist is the memorial of Christ whereby the worshipper offers to God the perfect Sacrifice found expression in Laud's liturgical efforts. Sad it is to remember that the Book of Common Prayer of 1637, which in the interest of freedom was so bitterly opposed in Scotland, was a liturgy instinct with this richer and deeper apprehension of the Eucharist. This deeper reading of the Prayer Book did not appear to bear any immediate fruit, for the revision of 1662 only slightly altered the Book. Yet this mode of approach to the Sacrament has lived on as a characteristic Anglican trait.

Earlier I spoke of the Anglican rite as an attempted synthesis. We are now in a position to estimate this.

(1) The Idea of Sacrifice is not ignored in this rite, for while the early reformers repudiated the doctrine of Sacrifice in the Mass, they did not wholly let slip the conception. The sense that something is done is present in this form of worship. Worship is an offering of praise and prayer. The worshipper gives what is due to God and fulfils the duty of the creature. The atmosphere of

[1] Cf. Stone, *A History of the Doctrine of the Holy Eucharist*, p. 313.

this worship is the offering of devotion to God. In particular the Eucharist is regarded as sacrificial in three ways. There is, firstly, the commemorative sacrifice of Christ's death which is shown in the bread broken and the wine outpoured—this is offered by the priest alone; secondly, there is the sacrifice of praise and prayer in which priest and people join; and thirdly, there is the offering of the worshippers—the oblation of the individual life.

One feature of the sacrifice type of worship the Anglican rite shares with the Roman. In its origin the efficacy of the sacrifice involves the correct word and the right gesture or action. The instinct that everything must be properly ordered pervades the Anglican form, and the institutional element in religion appears as a sense of order in the Church's devotion. In the historic Prayer Book the attitude of the worshipper is devout rather than passionate, and his worship is the proper offering of his spirit rather than the soul's abasement before a miracle. In this I trace a subtle difference between Roman and Anglican worship. The former is more objective. Its words and ceremonies are not the choice of the human spirit selecting what is fitting in its approach to God, but are the inevitable and necessary response to the Divine Miracle in the Sacrifice. When the Anglican communion has laid supreme stress upon the element of Sacrifice in worship, she seeks as in the Anglo-Catholic movement to adopt the ways and methods of Rome. The reason of this is not far to seek. By her intense absorption in the Divine Sacrifice as present in worship Rome has won a power and an objectivity that do not belong to traditional Anglicanism. The passion of blood is not in the Anglican rite. The *via media* misses the stark and challenging mystery and therefore is robbed of emotional deeps and of piercing intensity. Thus while the Anglican rite is dignified, beautiful, and restrained, it is in Wordsworth's phrase about Goethe's poetry "not inevitable enough." To some tempers there is, despite its fair form, a certain chill in its spirit and a formalism in its speech.

(2) The Mystery Drama in worship enters into the Prayer Book in a less degree, but it is none the less present. The influence of the Eastern Liturgies affected somewhat the thought and the expression of Cranmer, and the record of Anglican interpretation

has shown a kinship with the East which broods upon the mystery of the Incarnation. The Prayer of Humble Access has Greek associations with its aspiration towards union with the Lord. There is shadowed rather than expressed a mystical background to the Prayer Book. The mystical element which is implicit in the Prayer Book has been made explicit by its interpretation. Gore's teaching that the Eucharist is one with the Incarnation is developed from this tendency. Yet while a real spiritual sympathy exists between Anglican worship and Eastern devotion there are two distinctions. These both spring from its position as a *via media*. The liturgies of the East represent through symbol and word the coming of the Divine Presence and the approach of the soul. The Anglican rite does not so delineate the spiritual drama in its worship. This is not only because the order of her eucharistic service is faulty and its framework mutilated ; it is also because the Anglican spirit will not admit of the unrestricted appeal of symbolism. This rite lacks the glowing colour, the richness, and the impressiveness of the East. The East delights to pour forth its ecstasy of praise, its intimate yearnings, its unrestrained petitions. The language of the Prayer Book is marked by dignity and sobriety and a still beauty. The exuberance of the East is wanting, and with it also there is lacking that passion of adoration which can so uplift the soul. Thus while Eastern thought in its richness and width casts its spell over the devout thought of this communion, it can find no means of liturgical expression for its warmth, its throbbing life, and its coloured beauty.

(3) The Oracle type of Worship comes into the Prayer Book through the movements of the Reformation in the midst of which it was framed. The Word is highly honoured in this rite. A place is given to the preaching of the Word, but still more marked is the position given to the Bible. This is the Oracle of God and is to be received by the worshipper as such. Therefore great care is taken to provide for the reading of Holy Scripture in Morning and Evening Prayer. The exhortations that are found in the Prayer Book are evidence that it was obedient to the reformers' desire that the Word of God should be understood and all that was done in worship apprehended. So also the reformers' interpretation of

the Mass as communion enters into the fibre of the Prayer Book, and the fellowship aspect of the Sacrament is shown by the fact that communion becomes the testimony of an existing fellowship rather than the discovery of that fellowship through the Sacrament. Yet when we compare this rite with the reformed modes of worship there is a marked divergence. The Anglican has all the qualities that belong to balance and proportion. However, there is wanting that narrow but mastering force which belonged to those who receive the Word of God. In her worship the Church of England escapes the defect of one-sidedness, but loses something of the driving power that comes to those whose worship consisted in its essence in hearing the Sovereign Will of God.

One notices also in the episcopal form the interplay of the two movements in worship. There is the ascending scale running through the Anglican eucharistic form as through the Eastern and Latin rites. This represents the mood in which the soul after purification reaches upwards in the resolve expressed in "Lift up your hearts. We lift them up unto the Lord" to union with God's Spirit. There is also the descending scale emphasised anew by the Reformation which hearkens to the Voice of God speaking in His Oracle and responds in awe, gratitude, and obedience of will. It is one of the richnesses of the Prayer Book that these two essential movements in worship are recognised and in part balanced. The two poles around which this rite circles—mediæval practice and reformed thought—were disastrous to the structure of the Mass, but they ensured the presence of these two moods in the Prayer Book. I do not mean that there was any conscious attempt to balance them, nor do I assert that the reconciliation is perfect, but all unwittingly the problem has been faced.

I would take one illustration of this interplay and I take it from what has been condemned by distinguished liturgists. My example is the double use of the Lord's Prayer in Morning Prayer. The historical origin of this fact is of course that two services are united. In the first use of the Lord's Prayer we see how the mediæval usage of repeating this prayer in silence as a preparation for worship has been made a definite part of public worship. In an audible voice this prayer is to be said, and this shows the

14

influence of reformed thought which struck out everything private or secret in the Church's service. But the prayer remains as the wings by which the soul is raised after purgation from sin to the high duty of glorifying God. This is in accord with the mystical development and is the ascending movement. In the second use of the Lord's Prayer we have the prayer of the worshippers who have heard the Word of God in Scripture, and in the Creed have declared the great acts of redemption God has wrought. This is the mood in which the children of God respond with gratitude to God's revelation and in which they seek to make God's Will be done on earth. This mood leads on to intercession and to surrender of our will to God's purposes. This accords with the descending movement in which the spirit of man receives and obeys. Since the revelation of God is for all men there belongs to this use of the prayer a more universal and less personal aspect. The prayer is said by all. In the same service we find the Lord's Prayer set in the first case within the mystical development from purgation through illumination to communion, and in the second case within the revelational development starting from the Act of God Who speaks to the response of gratitude and obedience in man. Since the relation of these two moods in the Anglican rite is largely unconscious and the fruit of circumstance, the perfect poise is not achieved. Soaring adoration and the mystical absorption of the soul in the Divine do not find a full expression here. For the loss of self in worship we must go elsewhere. On the other hand, the characteristic of the revelational type of worship is also lacking. The sense of self intensified and heightened before the Presence of the Supreme God Who apportions to this self its tasks and duty in His Kingdom does not burn in the Anglican Prayer Book with that flaming fervour with which it has burnt in evangelical and reformed circles.

Thus, though the Anglican form points the way, it does not itself provide the solution. This rite dulls the spiritual characteristic of the three types we have considered and does not reproduce their power and poignancy. The soaring height of the mystical movement and the profound and shattering depth of the revelational movement are lacking in the Prayer Book. In short this *via media* is a compromise leaving out valuable elements and not a true reconciliation. The final liturgy of reconciliation lies hid as yet in a future shrouded with mist.

There is one criticism to which the Prayer Book with its offspring rites is exposed. Morning Prayer and Evensong derived from mediæval sources which were largely monastic have become the characteristic services of the Anglican Church, while the one great public service of mediævalism—the Mass—is no longer the public service in which all worship. Perhaps the leading defect in the practice of this Church is that communion, which in the primitive Church was the specifically Christian form of worship, has become secondary to Morning Prayer. Happily Anglicans are alive to this unfortunate consequence which the use of the Prayer Book has entailed.

One permanent contribution has been made by the Prayer Book to the devotion of the universal Church. This is its distinctive beauty of expression. It was fortunate that when the prayers of the Roman Missal and Breviary were translated for use in public worship it was by a genius in liturgy like Cranmer, and at a time when the wells of English speech were pure and undefiled. A skilful selection and a wise adaptation of liturgical material, an exquisite diction and a sensitive devotional spirit characterised the first Book, and the later additions have in the main not fallen greatly from this high standard. Not only are the translations made in noble English but in not a few cases the original is excelled. But on this merit I need not spend further words. One or two examples will speak more conclusively. How could " ut inter omnes viæ et vitæ huius varietatis " be more happily rendered than by " that among all the changes and chances of this mortal life." Compare the Collect for the Sunday next before Easter : " Almighty and everlasting God, Who of Thy tender love towards mankind hast sent Thy Son, Our Saviour Jesus Christ, to take upon Him our flesh and to suffer death upon the cross that all mankind should follow the example of His great humility ; mercifully grant that we may both follow the example of His patience and also be made partakers of His resurrection," with a literal translation given in the Roman Missal, " Almighty and Eternal God, Who didst cause our Saviour to take upon Him our flesh and to suffer death upon the cross that all mankind might imitate the example of His humility; mercifully grant that treasuring the lessons of His patience we may deserve to have fellowship in His resurrection." "Whose service is perfect freedom" translates "cui servire regnare est." A phrase like "such good things as pass man's understanding" transcends "unseen good things" ("bona invisibilia").

Yet despite the excellency of the Prayer Book's style and language, there is perhaps a certain risk of monotony. There is less variety than in the Roman service, and there is the peril that in her devotions the Anglican Church may be stereotyped. Perchance the worship of the Church calls for greater variety in utterance and in mood than is given in this English book. The prayer books of episcopal Churches other than the national Church of England have followed with varieties in detail the path laid down by the Book of 1549.

One liturgy there is of modern times which contains all the virtues and escapes almost all the blemishes of the Prayer Book. I refer to the liturgy of the Catholic Apostolic Church. This book is largely based on the Prayer Book, but it has a width, freedom, and variety which the Anglican form lacks. This is caused very largely by two things: (1) A greater use is made of Oriental prayers with their poetic and mystical appeal. The framers of this liturgy had a far profounder knowledge of Eastern devotion than had Cranmer, and were not afraid of more emotional utterances. Consequently this book has an intimacy and a horizon not restrained by racial reticence nor limited by national outlook. (2) In this communion there is a much stronger emphasis on revelation in worship. This finds expression in the part which the "angels" take in the service, and corresponds to the prophetic ministry of the early Church. This expectancy of spirit moulds the liturgy and gives to it a fresh and living freedom. The atmosphere of waiting makes every act of worship the response of the soul to the Call of God. Of all liturgies of this type this is the most adequate.

CHAPTER X

THE QUAKER RECONCILIATION, OR WORSHIP THROUGH SILENCE

THE Lutheran and Calvinistic types of worship which carried within them the seed of individual liberty accepted the assumptions of the mediæval Church whose form of worship they sought to displace. The idea of the Church is part of their inheritance. It is from another centre that the real repudiation of the development in worship comes. The groups and sects like the Anabaptists created in the ferment of this great reformation movement are the fathers of individual liberty, of individual interpretation, and of the assertion of individual experience. Amid the rebirth of religious feeling and the recrudescence of the prophetic ministry there is no specifically fresh contribution to the art of worship. Yet amid the movements which the spiritual activity of post-reformation life has called into being there is one group whose contribution to worship must be noted. The Society of Friends, commonly called Quakers, did not only revive a practice which had fallen into abeyance ; they found a method of worship which is distinctively their own. From the vivid experience of George Fox Quakerism dates its origin, and the response which his experience found proved that he was the spokesman and interpreter of a latent need. This method of worshipping through silence is based on the idea of the Spirit's presence in the minds and consciences of the worshippers.

Theologically the Quaker worship implies the doctrine of the inner light. " The light that lighteth every man that cometh into the world " becomes manifest through the quiet of silence. Here we have a worship that is based on the immanence of God. The mediæval adage, " The age of the Father has passed, the age of the Son is passing, the age of the Spirit comes," might be applied to the sphere of worship. The sacrifice idea and the oracle type alike start with the transcendent being of the Father, and by different methods reach the experience of communion; the mystery drama circles round the process whereby the Divine becomes human and is orientated around the activity of the Second Person of the Trinity; the Quaker form of worship starts from the presence of the living Spirit. It may seem incongruous to place this form of worship under the title of "the Oracle type." Barth has remarked on the distinction between the word of revelation and the silence of adoration. There is, however, a real kinship between Quaker silence and the thought of the revealed Word. The reformed service and the Quaker service are complementary. They both rest ultimately on the idea of revelation, but in the reformed rite revelation is an objective act of God in history which is declared anew and experienced afresh in the reformed service, whereas in Quaker worship revelation is an inner experience which lights up external events. Speech and silence, declaration and waiting, are two methods of reaching the revealed word. Silence in the Quaker use of it implies speech, for it is the silence of waiting preparatory to revelation.

The first characteristic of Quaker worship is the silence of waiting, which is the condition as well as the anticipation of revelation. A second characteristic is the silence of fellowship. Also we find a silence that is akin to the sacramental silence of the Eucharist and of the Mass. Indeed, the celebration of Low Mass has a psychological effect not unlike that of a Quaker gathering. A stillness reigns as the murmur of the priest's voice melts in the silence, broken only by the sound of the bell or the server's low response. A silence also accompanies the celebration of Holy Communion in the rites of other Churches. This is the silence of union which is a definite trait in the worship of the Friends. The silence of preparation finds its fulfilment in that silence of divine union. To this there is linked the silence of corporate fellowship. These three characteristics of Quaker silence must be observed if we are to appreciate the depth and spontaneity of this simple worship.

In addition to the elements involved in the Quaker silence we must note also the movement in their form of worship. In the first place the worshipper escapes in the time of waiting from the limitations and distractions of mortal existence by an inner withdrawal and a concentration upon the life within. This is the cleansing of the soul and the purifying of the spiritual faculties. This cleansing and this entrance into silence are the preparation for the soul to receive. By the action of purification the soul becomes the vehicle and the medium of the Spirit's expression. There comes then to this waiting spirit the luminous sense of God. There is the immediate and direct experience of God's Presence. The unity of human fellowship is now achieved, because through the disappearance of the temporal separation it is now unveiled in the experience of the Divine. Thus the Quaker silence is not empty but contains this inner movement of the Spirit.

This method of silence is not the communion of the "Alone with the Alone," for it is a silence of fellowship; nor is it a silence of discipline, for there is no constraint in this worship. "I do not so much commend and speak of silence," says the seventeenth-century Quaker George Barclay, "as if we had a law in it to shut out praying and preaching or tied ourselves thereunto. Not at all, for our worship consisteth not in words, so neither in silence as silence but in holy dependence of the mind upon God from which dependence silence necessarily follows in the first place until words can be brought forth which are God's Spirit." There is no constraint. The silence may be preserved for the whole meeting or it may be broken at any time by the word that is revealed. We see in this worship the reconciliation of the idea of the God Who reveals and the idea of the God with Whom there is mystical communion. For fellowship of soul with soul in worship is not something to be made by man's effort; it is something to be discovered, and this discovery is made by the revelation of the Spirit. George Fox speaks of the "hidden unity in the Eternal Being," and the discovery of this "hidden unity" is at once the fellowship of soul with soul, and the mystical union with God. Quaker worship is a puritanism that does not fetter personal liberty and a mysticism that through its fellowship is free from eccentricity of spirit. The mystical spirit wears the garb of puritanism, and the puritan soul finds its mystical expression. On this high altitude of spiritual fellowship there is the union of the protestant or puritan sense of revelation and of the mystical aspiration towards adoration.

In this worship we see the blending of the two movements in worship—the descending movement from Divine Revelation to human receptivity, and the ascending movement from human aspiration to Divine Union. This worship is both "prophetic" and "mystical." But not only does the Quaker service achieve this harmony of these two movements, it also unites on a wholly spiritual plane the values expressed by the three types of worship we have considered. The oracle type of worship is present, for it is the Word that the Spirit breathes and which is declared. The mystery drama is figured by the movement of the soul in this time of silence and by the consummation of the soul's progress in Divine Union. The sacrifice type is represented by the offering of the soul stripped of earthly thoughts and divested of all associations of time to the guidance and leading of God's Spirit. This reconciliation is on the high level that conserves the freedom of the individual. No external authority such as the tradition of the Church or the Bible is needed. Experience is its own authority and the revelation carries in it its authentic evidence. The sacraments are treated as external rites which do not belong to the realm of the Spirit. Quaker worship thus turns its back on the tradition and on the sacraments of the Church, not as evil things but as irrelevant. All life is sacramental and every meal a remembrance and a communion. No form of words nor any symbol is required in this worship, for it is a worship at once pure and free. It is purified from the subtle associations of symbolism that may chain the soul to things of this earth, and free from all constraint of obedience to any external standard. Surrender of self, freedom, and fellowship are distinctive marks in the Quaker meeting.

The Universal Church owes much to the Society of Friends, for this company of quiet souls have contributed two precious things to the service of the Church. The first is their method of worship by means of silence. The Quakers in their use of silence did two things. They formulated their own unique application of silence in worship as ministering to freedom of spirit, as revealing fellowship of souls, as waiting upon God, and as expressing the highest adoration. They also brought again to remembrance the practice of silence in worship. Silence had been a trait in worship from the first, but it had been used largely without conscious intent and not sufficiently used. The significance of silence is now appreciated as an element in and an instrument of worship, and for this we owe a debt of gratitude to the Society of Friends since their persistent use of this method brought it at length before the mind and imagination of the Church.

The second gift is the spirit of their worship which in its purity and simplicity was a revolt from an exaggerated dependence upon ceremonial and a protest against the tyranny of the idea of a revelation that was enforced as an external law. The part this restrained and disciplined mysticism has played in the lives of Quakers is obvious, and from the practice of their worship they have gained that atmosphere of quiet and reverent certainty and that spirit of active beneficence which their history as a sect so clearly evinces. High praise has their worship won in many quarters. " It is the most spiritual form of divine service," says Dr. Otto, and the late Dean of St. Paul's has commended their way of life and worship as essentially Christian. Before I pass any criticism, it is well to note the wonderful power of their worship in impressing and moulding the spirit of men. This worship has been undisturbed by the storms that critical science and historical investigation have caused. Tied to no theory of Biblical inspiration, linked to no belief in the efficacy of anything external to the inner spirit either of ordained priesthood or of sacramental observance, it has ridden safely the waves of destructive criticism and historical research, for it is anchored only to an experience which is unassailable. The spiritual power of this worship has been manifest in what it has created: a temper pacific, an outlook that refused the controversies of one-sided bitterness, a toleration wise, noble, and patient, an ethos true to the " kindred points of heaven and home," and touched to the finer issues of a holy reverence and an enlightened kindness. It has preserved precious notes of that spirit found in the Gospel narrative.

There are certain limitations in this most spiritual form of worship.

(1) Quakerism is a form of worship pre-eminently suited to a particular type of nature. In short, it is not a universal form of worship. Dr. Thomas Hodgkin, whose testimony is worth much, said of silent worship: " It is not equally adapted to all mental conditions; it needs to be introduced with discretion, it will not compensate for the neglect of the gift of teaching, it is as a rule more fitted for those who have made some advance in the Christian life than for those who are still on the threshold." [1] Is not this tantamount to an admission that this method of silent worship belongs to a special class? This worship is the worship of a company of select souls who have found a method, conducive of good to them, and opening to them the entrance into a deep fellowship. But it is the characteristic of the Church's public worship that it is for all sorts and conditions of men and not for a coterie of noble spirits. Religion meets man at every level of spiritual and intellectual development. There is something universal in its appeal, and there must therefore be something universal in its expression. The spirit of religion must be capable of an utterance that is for all and of a range that embraces all. The worship of the Church ought to be that universal expression.

(2) The repudiation of the sacramental is the aristocratic gesture of the emancipated spirit. Of course it is not strictly correct to say that Quakerism denies all symbolism in worship. It does set aside the appeal to the eye through ceremony and image, and the appeal to the ear by the ordered rite of a spoken and musical service. Yet none the less symbolism is present. The very silence and the atmosphere of quiet are not merely instruments that prepare the soul for worship; they are also symbols of that revelation. The atmosphere is not only a preparation for, it is also a representation of God's Spirit and Presence. The Silence of the Eternal from which the Word comes is mirrored by the silence of the worshippers. There is not here an escape from symbolism; there is rather the negative use of the symbol. If then this most rarefied service has to admit the symbolism that represents God's Infinity, why should only the negative symbol be used and not also the positive symbol that speaks of God

[1] Hodgkin, *Fellowship of Silence*, p. 87.

incarnate in life Who uses things of sense to speak to the Spirit of man ? This type of worship appeals only to one side of man's nature. It appeals to man as a disembodied spirit. Yet if the Incarnation be the central thought of Christianity, the Christian religion must touch the whole nature of man, and therefore the art of worship which is the expression of the spirit of religion must make an appeal to all sides of human nature. I therefore see in Quakerism the exhibition of a most valuable form of worship, but it is a method that is not for all nor does it include the whole of man's nature.

The attempt to escape from symbolism bore certain fruits. The sacramental side which is the incarnational side of worship is set aside and the hallowed symbolism is rejected. Yet testimony is borne to the invincible need of human nature for the symbolic element. This is seen in the early dress and speech of Quakerism, but it comes as a symbolism that separates and not as the symbolism of the historic sacrament that unites.

(3) This type of worship rests on the assumption that the experience of all souls is alike in this, that to all will be given the immediate sense of the Spirit's Voice within. Perhaps this belief springs from the high faith that God opens His Hand freely to all His children, and from the noble motive that no one would choose to possess spiritual gifts that were not appointed for all. This assumption, however, seems to deny the diversity of the spiritual world. There are times, so history insists, when there is no open vision. " It seems a safe generalisation to say," writes Professor E. W. Watson, " that days of great action have not been days of deep religious feeling. In few periods has religion in England been less conspicuously effective than in those of the Black Prince, the elder Pitt, and the Duke of Wellington." [1] If this be so of periods, it is true also of individuals. Worship is not the concern only of those whose religion is tingling with consciousness of itself. Religion is, I believe, implicit in all, and public worship has a relation to those whose religion is implicit in their doings rather than explicit in their conscious experience. If worship be, as I contend, an essential human attitude, and the complement of external activity,

[1] *The Christian Faith*, p. 252.

it must be adapted to the extro-vert as well as to the intro-vert. Many are the souls whom the Lord God has made and loved, whose centre of inner activity does not lie within the explicit self-consciousness of an immediate experience. One cannot imagine Shakespeare without religion, but one cannot conceive that Shakespeare could be Shakespeare and possess in worship the immediacy and directness that belong to St. Theresa or John Bunyan. This seems to imply that for natures whose inner core lies in the sphere of activity or creative art, public worship must provide a mediate and not an immediate experience of God. For this purpose Quaker worship is ill adapted, for either there is this direct and luminous experience, or the worship is empty and dull. This criticism amounts only to this, that Quaker worship is not a substitute for the catholic worship of the Church.

(4) Finally, the Quaker method of silence is connected with a particular realisation of God's Being. As I have said, the doctrine of the inner light is linked to the idea of the Spirit's activity. The value of this can scarcely be over-stated ; yet one note seems to be unduly faint in this worship. There is the sense of adoration and of union, but the sheer transcendence of God Who stands over against man's purity and creatureliness is not prominent. This is caused by the fact that the revelation of God in the facts of history and the Word spoken beyond our experience is not the foundation of this worship as it is of the reformed type, but the basis is the revelation of God here and now in present experience.

I would therefore judge that this high type of worship seeks the reconciliation between the sacrifice idea, the mystical movement, and the revealed word at a level that is too ideal and abstract. It is a reconciliation that only succeeds by narrowing its range to those who are specially equipped with a particular temperament. While therefore this worship does conserve the values of the sacrificial offering, of the mystery movement and of the revelation to the inner spirit, it is too ideal and abstract in form to be the universal form of God's widely differing children. Such criticisms are not directed against the practice of the Society of Friends, but against the idea which doubtless they would be the first to deny

—that this worship could take the place of catholic worship. While there are elements, I believe, in the catholic tradition that have been omitted by this silent rite, the Friends have made a most valuable contribution to catholic liturgy not only by their own unique application of silence, but also in this, that they are largely responsible for the revival of this note in worship.

Let us turn to the use of silence in worship which Quakerism made prominent, and in the first place let us observe how the practice of silence is rooted in the past. It belonged to Hebrew devotion and to the Hellenic mystery. Ignatius[1] suggests that Christ the Word comes forth from silence which therefore is the symbol of the Godhead beyond and outside of human experience and is the representation of the Unknown in God. It is therefore natural that silence should be the medium in the adoration of the Ineffable. This silence before the Infinitude of the Unknown belongs to the worship of all the higher religions. Silence is rooted in the three historic types of worship. The sacrificial idea which is the institutional aspect of worship has the silence of the offering and the silence of communion. The Mystery type has the silence of adoration as its apex. The Oracle type has the silence of reception: "Be still and know." These different aspects are found in the liturgies of the various types.

In the first place we find the liturgical silence of the Eucharist. There is silence before the Mystery of God's presence. The inaudible prayers of the Eastern Church and the secret prayers of the Mass are testimony to this silent worship which leaves the soul alone before its God. A different quality can be distinguished in these silent devotions. There is, for example, in the Roman Mass, the silence of waiting heralded by the sound of the bell which is preparatory to the Divine Coming. There is the silence of adoration at the elevation. There is the silence of union at the partaking of Holy Communion. The first and the last—the silence of expectancy and the silence of union—belong to the celebration in Lutheran and reformed Churches. These three qualities in the sacramental devotion are capable of very varied expression, but the three moods—expectancy, adoration, communion—find in

[1] *Ad Magnesios*, viii.

silence their most adequate form of expression. The silence of preparation and of discipline is also found in the Hours. The very effective method of saying together in silence the Lord's Prayer and the Apostles' Creed is an illustration. Directed silence is found in the Eastern rite, and from the ancient service of Good Friday we see that in the Roman rite there used to be bidding prayers in which the worshipper prayed silently and freely along with his fellow-worshippers. The practice of the Orthodox Church and the Roman Obedience provide in the liturgies definite occasions for silent devotion. It is apparent that the silence of adoration and the silence of union have a kinship with the mystical or aspiring mood, while the silence of expectancy and of waiting belongs to the receiving mood or the temper that awaits revelation.

It seems to me somewhat remarkable that so little use save at Holy Communion was made of silent worship by the branch of the Church that bears upon its forehead the stamp of the Reformation. Even the Anglican Prayer Book, which sought the way of compromise, contains only one rubric enjoining silent prayer when in the Book of 1661 it is enjoined in the ordering of priests, "after this the congregation shall be desired silently in their prayers to make humble supplications to God for all these things, for the which prayers there shall be silence kept for a space." In Presbyterianism there is one token of the value set upon silence in worship in the Order and Doctrine of the General Fast (1565). After reading the twenty-seventh and the twenty-eighth chapters of Deuteronomy "the minister shall invite every man to descend secretly into himself, to examine his own conscience whereunto he findeth himself guilty before God. The minister himself with the people shall prostrate themselves and remain in private meditation a reasonable space, as quarter of an hour or more. Thereafter shall the minister exhort the people to confess with him their sins and offences." [1] In the former there is the silent prayer of supplication and intercession, and in the latter the silence of self-examination as the prelude to confession. The practice of silence before the reception of the Word seems congruous to the reformed type, and it seems curious that a form of worship which

[1] *Knox's Works*, vol. vi. p. 419.

drew so largely from the prophetic spirit of the Old Testament should not have made use in public devotion of that silence which is the way of approach to Divine Revelation. "Let all the earth be silent before the Lord." But the insatiable love of exhortation seems to have left little room for this means of worship.

The modern spirit is alive to the worth of silent worship. Every communion seeks to utilise this method. In the worship of New Thought Groups and Christian Science meetings silence is used as a means of the soul's approach to the Divine. The mystical spirit which created "the prayer of quiet" and "the prayer of interior silence" has touched with its wings the devotions of public worship. If corporate worship is to preserve the traits of its three historic types, it seems certain that silence must be used, and the different qualities and aims of silent worship given a place in the public service.

I would therefore sum up the uses of silence as a means of devotion.

(1) There is the sacramental silence which embraces the three moods of expectancy, adoration, and union. These three moods need to be treated as distinct in silent worship or else the mind falls into a void and is lost in vagueness. Whether or not Holy Communion be celebrated, these moods belong to the Divine Service, and there is no more effective means of preparing the soul to receive spiritual truth than silence, no such adequate method of uttering adoration as through silence, no such fitting medium for representing the strange and wondrous experience whereby the soul in time has union with the Eternal as silence, no more potent way by which the sense of human fellowship can be poignantly felt than silence.

(2) There is the true Quaker silence in which the element of guidance is present. This is a real human need in worship, but it would seem to be impossible to retain the Quaker freedom of utterance in a service obedient to the order of the historic tradition and to the command of declaring the Word made flesh. One element of the Quaker silence can be preserved in a silence before the Word is read or is preached, or the Word is made present in the blessed sacrament. Also the surrender of self in the oblation

of the soul can be expressed by a silent pause in prayer for this offering. The Quaker practice of uttering the individual guidance given to the particular soul, however valuable it may be in a group meeting, finds in the Divine Service its counterpart and fulfilment in that proclamation of God's Grace and Goodness to all men which is the Gospel and which is declared in the Scripture lessons, the sermon, and the praise.

(3) There is directed silence. Here the silence is kept, but a subject is given for meditation and all are united in this endeavour. By this means the thought and desire of each worshipper are enriched by the presence of other worshippers. In confession the steps of self-examination are given and silent pauses made before the voice of united and corporate prayer beseeches forgiveness, and the word of absolution is spoken. Or in thanksgiving the subjects for gratitude are rehearsed with silent pauses, and through this silence of prayer or meditation a corporate worship is offered. Or there are silent intercessions in which are named the objects of prayer, and then silent devotion follows, concluded with a collect. The historic bidding prayers are illustrations of this method.

(4) There is free silence in which there is no common object of prayer or of meditation announced, but in which silent prayer is made by each. This has a value in creating the mood of fellowship and is of worth following upon the reading of Scripture, the preaching of the Word, or after Holy Communion. This too is a silence in which the individual soul within corporate worship can receive direct guidance.

(5) There are brief intervals of silence wherein the movement of the service from adoration and confession to thanksgiving and intercession is realised and made vivid to the worshipper. How we may apply the method of silence allows of much discussion, but the necessity of silence in the art of worship is plainly urgent. Let us not be deluded by making the false contrast between the Word of Revelation and the silence of Mystery. The Word comes in silence as in speech. "He that truly possesseth the word of Jesus," says Ignatius,[1] "is able to hearken unto His silence." If the service of the Word is to be enriched with the depth of mystical

[1] *Eph.* 15.

communion, the way of silent worship is the surest. If the sense of corporate unity is to be felt, then the stillness and the quiet of souls united in unspoken prayers are most powerful. Therefore I find in this method practised in the meetings of the Friends a real gain to the liturgy of the Catholic Church.

CHAPTER XI

EUCHARISTIC WORSHIP

THE Eucharist is the central rite in the Christian Church, and despite the variety of forms in which it is celebrated it is the common heritage and common worship of the Universal Church. This act of worship which ought to be the uniting link between the several branches of the Church has, owing to diverse interpretations, become a cause of separation and a source of schism. Yet it is the primitive and characteristic act of Christian devotion. The history of the Eucharist proves the truth of Troeltsch's statement—" the essence of all religion is not the dogma or idea, but the cultus and communion." The three cultural forms of human religion, the Sacrifice, the Mystery, and the Oracle, have been employed to express the fact which lies within the circle of sacramental ideas.

To the detached observer of religions the Eucharist is but a social meal using symbols with rich religious associations ; to the faithful the Blessed Sacrament is the special and appointed way of the highest worship. The fact that it is a social ceremony means that it is the worship of the Church, and thereby it is rescued from the one-sidedness of individual devotion. The fact that it is symbolic means that it unites men in the region of the inexpressible where inarticulate desires and feelings find their home. But this is not all. We must add the words, " the special and appointed way of the highest worship," in order to describe the rite. The word " special " implies two things. The first is that the Presence of the Lord is the basal fact of this worship, and this Presence alone gives meaning to the different acts. How that Presence is to be conceived is a question on which men differ, but that the Presence is experienced is the testimony of the faithful, however they may explain this fact or to whatever communion they belong. The second is that this worship is not only symbolic but sacramental.

A symbol is a kind of language in action, it signifies and represents; but a Sacrament is an instrument as well as a didactic or dramatic symbol. The essential difference between the significance of the symbol and the effectiveness of the instrument is pointed out by Canon Quick.[1] "Instrumentality is the relation of a thing to that which is effected by it; significance the relation of a thing to that which is suggested by it." The Sacrament is at once a symbol and an instrument. It is something through which God speaks and something through which God works. We may not neglect either aspect of the Sacrament. The Sacrament may not be treated purely as an acted parable or an act of piercing and poignant meaning. Our Lord spoke many a parable, and we recognise the beauty and the adequacy of the simile between the natural order and the spiritual realm. These word-pictures taken from the normal course of natural and human life illustrate the workings of a spiritual principle in the life of man. This is not all that we find in the Sacrament. Definite associations are made and promises spoken by Jesus, and without reckoning on these we have no Sacrament.

This brings us to the next point—the sacrament is appointed. It is not symbolism selected by man's spirit as suitable; it is given to man and chosen for man. Behind the sacramental observance lies the promise of the Lord that He will be with His own and will give His strength and His faith to them. This is the general promise. There is also the specific institution and command, "This do ye." I have discussed the institution earlier. Whether or not the words "this do" came from the lips of Jesus on that fateful night, the Sacrament is appointed whether the institution be by explicit statement or implied in the very act itself. The authority for its appointment rests in Jesus Himself, and it matters little whether in word He bade His disciples repeat this act or whether He so acted that He made them know that this was a perpetual rite.

We may therefore now say the Sacrament means a Divine Presence, implies a sacramental principle whereby the physical may be the symbol of and the instrument for the spiritual, depends

[1] *Christian Sacrament*, p. 12.

on a Divine institution grounded in history. These preliminary considerations had to be mentioned ere we glanced at the types of worship that have been used in eucharistic devotion.

I. First there is the idea of sacrifice and of offering. As the name Eucharist implies, there was from the first the offering of thanksgiving in this worship. From the *Didaché* onwards this note of offering in the Sacrament is sounded in this service. The purely spiritual sacrifice is there, and prayer becomes the sacrifice of thanksgiving. In addition to this there was the offering of material things, bread that strengtheneth man, and wine that maketh glad the heart of man. Material offerings were made in the early Church, and these offerings were used for two purposes. These offerings originally supplied what was necessary for the common meal and the sense of brotherhood was thereby assisted. It is well to recall to-day this note in the sacramental service. The gifts which minister to the needs of the poor are part of the sacramental offering. The assertion of Christian fellowship made in this offering on God's altar is an essential aspect of Holy Communion. But a part of the material offering was set aside for a special purpose. To a Jew the offering of bread and wine, of what is essential to man's physical life, would be a thanksgiving to God for His goodness in creation and for His gracious care towards man; but to the Christian conscience these material things, bread and wine, are inevitably linked to Christ through the use He made of them. "This is my body" is the phrase that is regulative of our eucharistic thought.

What can we offer to God? There is nothing man has to offer but himself—his will and his life. Let us then be quite clear on this point; we have something to offer in the Eucharist, and none even of God's shining spirits can make our oblation. And equally definite is the other aspect, that we have nothing else to offer.

Now the idea of sacrifice does not necessarily involve the giving of something other than ourselves. Popular speech does not wholly err in counting self-sacrifice as the crowning gift. "When the Jewish," writes Gore,[1] "passed into the Christian Church, it became a first principle that there was no more need for pro-

[1] *The Body of Christ*, p. 164.

pitiating God." There remained no longer any sacrifice as in pre-Christian times. There is nothing to add to Christ's sacrifice. But the disappearance of propitiation does not mean the end of sacrifice. There remains, as we have seen, the sacrifice of thanksgiving, and before the Vision of the Divine Sacrifice in Christ the offering of ourselves to God. "For we offer to God," says Irenæus, "not as if He needed anything but giving thanks to His Supremacy and sanctifying the creature." Here is the Church's priestly duty and her perpetual task of glad praise. But what is the highest thanksgiving she can render? Is this not linked to the life and death and victory of Jesus? And how can the Church offer herself to God's service and the worshipper offer his life and being to the Eternal Will? Is it not through the mind of Jesus and in the spirit of Christ? The Church offers to God the Creator and Redeemer the highest and noblest in human life—the life and doings of Jesus of Nazareth. What human life can be is the offering of man's imperfect little life, and what human life can be is seen in the historical Jesus and is experienced in the indwelling Christ of Whom St. Paul speaks. In the Sacrament these two aspects of Christ's being are one. The prayer the Church offers is that in Christ may be seen, through the power of God's Spirit, the revelation of the Heart and Nature of God. Man offers himself—his highest and best—which through God's revelation and redemptive Grace is made Christ. The offering is the priestly act of the Church, and God in His acceptance of man's poor wayward striving has made man the body of Christ, the instrument and organ of His Will. "If then," says the great St. Augustine,[1] "you are the body of Christ and His members, then that which is on the altar is the mystery of yourselves; receive the mystery of yourselves. You hear what you are, and you answer Amen and confirm the truth by your answer; for you know the words the body of Christ, and you answer Amen." We cannot dissociate the sacrifice of Christ as represented in the Eucharist from the communion of the Church with Christ in which she offers herself. There is in this wondrous rite the identification of ourselves as belonging to the Church of God with Christ the Eternal Offering of all that humanity

[1] Sermon lvii., quoted Brilliot h, *op. cit.* p. 33.

is or can be. The Church offers nothing of herself; not her merit but her trust and faith in Christ's sacrifice, which is at once an historical fact and an inner experience. In her oblation she offers to God the Eternal Christ Who is alike without as the object of devotion and within as a creative power.

But what relation has this to the bread and wine, the visible elements? They are the vehicle of this offering. On the human side they are the gifts of God in Nature—corn and the vine made by human labour into bread and wine. By the act of consecration all that these elements represent is consecrated—all that man has received from the bounty and the beauty of the earth and all that man has achieved by his labour and by his love. This consecration of these gifts declares the great sweeping truth that all the gifts of Nature and all the activity of man are to become the body of Christ, that is the means and vehicle of His Spirit. Further, these elements are set apart and thereby dissociated from all other purposes but this, that the soul may ascend through them to God. The only basis for that ascent lies in Christ the author and finisher of faith, the Word of the Father. Only by His authority and through His promise can these elements be more than material things. Now bread and wine from the human point of view have their purpose, value, and meaning in ministering to bodily need, but by the oblation these elements, bread and wine, are given a Godward direction. Then through the prayer of consecration, that is by the Power of the Word and the Action of the Spirit, their purpose, value, and meaning are changed. They no longer exist for their human purpose, but for a Divine end. Their purpose is now no longer the satisfaction of bodily need but the feeding of the soul. Their meaning is now altered and their value transformed. This is not magic, for the potency of the Church's prayer rests upon the Lord's promise, upon that Word that never passeth away, and upon the gift of the Spirit. These material things are made by God vehicles of His Presence, and although still existing in the world of sense and of time they are transformed to another purpose. They become the instrument of God—the Body of Christ. Now the essence or being of anything rests in its meaning or value or purpose; things exist for us mortals in virtue of the purpose they fulfil or the meaning they have in our universe of knowing. If then the purpose and the meaning of these elements be altered, they are no longer merely bread and wine. Their form of existence is changed because their purpose is altered. The word "substance" belongs to an antiquated philosophy, and what corresponds in the language of to-day to the substance which could not be seen, touched, or felt, is the meaning or essence.

This change in meaning and direction depends upon the two truths which the Incarnation declares. The first is the general principle, "the Word became flesh." God uses the material offering, which is made in obedience to trust in Christ, as the means whereby He gives a rich experience of Christ. The spiritual is incarnate in the material. In this sense the Sacrament is the extension of the Incarnation, for the Spirit of God comes near to man through the things of sense which are His vehicle and instrument. But the second truth carries us further. Creation is the work of God and the medium of creation is the Logos. "Without Him was not anything made that was made." The principle of Christ's life and death is the principle on which this universe is based. This may seem a hidden truth; but it is the assertion of the Christian Faith that the Creator and the Redeemer are one, and this great affirmation is made in the Blessed Sacrament. The spirit of Christ is the spirit that lies within all that exists. We see not this; by faith alone can we grasp it. Only in Christ has this Spirit found a self-conscious expression; in all else this creative Spirit lies concealed. Now the reality of any thing depends on its Godward direction. Behind these material things, bread and wine, lie the creative forces of God in the world of Nature and in the energy of human nature. By God's Power and Being they exist, and for their being they depend upon that God Who created and is creating all things through the Spirit that in man's little life appeared as Jesus Christ. Thus in the Eucharist we identify the Jesus of history Who lives again in our experience as the Risen Lord with the Creative Word of God, the Logos, expressed in the external world. God uses the reality of the bread and wine which is the creative activity of the Logos as the means for giving to our conscious and subconscious mind the fact of Christ. In the Sacrament the offering of man's thankfulness and his oblation of himself becomes the reception of Christ. This involves that in our service there must be an act of offering and a consecration by the Word of Christ and through the Spirit's Presence.

That is the line of thought by which Christ's Presence is embodied in the bread and wine, and is the approach to the Eucharist through the idea of the Incarnation. As far back as Justin Martyr the thought of Christ's Incarnation and the thought of His Passion and Death were linked to the celebration. The second line of thought is the definite relation of the Eucharist to Christ's Death. The connection between the Eucharist and Christ's sacrificial death is made by Jesus. The Last Supper is the interpretation of Calvary and it is an interpretation expressed in symbol. At the Last Supper there were the visible bread and wine—tokens of that body of Christ which was present in the flesh. In the Eucharist there are the visible bread and wine—also tokens of the body of Christ which is present, for the Church is the body of Christ. The fact of Calvary is expressed anew in the rite which gives the interpretation of that death. This fact of Calvary is that Christ died there and that a brutal and cruel judicial murder took place. Jesus united His death to the Last Supper and thereby gave the meaning of His death. The Eucharist is the statement expressed in symbol of that death, and is its interpretation. A sacrifice implies a priest, an oblation, a victim. The Church in her priestly function is the priest in obedience to the Word of Christ and acting wholly by the authority and through the power of Christ, the bread and wine are the oblation of man's thankfulness, and the victim is Christ, still by the evil and sins of men crucified. "The Eucharist," says Dr. Spens,[1] "is that part of the sacrifice of Calvary which by our Lord's appointment expressly invests His death with its significance, and thus renders it such an acknowledgment. By it He ensured that Christian worship should be centred in the confession of God's Infinite Holiness and the awfulness of sin, and that His worshippers of all times and places should only on the basis of that wholly evangelical confession stand secure in the fellowship of Grace." The Sacrifice of Calvary is an act to

[1] *Essays Catholic and Critical*, p. 436.

which nothing can be added, but our recognition of it is required. The Eucharist is this recognition. Nor is it simply the recognition of a past event in history, but the acknowledgment of that Eternal Process which in that act is made manifest. The Sacrifice of Christ is then not a past remembrance but a present fact. Christ is not sacrificed anew in the Sacrament, but in the Sacrament the sacrifice of Christ is acknowledged, and through the Word and the Spirit's Power this sacrifice is recognised as a present experience to the believer. The consecrated bread and wine—the offering made—are therefore by God's Grace the Body of Christ, for by the might of His Spirit God makes present and actual Christ's Body.

It was the staunchest of Protestants, Professor James Denney,[1] who in a letter wrote these words: "It (referring to the idea of mystical union) is just like the language of passion in which the sacramental bread and wine are called the body and blood of Christ. No other language would satisfy Christian feeling. Yet they are not the body and blood of Christ." But in this high realm is not the language which satisfies Christian feeling more likely to be truth than language shaped by our scientific theory and our metaphysical outlook? Surely Christian feeling must express itself in the language that satisfies, and is not subject in its expression to any standard beyond itself. We ought to adapt our theory of the world to the authentic expression of eucharistic Worship.

The element of sacrifice belongs to the eucharistic feast, and this aspect has been specially made prominent in the Roman Mass. While we see the insufficiency of the Roman statement which is tied to an effete metaphysic, we must recognise that under the ægis of the Aristotelian philosophy, with its distinction between the substance impenetrable to sense and the accidents which were perceived by sense, the doctrine of transformation is a method of conserving a rich and full sacramental experience.

II. The Mystery Drama makes its contribution to the celebration of the Eucharist, and this contribution has three aspects. The first concerns the symbolic elements in the celebration, the second is the dramatic movement of the celebration, and the third the atmosphere of the Christian Mystery.

[1] *Letters*, p. 38.

(1) First there is the symbolism that represents and presents the Mysterious Presence. Now symbolism is of three kinds in this service. (*a*) There is symbolism whose use is didactic. The image says to the unlettered what words say to the more educated. This function of symbolism must not be wholly ignored, for the Eucharist is for all sorts and conditions of men. Action and ceremonial and picture and form are needed to make the service comprehensive in its appeal. (*b*) Secondly, symbolism has a dramatic use. It expresses more powerfully than words, and it accomplishes something that words cannot do. Such an action as the elevation, or the fraction, or the distribution of the consecrated elements says what no word can utter. The actions in the Eucharist have this dramatic and poetic value and they must not be robbed of their power. (*c*) Thirdly, symbolism has another use. In this an act is symbolic of a will or a purpose to give or confer something and to achieve some end. This is essentially the sacramental symbolism. The Christian Mystery is the expression of the purpose of a Mind. It is the picture of God's Approach.

(2) This brings us to our second aspect. In the Christian Mystery there is a dramatic movement, and this movement must find expression in our service of celebration. There is an order and a sequence which correspond to the movement of the spirit. The essentially dramatic nature of this movement must be made evident. The story of God's search for man is recounted. The drama of Divine Revelation is unfolded. The Eucharist is not narrowed to one point in time, however significant that point, nor to one fact, though that fact be the dominating fact in spiritual history. Not simply the Death of Christ is its message, but the remembrance of His Whole Work: "remembering therefore His passion and death, and resurrection and ascension into the Heavens, and His future second coming, when He shall judge the living and the dead."[1] But further the Eucharist gives the Death and Victory of Christ its place in the whole Revelation of God, and recounts the Drama of God's Coming to man, and of man's redemption.

(3) The third aspect is the atmosphere of the Christian Mystery. There is the sense of a Presence mediated through the rite. In an

[1] *Apostolic Constitution*, Book viii.

earlier chapter I pointed out how we find in the New Testament three attitudes to the Sense of the Presence, and the Mystery has developed all three.

(*a*) The first attitude is enshrined in the sacramental teaching of St. John—to eat the flesh of the Son of Man, and to drink His blood, and is derived ultimately from the saying of Jesus, " This is my Body." The Presence of the Lord is in the Sacrament—in the whole action of the Sacrament, or more specifically in the elements. To eat His flesh means mystical union with Christ's glorified Body. Yet we must not distinguish between the glorified Body and the garment of His mortality as though we would divorce the Christ of Glory from the Jesus of history. We are united with Christ as the human expression of the Eternal in this act of Holy Communion. The Church has carefully kept this sense of the Presence in her celebration. Indeed, sometimes men have thought of the Lord as imprisoned and localised in the consecrated element. To correct the extravagances of popular devotion (for example, the little Host which the priest will give one under the form of bread is," You, my Adorable Jesus "),[1] and the survival of paganism in man's heart, one needs to recall the profound words of Newman—" If place is excluded from the idea of the sacramental presence, then division and distance from heaven are excluded also. . . . Moreover, if the idea of distance is excluded, therefore is the idea of motion. Our Lord then neither descends from heaven upon our altar nor moves when carried in procession. The visible species change their position, but He does not move. He is in the Holy Eucharist after the manner of a spirit." The mystery of Christ's Presence in the Eucharist must remain a mystery. There is evidence in the Eastern liturgies as in the Gallican and even in the Roman, that the Presence is not simply in the elements. The mystery is the Presence of Christ, the Sacrifice by Whom the souls of men are fed. This sense of the Presence involves its own ceremonial and ritual. The Church fulfils here her priestly function in obedience to Christ's command, and gives to her members the gift of God. Such an attitude to the Presence means that the emphasis of the service falls on the gift of God to us. Christ is the Bread of Life.

[1] Quoted Bourget, *Real Presence.*

(*b*) The second attitude to the Presence is that in which Christ is the Host. "Thou only art the Priest," as the hymn says. This sense was alive in the early Church. The Lord Jesus is present and He presides and dispenses His own Sacrament. Signs of this survive in liturgical usage. The Armenian liturgy[1] speaks of seeing "the King Christ sitting and surrounded with the heavenly host." In the Mozarabic rite of to-day we find the prayer "adesto, adesto Jesu pontifex in medio nostri secut fecisti in medio discipulorum tuorum."[2] The same tendency is shown in the Mass for Epiphany in the same rite where the whole Mass is addressed to the Lord Jesus Christ. The Syrian Jacobite offers the sacrifice to Christ. "We therefore, O Lord Jesus, offering this bloodless sacrifice, implore Thy love towards men." This sense of the Presence also has its own appropriate ritual and ceremonial. It implies that the mortal celebrant is on the same side of the Holy Table as the people. This attitude is valuable and original for it belongs to the Synoptic tradition. To express it we must suggest the fact that the Lord is the Host and He only is the celebrant. This perhaps might be done by the Cross, the symbol of Christ, set over the Holy Table, or by the representation of the Lord behind the Table, or perchance best of all by leaving vacant and unoccupied the chair behind the Holy Table. Here the emphasis falls on the Lord Who broke bread with His own.

(*c*) The third attitude to Christ's Presence is in the fellowship of the worshippers who are made one bread. St. Paul speaks of the Church as the Body of the Lord, and in the communion of Christians one with another there is the mysterious presence of Christ. "Where two or three are gathered together there am I in the midst of them." This sense of the presence through fellowship must also find its expression. Our presbyterian celebration seeks to proclaim this attitude. Holy Communion is the act of the whole congregation —not a few celebrating together, but a celebration that asks all members to be present. This profound sense of Christ's Presence needs to be preserved, although in our Scots worship there is need for emphasis of the other two attitudes. If we had in Scotland far

[1] Brightman, *op. cit.* p. 431.

[2] Probably not original; cf. King, *op. cit.* p. 301.

more frequent celebrations it would be possible to express these different aspects of Christ's mysterious Presence. They are, of course, all ultimately one, for there is One Lord. But so rich in meaning and so vast in content is the Eucharistic Mystery that it seems scarcely possible to bring out all its fulness in one service. An attempt to do so sometimes leads to a celebration that lacks the personal appeal and poignancy of any one of the three attitudes.

III. The final type of Religious Cultus is the Oracle. This assuredly is needed to give us the whole meaning of the Sacrament. The Word is proclaimed. The Sacrament is the preaching of the Word not by human lips but by action and by the written Word of God. The Sacrament is regarded by this type of worship from the standpoint of Revelation. God speaks to men in the sacred rite. The Eucharist is primarily declaratory of God's Grace, and its effectiveness rests in the Word of God set forth in the rite being grasped by the soul. The historical is here prominent, for it is in history that God has spoken. "The night in which He was betrayed" roots this experience of God's Grace in this actual life, and in the world of mortal happenings. The Eucharist is redemptive, is effective in bringing Christ to men because it is the revelation of God's Love and Holiness. "The supper declareth," says the Confession of the Genevan Congregation approved of by the Church of Scotland,[1] "that God as a moste provident Father doth not only feed our bodies but also spirituallie nourish our souls with graces and benefits of Jesus Christ; which the Scripture calleth eating of His flesh and drinking of His blood." "The bodie of our Lord Jesus," says Calvin's catechism, at one time authoritative in Scotland, "for so much as it was once offered up for us in sacrifice to bring us unto God's favour is nowe given unto us to assure us that we are partakers of the reconciliation." In one of his sermons Robert Bruce speaks of bread and wine as being signs not only because they represent but also because they have the body and blood of Christ joined with them. "The sacrament is appointed," says the old Scots preacher, "that we may get a better grip of Christ nor we get in the simple word." Let no one imagine that the Word

[1] Macleod, *The Ministry and Sacraments of the Church of Scotland*, quoted, p. 284.

of God idea in worship does not leave room for the Real Presence. Dr. Wotherspoon[1] has pointed out that while the Church of Scotland denies transubstantiation it asserts in its own terms the Real Presence.

Let me sum up the ideas or notes that are voiced in the Eucharist as we have considered it. (1) All three types give the note of thanksgiving in the Eucharist as the name suggests. This song of praise has a wider range in Eastern worship, and we in Scotland have followed too narrowly the Western emphasis on Christ's death. The Eucharist belongs to the Hope of Christmas, to the triumphant joy of Easter, the abiding inspiration of Pentecost, as well as to the Thursday of Holy Week. (2) The second note is the offering. The supreme worship of the Church is offered in the Eucharist, for there she shows forth Christ's death and makes the memorial of His sacrifice. This act of memorial is made an act of sacrifice wherein the Church gives herself in union with Christ and presents a living sacrifice unto God as her oblation. (3) The third note is that of the Presence mediated especially by the Mystery Mood. (4) The fourth note is that of communion and fellowship; and (5) finally there is the historical note which commemorates Christ's Work. These notes then must be struck in the celebration of the Eucharist. Let us see how this is done.

The Divine Service of the Sacrament in its classical and historic form has three divisions: (1) The Ministry of the Word; (2) The Oblation and the Consecration; (3) The Communion and the Reception. This form is but an elaboration of the Scriptural warrant and is derived from the account of the Last Supper. Reduced to its simplest expression the Eucharistic Service has the following elements. There is the setting of the celebration and its authority. This is represented by the account of the Institution which proclaims the Word and establishes the rite in the historical revelation. After the circumstances of the Eucharistic Feast are declared there follow six actions. (1) The Lord Jesus took bread, and after the same manner also He took the cup. This taking of the elements is the freeing of them from all other purposes and associations and the separation of this bread and this cup unto

[1] *Religious Values and the Sacraments*, p. 282.

God. This is the offering and oblation. (2) When He had given thanks.[1] This is the thanksgiving or Eucharistic Prayer. (3) He took bread and blessed,[2] " the cup of blessing which we bless." [3] This blessing of the elements is the act of consecration. (4) He brake. This is the fraction. The breaking of the bread and the lifting of the cup are linked to the great declaration, " This is my body " and " this cup is the New Testament in my blood." Here is the action that we do in remembrance of Him. This is the act of Memorial. (5) He gave to them. This is the action of giving to one and to all. Christ's act is symbolised in the giving and distributing of the holy elements. (6) Take eat [4] . . . drink ye all of it.[5] This is the reception and the communion.

From this we see clearly that there are two main actions in the Eucharist—the Consecration and the Communion. The Roman Church has attached such importance to the act of consecration and of memorial that the action of communion has not received sufficient prominence ; but the Reformed Churches have paid such scant regard to the act of consecration that the action of communion is alone conspicuous. Yet both Consecration and Communion are essential to the Eucharist. The former is the Godward aspect and the latter is the manward aspect of the Eucharist. They may not be separated. These acts must enter into all our celebrations, be it the communion of the whole congregation or the communion of individuals, for the meeting-place of God and the soul is beneath the shadow of what these acts figure.

I. I now turn to consider in greater detail the Divine Service of the Eucharist which follows the sequence and elaborates the actions of the New Testament Institution, and adumbrates the eucharistic ideas already mentioned. The first division is the Ministry of the Word, in which the teaching function of the Church is given its place and which is not opposed to her priestly function but part of it. To make the crisp distinction between instruction and worship is to forget the tradition which the reformers of the sixteenth century revived—the place of the Word in worship. This emphasis on the Word has been somewhat blurred, but it

[1] 1 Cor. xi. 24. [2] St. Mark xiv. 22. [3] 1 Cor. x. 16.
[4] St. Matt. xxvi. 26. [5] St. Matt. xxvi. 27.

was no invention of the sixteenth century, for it belongs to the catholic tradition. It is very significant that the service starts with the revealed Word. In the Eastern Liturgy the Little Entrance shows the importance attached to the Word of Revelation, for this entrance is associated with the fellowship we have in worship with the invisible hosts of God. " O Master, O Lord our God, Who hast established in the heavens orders and armies of angels and archangels for the ministry of Thy Glory, grant that with our Entrance there may be an entrance of holy angels ministering unto us and glorifying with us Thy goodness." So too the same high place is given to the Word in the Mozarabic Rite, which began originally with the lessons, " as it may be assumed did all other liturgies." [1] Prayer of confession and song of praise were added as the approach to the Word of Revelation. What I wish to urge is this. The beginning of the service is not simply for instruction and for edification ; it rests on the fact of Revelation. From above and beyond the life of man's curtained day comes the Eternal Voice, and out of the impenetrable void there is the revelation of God's redemption. God with man and God in man will be the notes of the consecration and the communion, but we begin with God high and lifted up. We wait in the first place upon His Word. Therefore it is that the Scripture lessons must be surrounded by an atmosphere of reverence. The Gospel which Origen describes as the " crown of Holy Scripture " was read last, and before it a lesson from the other portions of the New Testament (the Epistle). The first lesson is from the Old Testament which sets the Eucharist in the stream of human history and serves to remind us of the wider revelation of God which eucharistic worship fulfils. If we are to do justice to the Catholic thought of God's message, we must have a service which, through the preparation of confession, seeks to provide the attitude of soul in which to hear, and through thanksgiving establishes the mood of faith resting upon God the Eternal Who will speak to us. The lessons ought to be short and to bear upon the nature and character of God Who reveals Himself and Whose word is Christ.

The first note in the service, to my mind, ought to be the sense

[1] W. C. Bishop, *Mozarabic Rite*, p. 21.

of God's Transcendence before Whom man is a creature of time. From such a God it is that we receive the revelation of His Being and Purpose. How this is done may vary. Through praise, or call to worship, or in prayer it may be effected. But if we are to be faithful to the idea of revelation, this must be the starting-point. Then follows the element of edification—the instruction as to our duties and as to the Nature of God. The rhythm of the service begins on the descending scale. The sense of the Transcendent God is followed by the confession of sin and the purification of desire, by the petition for our needs and the thanksgiving for God's Grace and Goodness, for the hearing of His Word in Scripture, and by the recognition of our vocation in this life expressed through the Church's intercession for the Kingdom, the world and for all human needs. There ought, I feel, to be something in this part of the service that expresses in worship the unity of the Church. The use of Kyrie eleison is found in this part of the service from the sixth century in the West and from the second century in the East. This phrase, probably adopted from heathen worship, has been baptized into the tradition of the Church's devotion. By its use the unity of the Church in confession would be expressed. So also the Gloria in excelsis has found a place in the Western service. Its use would make for unity in praise and utter the catholic note in adoration.

II. We now come to the second main division of the service, the Oblation and the Consecration. In the ancient liturgies there were in the Liturgy of the Faithful two parts, the pro-anaphora and the anaphora. In the former there are differences in sequence, but the service is around the offering of the elements. Here in the East is the Great Entrance, and in some of our own Scots churches at this point the elements are carried into the church. This practice has been adopted in some African missionary churches in which the spontaneous growth of a liturgy is reminiscent of Eastern worship. In Scotland the psalm used while the elements were brought in was the 24th, "Ye gates, lift up your heads." In this offertory act the Scots practice follows the East where the bread and wine are made ready before the beginning of the Divine Service, while in the Roman Mass the bread and wine are prepared during the service as must have been the way of the primitive Church.

At the beginning of the pro-anaphora we find the Benediction. This originally may have been the dismissal of the catechumens and penitents, but the invocation of the Triune God as this service begins, wherein through the Spirit we receive Christ the Gift of the Father, has become the fitting note of this new starting-point. There is some considerable divergence in the various liturgies. General intercessory prayers are sometimes offered here. To do this would be in accord with the reformed usage of having intercession after the sermon. Then the offertory act is made. The setting apart of the elements for their sacred purpose is the prelude to the act of offering. This ancient custom of offering to God these gifts is also an act in which the worshippers offer their minds to God's truth, their wills to His Will, and their lives to His purposes. Here too we must remember was the primitive offering of bread and wine, of which part only was used in the service, as the rest was for the benefit of the poor. What to-day takes the place of the original offering in this respect is the offering of money or the collection. This makes the collection a true offering to God's Church and turns it into an emblem of the offering of our wills to God. The other place for the offering of money that might be deemed suitable is after communion at the close of the service when the offering is united with the prayer of thanksgiving.

To this section also belongs silence for prayer. The soul ought to have time to recollect itself. In addition to silence for private devotion there are, as we have seen, the offertory prayers. In some liturgies, for example the Syrian Rite, the prayer of the veil is voiced when in the East the curtain that concealed the Holy Table is withdrawn, or when in the West the elements are uncovered. In the Lyons Rite while he uncovers the chalice the celebrant says, "What shall I render to the Lord for all He hath given to me? I will take the cup of salvation and call upon the name of the Lord," and then extending his hand over the bread he says, "Jesus said to His disciples, I am the living bread which comes down from heaven. If any man eat of this bread, he will live for ever." [1]

[1] King, *op. cit.* p. 124.

In the Roman Mass the first offertory prayer, "Suscipe Sancte Pater," which is a secret prayer, gives the horizon of the service, "for mine own countless sins, offences and negligences, and for all here present, and for all Christians living or dead." Perhaps it would be a good thing if we had prayers printed for private devotion that would give such a range of devotional aspiration.

Here also occurs the Pax, or Kiss of Peace, as the expression of the fellowship of those who are about to partake of this blessed sacrament. It is regrettable that we have no outward emblem which would express the unity of the congregation. The early practice being native to the East was long since abandoned. Our modern salutation—handshaking, seems somewhat trivial and commonplace. Some gesture or action is required, and certainly a response from the congregation acknowledging their fellowship is needful. It is noteworthy the emphasis laid in all Christian rites on this idea of peace and goodwill, and it is a tradition which we need to preserve. Our worship in the Eucharist ought to say this definitely by word if in no other way. Finely, the Mozarabic rite[1] phrases this. "O God, the abounding Source of all good things and the unfailing concord of the saints, grant such peace on earth that we as peacemakers may alway follow and fulfil Thy commandments. ℟. Amen. For Thou art our true peace and unbroken charity, and with the Father and the Holy Spirit livest and reignest One God for ever and ever. ℟. Amen." This practice seeks to obey the word of Jesus, "first be reconciled to thy brother and then come and offer thy gift."

Here, either before or after the Peace, in many rites is placed the Creed. The declaration of faith is linked to the fellowship of the worshippers. They are one in spirit and in doctrine. But the fact that the Creed has an indeterminate place in the liturgy arises from the fact that it is a late importation into Western Worship. It was introduced first in Spain by the order of the Synod of Toledo (589), and from Spain its use spread to Gaul. It only appears to have been added to the Roman Mass in the time of Benedict VIII.[2] It cannot therefore be regarded as of the essence of the service. "Its liturgical use," says Dr. Fortescue, "is an

[1] Oratio ad pacem.

[2] 1012–1024.

afterthought," and this distinguished Roman adds, "no creed contains the whole faith from any point of view," "the old use of creeds is not at the holy Eucharist." This seems a sound conclusion to draw from history, and it is well to assert that the recital of a creed is no intrinsic part of eucharistic worship. On the other hand, what makes for unity has a place at this point, and a creed as the epitome of the faith of earlier generations may help to give the sense that we are knit together by a common faith, belong to a great tradition and walk in the footsteps of those who have, in their day and generation, witnessed unto the Grace and Love of God made known in Christ. The creed in use for the eucharistic service is the Nicene. John Knox's liturgy, however, uses the Apostles' Creed in accordance with the reformed custom. The point of importance to note is that the mood of the offertory is that of peace and reconciliation.

(2) We now come to the second section of the division, Offertory and Consecration. This is the anaphora or the illatio of the Spanish rite, the contestatio (the testimony of thanksgiving) and the immolatio (offering or sacrifice) of the Gallican Rite, and the original beginning of the Roman canon. This is the consecration. The call to the soul to ascend is sounded in "lift up your hearts," and "it is verily meet, right, and our bounden duty" is the beginning of the prayer which gives thanks for God's Glory, for creation and for His providence, and culminates in the Ter Sanctus, "Holy, holy, holy, Lord God of Sabaoth, heaven and earth are full of Thy Glory." The Benedictus, "Blessed is he that cometh in the name of the Lord," which was the cry of the people on Palm Sunday, is added in the Roman Mass to the adoring praise of Isaiah. This is not the original place of the Benedictus, which in the *Apostolic Constitutions* [1] comes later in the service as the cry of the people at the elevation. Some [2] have suggested that this is originally the cry of acclamation with which the people hailed the emperor, but the presence of the phrase in the *Apostolic Constitutions*—an Antiochene Rite—is rather against this view. Yet even if this were the original occasion of the cry, I cannot agree with those who would therefore omit it. For it has been assuredly baptized into the

[1] Brightman, *op. cit.* p. 18. [2] Atchley, *Ordo Romanus primus*, p. 91–95.

Western Liturgy. The prayer continues after the hymn of Isaiah to give thanks for the Incarnation and the Redemption ; and after this brief commemoration of redemption the words of the institution are given. This method of introducing the words of institution in the eucharistic prayer by means of a relative clause (" who in the night He was betrayed," " who in the night He gave Himself," [1] " who the day before He suffered " [2]) is common to all the rites. The actual words of the institution vary curiously. The mind of man has been unable to leave the formula in the simple and mysterious words of the Master, and there is the tendency to add and amplify. The words of the institution are a feature in all the later [3] liturgies and are the common [3] element in all celebrations. This is one of the points where our service is anchored in history. The bare words of the New Testament are therefore to be jealously guarded from interpolation. However suitable to the mood of the Church such phrases as in the Syrian Jacobite Rite, " in the same night in which He was betrayed to death for the life and salvation of the world," or the unhistorical statement of our Scots paraphrase, " that brings my wondrous love to view," may be, the historical words of the New Testament must be preserved in all their purity from man's interpolation and interpretation in this prayer. The words of institution may be read as the warrant, but it seems to me that this ancient custom of inserting them into the prayer ought to be retained, as Dr. Wotherspoon [4] does. After the words of institution there follows the anamnesis or prayer of memorial. This brief prayer recalling Christ's most blessed sacrifice presents before the Eternal Father this memorial of Him in accordance with His appointment.

The next element common to the liturgies [5] is the invocation or epiclesis of the Holy Spirit. As a rule, God the Father is invoked to send down the Holy Spirit upon the offering and upon the worshippers, so that the offering may be the body and blood of the Lord. The Coptic Rite, however, invokes Christ, " We beseech

[1] St. Chrysostom. [2] Roman Mass.

[3] Omitted in Adai and Mari, the East Syrian Nestorian Rite. Wetter bases his argument on this for the original Eucharist having no relation to the Passion.

[4] *The Divine Service.*

[5] There is evidence that the Roman Mass once possessed an invocation.

Thee, O Christ our God, we Thy sinful and unworthy servants, and worship Thee by the pleasure of Thy Goodness that Thine Holy Spirit may come upon us and upon these gifts here present, and may purify them unto us." In the ancient liturgy of Serapion the petition is that the Word may descend, "O God of Truth, let Thy Holy Word come upon this bread that the bread may become the Body of the Word, and upon the cup that the cup may become Blood of the Truth." Traces of invocation of the Word are found in Spain, "Mitte Verbum tuum e celis Domine,"[1] and in the Ambrosian Missal on Maundy Thursday there is a logos epiclesis. Perhaps also in the Roman prayer "per quem hæc omnia" we can see vestiges of a logos epiclesis. "The Logos epiclesis," says King,[2] was apparently earlier in date, but it was displaced through the development of the Holy Spirit as the source of grace." For us what is of interest is that the consecration is looked at from two different aspects. The Logos epiclesis links the consecration more closely with the Incarnation, and the Spirit epiclesis has more reference to the Day of Pentecost. Perhaps the mystery of the Eucharist calls for both standpoints. The elements are so changed in significance and value through the creative Word that they become to the worshipper the Body of Christ, and the hearts of the worshippers are so inspired by the Holy Spirit that the elements have the significance and worth of the Lord's Body. We need to approach both objectively and subjectively the mystery of the Eucharist.

To the epiclesis succeeds the Great Intercession. This is a short prayer before the bread and wine now consecrated, wherein the great desires of the Church are held aloft in the presence of God. The mood of this is the inevitable fruit of beseeching God's immediate presence. The work of God's Kingdom, the need of mankind and the fellowship of the departed, are borne into the mind of the worshipper by the sense of God's nearness. This intercession is repetitive for it summarises the petitions that have been made earlier. Its significance rests in this, that the prayer insists that God cannot be experienced apart from His purposes. It denies the truth of an individualistic communion of the soul with God.

[1] King, *op. cit.* p. 365. [2] *Op. cit.* p. 431.

I would note the importance of the remembrance of the departed. It is part of eucharistic worship to feel the unity of all the faithful, be they in this life or in the life to come. A noteworthy feature in all liturgies is the sense that our worship is part of the worship of the triumphant spirit. The Saints in glory and the humbler souls in the hereafter are present, for they are where Christ is and Christ is here. It was the universal custom of the ancient Church to offer prayers for the dead. They are specially marked in the Celtic Church, and the memento of the dead is an integral part of the canon in the Gallican and Irish Mass books. The place of the prayer for the dead has varied. Up to the fourth century, says Mr. Edmund Bishop,[1] the memento of the dead was contained in the long prayer for all sorts and conditions of men which was said at the beginning of the Mass of the Faithful. At a later date this memento was transferred to the eucharistic prayer, of which it became the closing section. The novelty was also introduced (perhaps in the Church of Jerusalem) of the public recital in the Great Intercession of the names of certain dead persons. This new devotion spread among the Greek-speaking peoples, and the practice of reciting the names of particular persons was adopted in the Western Churches of Gaul and Spain and North Italy. Finally, owing to Franco-Gallic and Celtic influences, the custom was adopted by Rome. In the Stowe Missal the nomina are found within the canon though perhaps as in the Mozarabic their original place was with the offertory. The custom therefore of some Scots kirks of reading at the Holy Table the names of those who have died since the last Communion is true to this Celtic tradition.

The question that interests is not so much the original place of this prayer for and remembrance of the departed in the eucharistic worship as its significance. There are two types of prayer—prayer for the departed and prayer for the help of the saints. The reformers of the sixteenth century abolished prayer for the dead which had been the practice of the universal Church. This they did as a protest against the shocking abuse which reduced masses for the dead to a means of extracting money. In the reaction from a commercialised view the idea of purgatory was thrown away,

[1] *Op. cit.* pp. 100–102, 113–115.

and with it went these prayers. But men cannot live in a reaction, and we cannot always worship in the spirit of protest. The question really is, are we or are we not to exclude all thought of our departed from eucharistic worship? It is a psychological impossibility to remember before God those we love in the Unseen and not to wish them well and to desire for them all good. What is prayer but desire directed to God? We do not know what they need, but we believe that like us in our humbler spheres they ever need the light and peace of God. It is said that the Blessed need not prayer, and that the departed are in the hands of God, and hence our prayers are bootless. This argument would cut the nerve of all intercessory prayer. Who are we to dare to assert limits to God's Grace and Power, and to profess to know the Eternal God's way with His children who are hid in "death's dateless night"? It is because we are ignorant, knowing nothing of the Beyond save that God is there, that we must lift up our hearts to our Father's Love in prayer when we remember our departed. We no longer dare to hold the rigid and audacious distinctions the reformers made. Is it for us to deny the purification of the life beyond? A humbler attitude amid this great and mysterious universe befits the littleness of man. How can we profess to know whether prayer for the living or the departed is of avail? God only knows, and leaving all things in His hand it is surely becoming that the Church remembers and prays for, in her eucharistic worship which transcends space and time, the saints and heroes of the faith and all departed souls, as she prays for the leaders of men in this our earthly conflict and for all who strive beneath the shadows of mortality. What glorious tasks God bids the Blessed do we may not know, but the prayer of poor struggling humanity, the petition of the Church militant, may through God's Mercy and Power be of avail.

The second question relates to the petition for the help of saints. Only to God can worship be offered. There is not for this practice any ancient evidence save perhaps a reference in Origen. Yet the supplication of the saints, Ora pro nobis, became prevalent both within and without the liturgy. Is this quite extraneous to the worship of God? And is it wholly out of place in eucharistic worship? Having mentioned the saints with whom we seek to be in communion the Ambrosian Rite proceeds: "by whose merits and prayers do Thou grant that in all things we may be defended by the help of Thy protection through the same Christ, our Lord." The actual phraseology is open to criticism, but what of the underlying idea? Are we going to take seriously the idea of communion between the seen and the Unseen? We ask the prayers of those who live with us the life of time, may we not ask the help of those who with undimmed eyes behold God's Glory and Love? Do we not desire that the words of the great prophets of old, of St. Paul and the evangelists and of the mighty-souled, help and succour us, do we not desire that our spiritual heritage built through God's Grace by brave and faithful lives and by the shining nobility of God's Greathearts be defended and protected by their influence? If we do so, may we not say so before the Face of God? We are not solitary gipsies wandering through this life of time; but we are in God members of a fellowship unbroken by death and by the passage of time undestroyed. This practice may have led and may lead to grave error and veil the Face of God, but in its essence is it not the assertion that men are not waifs nor mere individuals but dependent upon one another whether in this life or the life to come? The Glory of the Redeemer breaks the limits of our little minds, and we call to our aid the help of those who have triumphed to declare that Glory and to worship the stupendous mystery of God's Love. In the Eucharist neither life nor death can separate from the Love of God which is in Jesus Christ. Here therefore the interdependence of all souls —the fellowship of all saints—must be declared.

III. The eucharistic prayer contains the Lord's Prayer, which is the beginning of communion. The words Jesus taught His disciples we take upon our lips at this high point of Christian worship. This prayer finds a place in all the later liturgies, but it is not mentioned in the earliest documents. The so-called liturgy of St. Clement contained in the eighth book of the *Apostolic Constitutions* omits it, as do the Ethiopic Church orders and the Testament of our Lord which, however, has as a private communion prayer a kind of paraphrase (showing that the evil habit of the reformers of meddling with the Lord's words has a precedent). Nor does Serapion contain it. "Brightman sees traces of it both in Serapion and in the Ethiopic Church orders, but this is far from obvious."[1] We cannot therefore say that this dominical prayer can be proved to have a primitive connection with the Eucharist. The omission may be explained in some cases on the hypothesis that reference to its inclusion was thought unnecessary; but it did become a necessary portion of the rite. Perchance the phrase "give us this day our daily bread" suggested the fitness of its use at Holy Communion. The prayer is introduced by a petition to be allowed to pray the prayer of Christ. "Sanctify, O Lord, our souls and our bodies that with a pure mind and with soul enlightened and with face unashamed we may make bold to call upon Thee, O God, Heavenly Father, Almighty and Holy, and to pray and to say 'Our Father.'"[2] The prayer ends with an embolismus. "Deliver us, we beseech Thee, O Lord, from all evil past, present, and to come" is the beginning of the invariable Roman embolismus. The Gallican embolismus seems to vary with every Mass. "Delivered from evil and strengthened always in good, may we be made to serve the Lord our God. Bring to an end, O Lord, the tale of our sins," says the Mozarabic rite. The spiritual mood of the embolismus is quite plain. Man is conscious of his own weakness and of the perils and snares of life. The great words of Christ sound in his ears: "Lead us not into temptation, but deliver us from evil"; and the soul knowing that Christ is the Only Deliverer from evil, dwells upon the thought. In the eucharistic prayer this seems to be a true reflex of the Christian mood, and the embolismus appears a more fitting ending than the doxology which is added to the words of the Lord in our Bibles. In the East the prayer is said by the people, and this, which seems the original custom, is certainly fitting.

In some rites we find here the Agnus Dei. The appropriateness of this as a preparation for communion has been questioned, but I cannot but feel that at this point in the service it is fitting for Christian feeling to express its prayer to Christ. The cry of the Baptist when he saw Christ becomes an adequate prayer of the Church at the breaking of the bread.

[1] Maclean, *Ancient Church Orders*, p. 42. [2] Syrian Jacobite.

"He took bread and brake it." The practice of the breaking of the bread is an essential gesture in this service. We are following the example of the Lord, and this action is the symbol of what Christ did for us. The importance attached to this feature is excessive alike in the Eastern and Roman rites, but that is no reason why we ought not to give the action its due place. Our presbyterian forefathers were not regardless of ceremonial in this respect. "He taketh the bread." Some presbyters touched the elements before blessing, others lifted the bread, and to certain it was a matter of such import as to justify secession. Others again held in their hand the bread during the blessing, not wholly unlike the action of the Dominican priest, who holds in his hand two particles from the fraction until his communion. This meticulous observance may be misspent, but on the other hand it heightens the sense of communion when we consciously recognise that we are obeying a great order, following a universal tradition and doing what our fellow-Christians do.

The elements used in communion are bread and wine. Bread has always been the element, but the tradition as to wine is not so certain. Christendom has used many varieties of bread—leavened and unleavened, the wafer in the Roman Mass and the bread that is so elaborately divided in the East. Scotland has shown the same diversity. Usually wheaten bread was used, but we find also oaten, and in Galloway as in Ireland an unsweetened shortbread. Wine seems to have been generally red wine, as at the pascal feast. The wine was mixed with water as was the Jewish habit. This has prevailed as a custom in the churches most sensitive to the catholic tradition. It is unfortunate that this catholic practice was not more widely used in Scotland,[1] as it might have solved the vexed question of what ought to be used. Unfortunately controversy has entered the modern Church as to whether wine be used or some substitute made to appear like wine. To this there has been added division as to the common or individual cup. It was unfortunate that the Church in this land took no thought and neither considered the mingling of water in wine, nor the fitting cup or chalice. The

[1] Dowden, *Scottish Communion Service*, p. 43. "This custom of mixing water with wine was almost universal in the North."

sad situation has now been reached that it is unlikely that there will be agreement. Since Christians cannot unite on this and insist on departing from the original institution, only one course seems open to the Church of the future if she would maintain the unity of her practice in this feast of fellowship. This is to follow the method of the Roman obedience and to communicate in one kind only. For if a Church cannot agree, then it surely is better to refrain from division and humbly to acknowledge that by our dissension we have made it impossible to distribute the cup.

The giving was part of the ordinance, therefore the bread and the wine must be given and distributed. The bread and the cup are passed from hand to hand. This keeps at once the sense of fellowship and the sense that through our fellows comes to us the Presence of Christ, God's gift to us. The modern practice of communion in which there is no distribution is as unscriptural as it is uncatholic, and it sins in its prosaic love of a suburban comfort against the symbol of our dependence upon our fellows.

What follows the partaking is very brief, and is thanksgiving. Knox uses Psalm ciii. as the act of thanksgiving. The note sounded is our humble and glad gratitude with the petition that the feast may be consummated by a faithful witness. Then the dismissal and benediction.

The movement of the service may be summarised thus: the reverence before the transcendent God, the confession of our sins and frailty, thanksgiving, the hearing of the Word and its application to us, the recognition of our place and duties in the world, our aspiration for union in will and desire with God's Will in the prayer of intercession, our sense of unity through the peace Christ brings and through the faith He gives, our common offering and our prayer to go to His presence, the ascent of the soul towards union with God in Christ through the thankful remembrance of God's great works and of God's mercy in Christ Who lived and died for us, the aspiration that God's Presence in Christ may be ours in the consecration, the sense of the Divine approach and the experience of union in the communion, the dismissal with thanksgiving to life and its duties. The contents are: the gathering Psalm, prayer for Holy Spirit, confession and absolution, praise, Old Testament lesson, praise, New Testament lesson, Epistle and Gospel, Nicene Creed or Te Deum, general intercession, praise, Sermon, praise, the invitation, the peace, the offertory prayer, Salutation or benediction, eucharistic prayer containing Sursum corda, commemoration of creation and providence and redemption, words of institution, anamnesis, invocation, great intercession, Lord's Prayer, embolismus, communion, thanksgiving, benediction.

Two observations I would make about the eucharistic service. (1) The first is the need of silence. The soul needs to be left alone. Moments of silence are needed at the beginning to realise the God of revelation, in the confession of sins, silent prayer that is summed up in a collect of thanksgiving, the silence of waiting when the presbyter is at the Holy Table to hear the invitation of God, the silence of offering when at the offertory prayer we offer ourselves, the silence of adoration in the eucharistic prayer after the great intercession, silence after the embolismus to recall our special need of deliverance, the silence of communion. Such are suggestions, but however we arrange it there is a great need for the ministry of silence in this high worship in order that the depth and mystery of the Eucharist be experienced.

(2) The second remark is that there is a great need for the congregation taking a fuller part in the service. The eucharistic prayer and its varied divisions call for responses. It was the ancient custom of the early Church for the people to respond with Amen. But I think we must go much further than that. It is hard for the worshipper to follow the movement of the service. Perhaps the different stages could be made known. We have not in Presbyterian worship sufficiently recognised that the body influences the mind and the different attitudes of standing, kneeling, and sitting should be used more than they are. All three attitudes are used at Holy Communion. Communion is received standing in the East as once also in the West. It is received kneeling by a Western practice and sitting by a reformed usage. These all bear testimony to an aspect of eucharistic worship. Kneeling is the attitude of prayer, and by this attitude the offering of the soul in the Church's oblation is most easily expressed. Standing is the attitude of adoration. Sitting conveys best the fellowship

of communion. All these notes are in the Eucharist, and we ought to use our bodily attitudes to help our soul's ascent to God and our soul's reception of God's truth.

We need to emphasise anew the importance of this central service. Our Scots forefathers in bygone days honoured the sacrament by surrounding it with many services, fast-day observances and much preaching. In the accent of the future we need to make it felt how supremely important for the culture of the inner life is this worship and how essential to the Church's life. I feel that until we introduce more symbolism we shall fail, for we live in an age dramatic rather than speculative, in a period where men learn by other senses than the sense of hearing. May we not consecrate to this great celebration all the beauty of colour and of form? Ought we not to have a cross prominently before our eyes from the beginning of the service? The cross by which our Lord wrought the great victory is the symbol of the Christ Who died and conquered.

Types of communion service vary. There ought to be no dull uniformity. There is a common element, but there is a variety of types. A service of Holy Communion at Easter has a different tone from the celebration at Christmas or at Pentecost, or the celebration that is the memorial of Passion Week. We belong to the Western Church, and the Gallican Liturgy had manifold prefaces and variety in each Mass.

The possibility of variety depends on frequency. Rome celebrates every day, though, of course, on Good Friday it is the Mass of the Pre-sanctified in which there is no consecration. The East, maintaining the custom of the early Church, celebrates weekly. We celebrate for the most part from monthly to half-yearly. Now in Scotland we have developed a service of Holy Communion which has very great value and ought to be preserved. It is the service of the full congregation, where all partake. This type of service emphasises the fellowship of the Church and represents the historic feast perhaps best of all. It should remain with the element of the mysterious Presence deepened, with the aspect of glad thanksgiving more stressed and the Church's oblation made more manifest. But there surely could be developed other forms of service so that the feast could be kept every Lord's Day. I do not consider now how this would affect weekly worship, but Holy Communion could be celebrated before or after morning service. In such celebrations it would be possible to emphasise the different aspects of this great feast.

Finally, let us glance at what is called the Reservation of the Sacrament. Perhaps such a name is scarcely happy, as this might more correctly be called the reservation of the elements. It is in line with Christian tradition that we reserve the consecrated elements for those who are sick. Why because of infirmity should they be debarred from partaking of the Lord's Table. The bread and wine that have been consecrated in the Eucharist service are their right. Then it is no private communion, but they are linked to the fellowship of the Church in her chiefest service. There is also the reservation of the elements for the purpose of adoration and of worship. Now it seems to me that in our morning service if there is no celebration we need a point in which in silence we can focus our adoration. What is more fitting for this purpose than the element that has been consecrated and used in the Eucharist? Does not that more definitely than cross or picture or statue bring before the mind and spirit the wonder of God's Redemption? I would therefore argue for the use of the reserved element—the consecrated bread—in the weekly service. There upon the Holy Table would rest the holy bread, and before this and through this we would adore God. This form of devotion is no return to the past. I do not think we can find such a practice in the early Church, and in the Middle Ages the elements were reserved not for adoration but for use as a kind of charm. This devotion belongs to modern times, and it is to meet a need of to-day that it exists.

Ought we not to be bolder far in our eucharistic worship? Ought we not to face the world in which we live and not allow our minds to be scarred and our imaginations blistered by old, unhappy, far-off things? Surely we need all the help we can find to make the sense of the Unseen felt. Why not make use of God's ministry of light? Jesus spoke of Himself in words that were pictures. May we not represent our Lord's presence by the symbol of light? Candles upon the Holy Table suggest that mystery which makes

God's Presence felt. Of course all these things are externals. But our problem to-day is to make more real the sense of God and more actual the presence of Christ. No branch of the Church has a better right to be bold than the Scots Kirk, for we have in our history learned the distinction between what was external and what was essential. Therefore it is that, having learned the lesson of our history, we are free with open faith to use and to adopt every means and all methods that minister to man's soul the strange and glad message that God is with His children.

CHAPTER XII

WEEKLY AND DAILY WORSHIP

I. Let us first turn our attention to the weekly worship of the Church, and our first consideration must be the Divine Service on the morning of the Lord's Day. What is the aim and what is the function of the morning service? Every Church is seeking to perpetuate according to the circumstances of its life and the outlook of to-day the worship which came into being with the Christian Faith. At the meeting of the first followers of the Lord on the first day of the week there was the "Breaking of Bread," and undoubtedly it was the primitive practice that the Holy Eucharist was celebrated. The Reformers, especially Calvin, sought to step past the mediæval growth and to return to the primitive form of worship. This was their intention though they may not wholly have understood the nature of that early worship. We therefore who walk the great roadway of the Christian tradition must acknowledge that our morning service takes the place of this worship of the early Church, and must admit that the aim and function of our service ought to be the aim and function of a eucharistic service. We therefore are faithful to the Reformed tradition in making this assertion, for the purpose of the Reformers was to revive the primitive worship. This gives us the general outlook on our morning service.

The relation of the Reformed morning service to the Eucharist has been discussed by Dr. Maxwell,[1] and he, following Professor Doumergue's contention ("for Calvin the complete order of worship on Sunday morning is the order which embraces the celebration of the Eucharist"), traces the descent of the Book of Common Order from the mediæval Mass. The Reformed service then is not a completely new form but the simplification—to the extremest

[1] *John Knox's Genevan Service Book.*

limit I admit—of the mediæval Mass. The morning service in the Reformed Church is the Liturgy of the Catechumens, or it might be given the mediæval name "dry Mass" (Missa Sicca)—that is, a service at which the prayers of the Mass were said while the Offertory, the Consecration, and the Communion were omitted. Apparently there were two kinds of dry Mass: the one, simpler and shorter, consisted of the Epistle, Gospel, Lord's Prayer, and Blessing; the other, in which the priest wore full vestments, contained the whole Mass with the exception of the Canon.[1] The latter form is not unlike the Mass of the Pre-sanctified wherein there is no consecration and where Holy Communion is distributed to the worshippers.[2] "In some places," says Schuster, "a relic was held up for the veneration of the congregation instead of the elevation of the sacred Host." We may not, however, hold that there was a conscious derivation on the part of Calvin. But it is enough for our purpose to know that the roots of this service go back to the morning eucharistic service of the mediæval Church, and to recognise that the Reformers' desire was to imitate more exactly the worship of the early days. The general truth remains that if our morning service is to be in line with the service of the first century it must fulfil the aim and function of the Eucharist. If it be only a liturgy of the Catechumens or a dry Mass in the narrower sense, it is then a service of the Word in which there is reception of God's message, followed by prayer and instruction. It would then be a service wholly in the descending movement and the emphasis would fall on God Who has spoken in revelation. The ascending movement in which the soul rises to adoration would be wanting. My contention is that if we are to make our morning service the successor of and substitute for the service in the early Church, both aspects of revelation and redemption must be retained, and psychologically we must both bow down before the Word which has been spoken and lift up our hearts to find union with the God Who redeems man from a life of passing shadows.

When we glance at the morning service in the diverse branches of the Church we recognise the tendency of each to concentrate

[1] Durandus. Cf. Fortescue, *op. cit.* p. 192.

[2] Cf. Schuster, *The Sacramentary*, vol. v. p. 316.

on its special characteristic. We might distinguish the forms of Christianity that divide the religious life of Scotland and in a swift generalisation say that an Episcopalian goes to church to say his prayers, and a Roman to be present at the mysterious offering of the miraculous sacrifice, and a Presbyterian to hear and to receive the Word of God. Thus historically the first has tended to emphasise the devotional worship of prayer and praise which is due to the Divine, the second to dwell on the Divine Presence in the sacrifice, the third to concentrate on the appeal of God's Word to heart and mind. We all recognise the value of the idea which is behind each, and also the peril of one-sidedness that belongs to each. Our concern ought to be to make the morning service the richest expression of man's devotion to God, the deepest sense of the Eternal and of the superhuman Presence, the clearest perception of God's sovereign Will of Grace.

It is of the essence of Christian thought that Christianity is the religion of the Incarnation, and Christian worship must, if it move on parallel lines to Christian truth, embody this kernel thought. The Eucharist is the assertion of God's presence with man which is the fruit of the Incarnation; and the morning worship which represents the Eucharist ought to be such that it mirrors the Incarnation, the presence of God with the human soul. Thus such a worship is not simply the expression of man's gratitude, penitence, and praise, nor only the experience of a strange miracle in the dim twilight of ceremonial, nor solely the reception of God's Word in speech and the response to it in prayer. It is also the representation of God's presence through word, gesture, and rite, which are used by the Divine as the means and vehicle of the spirit. The idea of the Incarnation is not only a doctrinal axiom, it is also the gauge and test of the means of worship.

We then take as our two guiding facts for our morning worship: (1) that the service must mirror the Incarnation, and (2) that it is a 'shadow eucharist.' What then ought to be the contents of the morning service? To answer this question we must recall what are the ideas that have been expressed in the Eucharist, and if we are to make this offering of worship richly coloured and spiritually complete it must incorporate in some measure the ideas that lie behind the various rites and liturgies. We have seen that there are five ideas which are expressed in the celebration of the Sacrament, and each must find some place in this service.

(1) The first is the historical aspect. Our morning service commemorates a supreme fact. It asserts the Divine intervention in history. The particulars of history are the medium of the Divine action and of the manifestation of God in human life. The life of Jesus of Nazareth is at the same time the fulfilment of the Hebrew aspiration and the beginning of a new era. This emphasis upon the historical revelation is given in the lections of Holy Scripture. These are of course for edification, but they are not simply truths about God or ethical instruction. This is the Word expressed more or less adequately through the minds of men, and exhibits the Divine energy of grace at work. Parts of Holy Scripture are not suitable for this purpose because they do not sufficiently manifest this Divine revelation. The Old Testament lesson represents the energy of God working through the course of history, the revelation of His Will. The New Testament lesson is the fulfilment of that purpose. In my opinion there ought to be two New Testament lessons, Epistle and Gospel, which can be read together. The one from the Epistles shows the creative power of the Spirit in renewing human nature, the other revealing the words and deeds of Jesus as the evidence of God's Grace gives us that handbreadth of human history which was lighted with the pure radiance of the Divine. Greater prominence should be given to the reading of Scripture. The lessons should be surrounded by an atmosphere of reverence which might be suggested by a brief prayer or an exclamation of praise. We announce that it is the Word of God which is read. There are those who do not like this phrase, for they say the Bible is not the Word of God, but contains the Word of God, and by that phrase we are perpetrating a mistaken view of the Word. The answer to these critics is that the passage read does contain and therefore is the Word of God; and we ought so to select our readings as to make this evident. There ought to be a response to the reading of the Word, and it would be well to make a distinction between what is said after the Old Testament lesson and what is said after the Gospel. After the lesson

other than the Gospel might be said "Thanks be to Thee, O God," and after the Gospel "Praise be to Thee, O Christ," which is a phrase reminiscent of the Gospel lection in the East. By the reading of Scripture our service is anchored in history. We commemorate at the same time God's revelation in the historical past and we hearken to this word as a revelation to the mind and conscience of to-day.

There is, however, another way of emphasising the objective character of our worship. This is by following the Christian Year. The varied moods of the worshipping spirit find expression as we move through the hope and awe of Advent, the joy of Christmas and Epiphany, the discipline and humility of Lent, the triumph of Easter, the aspiration and assurance of Ascension, the bounty and grace of Whitsuntide, the mystery and richness of Trinity. The feelings and moods of the worshippers have an anchor in the events and experiences of history; we are thus not making simply the offering of our immediate mood, but are rendering our offering through obedience to the discipline of God's revelation. This too provides the variety which is often so wanting in our service, for no two Sundays ought to have quite the same tone or colour. Here also the remembrance of the Saints as the embodiment of God's Will has a place. Unfortunately there is a tendency to-day to turn from the reverence due to God's Mind incarnate in human personalities to the commonplaces of the bourgeois mind which prescribes abstractions like Youth or Foreign Missions to special Sundays. Fortunately the heart of man is inherently poetic, and these modern pedestrianisms are bound to die. There is no great subject like Peace or Missions which has not within the pages of Holy Writ or in the history of the Church its chosen representative. In one age or another God has inspired his great-souled servants to special tasks. If we wish to emphasise these tasks in our worship, it ought to be around the thought of God's revelation through human lives. The observance of the Christian Year therefore has value for its historical significance. It confirms our subjective feelings by the objective revelation of God. It consecrates this present life by showing that human life has been the vehicle of God's Speech. It has worth because it bids us worship before the central facts and experiences of the faith. It is educative because it teaches us the range of our religion. It is disciplinary because it bids us at times step forth from the limit of our own mood into a wider and deeper emotion.

(2) The second idea is that of fellowship and communion. Just as the historical in worship brings us before Jesus Who lived and died and triumphed, and before the forerunners and the followers of this revelation, so this idea of communion brings us to the Christ in men, to the Holy Spirit that is the Spirit of truth and peace. All the worshippers, despite their differences of nature, culture, and experience, have something in common which ought to find expression in some common action or attitude. The mood of fellowship ought of course to pervade the whole service, and audible responses to the prayers of confession, thanksgiving, and petition are useful. So also there is value in bidding prayers. The praise too is a fitting means for expressing this idea and sentiment, and the use of one or two familiar tunes is helpful. The repetition of the Creed ought to create a sense of fellowship, but unfortunately it does not seem to do so. The saying of a creed ought to be an act of faith in fellowship one with another, but a creed is inoperative so long as men regard it as a document to be treated with the caution of a lawyer reading a deed. It must be taken whether sung or said as the symbol and expression of what is beyond utterance if it is to be a bond of fellowship. It seems unfortunate that we cannot find some external act or attitude that will make dramatic the sense of fellowship. A sermon too has a real place in helping to create a common mood or feeling. The practice of providing pauses in the service for silent prayer has a strange power of quickening the sense of human fellowship.

But our fellowship is not simply with one another, but with the whole Church in heaven and on earth. To dwell on the presence with us in all worship of the spirits of the departed, to have some part of the service that is known to belong to the worship of far-off days, to have something in the service like the Lord's Prayer that is common to all Christians—these things are of avail. Yet the sense of fellowship ought not to have only a backward look across the pages of a glorious past, but a forward reference to the unexplored gifts God holds for His children in the days to be. There ought to be in worship an act of hope for mankind and for the world in which we find our fellowship through a common aspiration. The horizon of worship is God's deathless kingdom.

The source, however, of our sense of human fellowship rests on communion with the Divine. It is when the spirit within seeks the Spirit around and above us that there is fellowship. In an act of adoration there is union. This is one reason why I advocate that there be some visible and central sign of God's Presence. The Sacred Elements on the Holy Table might fittingly be the symbol for this act of common adoration, and if Holy Communion were celebrated before morning service this would be possible. Or, as I mentioned, a cross might be used. This act of adoration would be at once Divine Communion and human fellowship, and would correspond to the elevation of the Host in the Roman Missal, or the Great Entrance in the Eastern Rite. It is perhaps the greatest difficulty in any service to utter adoration in words. Words which can express so many moods fail here, for the height of adoration is speechless, too full for spoken words.

(3) The third idea which has to be expressed is thanksgiving. The whole atmosphere of the Christian service should be permeated with the mood of gratitude and praise. This is the temper that the Eastern Liturgies have most faithfully preserved. The prayers of all kinds—confession, petition, and intercession—are bathed in the mood of praise to God. Perhaps the evangelic worship of little companies preserves this mood better than the ordered service of our Church. If our morning service is to take the place of the Eucharist, thanksgiving must not only be present but have a wide range. The Church has taken not a little of her eucharistic praise from Jewish sources and thereby escaped from the narrowness and intensity of a purely Jesus-cult. For into the Hebrew thanksgiving flow the praise and gratitude due to God the Almighty Creator, the Lord and Father of all flesh, the Guide and Sustainer of all life. This note of universal thanksgiving must be kept in our service. I am not arguing that this general thanksgiving must use always the language of Old Testament praise, but it must have the same wide sweep.

There ought of course to be definite acts of thanksgiving in prayer and in praise. " Joy," said Dean Inge, with pardonable exaggeration, " as a moral quality is a Christian invention," and this joy must enter into our service far more than it does. There is room in all modern liturgies for spiritual imagination to find and feel new modes of uttering the soul's gratitude to God for His gifts in creation and His redemptive Grace. A bidding prayer of thanksgiving allows liberty to the soul to make special and individual acts of gratitude. Our thanksgiving tends to be too vague and general and not always to touch the chord of gratitude with fresh and authentic power.

(4) There is the idea of sacrifice. This idea affects our worship in that the service is both the memorial of the Divine Love and the offering of the Church's oblation. That redemption is the Act of God is the essence of the Christian offering in praise and prayer. Our offering, as we saw, is our response to God's Act in Christ. Naturally in every service the sense of the Divine Sacrifice and the human response pervades the whole devotion. The Vision of the Divine Sacrifice is no isolated experience or " far-off theological mystery." The God made manifest in Christ's sacrifice is the omnipotent God " Whose atoning love unweariedly creating good out of evil "[1] creates " a triumph which but for the wrong or treason had never been." The principle of the Atonement is the redemption of life from evil, not by forgetting evil but by making it the opportunity of a greater good. In the response to God's sacrifice must be the human sacrifice. This has relation in the first place to the confession of sins. The forgiveness of sins means that by God's Grace our evil will be changed and transformed into a nobler opportunity of life and of service. Our sin which has brought evil into the world can only find atonement by God's Act whereby a greater good is brought into the world than could have been possible without our sin. This is wholly the work of God's Grace, but our response to it affects our confession of sinfulness. Confession must be linked to resolution. In confession we accept God's Gracious Will and we place our wills in obedience to His. The change wrought in us by God's Grace which is part

[1] Pringle Pattison, *Idea of God*, p. 417.

of the atonement must find expression in new resolves and deeper insight. Therefore if we are to worship before the sense of God's sacrifice our confession must be transformed into resolution. The vow of obedience and of service ought to follow absolution or the declaration of God's Pardon. This may find symbolic expression, but it is essential that the worshipper should know what is happening in the service.

In the prayer of intercession the thought should be made definitive that in her oblation the Church gives herself through the sacrifice of Christ to the work of God and the furtherance of His Kingdom. Her intercession becomes then not simply petitions, but resolutions of the will, and vows of service. The Church in her oblation represents mankind. It is therefore the Church's part to recognise and to confess the sins of the world and of the age and of this present civilisation as her own sins, for all men share therein. She stands in the world's stead, she acknowledges the sins of her own day, she makes herself one with all creatures in her prayer of intercession. So too in her thanksgiving the Church renders thanks to the Creator in the name of all creatures, for to her alone has God given through His revelation the voice to speak to the Redeemer, since to her alone is given the vision of the Redemption in Christ. Thereby the Church before the Vision of God's Love makes herself the vehicle of creation's praise. This can only be when the Church is conscious of the oblation she offers. I feel that much could be done to stimulate this consciousness by the ministry of the eye.

In the early Church the material offerings were the symbol of the Church's thanksgiving. Gore[1] makes the remark that a Christian Eucharist in the first age must have frequently resembled a modern harvest thanksgiving. What the practice of such an offering accomplished was to furnish a visible symbol of the Church's offering. To-day of course the money offering takes the place of the early offerings in kind. Thus to mark that it is a real offering it should be set on the Holy Table and dedicated with prayer, to which there should be a response. For this act should be a real offertory act in which we anew offer ourselves to God. But there is another

[1] *Body of Christ*, p. 172.

suggestion concealed in the custom of the early days. These visible and material things were not only man's offering for God's purpose, they were also manifestly God's gifts to men. The sense of thankfulness is stimulated and made definite by the sight of God's gifts and thereby the offering of gratitude is full. Now our form of money offering to-day does not speak, as did the ancient offering, of God's creative power, of the wealth and largesse of His Bounty. We need something that does so in order that our sense of thankfulness be increased. Ought we not then to have within our churches things of beauty and of worth that speak of God's gifts to men, that remind the soul of the wonder of God's creation so that our offering of thanksgiving may be richer ?

(5) There is also the idea of mystery and the Sense of the Presence. The Roman obedience in order to stress this note of mystery has seemed to make the Presence definite by localising it and to make the Presence real by the use of a precise set of words. The Orthodox Church also lays great weight on the sense of God's Presence and His Coming in the two Entrances. Professor Otto in his suggestion for worship sketches a service which has at the heart of it an act of adoration made in silence. His suggestions I must confess seem a little precious and artificial, because it is not possible by the use of the great hymns and prayers of eucharistic worship unrelated to that worship ever to rise from subjective feeling to the sense of an objective presence. But he does point to a real need in worship when he urges that there must be a definite act of adoration. Profesor Will [1] also, from a different standpoint, makes a similar proposal. I feel that both these distinguished thinkers relate the sense of mystery wholly to a moment in time rather than connect it with a symbol in space. One must acknowledge that there is a blank in reformed worship in this regard. It is doubtless true that the Presence of the Risen Lord so clearly realised in the early Church has in the forms of Rome and of the East been influenced by thoughts outside the circle of the original Christian experience. If, however, there be religious modes capable of expressing the sense of mystery it is surely right that they be baptized into the worship of the Glorified Christ Whose fulness filleth all things.

[1] *Le Culte.*

An act of adoration in public worship seems to be necessary in order to make real the sense of the Presence and to express the experience of Divine Union. It is the apex of the service from one point of view, for it is the point to which the ascending movement leads. Such an act appears to require two things. The first is silence which stills the spirit. The second is some object or action on which there is a corporate concentration of attention. In the Eucharist this object is found in the elements upon the Holy Table, and I have therefore argued for the presence of this sacred symbol during public worship. This act of adoration would not then be a vague mystical mood but it would be focused upon what represents Christ as the Redeemer and as the Present Lord. In the thought of Mystery in public worship we must bear in mind the distinction that I made earlier between the ascent of the soul and the descent of the Spirit. The former or ascending movement has its focus in an act of adoration in which the soul is lifted up to Divine Union. This is what we have discussed above. In the latter or descending movement there is the prostration of spirit before the sense of God. This is not the culmination of the soul's ascent; it is the sense of God's Transcendence from which the movement of worship flows. These two poles in worship must be recognised and kept distinct although the sense of mystery belongs to both.

Such are the elements that have to be interpreted in our morning service. We have to consider how this is to be done. The practice of conducting the devotions of the congregation from the Holy Table is one that ministers to the spirit of worship and suggests the true original of our service. This is not really an innovation in the Reformed Church, but a return to an earlier practice. "It is clear that in the French Church at Strasburg the service was conducted, as in the German Church, from the Communion table."[1] It is well to make the distinction between the pulpit as a place of prophecy and the Communion Table as the place of offering. The habit of pronouncing the Benediction from the Holy Table suggests that the service is the prelude to the Eucharist; but it is not enough for this service to be the preparation for eucharistic worship, it must be the substitute.

[1] Maxwell, *op. cit.* p. 37.

A service has variable and invariable elements. (1) Let us take the invariable elements. As the Eucharist is a rite common to Christendom there ought to be in every morning service some part of the worship that is the common heritage of all Christians. For this there might well be a liturgical book in which the catholic or universal expressions of devotion could be found. The Lord's Prayer does serve this function, but the addition of the Sanctus and the Agnus Dei would help to increase the sense of unity. There ought to be an invariable element so that wherever the worshipper may be he hears the familiar words which have the association of home for him. The structure of the service remains the same from Sunday to Sunday, and some elements should not alter, as for example the Benediction.

(2) There are the variable elements. These are of two kinds: (*a*) There is the uniform variation. In accordance with the season of the ecclesiastical year there should be variety which marks the seasons. For example, there should be a collect that is used in Lent and another that is used through Whitsuntide. This marking of the seasons may be done through hymn and chant or by the call to worship. One of the advantages in the use of ecclesiastical colours is that the time and circumstance of worship are announced to the eye. (*b*) There is the constant variable. Within the same architecture of the service there is constant variety. For example, in the intercessory prayers certain subjects always are present though their expression may alter, but certain others change from Sunday to Sunday. Where I think most of our Presbyterian forms of service fail is just in this, that they are not based on the distinction between the invariable, the uniform variable, and the constant variable. The distinction that the Church of Rome makes between the ordinary of the Mass and the proper is wise, but in addition to that we add the constant variable which in the Roman Rite is mainly only the homily and the lessons, while with us it would include as well differences in prayer and in praise. But while the goodly custom of the Reformers as of the early Church is preserved in that there is a place for free prayer as well as for the introduction of the devotional heritage we have received, at every point in the service the worshipper would know just what is being done.

Let us trace the sequence of the service. Here again I revert to the distinction I have frequently mentioned between the two movements in worship. The first aims at giving us power and the sense through God's revealed Grace of being able and fit to meet and overcome the menace of life. The second aims at union with the Divine above the harass of daily living and seeks to find eternity in time. In the first, our meditation is the fruit of revelation ; in the second, revelation is the outcome of meditation. The first starts with God the Revealer, and from this we move on to dwell on His revelation. From this flow the prayer of abasement and the prayer of confidence, and then follow the hearing of His Word and its implications for us. The second begins with the God of mystery and to this God we lift up our hearts and seek through purification to find what He has to say to us, and then by the light of this knowledge to gain union with Him. Now the supreme experience of the Eucharist is union with God, and therefore this must be in our morning service. But our service cannot begin with the mystical movement because our service is founded on revelation, nor can it end with it, for the aim of the mystical movement is union and our service must conclude with the sense of power to meet life and face its possibilities. We may then say that our service must begin with the God of revelation Who in the past of the race and of our own experience has spoken. This is the ground or warrant of Christian worship—no trembling step of approach but the assurance that the God of revelation in Christ is over all things.

We begin then with the Word spoken by God in the past and we advance to the consequences of this revelation—our present need, our past sinfulness, and our causes for thanksgiving. Then moving from the past we turn to the future and in our supplications and intercessions make our offering. Here the soul begins its ascent to the God of Mystery Who ever reveals Himself anew, and through purification and illumination it advances to union. This is the apex of adoration. Thereafter we recall this experience and seek its revelation. Worship now takes up the first movement and gives to the mystical experience the orientation of present-day life. As in the liturgies the post-communion prayer is a prayer for faithfulness and power through God's Grace to live in accord with His

Will, so our service strikes the same note. Then finally there is the blessing from God on His children as with a new strength from the Unseen they return to life. In this sequence of worship we have heard an oracle, offered a sacrifice, experienced a mystery, and finally as the result the worshipper gains power and strength to live. As in the full Eucharist so in this service we use the three historic types of worship—the oracle, the sacrifice, the mystery—and finally return to the mood in which the oracle or revelation calls for obedience to its behests.

Such is the general statement about the sequence of the service. Let us examine this in greater detail. We start with the thought and word of revelation. This means that after the gathering psalm there is a call to worship. This may be taken as the call of the Church to her members to worship God, but I think it ought rather to be the call of God to the Church. At the beginning of worship there is the sense of God the Transcendent Whose revelation of His Will and Holiness gives rise to the response in man. There is a double response—a sense of our nothingness which Kyrie eleison expresses, and the sense of God's Glory and Majesty which the Gloria proclaims. These two thoughts are linked together, for God's Greatness reveals our frailty and the sense of creatureliness extols God's Sovereign Power. Here in worship we bow down before God and are conscious of ourselves as very little before Him. This is not the confession of our faults and sins, but the sense of our sinfulness and frailty. Then follows after this recognition of God's Wonder and Glory in Creation and Redemption, the confession of the sins of the past week. An opportunity for silent recollection must be given, and this is followed by the absolution which asserts our confidence in God's forgiveness. Thanksgiving is made for the past in answer to God's gifts in creation and in salvation. The lessons give the message of the Word and between them there is a song of praise. After the lessons a confession of faith either in creed recited or praise sung. We move now into the mood of the future and we present our supplications. This is the beginning of the offering of the sacrifice. The offering is taken which is linked to the intercessions. The offering of intercessions wherein the Church makes her priestly prayer for the world, for human needs, for God's Church and Kingdom, needs an introduction such as the Sanctus or the kind of thanksgiving we find in the preface. The recognition that it is our duty to give thanks and to intercede marks this sacrifice of prayer. We move now into the atmosphere of mystery and we are bidden anew lift up our hearts unto the Lord as we approach through brief stages of purification and illumination to union—the point of silence and of adoration in our worship. Thereafter follow a prayer and praise of thanksgiving containing a vow of faithfulness and obedience, and the dismissal by the Benediction.

Two points I wish to mention. The first is that this scheme does not involve setting aside our customary service. It only means that the praise and the prayers are so chosen that they correspond to the movements that run through the service. It is a mistake to imagine that the beginning of worship is its lowest point. It is not; for the mood of the worshipper at the beginning is fresh and ready to receive the sense of God though not prepared for the experience of adoration in union. From God the Subject and Creator of all worship we move through the sense of God's Glory and confession and power to the proclamation of the Word. Then there is the offering of prayers within the mood of humble dependence and then the ascent to the sense of mystery and absorption which leads to the mood of resolution. I am sure we have all been present at a service in which this movement was kept. It is in the power of the spiritual artist to create this and to follow it all unwittingly, but most of us are not spiritual artists and have not the power to capture and to guide the minds of the worshippers. For this reason I argue that the analysis of our services should be known so that it might be possible for all the worshippers to follow. One suggestion I would make that is an innovation. Between the different parts of the service, the Oracle or the proclamation of the Word, the Sacrifice or the offering, the Mystery or the act of adoration through silence and symbolism, there should be intervals which would be used for singing. During these singings it would be possible, if necessary, for people to leave and to enter the church; and young children for whom the whole service would be too long could be present at one or other part of the service. At present young children who do not remain for the whole worship commonly hear the same part of the service each Sunday, but by this arrangement they would be able to attend different portions of the worship. The second and especially the third part of the service would admit of—indeed call for—symbolism which would allow children to worship, for the symbolic is as near the mind of childhood as of experience.

The other point is obvious. One thing that at once strikes the mind of every one is that I have not assigned any place to the sermon. This I have deliberately omitted, not because I would cast any aspersion upon the high office of preaching, but because I believe that the sermon is the one item in the service that must be free if it is to fulfil its greatest usefulness. Upon the nature of the sermon depends its place in the movement of worship. A sermon may be an act of faith—the declaration of God's Will proclaimed in Scripture and related to the life of to-day; then the sermon belongs to the oracle division of the service. A sermon may be the explanation of and prelude to the offering of our intercessions in creating wider sympathies and deeper longings; then the sermon will belong to the sacrifice division of worship. A sermon may be an act of edification and a call for resolution, the direct application of the mood of worship to life and its duties and problems; then the sermon will belong to the very last stage—the recollection of what we have experienced in worship. A sermon may be the preparation of the soul for adoration moving through the appointed stages; then the sermon will belong to the mystery portion and will appeal to experience. Have we not heard sermons that instructed us and opened our eyes to new truths in Scripture, sermons whose fitting end was in prayer for God's world and God's Kingdom, others again that braced us for life, and others whose fitting end ought to have no spoken word or sung hymn, but the silence of the soul before God in adoration? How often too have the prayers and praise of the Church been a little unmeaning because the soul had not been made alive to their meaning. This surely is the function of preaching, but to achieve this the sermon must come early in the service.

II. We have been considering the Sunday Morning Service as

the substitute for the Eucharist, which means that it is a service complete in itself. By that I mean it is a service which contains all the elements or acts of worship. The other services which we find in pre-reformation days such as Matins, Lauds, were not complete services. They are, for example, wanting in the offering of direct intercession and, save Prime and Compline, there is no definite confession of sin. The question now to be answered is, are the other services on the Lord's Day to be complete or incomplete ? The advantage of the incomplete service is that it can be given a point and urgency. It can be specially addressed to a particular end or adapted to meet differences in age and in outlook. The argument for the second service being a complete act of worship rests on the fact that it may be regarded as an alternative service. Some people are debarred by vocation and other causes from attendance at morning worship, and they have to be provided with an alternative service as complete though perhaps shortened in form. I admit this difficulty ; but it could be met by having in one church in a district this complete service which would give an opportunity to all hindered from attending morning worship.

If then we accept as our principle that the second service is the complement of but not the substitute for the morning service, we shall observe several possible varieties in this second service. (1) There is a service whose main purpose is the preaching of the Word. Such would be the service in which there are praise and prayer but where the sermon is devoted to a special purpose—it may be apologetic, dealing with the defence of the faith from present-day attacks, or hortatory, pointing out our duties in our life and station. It is the preaching of God's Word in relation to the circumstances in which we are set. Or such a service may be fundamentally instructional, in which the sermon or homily deals with the explanation and exposition of the Bible, or with the teaching of the Church. This would cover the ground taken by many Bible classes. The reason why I advocate such a service is that there are many subjects which ought to be dealt with by the Church but which require a considerable time. Often what happens is that the devotions and the reading of Scripture are curtailed for the sake of the sermon, or if adequate time be given to them there is no room for a sermon which can do justice to the theme. People listen to lectures on literary and scientific subjects for forty or fifty minutes, and a political speech is as long. Why then are so many sermons counted dull although shorter ? Is the reason not frequently this : that since a sermon is embedded in a service it cannot deal with the type of subject which calls for full treatment, or else it can only touch on such a subject and therefore scamp it ? In Scotland we used to speak of a preaching, and such a second service consisting of prayer, praise, a short lesson, and sermon would help to meet the need of those who are quite lost as to what the Church stands for and are in sore need of instruction as to what the faith is. It is a menacing fact that so many minds who mean well by their fellows are in abysmal ignorance of what Christianity is.

(2) The second type of service is devotional. We meet at the hour of evening sacrifice to make our offering of thanksgiving. This service is the saying of our evening prayer and the giving of praise. Here the form of the service is governed by its aim. Devotions in which the prayer of silence and the bidding prayer have a place are offered and responses are freely used. The atmosphere of such a service would fit into the yearly season and the evening hour, and the sermon would be devotional in character. Such a service is suited for another mood and temper than the first type and has a different objective. As the first type was predominantly a service of preaching and teaching, this is fundamentally a service of prayer and offering. Apart from these two types there are others. There is the evangelistic service which has occasional place within the Church. The object of this service is to arrest those who are without. It has always appeared to me that the fitting place for the sermon or speech that is addressed to those outside the Church should be preached outside the Church. I do not advocate the holding of services in places where there is not the atmosphere in which public prayer ought to be offered or in situations which may encourage profanity among those who do not share our faith, but in such places the sermon or speech which advocates our Christian faith and the kingship of the Lord Christ should be spoken. I cannot but think also that the Church might

make greater use of modern inventions in her special services. A cinema screen by a dramatic presentation of the life of Christ can make, if properly used, the kind of dramatic appeal which the mystery drama made. So also religious plays can be used as a Church service. We must recognise the distinction between the complete or eucharistic service which is the Sunday morning service and the incomplete service which has its own specific end.

But in addition we must face the fact that the habits of this generation and of the coming generation have changed as to the keeping of the first day of the week. I do not argue as to what is permissible and what is not upon the Lord's Day. We cannot fix our standard upon a negation, for that is like trying to stand upon nothing, but we can assert the duty of worship upon the day of worship. I would fain see this duty of worship far more strictly advocated, but before we can do so we must provide opportunity for all. To this end I would like to see a short early morning Sunday service of devotion, and also a late evening Sunday service which would be like Compline. Those who are spending their Sunday abroad would thus have the opportunity of beginning or ending the day before the Face of God, their Creator and Lord.

As I suggested, earlier Holy Communion should be celebrated at least once every Sunday. The most fitting time would be in the morning before Divine service. This might be the simple form of Holy Communion emphasising the fellowship of the upper room in the breaking of bread. It might be the Mystery in which the Lord Christ breaks to us the bread of life, and Himself the Unseen Priest bids us keep the glad feast of His Presence. It might again be the Sacrifice type where the Lord Christ, like the broken Bread, gives Himself to us in His Sacrifice, and asks from us the offering of our obedience. According to the circumstance such a Holy Communion would have a distinctive note. Then it would be possible for the hungry soul to receive each Sunday, as in the primitive Church, the joy of the Blessed Sacrament.

I think that in addition to the congregational service there should be the encouragement of group worship. There are those who through a common experience or by reason of a common outlook or by the circumstances of age and of station have a natural community in worship. " If two of you shall agree on earth as touching anything that they shall ask " is a word of the Lord which points to a fellowship in intercession. But the worship of selected groups, both in prayer and in waiting upon the word, is additional to and not instead of the Church's morning service, where all sorts and conditions of men present their common offering.

I do not advocate this suggested programme as possible for all, perhaps not even for any, of the parishes of our Church ; but I do suggest that some such ideal should be in our minds so that in God's time our dear Church will be to Scotland the Catholic and Evangelic household of the faithful.

III. The Daily Service.

The idea of a daily service is no innovation in the Reformed Church in Scotland.[1] The Reader's service to begin with was a daily service, and is taken from the Hours of the mediæval and ancient Church. The custom of morning and evening prayer is well established. So there is reformed precedent for the daily service if such be required. How are we situated as regards this service ? The daily service may be either the substitute for or the complement of the weekly service of worship. There are a certain number of people who are prevented by their work from attendance at Divine Worship on the Lord's Day. This fact, however regrettable it may be, lays a responsibility on the Church. It ought to be possible for any one who cannot worship on Sunday to find in the district in which he lives a complete service of worship during the week. Since also a certain number cannot be present at Holy Communion on Sunday it behoves that in some church in the district there be a service of Holy Communion. I do not suggest that the Sacrament be celebrated daily in every church, but there ought to be a daily celebration in some church, so that those who have been debarred from partaking of Holy Communion, and those who desire more frequent communion, may have the opportunity to do so.

The daily service can also be regarded as the complement of the weekly service. There is a growing number of people who

[1] Macmillan, *Worship of the Scottish Church*, p. 136.

would choose to say their prayers in the atmosphere of the church ; for this the practice of keeping churches open as the place of prayer is the solution. There is a fact which, however much we may regret it, is very patent to-day. People live much less in their homes than was formerly the custom. It is therefore but a sign that the Church is adapting itself to the spirit of the age when it encourages the offering of prayer within the place set apart for worship. The habit therefore of holding morning and evening prayers within the church is one that is likely to grow and develop. But all such daily services will fail of their object if they be not conceived as subject to the needs and circumstances of the worshippers. They are not services that, like the Eucharist or its equivalent, the morning service of the Lord's Day, are complete acts of devotion picturing the worship of mankind. These daily services are framed for special and specific purposes. As more and more we see the spirit of the world encroaching on the claims of Sunday as a day of rest and worship, the Church must meet that attack not by a negative propaganda, but by her counter-assertion that all days are God's days and each day needs to be hallowed to God's purpose and blessed by His presence. The deep gulf that is dug in many minds between the first day of the week and the other days is fraught with peril ; some people even speak of Sunday as God's day, thereby leaving room for the fatal deduction that other days belong to the world. Yet all days are God's days ; the Lord's Day is the day of the Lord Christ. To keep and celebrate on this day the joyous memory of His victory over the power of evil and of death is the peculiar duty and privilege of those who are named by the name of Christ. The place of the short service on the week-day has significance and importance because it affirms that all days are within the Divine keeping.

If we are to recapture the rhythm of the Christian Year we must not only mould the worship of Sunday to it but must pay respect to the claims of the great days of the Church's life, Holy Week, Good Friday, Ascension Day, Christmas, etc. Here in these additional services we must be prepared for innovation and for change. This is the place for spiritual experiment. Our liturgical service must not be impervious to the mood and outlook of the twentieth century. In these incomplete services methods and means should be tried so that there may be evolved some way whereby the unity of the brotherhood, so broken by the present constitution of society, may discover itself, and the great things which all men and all believers in life and in God have in common be declared and made more potent.

CHAPTER XIII

SYMBOLISM, OR THE DRAMA AND BEAUTY OF WORSHIP

In all forms of worship there is a symbolic element and all public worship necessitates ceremonial. Just as you cannot escape ritual in a service, be it elaborate or simple, good or bad, deliberate or unreflective, so also you cannot avoid ceremonial. " Strictly speaking," says Dr. Frere, " a rite is a form of service, while ceremony is the method of its performance." An elaborate service like the Roman High Mass and a simple service like a prayer meeting have each form, but they have also a ceremonial, *i.e.* a way in which the form or rite is used. A Church using the Eastern Rite has a very meticulous ceremonial, but the Plymouth Brethren's Breaking of Bread also possesses a ceremonial—a manner in which the action is done. Ceremonial may be magnificent or grandiose, restrained or bleak, but it is always present. In some services like the Roman, the ceremonial is so prominent that it may even obscure or misrepresent the ritual, in others like evangelic preaching, the ritual or form of words is so emphasised that the ceremonial is scarcely noticed. Ceremonial can be called an external thing. So it is, and if it be separated from spiritual meaning it is merely external, just as " words without thoughts never to heaven go " ; yet an external thing may be made the expression of an inner mood. Ceremonial therefore, as the manner or mode in which we employ our ritual or form of words, includes all gestures or actions and all adornment or beautifying of worship.

It is impossible, therefore, to deny that there must be a relation between what is called art and what is called worship. One would naturally expect to find there was some real connection owing to the origin of both impulses. For it appears an incontestable fact that the instinct of worship and the art impulse were closely linked in primitive times. Out of religious ceremonial and ritual the art sense appears to have sprung. Worship as a public act preserves the recollection of this early bond. We rightly speak of the art of worship. For worship is an art rather than a science. Desires, impulses, spiritual cravings have to be given expression. The art of worshipping consists in expressing these adequately. We seek therefore what is significant for worship, and we discover that what is significant is beautiful. God is the God of beauty as well as of ethical goodness and truth, and His service must therefore be beautiful. But it is not our aim to introduce into worship actions or gestures or images because they are beautiful, but because they are significant. There are forms of beauty which are irrelevant to worship and therefore have no place in a service. It is not every type of good music nor all forms of plastic art that are appropriate to worship, but only that which can be expressive of the Godward relation of the soul. The art of worship may be magnificent like the starry heavens, or bald like the bareness of the mountain-top. Things of beauty may be deliberately brought into the service or the beauty may be present quite unnoticed as in the simple beauty of the old psalm tunes.

This raises another query to which we must pay attention in this chapter. The right method of doing anything affects not only the mind which observes it, but the whole consciousness of the worshipper. The art of a service is not merely an appeal to an abstraction called mind, but to the whole man. So we must reckon not simply with influences of which the worshipper is conscious, but also those of which he is quite unaware. There is an atmosphere conducive to worship; there are sensory appeals that increase the strength of the worshipful instinct. The phenomena of worship—the order of ritual, the ceremonial impressiveness, the ministry to the eye and to the ear, the experience of colour and of space—affect not only the field of consciousness but speak also to that hidden region of our being which is veiled from thought. "We think with words," said Anatole France, but into worship come other elements than the clearness of thought. Indeed before thought can be worshipful it must become, in Merejkowski's phrase, "impassioned thought." The abstractions of the mind are made vital by contact with phenomena, and the thought that God is becomes through the phenomena used in worship the realisation of His Presence. "There are in fact," says Unamuno[1] "people who appear to think only with the brain or whatever may be the specific thinking organ ; while others think with all the body, and all the soul, with the blood, with the marrow of the bones, with the heart, with the lungs, with the belly, with the life." So we worship with our whole being, for the God we worship is at once the God of Revelation and the God of Mystery—the God Who from the beyond has spoken to us and the God in Whom we live, the personal Will and the super-personal End and Goal of all existence. Speech then is not the only medium of worship, but we must bring into its embrace actions which enlist bodily movement and symbols that shadow the inexpressible.

We begin with ceremonial, which can be of several kinds. Dr. Frere[2] distinguishes four types—utilitarian, interpretative, mystical, and symbolic. We see in the growth of ceremonial how one thing can pass from one type to another. For example, the use of candles was originally for the purpose of giving light ; but it acquires from usage an interpretative value. Jerome tells us that " throughout the whole Eastern Church . . . whenever the Gospel is to be read the candles are lighted." Physical light becomes the interpretable accompaniment of the Gospel which tells of the Light of the world. Or incense, which came into use from pagan sources as an honorific sign, becomes not simply interpretative of the honour due to God's altar and God's book, but symbolic of prayer which rises like incense to the throne of grace. Acts of ceremonial which were in their origin utilitarian or interpretative may survive owing to the innate conservative instinct in public worship after their use has vanished or their meaning is forgotten.

(1) Utilitarian ceremonial arises from the fact that if an action is to be performed it must be performed in some particular way. Whether is it better that each choose his own method or that there be a recognised and universal way of performing the action? For example, in Holy Communion certain actions must be performed, and it seems not unreasonable that Christians should try to do these

[1] *Sense of Tragic Life*, p. 14. [2] *The Principles of Religious Ceremonial.*

in the same way. An attitude again must be taken during the different parts of the service, sitting, standing, or kneeling. There is the need of conformity whether we stand at prayer as did the early Church, or kneel as was the later practice. The Council of Nicæa prohibited kneeling during Eastertide and on Sundays, as at the time of rejoicing and on the day of the Resurrection human confidence in God's victory was better expressed by standing than by kneeling. I cannot but feel that our utilitarian ceremonial could be made more interpretative than it is. Some Churches like the Lutheran receive the message of the Gospel standing. Is there not room in our service for a greater variety of attitude ? Worship is an act of the whole congregation, and could this not be emphasised by the attitude taken by the worshippers ? The congregation is not receiving the Word the whole time, it is sometimes making an offering of petition and intercession or an offering of confession and thanksgiving. The same attitude is not appropriate to all these acts. I wish that thought were given to these externals of worship, so that they might be the vehicle and the announcement of the inner reality.

(2) Interpretative ceremonial is that which is added in order to make the meaning more impressive. What this means is that the eye as well as the ear is enlisted in the worship of God. I have already argued that some visible object and some definite attitude are of value in the act of adoration. This is the interpretation of a mood which otherwise might be dissipated in vagueness. That prayer be offered in a different place from where the lessons are read, or from where the sermon is preached, really interprets what is being done, and marks the triple distinction between what man offers to God, what man hears of God's revelation, and how man applies that revelation. People certainly vary greatly in their sensibility to the external accompaniments of worship ; there are those who would be helped thereby and no one would be harmed.

Two reasons exist for the greater use of interpretative ceremonial. The first is that it would make more patent the fact that worship is a corporate act in which the whole congregation joins. The second is that it would help to explain to the young what is being done in worship. It is sound psychology which we find in the Hebrew Law whereby, in the Feast of the Passover, certain acts were performed which could be explained to the youthful. "And it shall come to pass when your children say unto you what mean ye by this service."[1] The act which is interpretative to the Jew he explains as a symbol to his child. While I am persuaded that there is a real need of interpretation in our service, we must beware of the snare set by the pedant who would preserve usages simply because they are old. The one justification of interpretative ceremonial is that it interprets. Our age calls for interpretation in action since its favourite form of expression is dramatic, but we must not foist upon to-day the interpretation suited to another time. Dress is one most obvious sign that interprets ; the gown of Geneva with full sleeves is probably the "priest's outdoor habit,"[2] and has become the garb for the Divine Service in Scotland. We need, however, in addition a distinctly eucharistic sign. The use also of ecclesiastical colours would be a valuable piece of interpretative ceremonial.

(3) Let us take next mystical ceremonial. This consists in the attaching of a new meaning to ceremonies which already exist on other grounds.[3] This has flourished abundantly in the East, but also it has been prevalent in the West. The custom of adding water to wine in the service of Holy Communion goes back originally to the fact that thus Jews drank wine, and this would probably be the practice at the Last Supper, but this mixture of wine and water has found many mystical explanations. Water and blood flowed from the pierced side of the Saviour, the Evangelist relates. St. Cyprian sees in the water and wine the mystical union of Christ's people with Christ. Again the water and the wine are emblems of Christ's two natures. In mediævalism this tendency became luxuriant. Durandus explains mystically the whole service of the Mass. For example the reading of the Epistle is the preaching of John the Baptist who preaches only to Jews, so the reader turns to the north—the region of the ancient law. The reading ended, he bows before the bishop, as the Baptist humbled himself before Christ, and so it continues.[4] This habit of attaching mystical meanings to ceremonial acts is also used extensively by the Roman Church of to-day. We too are indulging in it when we say that the

[1] Ex. xii. 26. [2] Maxwell, *op. cit.* p. 213. [3] Frere, *op. cit.* p. 145.
[4] Cf. Taylor, *The Mediæval Mind*, vol. ii. p. 104.

recital of the Creed follows the Gospel as the response of faith to the revelation of God. If this tendency does not outgrow the bounds of devotion into the trivial and even the ridiculous, it has a real value for worship. It can make spiritually dramatic the order of the service, but it must not be mistaken for the historical cause of the order, nor must it be allowed to turn the acts of devotion into a spectacular movement. If, however, we make these reservations I can see a place for this mystical interpretation in our service. The Divine Service implies a view of God and of the World. There is a theology of incarnation and redemption, a philosophy of God and of man, a revelation of the eternal in history behind the act of worship. Ought we not to make some attempt to express this? "The perfect philosophical poem," says Professor Reid,[1] "is only possible when philosophy is visualised in a sustained dramatic myth." Worship should be nearer the mood of poetry than aught else, and if God's transcendent nature and man's redemption through grace are to be declared it is surely possible to attach mystical interpretation to the order in our service. Then by word and through symbol we could show how the service starts from God the Creator who has revealed Himself and with Whom the creature can have fellowship as His child, continues through confession which unfolds the helplessness of the world apart from God, and through thanksgiving and intercession which reveal God in nature and in human life, through the reading of His Word in the Old Testament which makes known His revelation in history to man's seeking heart, in the Epistle which shows the effect of the presence of God's Spirit, and in the Gospel which is the utterance of His Glory. Then follow the answer of the Creed, the ascent of the soul to meet God in the eucharistic worship of adoration wherein are the specific Christian fellowship and union with Christ, and finally the dismissal of blessing to our life and its duties. Are there not great dramatic possibilities in this movement? The deliberate attempt to represent it through ceremonial would increase the horizon of worship, as in the East, and would also be psychologically congruous with the temper and mood of to-day.

[1] *Wordsworth*, p. 247.

(4) There is finally symbolic ceremonial. This is distinguished from the other forms of ceremonial because it does not merely interpret or attach a new meaning to ceremonies that are there; it adds a new meaning and a new expression—in short, it adds a symbol.

Now we must observe that a symbol can perform two functions; a symbol may be used to represent God's Presence and God's Word. This is to view the symbol from the Divine side. Such, for example, is the consecrated bread—the sign that Christ is with the worshipper. A cross is the symbol of God's great act of salvation. On the other hand, a symbol may be the expression of the spiritual aspiration and experience of the worshippers. We saw how incense came to symbolise prayer and the floating and mounting smoke the upward yearning of the human heart toward God. The Holy Table is a symbol of the fellowship that Christ has brought to us, for to the same table He bids us all come. The cross above the Holy Table, or the Elements on the Table, would then have the double symbolism of God's grace in Christ reaching toward us, and of our union one with another aspiring to Him. There is, then, as Professor Will has pointed out, this double use of the symbol. The first he calls the transcendent and the second he calls the psychic. The first sees the symbol as the object that signifies or embodies God or Christ, the second feels the symbol as the object that expresses the need and the aspiration of man's heart. There is surely a place for both these forms of symbolism in our service.

Let us glance then at the two types of symbol that are found in worship.

I. We look first at the transcendent symbol. There is a region where speech fails, for speech defines. The otherness of God cannot be expressed; the unlikeness of God to man, God's utter Transcendence which baffles our thought—this sense of the Infinite outruns our language. "We see in a glass darkly," says St. Paul, and this mood must enter into worship. "Worship indeed," writes Professor H. F. Taylor,[1] "is not mere abjection and abasement before something which baffles our intelligence, but without the element of

[1] *The Faith of a Moralist*, p. 208.

the baffling there is no worship." The God of Revelation has spoken His Word; but the God of Mystery is silent. As in the material universe we stumbling humans touch the Infinite, "the silence of the starry skies, the sleep that is among the lonely hills," so in the universe of the spiritual we are in the presence of what cannot be spoken. If then our worship is to be as deep and as expressive as the horizon of the Eternal, we must dimly grope after the Infinitude of God that is not exhausted in the revelation in history and in Christ Jesus. How can we express this but by a symbol? "Some men," says Mr. Galsworthy with the hauteur of the sceptic, "naturally root themselves in the inexpressible for which one formula is much the same as another." But it is not a case of man's choice; it is the circumstance of our existence. The inexpressible can only enter into worship through the means of symbolism. "The symbol itself," says Baudouin, "is always richer in meaning than any of the explanations one may give of it." Here our writer is referring to the symbol in psychology, but what he says applies also to the symbol as it enters into worship. For this purpose of worship we must choose a symbol that by its associations is inexhaustible and through its objectivity conveys the sense of reality. Hence it is that the type of art which worship employs here is non-representational. God, in human form, was the expression of the clear open-air mind of Greece, but there has ever been the attempt to transcend the anthropomorphic tendency. The animal-headed deity is a grotesque example of this. The first tide of artistic feeling that touched Christianity appears to have been of this non-representational character. "Among historical forms of religion," writes Strzygowski,[1] "Monotheism appears to favour a non-representational system. Judaism and Islam are examples; we shall see that in its origin Christianity inclined in the same direction." In the endeavour to seek a fitting symbol for the Infinite it is in accord with the modern spirit as it is consistent with the earliest tradition to seek no representation but an arrangement of form and of colour that will give to us the sensation of the Infinite. We must not be tied to the symbols of the past for the historical does not enter into this perception.

[1] *Origin of Christian Church Art*, p. 104.

Modern art-forms could be summoned to the aid of worship and a satisfying symbol could be devised for us of these modern times. Unfortunately much of the art symbolism employed by our Church belongs to a past era, and we appear to be blind to the possibilities in worship of modern art which by its spirit of naked sincerity is cleansing art from cloying sentimentality.

On the other hand, since Christianity is the religion of the Incarnation, there is the need of representing Christ. The historic representations of Christ have been three.

(1) The cross has preserved by its purely symbolic character the mystery and the wonder of Christ's life. It refers to an historic event, the crucifixion, and there is the suggestion of the Risen Christ in the empty cross; but the very shape of the cross has an inherent appeal, for the cross is no invention of Christianity, and the roots of its unconscious appeal go back to primeval nature. It is to the mind the sign of the Risen Lord Who triumphed through the cross, but it also speaks to the unconscious side of man's nature as the representation of mysterious life.

(2) There is Christ depicted as the ruler and the judge. God is personified as the Lord of all in the person of Christ. Christ is represented with beard and long smooth hair. There is no attempt to set forth the actual and historical appearance. The form of Christ is hieratic, seeking to express all He was and is and not what He looked like.

(3) There is the Hellenistic depicting of the Founder of Christianity. "These two Hellenistic unbearded types of Christ, the long-haired of Asia Minor and the short-haired of Alexandria, have been completely superseded in the West." [1] These two types delineate Christ as the perfection of humanity. These have no intention of depicting Jesus as the Jewish leader. They represent the ideal man.

There is value in each of these representational forms as there is value also in the realism of history, but for the ends of worship the hieratic form has greatest worth and the humanly perfect excels in value the historical. Historical imagery is useful mainly in informing the mind through the eye and being a kind of visible

[1] Strzygowski, *op. cit.* p. 162.

lesson. It appears to me that our worship would gain if our eye were engaged as well as our ear. Hence I would advocate the use of pictorial representation as well as the form of the cross. Pictures would vary according as the season of the year emphasised Christ the teacher and example, Christ the voluntary sacrifice, Christ the conqueror, Christ the judge, and this variety would necessitate different types of representation. As our aim is to reach the significant in worship, the didactic element is not to be neglected in the symbol. The deliberate lessons taught by the pictures fulfil the function of a sermon or are illustrative of historical events or doctrinal truths, but as well as the appeal to the intellect there is the appeal to the feeling which is partly subconscious. This must not be ignored. The influence on feeling and on the unconscious united with the shadowing of some religious idea makes a symbol significant for worship.

II. The other type of symbol is psychic. This symbol expresses the inner mood of worship. Now public worship calls all sorts and conditions of men to the altar of the Unseen. Such is the variety that it is almost impossible to get one intellectual expression for the varied experiences. The forms that are suitable for one level of culture are not adapted to another. There are differences of youth and of age, divergence between the varied temperaments of men and distinction between their abilities. Yet there is an essential unity in Christian experience which must find its way into the service. It is a fatal error to put into the Divine service as a concession to the ignorant what is helpful to them and is not needed by the more learned. Such a procedure is a discrimination between the creatures before their Creator, and sins against the supreme necessity of worship which is the sense of humility.

Now I claim two functions for the psychic symbol, be it object, action, or gesture. (1) The first is that the symbol steps past the distinctions between men. It appeals to the natural instincts of the untrained mind as it does to the highest culture. Like great poetry it can have a universal appeal. The Lord's Supper is the chiefest example of this. Men are divided when they begin explaining what it means, but within the atmosphere of the celebration there is a unity which overcomes mortal differences. Why may not this unitive symbolism be used in other services than that of the Eucharist? Would it not be for the growth of humility to have something in our service that reduced all to one level? Can a Church be really conscious of its world mission to all souls that adapts the whole service to one type of mind? Symbolism is the uniting feature. Why do we not make fuller use of it?

Our fellow-Christians of the Eastern and Roman Churches have made much of the symbolism associated with the Virgin Mary, the mother of our Lord. The Divine Mother who comforts has been a potent symbol in the history of devotion and it still has a strong attractive power. "I need a mother," were words Carlyle as an old man is reputed to have uttered. Now I suppose we all share the feeling that the mediæval development of Mary veneration runs the risk, if it does not actually fall into the error, of making the maid and mother of Jesus into the pagan queen of heaven, and of losing the historical thought of her who was most blessed of women in the trappings of ancient and discredited deity. Yet the mother thought has a great appeal to the instincts of the human heart and carries with it an ennobling comfort. Can we not use something of this symbolism? The Church has been called by many great teachers the mother of the believer; and did not Calvin of Reformed orthodoxy declare that he cannot have God for his Father who has not the Church for his mother. Now if we regard the Church not as a visible institution whose policy of timidity is only too apparent, nor even as a company of very imperfect Christians who seek to worship God and follow the Lord Christ, but as the abode of God's Holy Spirit that enlightens, comforts, and strengthens our souls, then may we not, recalling God's gift of light and life to the Church, call her our mother in God. And was not our ever blessed Lord born from that ancient church of God's fostering in Israel? Can we not see in the Church the instrument of God's salvation, and may we not symbolise in our worship of God, the Giver of all, His gift to men—the Church, the mother of all souls? So feeble is our vocabulary of devotional thought that as William Watson has said, "We limit the Supreme with sex." Could we not bring into our worship that tender and maternal note that is so lacking in Protestantism, and boldly yet reverently acknowledge before God that we are not independent spiritual units but children of His Church, our mother ? Is not the Virgin Mary, the mother of our Lord, the fitting symbol of that Church of the Spirit from which we, the followers of the Lord, are born ?

(2) The second function of this psychic symbol is to maintain the liberty of the individual worshipper. He is permitted to bring into the service his own particular vision of truth, his own experience of goodness, his own yearning for peace and purity. He worships in fellowship with others, but he worships also in the freedom of his own nature when he worships by means of the psychic symbol. I would urge that symbolic action has a place in expressing the soul's ascent to God. We must all climb alone the staircase of our own experience. We do so together in corporate worship, but we need to be let alone to do so. Here the use of the symbolic is of great worth. Our services suffer from too much expounding and talking which sometimes meddles with the soul's lone communion. This is our unfortunate legacy from the Reformers who had a great gift of exposition but lacked appreciation of worship as an art. In the offering of the prayer of seeking or the prayer of contrition or of thanksgiving or of intercession, we obtain unity with others through silence which also gives us this freedom to pursue our own appointed way, but in addition to silence there is the need of something that is shared by all and yet leaves the soul with its own approach to God. I would plead for greater boldness in our use of symbols so as to provide for all needs and so as to make the Church what God has called her to be, the home of all souls. There is the symbol of the candle burning before the altar ; is not the flame a symbol of the inner aspiration of the soul ? Here in the house of God burns the flame which signifies our deepest life. Think of the symbolic use that could be made of the door and the steps of a church, the attitudes of standing, walking, and kneeling, the table, the fair linen cloth, the chalice and the paten.[1]

I would not pass by the objection which may be launched against the whole attitude that I desiderate. There is in some minds a definite dislike of all that is ceremonial, and in the interests of

[1] Cf. *Sacred Signs*, Guardini.

simplicity symbolism of all kinds is condemned. Let us recall, however, that ceremonial is in its essence neither elaborate nor gorgeous, but is " reduced to its simplest elements just the tendency to confine the expression of a specific human activity to one artificial form prescribed by convention ; the antithesis to it is not simplicity or baldness but free spontaneity, permission granted to the activity of the moment to find its expression for itself unhampered by precedent, convention, or custom." [1] Now part of the price we have to pay for public worship is simply this limitation of spontaneity. This is the discipline imposed upon the soul when we worship as the family of God. Common worship is only possible when we use artificial forms—that is, forms chosen by man for their suitability for this purpose. I recognise the revolt against order that exists in many minds who evidently do not feel the need for or the value of a rigorous restraint upon their crowding impulses and disorderly intuitions. One of the reasons I put forward as a plea for the use of symbolism is just to meet this difficulty and to give an occasion for spontaneous thought within the embrace of an ordered worship. This tendency to revolt from the ordered or ceremonial is characteristic both of Protestant individualism and of mystical contemplation.

(1) To meet the objection brought by a rigid Protestant outlook we have to make our symbolism capable of a rational interpretation. The symbolism must therefore be intelligible, " an unintelligible obscure religious art is about as absurd as a house without a staircase or a cathedral without a porch." [2] The individual worshipper must not feel that his personality is swamped in vague emotion, and his freedom crushed and limited by the unintelligible. He must find that through union with others in worship he achieves an increased sense of personality and a new feeling of liberty from self-constraint. This means that, as we saw earlier, the symbol must evoke both a conscious and an unconscious response simultaneously. The symbol must be capable of being rationalised and at the same time it must touch the hidden forces in man's nature. Of course the attitude of sheer individualism can never be satisfied, for it is a

[1] A. E. Taylor, *op. cit.* p. 247.

[2] Maritain, *Art and Scholasticism*, p. 144.

pure abstraction. We must be prepared in public worship to forego the safe harbour of self in order to launch upon the limitless ocean. As a rule the use of ceremonial and of accepted symbols in worship is repudiated by those who wish to remain within the safe convention of their own outlook. They do not care to risk the possibilities that lie beyond. Now it is to my mind the plainest spiritual axiom for worship that if we are to gain the sense of utter humility we must escape from the reserves and restraints of our individual attitude. By its mystery the symbol helps us to reach forth to what is beyond and by its meaning it enlightens the mind.

(2) The objection of the mystical temperament springs from the qualities of sheer mysticism which ever tends to nourish the soul in isolation, to deny the worth of external things, and to value slightly the historical or movement in time. Now it is here in symbolism that the errors and perils of one-sided mysticism are checked. There is a common worship, there is the reality of the external, there is a symbol with a historic significance. It is through a symbolic ceremonial that this profound need of man's nature can be used in Christian worship. But in order to bring the mystical temper into the public worship of the Church it is necessary to have symbols that are congruous to the spirit of mysticism. Historically, mysticism has made use of three symbolic figures which correspond to three temperaments :[1]

(*a*) The first symbolic figure that mysticism uses is the search of the soul. There is the mystical quest for that distant peace ; the pilgrim soul of man is ascending to God. Dissatisfied with the world of sense the pilgrim seeks his home. Dante's *Divine Comedy*, as Bunyan's *Pilgrim's Progress*, is the story of the mystical way. The soul seeks God because He is already within the soul. This may be represented as man's ascent in his search, or it may be the quest of love for the human soul which in modern times Francis Thompson has repeated in the mediæval thought of the *Hound of Heaven*. " Earth," says Eckhart,[2] " cannot escape the sky ; let it flee up or down, the sky flows into it and makes it fruitful whether it will or no. So God does to man. He who will escape Him only

[1] Cf. Underhill, *Mysticism*, p. 126 f.

[2] *Pred.* lxxxviii., quoted Underhill, *op. cit.* p. 136.

runs to His bosom, for all corners are open to Him." The search of man and his ascent, the search of God and His inevitableness, are symbolic thoughts that can be brought into worship. This analogy of man seeking his home does not belong to the surface of the human mind, but is an instinct embedded in the racial heritage from far-off days as well as a deliberate and conscious choice. We have seen how the Sursum corda is the beginning of this mystical ascent in the liturgy and in our service, but something more than words is needed. Some action is required that symbolises the lifting up of our hearts as man sets forth to his inevitable goal which is God. I could wish that the mystical motif was made plain in our service, for it seems an almost universal mood in man, and also I would fain see the Divine seeking represented in ceremonial. I know that in the deeps of the Eucharist all this and more is shadowed, but in the Divine Service of the Lord's Day morning I feel that the spiritual imagination of a new generation, unhampered by the weight of a negative tradition, will discern and discover a fitting presentation in form and colour of this great experience. Perhaps this may only be achieved by the penetrative insight of those who are alive to the spirit of art in these days and therefore are able to use it.

(*b*) There is the mystic marriage of the soul with God—the intimate and personal albeit solitary experience of Divine Communion. This craving for union is stamped upon the face of all mysticism, and the analogy of marriage supplies the language of this Divine embrace. Here also we are dealing with a craving that is deep as life itself and whose roots encircle the basic human needs. True it is that the New Testament emphasises not the marriage of the soul with Christ but the Divine Bridegroom whose bride is the Church. This thought belongs to the sphere of worship. The Christ Who is the Head and Husband of His folk is present. Here too I see the place for symbolic representation, for words are but clumsy things. Nothing sentimental or mawkish is in this idea, for it is the Church's absorption in her Lord. Public worship if it would appeal to the mystical soul must not set aside this profound experience in which the individual loses himself in a Divine Union through a corporate communion with others to find himself in Christ arrayed in new experience and accoutred for fresh responsibility. I do not see how this experience can be potent in public worship except through the symbolism connected with the act of adoration. Here too I feel that the application of this symbolism must be left to a new generation freed from the pruderies of the nineteenth century and cleansed from the indecencies of sentimentality.

(*c*) There is the third mystic impulse—the longing for inner perfection and purity. This is the birth of that higher spirit which alone can reach the "far country of the soul." There are the changes of the soul as it grows towards God. The root mystical idea begins with the sense of the unreality of all things even of life itself. Then by the birth of the Divine there takes place a spiritual alchemy—the transformation of life. Public worship is no stranger to this mood that only the pure in heart can see God, that God's gift is only to those who are called. But could we not more emphasise this motif. Then we would express the great and general truth that only by the transformation of man's natural life into a spiritual existence can he rise to God, and also the particular and relevant truth that only by the soul's thoughts and desires being changed from the passing and thronging concerns of to-day into thoughts and desires that reach towards the eternal, can worship be a real thing. The time and occasion for this recollection of what worship means are at the beginning. Could there not be something that would impress upon all worshippers that they are in the court of the Great King? Nothing can be received if there be not an inner transformation. The Roman Hours begin by the silent repetition of the Apostle's Creed and the Lord's Prayer. This is an attempt to realise the presence of God by transforming our thoughts and desires and lifting them to the level of Christ's prayer. The use of holy water at the entrance to the Church serves the same purpose for devout souls. Could there not be a corporate preparation for worship? Perhaps the discipline of silence might suffice to give entrance into the soul of this higher life. Yet I cannot but think there is here an opportunity of capturing for the service of the sanctuary a powerful impulse, and that through a symbolic act like the uplifting of the cross the Church, which is the bride of the

Lord, might prepare to meet her Lord. Sad certainly would it be if the Church could not provide for those who have been given this mystical temper. I am persuaded that this temperament has no small sway in the lives of men to-day within and without the Church and is implicit in all men.

If worship be an art we must remind ourselves what kind of art it is in order to distinguish between those symbolic forms which are appropriate and those which are not. Worship as an art is the expression of what is universal and common in man and therefore it must exclude what belongs only to special natures. It must not contain for public worship what is precious or limited, and the symbolism employed must not exclude any save those who do not worship. Divine Service is in this sense a mystery. It is a meaningless thing to those who do not know and desire the divine communion, but to those who possess the inner life of faith it is an open secret.

This art of worship, however, is not only the utterance of the universal cravings of man's spirit, it is also the means chosen by God through His providence in history for giving to His creatures and children the experience of His own life and power. With this thought in our mind we turn to the " material " which the art of worship uses. In Divine Service words are spoken or sung, actions are performed, there are visible objects, there is the influence of space as mediated through the form of the building. Worship contains elements that are rational and knowable, and elements that are non-rational and beyond the range of knowledge. The art of worship consists not simply in arranging the order of what is intelligible but also in relating in due proportion the appeal to the intellectual and conscious with the appeal to the instinctive and subconscious.

I. Let us take, in the first place, the use made in worship of the sense of hearing. Public Worship in order to be intelligible involves the use of words. Christian worship in its beginning employed the language of the people, and the sixteenth-century reformers made use of the vernacular so that the words of devotion might be " understanded by the people." The most essential use of language is to convey meaning, and the appeal to the ear in this respect is a fundamental thing. The symbolic aspect of the word is noticeable in the youth of language when the word or name carries with it a dreadful and awe-inspiring power. Something of this early atmosphere clings to the language of devotion, for words have not only meanings but they carry with them an emotional tone. For this reason we find a tendency to use a special language in worship. Even when a liturgical language is not used we observe the influence of this tendency. Sir Walter Scott has pointed out how in moments of high passion the Scot " takes to his English," and does not use the familiar dialect of every day. We too in our Scots service have adopted a form of speech that is largely confined to worship—a language shot through with scriptural phrases and Biblical associations. In public worship it seems well to use a form of language that by its cadence and rhythm makes the offering of prayer different from the casual expression of everyday wishes. In the sermon alone I hold there is place for a greater freedom of expression, for in the sermon we are seeking to make the word of truth incarnate in the ways and customs of this present age. The Church of Rome achieves through her use of a liturgical language the effect of distinguishing between the atmosphere of worship and the atmosphere of the market-place, but by using a language that is unknown to the people she pays too high a price for this result. Yet the sense of mystery must be given expression in worship and, as we saw, the unfamiliar and unusual sound of words assists in this purpose. I think, therefore, there is something to be said for following the practice of the early Church in expressing certain great feelings and experiences in another tongue. The early Greek-speaking believers appear to have used such phrases as Abba and Maranatha. Could we not follow their example ? The old phrase, Kyrie Eleison, is exceedingly beautiful and it conveys in repetition the suggestion of its meaning better than any translation. I also hold that the use of Maranatha would by its very strangeness suggest better to us than anything else the mysterious fact it announces.

We also observed that a liturgical language had value in ministering to the sense of the Church's unity and in emphasising the bond which exists between all followers of the faith. I would not lightly set aside the great service rendered by the employment of one chosen tongue, for in a world torn by national rivalries and beset by racial divisions there is nothing more important than the unity of the followers of the Crucified. The influence of the cultus is very great in creating a sense of spiritual kinship. But here again the price that is paid for this result is too great. However, I do feel that we might try to suggest the unity of all believers by rendering one act of worship throughout the world in one language. If, for example, the prayer of our Lord were offered in a tongue common to Christendom some hint would be given of our spiritual oneness.

According to St. Paul in the church at Corinth there was speaking with tongues. The apostle points out that these unknown sounds required to be interpreted so that the hearers might understand them. Probably we have in this phenomenon of inspired speech unfamiliar sounds spoken in a rhythmic cadence. The rhythmic character of words spoken in spiritual ecstasy belongs to mystical experience.[1] The situation in the Corinthian Church would approximate to the psychological state of the worshipper at Low Mass who says his devotions in unison with the muttered prayers of the priest. The inaudibility of the words is the accompaniment of devotion. The worshipper knows what the prayers are about, but hears only the rise and fall of the cadence. While Western and Eastern practice may not claim our imitation there is not a little to be urged in support of the practice of saying certain prayers in secret. The worshipper knows the general petition that is being offered by the representative of the Church, and he follows it and fills in the general phrases by his own particular devotions.

It is, however, predominantly in the Reformed worship that we find the greatest use made of the auditory appeal in the use of the spoken word. Congregational music also is the art which has greatly flourished in this circle just as the representational art of painting and sculpture has been prominent within the Roman obedience, and architecture and non-representational art most significant in the Eastern Church. The effect of a tune upon the mood of a worshipper is very marked, and the influence of music —the most disembodied of the arts—has been very real from the days of Luther and Bourgeois. We must reckon with this in worship and make use of its possibilities. Apparently the most effective

[1] Cf. Von Hügel, *The Mystical Element in Religion*, vol. i. p. 189.

praise is when the tune is known and yet not too frequently used. Perhaps one reason why our Christmas hymns and Easter hymns and those singings used only at Holy Communion are so effective is that they are at once known and yet not made commonplace through excessive repetition.

II. We now turn to the appeal to the eye. In worship some things are visible and I have argued in the earlier part of this chapter that we might well make greater use of the potential strength of this appeal. We recognise how in dress, in gesture, in images, and in pictorial representation the Church of Rome has employed this method. Undoubtedly the plastic arts have a real relation to worship, but we must bear in mind what worship is. I am not greatly afraid of a superstitious idolatry, but I tremble at the misplaced zeal of those who are seeking to make a service beautiful. A service must aim at being adequate for the offering of man's devotion and the reception of God's grace. If it be adequate it will be beautiful, but to aim at beautifying a service results not in significant beauty but in a heterogeneous collection of irrelevant things.

One of the greatest living art critics, Mr. Bernard Berenson,[1] has observed " it is probable that the Christian spirit cannot easily find embodiment in the visual arts." We have only to look at many pictures and forms in the Roman Church and much of the pictorial illustration used in our Sunday Schools to feel the truth of this remark. Unfortunately the harm that can be done by the maudlin sentimentality that is rife in so many representations of our Lord is not recognised. It is not enough to have a great subject—it must be treated greatly. This is one of the reasons why I advocated the use of non-representational art. However, we need not only in our worship the embodiment of the essential Christian spirit, the spirit of love, we need also to be reminded of the majesty and wonder of the Being whose essential nature is love. Here pictorial art can assist. By means of non-representational art the wonder and mystery of God, the vital life of the Divine may be presented. Bishop Gore [2] refers in his Gifford Lectures " to the old Christian

[1] *Northern Italian Painters of the Renaissance*, p. 30.
[2] *The Philosophy of the God Life*, p. 237.

hymn for the ninth hour," which begins with the invocation of God as " the persistent energy of things " (Deus rerum tenax vigor). This abundance of the Divine life, this mysterious vitality of the Creator, can be presented to us through abstract form or can be represented through the manifold wonders of His creation. So the figure of Christ can be symbolised as a hieratic Being or the perfect human, but not easily represented by the realism of history. The description of the historical Jesus is for words. We have also seen how the cross can be a symbol, and it is noteworthy to trace the development of this symbol. The cross becomes the crucifix, which at first is the representation of Christ the Victor, reigning from the tree. Then in obedience to the Western emphasis on sacrifice we have the delineation of Jesus as the Man of Sorrows in the dire grip of mortal agony. This is the victim, not the King. Save in Passion Week and on Good Friday when we specially recall the Crucifixion as a historical event, Christian thought should dwell on the victory of the Lord.

The use of pictures, frescoes, and stained-glass windows in a church has an influence on worship in two ways. Through setting before us some scene or form, or by means of an arrangement of decoration they make an impression on our feelings and bring a message to our minds. Their first function is to convey an atmosphere and to mediate spiritual truth. There is also another purpose which they fulfil. These representations stand before us still, patient, offering to be of service to the soul. Like the ladder of the soul's ascent they wait in aloof detachment until we make use of them. They are instruments which the soul can use. As well as this double function all visual appeal expresses a twofold truth. Every visible object that enters into worship has form which has a twin relation to the soul. Before every form the soul says, " I am different. This is not me. I am myself—a child of God." And yet before every significant form the soul also says, " I am like that. That answers to an inner chord of my being." [1] In accordance with this double function and this twin truth we must select the forms and the figures which we are to use in public service.

Colour makes its own special appeal. It may be used in two

[1] Cf. Guardini, *Sacred Signs*, p. 31.

ways: (1) The first is for the purpose of creating certain sensations which are suitable to the worshipful mood. Colour may be so arranged that it suggests in one part of the church the mystery of God's presence and in another part of the church it can minister to the sense of human fellowship. This is the æsthetic use of colour in worship and the worshipper is largely unconscious of its influence. The glory of colour suitably adorns the sanctuary to which the eye of adoration is directed, but is misplaced in the upholstery of the pew. This effect does not necessitate a cathedral. I have seen a church in Scotland where the worshippers sit on bare wooden benches and their eyes behold the flame and glory of colour ministering like the angels of adoration to God's Presence.

(2) There is also the deliberate use of colour as symbolic. The history of ecclesiastical colours is somewhat complicated. They are not found in the early Church. "Various sequences of colour have grown up in course of time to be in use in the Christian Church."[1] The old symbolic colours of pagan Rome, white as a signal of joy, a dark colour denoting mourning, and purple or gold expressive of dignity passed into Church use,[2] and apparently the colour sequence was developed a little differently in the Gallican and Roman sphere. It would seem that purple and white were specially used in the Celtic Church, and red and white are prominent in the Sarum Rite.[3] After not a little variety in use according to local preference a uniformity was reached whereby white is the symbol of joy and purity, red the symbol of love and sacrifice, green the symbol of hope, violet of penitence, and black of mourning. Surely if we are to give a place to God's great servant colour in our worship, we ought to adopt a scheme of colour that announces to the eye the note of that day's worship. Certainly black is singularly inappropriate for the joyous service of the Christian hope and redemption, and is not in congruity with the temper of the early days. Our Presbyterian service lacks colour. Would it not be better that the preacher of God's Gospel announced through colour the season of the Christian Year and one of the

[1] Warren, *Liturgy of Ante-Nicene Church*, p. 221.
[2] Cf. Atchley, *Essays on Ceremonial*, p. 90 f.
[3] Warren, *Liturgy and Ritual of the Celtic Church*, p. 125.

great facts of redemption rather than his own academic attainments ?

III. There is the influence of space upon worship. In the dome of the East there is the upward movement of the soul expressed. The enclosed space with its height gives rise to an æsthetic mood which is psychologically linked to religious aspiration. So in the long nave of the Western church use is made of distance in space. By the vista and through the rails before the altar there is suggested to the soul the mystery of what is within the sanctuary which we are called to enter in spirit. This is the ministry of the senses to worship. That the form of a building and the use made of it can influence the cultus and even affect the doctrinal interpretation of worship we see from the different development in the Church of the East and of the West. The main tendency of Eastern architecture is upward, for behind a screen the wonder is wrought, and so the eye and the mind do not penetrate but soar ; the tendency of the Roman form is an appeal to enter into the innermost where the miracle of Christ's presence is made manifest ; our Reformed type of church has tended to be the place in which the Word could be heard. The last therefore ought to symbolise the outgoing of God's spirit to man, but I fear this is but imperfectly achieved. There is another type of building, bright with light and the clearness of day, that has become associated with the modern development of Christian Science and of New Thought. We must not wholly ignore the message of such a building which is so different from the dim twilight and veiled silence of the old historic churches. Its message is the actual connection between worship and this present-day world.

What then is the type of building that ministers best to the sense of worship ? In order to answer that question we have to ask for what purpose a church building exists. A church building is the House of Prayer in which the soul's offering is made. It is sacred through great associations. Therefore an atmosphere of devotion should rest like a cloud of mystery upon the place where the soul meets God. A church is also the place where the Word of God is received. Therefore it is fitting that it should be adapted for that purpose so that men can hear in reverence and stillness the message of life. A church is also the meeting-place of God's family in Christ, and therefore there should be freedom from artificial restraint and friendliness should be a feature of the building. Finally, a church is the place in which the Blessed Sacrament is celebrated and therefore it should be hallowed as a holy place, for though God be everywhere He has revealed to us within these walls a sacred mystery. Can all these purposes be fulfilled by one building? I trow not, unless we dig deeper.

There are two attitudes to the church as a building that cripple the wings of worship. The first is the casual attitude which treats the church like a hall erected for a Sunday purpose. This attitude permits all kinds of meetings to be held in the church. It lays itself open to the bitter comment of a convert to the Roman obedience who is reported to have said, "that it was only in the north of Europe that men built a hall and hired a sophist and called it a church." Yet there is sometimes a need to use the church building for other purposes than those of worship—purposes that minister to the fellowship of the church. To adopt this casual attitude, however, sins against the innate reverences of the human heart and makes common that which is sacred through the associations of prayer. The second is the timid attitude that treats with conventional decorum the place of worship but is deaf to the sense of the Church's fellowship and blind to the fact that the early Church's meeting-places radiated friendship. This is the attitude of those who are not impressed with the joyous mystery of the Incarnation unfolded in the Eucharist, nor with the triumphant victory acclaimed in the celebration of Christ's sacrifice. This is the decorous dignity that denotes deadness of soul. To this kind of person I would like to quote the words of Dr. Percy Dearmer, "I might link this important subject on to our theme again by pleading for a revival of the Agape in a genuine modern form as a real friendly tea-party to be held in Church." This is perhaps a somewhat one-sided statement, but at least it shows a living attitude.

The solution to my mind lies along the line of separating different parts of the church and treating them as separate. There is the place where stands the Holy Table which must be treated as the place of God's Presence, and of the soul's offering. An atmosphere of mystery should hang over this. The place of the Holy Table and of prayer must be used for no other purpose. It is not fitting that the bright light of day be here, for in this place we symbolise the God of mystery Whose Presence man can experience. The pulpit or place of preaching and the lectern from which the Word is read should be in light, for here is the revelation of God. The place where the worshippers sit or kneel or stand can fittingly be in the light, for the significant thing is what the eye rests upon. Even the simplest building can be so treated that something of dim distance is there which suggests mystery, and something of the rising roof which suggests aspiration, and something of the light of revelation which surrounds the Bible and the pulpit. Then the Holy Table would be shaded from the light of this world, gleaming only with its own light. This triple division of the church would be in accordance with the practice of the East. If we were not so yoked to imitation we could find that a treatment of line and perspective and colour could attain these objects even in a bare place of worship. Indeed, one of the things that tends to interfere with worship in many of our churches is not their bareness which can be helpful, but the look of ease and comfort suggestive of a drawing-room which is scarcely conducive to the spirit of humbleness. By means of this division a church building could fulfil the various purposes for which it exists. Influences emanate from a building's form, design, and decoration, and these may be invoked in the service of worship.

I have sought to suggest and to illustrate that worship as an act of the whole personality has a side which touches art. Worship ought to be beautiful if we remember that beauty is not prettiness, nor the smooth satisfaction of the contented mind. Beauty is what satisfies a restless craving, not by reducing the beautiful to the measure of our natures and making the beautiful the desirable, but by lifting us outwith our smug satisfactions to the peace of the Infinite. " It seems probable," says a well-known art critic, " that we might reduce all forms of beauty, both natural and artistic, to series of relations expressive of the infinite." [1] Worship as our

[1] Vernon Blake, *Relation in Art*, p. 78.

relation to the Infinite ought therefore to have in our expression of this relation beauty which is expressive of the Infinite. In order that worship through ceremonial, symbolism, and ritual may possess beauty it must have a rhythm, a form, and a proportion.[1]

(1) The rhythm consists of the interplay between what is static and what is dynamic. (*a*) A static quality has to be expressed alike in the transcendent symbol and the psychic symbol. The Lord God, high and lifted up, has to be symbolised by something static, so also the God Who is the Source of all being, and Whose blessedness is beyond the reach of our little natures. The atmosphere of stillness, the quiet of silence, the immobility of stone, the repetition of the same words, the architectural line and form which clothe the idea of God's changelessness and the thought of God as the Author of immutable law, the light and shadow which symbolise God as the Eternal refuge—these one and all emphasise the static quality in the transcendent symbol. There is the same quality found in the psychic symbol. Silence, stillness, immobility, shaded light, suggest and interpret the mood of the soul wherein there is rest in God and peace beneath the everlasting wings. The static quality of God's eternity and of man's experience of peace requires to find expression in architectural form, visible shape, ceremonial, and ritual.

(*b*) The dynamic element also must find its utterance. God Who draws near, the Spirit that comes to man, the Divine Grace that reaches forth, this active quality must be set forth in ceremonial and ritual, through the visual and auditive senses and spatial perception. The idea of God Who hears and answers prayer, the thought of the Incarnation that renders the Divine near and present, the movement of the Divine Spirit through history are thoughts that require dynamic expression. This Divine Energy and Grace may be reflected in the Scripture lessons, the words of praise, and the sermon. The image of God's coming must be revealed in the rite of worship. The bread of the Eucharist is consecrated and then comes to the worshipper. The movement of the celebrant may signify this idea, or a change of posture in the worshippers may represent the Divine approach. This is the

[1] Cf. Will, *Le Culte*, vol. ii. p. 158 f.

dynamic in the transcendent symbol. There is also the same element in the psychic symbol which represents man's approach. The worshippers need to feel that they are not remaining still but moving toward God. Movement in procession or alteration of the worshippers' attitude may be utilised for this purpose. I have suggested already that the impulse of ascent should be conveyed by word and gesture, sign and image. Upon the equivalence and balance of the static and the dynamic in worship the beauty of the service very largely depends. These are ultimate relations of God to the soul and of the soul to God, and the clearness with which they are shown in use of ceremonial and in the ordering of the ritual constitutes the fitness of the rite.

(2) Worship must have form. This is the relation between unity and variety. (*a*) The sense of tradition, the fact that we are walking in the footsteps of those who have gone before, helps to constitute the feeling of unity. The service is no thing of threads and patches haphazard and accidental, but one central note echoes through it—the worship of God through Christ. This unity is no manufactured thing. It is given us alike through tradition and by the testimony of the Spirit. The unity is coloured by the circumstances of the time and by the conditions in which the service is held. The unity may sound through the hope of Advent or the harmony of Pentecost, through the morning's freshness or the dying of the day. It is a unity coloured by these dominant notes, but it is always one thing—the worship of God through Christ.

(*b*) The variety in the service consists in the use of all possible ways of expression and in the recognition of varied moods. The song of praise, prayer in all its forms, the use of silence, the ministry of the Word, the appeal to visual sensibility, the influence of the building—these are the various means through which the one tone of worship becomes a harmony. The changing moods of the Christian Year also contribute wealth to the great theme of worship. As the form of the service is constituted by the relation of unity and variety, its richness consists in the unity of worship being expressed through the greatest variety.

(3) Worship must have proportion of spiritual content. By

this I mean we must relate authority and freedom in public worship. The authority of the Divine Word that has been spoken, the authority of tradition, which is man's response in the past to the Divine authority, must be in due proportion to the freedom of God's Spirit here and now within his soul, and to the liberty of man's response in the present situation of his own life to God's revelation. There must be a poise of values between the restraint of worshipping God together in the ways of the past and the spontaneity of bearing testimony within our own soul. This poise may show itself somewhat externally in the proportion between liturgical prayer and prayer born of the immediate act of worship, or between the reading of Holy Scripture and the word of preaching. There is a relation between the authority of God that imposes restraint and the freedom of the Divine Spirit that calls for spontaneity, between the authority of the classic tradition in which man has worshipped and the freedom of the immediate mood which envelops the worshipper. To balance rightly restraint and spontaneity, authority and freedom, is to give proportion to a service, and that too is an element in the beauty of worship.

CHAPTER XIV

PRAYER, OR THE OFFERING OF SACRIFICE

As symbolism is the dramatic aspect of worship, so prayer in its widest sense denotes man's offering to the Eternal in which we make the sacrifice of thanksgiving and praise. From this standpoint the Eucharist is the supreme prayer because it is the supreme offering. Prayer is the spiritual sacrifice and through it the instincts that were expressed in the ancient sacrificial system find utterance. Like sacrifice, therefore, prayer in corporate worship is a public thing and cannot be the same in its language or in its atmosphere as private devotion. Yet while we must recognise the distinction between collective prayer and individual prayer, the same ultimate conditions apply to public as to private prayer.

Prayer seems to demand three conditions. The first is the Sense of the Divine Presence. This may range from a general feeling of awe to a vivid and definite experience, but without the immediacy of a Supernatural Presence our prayer is not prayer at all, but at best a preparation for prayer. It is at once apparent that all the prayers of mysticism involve this supramundane reference and experience, but so also do all forms of "ordinary prayer." The second is the experience of Personality in the Eternal. In the prayer of mysticism there is, if not the sense of definite personality, the experience of personality. "Mysticism," says Dr. Edward Caird,[1] "is that attitude of mind in which all other relations are swallowed up in the relation of the soul to God." Within this unitive relation there is the personal bond. This is seen in the stages of mystical experience given by St. Theresa—meditation, the orison of quiet, the sleep of the powers, and ecstasy. While the emphasis in mystical prayer falls on the immanent rather than the transcendent experience of the Deity, the sense of per-

[1] *Evolution of Theology in the Greek Philosophers*, vol. ii. p. 210.

sonality is not wanting.[1] When in some mystic like Eckhart the drift is towards a pantheistic unity which blurs the personal relation, we pass from the realm of prayer altogether into that of intellectual contemplation. This personal aspect is as evident in the region of ordinary prayer. Father Poulain [2] gives four types of ordinary prayer. These are (*a*) the recited or spoken prayer, (*b*) the prayer of meditation moving methodically from point to point, (*c*) the prayer of the affections in which the emotional colour has greater significance than the intellectual content, and finally (*d*) the prayer of simplicity in which there is the sense of resting upon the Divine and the feeling of activity is lessened. In all these prayers the *sine qua non* is the sense of God as present in a personal experience, however vague and inadequate. The third condition has been already touched upon. There is communion. We rise in prayer above the level of an awareness to Presence, even to a personal Presence. Prayer is more than a stunned sense of awe; it is a communion and a converse which may take many forms. It may be request and answer, desire and fulfilment (the spiritual dialogue), or it may be pure seeking (the search), or receiving (illumination), or the sense of harmony and rest (mystical union). These three things, the sense of Presence, the experience of personality, and communion belong to public prayer. The Divine Service must be of such a nature that it expresses these facts, and it also must be framed in such a way that it impresses them upon the mind and feeling of the would-be worshipper.

Prayer is the essence of worship; it is the high art of the soul. Sabatier has called prayer "religion in act that is real religion." Prayer in public worship has to promote and to express this mood. Three functions the prayers of the Church Service have to fulfil:

(1) The first function of public prayer is that it must be educative. It must teach men to pray in the only way they can be taught. When they saw the Master praying, the disciples said, "Lord, teach us to pray." This then is the permanent duty of the Church. The worth of what otherwise would seem formal repetition lies in this, that it is a preparation for the inner communion of prayer.

[1] Cf. Von Hügel, *The Mystical Element in Religion*, vol. ii. p. 325.

[2] *The Graces of Interior Prayer*.

The value of using the great expressions of the Christian tradition, such as words of the Bible, Agnus Dei, and Gloria, consists in this, that these Scriptural words and hallowed phrases laden with spiritual associations tend to create a sense of reverence and to induce the spirit of communion in the assembled worshippers. It is essential that whether we use a liturgy or not there should be a quite definite aim in the prayers used, and a quite distinct progress from stage to stage. To many the main function of public prayer is its power to develop in them the mood of prayer.

(2) The second function of public prayer is to voice a real experience. There is something which can only be expressed in prayer. The mystery and the wonder, the directness and immediacy of God's relation to the lives of men are abstractions when taken out of the prayer attitude, "Thou." There is that in Christian experience which can only be spoken in the second person. What we say to God is always deeper than what we can say about God. Further, there is despite all the disparity of human nature and the difference of religious outlook and experience something that all the followers of the Lord Christ share. This common element necessitates public worship for its utterance.

(3) The third function of public prayer is to stand between the finite and the Infinite and to bring together the past and the future. In Christian prayer the testimony of to-day is united with the tradition of the past and the prophecy of the future. Public prayer is the offering of the lives and wills of men in this present age, but it reaches out to the faith of those who have lived and to the hope of what will be. The communion of the saints and the prayer for the coming of the Kingdom belong to public prayer as the offering of the Church militant. The past out of which it grows, and the future into which it grows, are the two poles on which is poised the prayer of the sanctuary as an act of faith. In the sphere of devotion we find that the traditional element and the element of free individuality are not opposites but are complementary. The one cannot exist without the other. The value of a strong tradition lies in this that the inheritor has the strength of the past as well as his own. He is saved from futile and solitary adventures and delivered from caprice. For

this reason there is the persistent desire for an ordered liturgy. At this point a real diversity of temperament is revealed. " One of the principal differences between men," says Tolstoi, " consists in the different measure in which they are inspired by their own ideas or those of other people." Corporate prayer must meet the needs of both types, and therefore there must be a liturgical element and a free element.

The differences between men and the variety of human nature suggest that there must be different types of prayer. As we have seen, Heiler [1] has made the fundamental distinction between the " mystical " prayer and the " prophetic " prayer. " Mystical prayer has its roots in the yearning of the devout person for union with the Infinite ; prophetic prayer arises from the profound need of the heart and the longing for salvation and grace. . . . Mystical prayer is a pouring out of oneself, an entering and sinking into the Infinite God ; prophetic prayer is the utterance of the profound need that moves the inmost being." [2] Both of these approaches to God belong to the prayers of the Church. Without the first, worship is lacking in the feeling of the Divine Sublimity and the sense of human surrender ; without the second, worship is vague and wanting in ethical definition. Yet apart from this basic difference we can see four types of prayer which correspond to the four great needs of man.[3] Let us glance at these in turn.

(1) The first type of prayer is the " eudæmonistic " prayer, or prayer of desire, which corresponds to the primitive desire for life and safety. This is the cry for help and the uttered wish. This prayer as petition is ever present as an element in worship. Prayer is a desire referred to God. " Hoc licet orare," says St. Thomas Aquinas, " quod licet desiderare." We cannot separate the prayer for material gifts and physical succour from the prayer for spiritual graces and moral redemption. Both alike depend upon the recognition of God's Power and human need. The Hebrew psalter reveals this type of prayer as belonging permanently to human devotion. Public prayer has a double relation to this mood. (*a*) It has to give expression in a general form to the specific and

[1] *Das Gebet*, translated *Prayer*. [2] Heiler, *Prayer*, pp. 283, 284.
[3] Cf. Puglisi, *La Preghiera*, p. 204 f.

particular desires of the individual. These personal desires ought to find satisfaction in public worship wherein they are widened by sympathy and illumined by social contact. (*b*) Public prayer has also to direct the attention of the worshipper to those needs and wants of the soul which are only felt strongly in union with others. Thus public prayer has in the sphere of petition to train the individual worshipper in what he ought to desire. It is through the offering of the Church's petitions that the desires of the individual are elevated and purified.

(2) There is the æsthetic prayer which has its roots in man's desire to express his feeling and to describe or depict his emotions. This type of prayer has a contemplative aspect. It is not the product of the immediate mood and has not the practical aspect of the "eudæmonistic" prayer. "Most of ordinary worship," says Leuba,[1] "is a rudimentary mysticism." This dwelling on mystery, this extolling of God's wonders, belongs to worship. The wonder of the starlit heavens and the glory of the open skies arouse in man a spirit of glad appreciation, and this spirit in all its varied expressions must find a place in the prayers of the Church.

(3) The third type of prayer is the noetic prayer which corresponds to the deep-laid instinct to seek the light of knowledge. This prayer of knowledge is not asking for petitions to be granted, but is seeking to feel and know God. This knowledge is intuitive, like the penetrative insight of the poetic imagination, and possesses the strangeness that belongs to the familiar when a new light is shed upon it. This noetic prayer is of the nature of meditation.

(4) The last type is that aspect of spiritual communion when will meets with will. The acceptance of God's Will and the resolve to fulfil it is the ultimate offering of the self to God. This oblation of self must necessarily be of the very essence of public worship, for without it corporate prayer would lack its truly Christian character. These different types of prayer are of course not contradictory to one another but are supplementary. The public service that is to be not only real but rich must voice them all.

In the devotions of the Church six elements are commonly found: (1) Adoration or the Exaltation of God, (2) Confession,

[1] *Psychology of Religion*, p. 58.

(3) Petition and Supplication, (4) Thanksgiving, (5) Intercession, (6) The Blessing. These elements in prayer vary according to the centre of attention. Prayers of thanksgiving may be offered for what the worshippers have received or for what others have received. Petitions made for ourselves are supplications, but when made for others they are intercessions. Adoration is concerned neither with ourselves nor with others, but is centred wholly upon God. These three centres of interest, though they are logically separate, are in worship never held apart.

(1) "Adoration is the most characteristic and the one which gives the key to the understanding of the rest (of worship), though of course if considered in abstraction from the rest it is a key without the door."[1] I think, however, we must make the distinction to which I have already referred. Adoration may mean two things. It may mean the experience of union with God in which the sense of self disappears. This form of unitive experience is the culmination or apex of worship and not the beginning, as the eucharistic service most clearly shows. Adoration may also mean the Sense of God's Wonder and Greatness as compared with us, His creatures, in which the sense of self intensifies the awe felt before God's greatness. This meaning of adoration belongs to the beginning of the service. The note of praise and wonder sounds first. The Jewish morning service of to-day begins with praise, "Magnificent and praised be the Living God. He is and there is no limit in time unto His Being. He is one and there is no unity like unto His unity. . . . Behold He is the Lord of the Universe, to every creature He teacheth His greatness and His sovereignty." This is the setting forth of God's nature and power in the third person, and then the tone changes. "Blessed art Thou, O Lord our God, King of the Heavens, Who hast sanctified us by Thy commandments." Or take the beginning of Great Vespers in the Byzantine Office.[2] "Blessed be our God always now and ever world without end. Come let us worship and fall before our King and God. Come let us worship and fall before Christ our King and God. Come let us worship and fall before Christ Himself our King and God." This

[1] Streeter, *Concerning Prayer*, p. 244.
[2] *Byzantine Office*, Wainswright, p. 25 f.

invitation is couched in the mood of exulting praise, and this note of praise rings throughout the whole service. It is not quite the same as thanksgiving, for it is the glorifying of God's greatness. The wonderful Roman prefaces and the great glad prayers of the East show how praise exults in God's great works.

(2) Confession and pardon. Contrition is a constant element in public prayer, but while always present it varies in degree according to the kind of service. For example, in the service of joy and gladness in which the festival of the Incarnation or of the Resurrection is kept, confession enters into the service only as a means to an end. The worshipper confesses ere he can offer his offering of thanksgiving, but contrition does not belong to the intention of the service. In a service like that of Good Friday or of preparation for Holy Communion, and in the fasts appointed by the Scots Kirk of former days, there is a deliberate emphasis on human sin and guilt, and as in the Lutheran service the recognition of man's sin is the revelation of God's Grace. The place in such a service of confession is very different, for contrition belongs to the intention of the service. We must further distinguish between the confession of sinfulness and of creatureliness so characteristic of the Calvinistic service and the confession of our individual sins. The former confession really belongs to the extolling of God's greatness, before Whom man is naught. Its ultimate aim is to glorify God's unspeakable Holiness. In natures whose spiritual imagination works almost wholly with the fabric of the moral life God is adored by dwelling on the gulf between the human and the Divine. The latter confession is a spiritual discipline. Confession is not now the abasement of our unworthy and mortal nature, it is the cleansing of the life that has become spotted through contact with the world. The Book of Common Prayer exemplifies this. Confession with absolution precedes thanksgiving so that the soul confessed and pardoned may praise with joy. The confession is a prelude to worship; "that our consciences being cleansed through the blood of sprinkling we may at this time and henceforward acceptably serve Him and worthily magnify His holy name."[1] The place which confession and absolution occupy in all liturgies would be

[1] Morning Prayer, Catholic Apostolic.

unmeaning if we did not discern the thought of purification and spiritual discipline. "He that is washed needeth not save to wash his feet."[1] From the sins that wittingly or unwittingly he has committed since last he had absolution the worshipper needs forgiveness. The spoken words summarise the unspoken catalogue of commissions and omissions rehearsed by the conscience of the worshipper. These things must be acknowledged before with undisturbed soul gratitude can be uttered. The position that confession and absolution take in the sequence of worship varies somewhat. In the Roman Mass we find the resolve to worship, the thought of Who God is, and then the Confiteor. So the Book of Common Prayer invites to worship and then makes the public confession. In the Office of Oblation[2] there is an invocation of adoration and then the confession, and in this we see the mingling of adoration with confession. In the Coptic Rite[3] there is the sequence, adoration, confession with absolution. The fact that sometimes thanksgiving precedes and sometimes follows confession is determined by the nature of the service. In the former case thanksgiving is the prolongation of the note of adoration, and in the latter thanksgiving is the fruit and consequence of confession.

(3) Petition as Supplication. The essence of petitionary prayer is the appeal to the Will of God. "O Almighty and Eternal God, mercifully look down upon our weakness and stretch forth the right hand of Thy Majesty to protect us."[4] The petitionary prayer is the primitive but it is also the abiding prayer, for man ever needs succour in this mortal life. Yet we must not dissociate the petitionary prayer from the prayer of adoration,[5] for to do so makes our petitions an attempt to change the Will of God. By prayer it may be possible to remove that which impedes the Will of God, but it is a sub-Christian idea to think of the Divine Will as changeable. A difficulty arises also about what we may pray for whenever prayer is conceived only as the relation of the Divine Will and the human will. The simple faith that would ask for things material as well as

[1] St. John xiii. 10. [2] Russian Liturgy.
[3] Prayer of the Morning Incense.
[4] Roman Missal, Third Sunday after Epiphany.
[5] Cf. Heiler, *Prayer*.

for spiritual gifts is regarded by the more enlightened understanding as superstition, because it seeks to bend God's Will and God does not interfere with the laws of His physical universe. Hence the idea comes that there is a sphere which lies outside the range of prayer. This error need never have arisen if the separation between the prayer of contemplation and the prayer of petition had not been made. For God is not as man and the sense of His Infinity overshadows all our petitions which are the sincere and earnest wishes of the soul, offered to God, but are not demands nor counsels. When we study the petitions found in the Church's devotions they are by no means only for what are called spiritual blessings. They are petitions to ward off perils, famines, and disasters, to succour from the assaults of the Evil One, from the diseases of the body and the peril of death. The litanies which order and systematise the desires of the human heart are framed in the confident assurance that God's Power reaches to every sphere. Earthly and heavenly gifts come from the same hand and therefore they are alike objects of petition. There is a prayer in the modern liturgy of the Catholic Apostolic Church which well represents the mood of the ancient liturgies. "Look down in Thy compassion upon this and the neighbouring lands, and bless, we beseech Thee, the labours of Thy servants who have tilled and sown our fields. Vouchsafe to us temperate and seasonable weather; cause Thy sun to shine and let Thy rain and dew refresh the ground that the fruits of the earth may be matured, our garners may be filled with corn and our stores replenished with wine and oil and all good fruits, and that the abundance of food both for man and for beast may be supplied to us. So we Thy people and the sheep of Thy pasture will give thanks unto Thy Holy name, waiting for the time when with all Thy saints we shall be gathered into the garner of Thy Kingdom." [1] Such a prayer can be criticised by a certain type of mind because it asks for Divine action in the realm of Nature, and as we saw, if the relation of man to God be only the relation of the human to the Divine Will, such a request appears as presumptuous as it is unnecessary. But if the prayer be taken as laying the human desire alongside the Divine Purpose, as the confident resting of human

[1] Prayer for Seed-Time.

dependence upon God's Graciousness, then a quite different impression is given. The prayer assumes that God's purpose is one of gracious care for all His creatures, and the worshipper desires what he believes to be God's purpose in this natural world. If God's purpose of beneficence and of healing be checked by untoward obstacles beyond man's comprehending, human petitions are still prayer declaring the dependence of the creature upon God's constant care. The idea that the petitions in prayer have to pass the scrutiny of a logical and scientific investigation mistakes the nature of petitionary prayer, which is the utterance of desire. If the desires of the heart cannot be brought into worship, then our prayers will be hollow indeed.

(4) Thanksgiving is a form of praise. In pure praise the attention of the worshipper is concentrated on the Glory of God's nature, while in thanksgiving the form of consciousness is rather the effect upon us of God's Action. Praise dwells more on the Nature of God and thanksgiving on the mercies of God which we have received. Praise is therefore more contemplative than thanksgiving, which is more specific and definite. The distinction between these two elements in prayer cannot be precise, for praise melts into thanksgiving, and thanksgiving soars into praise. The great prayer of thanksgiving is the eucharistic prayer, which recounts the mercy of God as well as extols His Glory. This element in prayer is of course fundamental. But just as in Divine Service we have a general confession of unworthiness and a special confession of sins, so in thanksgiving there is the general thanksgiving for God's mercy and goodness and the special thanksgiving for particular things and happenings. The latter is provided for in the service by an opportunity of recollection in the thanksgiving prayer.

(5) Intercession is simply petition directed to others than ourselves. The range of intercession is very wide. As we have seen, the corporate sense gave rise in the early Church to prayer for groups—the sick, the workers in mines, etc. Prayer is also offered in the liturgies for those present, since before their dismissal the catechumens and the penitents are commended to God's care and grace. Prayer for rulers was offered long ere the governors of the world professed Christianity. The remembrance of the living

is linked to the recollection of the departed. This intercession for those who sleep is the assertion of *communio sanctorum.* Intercessory prayer is an integral part of Christian devotion, for it is the affirmation not only of the Christian brotherhood, but also of mankind's dependence on God.

(6) The Benediction, or the blessing, is the declaration of God's Blessing. It is not a pious ejaculation nor a devout yearning nor a petitionary prayer. It is an act that belongs only to the Church as the instrument of God. Not lightly therefore is it to be spoken, for it is a solemn act of bestowal.

In the history of Christian devotion many forms are found. In the first place we shall glance at free or extempore prayer. This form of prayer is quite a marked feature of the early Church. Perhaps we can see in St. Clement's prayer [1] with its scriptural phraseology and its simplicity and directness an illustration of what such prayers would be. This type of congregational prayer is the legacy of the synagogue to the Christian Church. It is the expression of spontaneous worship and its importance can hardly be over-estimated. This tradition of free prayer is a definite trait in reformed worship. "Congregational prayer is the centre and climax of congregational worship . . . originally the reading of Scripture and the homily had only a subordinate and preparatory value. Not speech about God, but speech to God; not the preaching of the revelation of God, but direct intercourse with God is, strictly speaking, the worship of God." [2] After the fourth century there was the tendency for Christian devotion to become stereotyped, but traces remain in the Eastern and Western Liturgies of free prayer. We must therefore recognise that free prayer is part of the great catholic tradition. Yet if this is to be congregational worship the worshippers must know the aim and movement of the prayer so as to be able to follow it. When Dr. Johnson, as reported by Boswell, makes the remark, "Sir, the Presbyterians have no public worship; they have no form of prayer in which they know they are to join. They go to hear a man pray and are to judge whether they will join with him," he passes the criticism of an unsympathetic hearer; but the remark has value in this, that it points to the peril

[1] Epistle to Corinthians. [2] Heiler, *Prayer*, pp. 306, 307.

of free prayer that is not framed in the movement of a liturgy or shaped to the purpose of common worship.

The liturgical development which fixed the devotions of the Church was not, I believe, anything but good. For one thing, it handed down the great classical expressions of the worshipping spirit, and thereby preserved these fruits of the first age. Think how miserably poor our heritage to-day would be if the iconoclastic spirit that repudiated written forms had existed from the beginning. The great sayings of the spiritual life would only have been handed down in tawdry paraphrases. It was not, I believe, an accidental happening but a real development of the Spirit which has bequeathed to us the forms of prayer extant to-day. Let us turn to these.[1]

(1) There are the longer prayers which are represented by the Euchai of the Eastern Church. These prayers are frequently tautological but at times they breathe an atmosphere of spiritual beauty. The same rambling, meditative prayer is found in the Gallican and Mozarabic Rites, and sometimes also in the devotions of the reformed Churches. Such a form of prayer calls for spiritual imagination, and it has a place in the services of the Church.

(2) There is the litany which is a form of responsorial prayer expressed in brief sentences. In the Divine Liturgy we find the classical example, the Greek Litany with the response, "Lord have mercy." Of the Petitionary Litany the following extract from the litany of Vespers is an example: "Let us complete our evening supplication to the Lord. ℟. Lord have mercy; Protect us, save us, be merciful unto us and preserve us by Thy Grace, O God. ℟. Lord have mercy; Let us beseech the Lord that we finish this evening in holiness, peace and innocence. ℟. Grant this, O Lord; Let us beseech the Lord for the angel of peace, the faithful guide and keeper of our souls and bodies. ℟. Grant this, O Lord." In the noble litany of the Catholic Apostolic Church there is variety in the responses. "Spare us, Good Lord." "Good Lord, deliver us," "We beseech Thee to hear us, Good Lord." The litany may have a penitential character or an intercessory. "Probably the litany is the simplest and most effective means of securing the co-operation

[1] Cf. Neale, *Essays on Liturgiology and Church History*, p. 47 f.

of a congregation in united intercession." [1] The terse directness of the litany prayer, alike in penitence and intercession, makes it an invaluable form of prayer.

(3) The Collect is constructed on a definite plan and consists in its full development of five parts: "(*a*) The Invocation, (*b*) The antecedent reason of the petition, (*c*) The petition itself, (*d*) The benefit which if it be granted we hope to obtain, (*e*) The conclusion." [2] The following Gregorian collect illustrates this scheme: "Almighty God Who seest that we have no power of ourselves to help ourselves, keep us both outwardly in our bodies and inwardly in our souls, that we may be defended from all adversities which may happen to the body, and from all evil thoughts which may assault and hurt the soul, Through Jesus Christ Our Lord." To this strict plan not all collects conform. Sometimes the petition is twofold, and frequently the form is less systematic, as, for example, in the Gelasian Collect, "Stir up, O Lord, Thy power and come and mercifully fulfil that which Thou hast promised to Thy Church unto the end of the world." The Collect is as a rule addressed to the Father, but not a few are addressed to Christ, and a few, especially in the Mozarabic Rite, to the Holy Spirit. The following Mozarabic collect is an example: "O Holy Spirit, the Comforter Who with the Father and the Son abidest One God in Trinity, descend this day into our hearts that while Thou makest intercession for us, we may with full confidence call upon Our Father." The Collect fulfils a specific function in the service. Apart from the fact that in the many collects of the Western Rite we have a valuable treasury of devotion, a collect, be it ancient or modern, summarises and expresses a definite devotional mood, and by its terse yet comprehensive statement gives a stability and a strength to a service. The puritanic objection to collects arose from inability to see their place in the service as the restrained and objective expression of Christian faith.

(4) In the Prefaces or illations which begin with the phrase, "It is very meet and right," and end with the Triumphal hymn, "Holy, holy, holy," there is a noble form of devotion. The eleven prefaces of the Roman Rite are but a tithe of the prefaces once in

[1] Perry, *The Scottish Prayer Book*, p. 73. [2] Neale, *op. cit.* p. 50.

use. These are part of the eucharistic prayer, but so long as celebration of Holy Communion remains infrequent, it seems unfortunate that these great statements of Christian faith are not used at other services. The familiar Roman preface for Christmas will serve as an example, "It is truly meet and just, right, and availing unto salvation that we should at all times and in all places give thanks unto Thee, O holy Lord, Father Almighty, everlasting God, for by the mystery of the Word made flesh the light of Thy Glory hath shone anew upon the eyes of our mind, so that while we acknowledge Him as God seen by men we may be drawn by Him to the love of things unseen."

(5) There are Responsory Prayers which are commonly called the preces. Such responses make use of Scripture. From the worship of the Offices we may learn how the language of Scripture may be made the expression of our praise. For example, in Lauds for Easter Eve in the Mozarabic Breviary we find the following: "Alleluia, I am the First and I am the Last and I was dead. ℟. And behold I am alive again for ever and ever, Alleluia; Thou art worthy, O Lord, to receive the book and to loose the seals thereof, for Thou wast slain and hast redeemed us to God by Thy blood out of every kindred and tongue. ℟. And behold I am alive again for ever and ever, Alleluia! Alleluia. The angel of the Lord descended from Heaven. ℟. And he came and rolled away the stone from the door of the sepulchre." Is there not a place in our modern service for using Scripture narrative as a prayer of praise? By this means could we not anchor our spiritual mood upon the historical revelation?

(6) Bidding Prayers are prayers of intercession. These were the prayers called "the bidding of the bedes" which gathered round the homily in the mediæval service called Prone. The bidding prayer is therefore a call to intercession. One great advantage of such a prayer is that while the mind of the worshipper is directed to the object of intercession the worshipper is free to express his own devotions in silence. Such a method as this unites the freedom of private devotion with corporate worship, and heightens the sense of reality in the intercessions of the Church.

(7) I have left to the last the most important prayer in the

service—the Lord's Prayer. No service of any kind but needs this prayer. "The Lord's Prayer," said Luther, "is the highest, noblest, and best prayer; all other prayers shall be suspected which do not have or contain the content and meaning of this prayer." I have already mentioned that we have no direct evidence of the early use of this prayer in public worship though it is enjoined for private devotion in the *Didaché*, but all the later liturgies recognise its paramount importance. St. Gregory the Great even says that it was the custom of the apostles to consecrate the elements by this prayer alone. The impious neglect of this prayer is one of the sad things in the record of puritanic devotion. This great prayer of our Lord can be used in many ways. In the morning service it should be repeated by all, as is the Scots custom following the practice in Frankfort. This is in line with the Eastern and Gallican and Celtic custom. As a rule in Scotland the Lord's Prayer is prefaced by another prayer, as is also the practice in the Eastern and Western Rites. This position of the prayer is to emphasise its significance as the highest act of devotion. Apart from the morning or eucharistic service, however, there are other services in which this prayer can be used differently. In accord with the custom of the Offices the prayer may be said in silence before the beginning of worship, or it may be used as the last act of worship at the close of the final service on the Lord's Day.

To whom ought the prayer of the Church to be addressed? The answer of course is God. But are all prayers to be addressed to the Father? The general catholic answer would be that prayer is addressed to the Father through the Son in the Holy Spirit. This is the attitude of most of the older collects, and this practice must rest on a tradition in devotion. This is perhaps the logical statement of the devotional appeal, and it is quite possible to construct public worship on these lines. Unquestionably this is Christian prayer, for it is offered to God through Christ Jesus the mediator.

When we turn to the New Testament we see that the strong monotheistic training of the Jew has entered the Church. The usage of St. Paul seems to be that prayer is addressed to God the Father. This may be called the norm of Christian devotional

21

practice. Christ liveth to make intercession for men,[1] but He is not the Hearer or the Answerer of prayer. In the Canons of Hippo [2] it is stated, " When we stand at the altar let the prayer always be directed to the Father." Perhaps to-day it is well to emphasise this aspect of Christian devotion, for there is a peril of making the Christian religion simply a Jesus-cult. The original Western tradition is founded on the authority of the New Testament.

But we also find within the pages of the New Testament that Jesus was invoked. There is the prayer of St. Stephen,[3] and the praise and adoration of the Lamb.[4] It is surely inconceivable that the Gentile converts would not address the Lord Jesus in prayer. " The cult of Christ," says Deissmann, " goes forth into the world of the Mediterranean and soon displays the endeavour to reserve for Christ the words already in use for worship in that world, words that had just been transferred to the deified emperors, or had perhaps been newly invented in emperor worship." It was in the atmosphere of devotion and not in the sphere of theological definition that Jesus was addressed as Lord and God in adoration. The unique thing in Christianity was not any new idea about God, but the belief in the present power of the Risen Lord. Therefore it was inevitable that the strong persuasion of the heart should be uttered in worship. In Gentile Christianity there was not the same sensitive fear of infringing a monotheistic tradition. Pliny reports that the Christians maintained that what they did at their meetings was to sing hymns to Christ. This praise of Christ in hymn is parallel to the prayers offered to Him. Doubtless the practice of praying to Christ was part of private devotion before it entered into the prescribed liturgy of the Church. As is to be expected, it is in the East where the idea of the Logos took firm root, that there is found in the liturgy a more marked emphasis on prayer to the Son. In the Coptic Rite we get phrases such as " Our Lord Jesus Christ, make us worthy to receive Thy Holy Body," " For Thou art our God, and unto Thee with Thy Good Father and the Holy Ghost." In the Orthodox Rite we find " O Son of God, receive me as a partaker of Thy mystical Supper." This Eastern development too has a basis in the early practice of the Church.

[1] Heb. vii. 25. [2] A.D. 393. [3] Acts vii. 60. [4] Rev. v. 9, 12.

Probably it was through the praise of the Church that the custom of invoking Christ in the liturgy entered the West. The introduction of Kyrie Eleison (about fifth century) from the East, and of the Gloria (sixth century) which is a translation of an ancient Greek hymn, and of the Agnus Dei, is evidence of this movement. The Western change of Kyrie into Christe when it is said or sung the second time gives the phrase a Trinitarian significance by making the second petition address the Son. The alteration also in the Gloria (which now definitely invokes the Son) from its original form in the Apostolic Constitution is significant.[1] The later collects, *e.g.* those of Corpus Christi (St. Thomas Aquinas) invoke the Son. In the offertory of All Souls' Day we find: "O Lord Jesus Christ, King of Glory, deliver the souls of all the faithful departed from the pains of hell and the deep pit." The same tendency is revealed in the evangelical hymns of Lutheranism and in the praise of modern days. So too the Holy Spirit is addressed in prayer. In the Mozarabic Rite for Whitsunday the great oblation is addressed to Him,[2] and in the hymns of the Church this practice also is found.

These two traditions in devotion exist to-day. They both have the authority of a tradition which is rooted in the New Testament and in the early Church. It is appropriate that at certain seasons Christ should be invoked, for example, Christmas, Holy Week, and Easter; it is fitting that in the eucharistic service the name of Christ should be on our lips in prayer; it is surely right that in every service there should be an invocation of the Lord Jesus. Yet it remains true that God the Father is the Hearer and Answerer of prayer. He is the God Who pardons our sin, He is our Creator and Redeemer to Whom we offer our adoration and address our petitions.

NOTE.—The ending of a prayer depends on the invocation. The conclusion of the historic collect form addressed to the Father is "through Jesus Christ Our Lord, Thy Son, Who liveth and reigneth with Thee in the unity of the Holy Spirit, One God for ever and ever." When the name of Christ is mentioned in the Collect the ending is "through the same Jesus Christ our Lord"; when the prayer is addressed to Christ the ending is "Who livest and reignest with the Father and the Holy Spirit"; when the Holy Spirit is mentioned the ending has the phrase "in the unity of the same Holy Spirit."

---

[1] Duchesne, 16 *op. cit.* p. 6.

[2] Bright, *Collects*, p. 201.

CHAPTER XV

THE DECLARATION OF THE WORD

In addition to the symbolic and devotional elements in worship there is also the declaratory. The Word of revelation is proclaimed and the Faith is enunciated. The declaratory element in the service, like the other elements mentioned, enters into every act of worship, for every symbolic action and all offering of devotion are based upon faith and are also the expression of faith. Yet in a special way three parts of a service are an explicit statement of faith, and their function is to declare, interpret, and make clear the faith. The Creed, Scripture lessons, and the sermon have this object. Let us look at them in turn.

I. To many minds the use of a creed in worship seems a matter of minor importance. Yet if we dismiss from our minds the debatable question as to whether the historic creeds are an adequate statement of the faith, we must surely admit that there is a real value in the Church affirming her faith as an act of worship. A form of words that links the worship of to-day to the devotion of the past centuries and declares the unity of the Christian experience is a valuable element in the Divine Service. A creed possessing the universal acceptance and authority which belongs to the Lord's Prayer does not exist and never has existed. "It is also a very naive mistake to think that all Christendom ever agreed in recognising one or two or three creeds as final, authoritative, and quasi-inspired documents." [1] Many creeds have been framed but only three have been used for this liturgical purpose—(1) the Apostles' Creed, (2) the so-called Nicene Creed, and (3) the creed which is known by the name of Athanasius.

(1) The liturgical use of a creed was not its original purpose. It is in relation to baptism that we come across the first employment

[1] Fortescue, *The Mass*, p. 286.

of a credal statement. Within the New Testament there are traces of this usage.[1] Baptism in the name of Christ [2] passes into the Trinitarian formula for baptism.[3] When this step was taken it inevitably followed that the interrogations at the sacrament of baptism became fuller. We find in the old Roman symbol a summary of these queries. This symbol did not appear to displace these questions, but probably was a statement of what was taught to those being prepared for baptism. This statement existed therefore for the purpose of instruction. When we compare what seems to have been the old Roman baptismal creed with the *textus receptus* of the Apostles' Creed we observe certain differences which are additions rather than amplifications. For example: (*a*) there is the addition, "he descended into hell." The reason for this is conjectural, but the addition was made before the fifth century. It became established in the West in the baptismal confession though not in the East. I do not mean that the East does not have this thought, but it is rendered in devotion, "we magnify Thee, O Christ, Giver of Life, Who for our sake wentest down into hades and with Thyself didst raise all things," [4] and not formulated into a creed. (*b*) The word "catholic" is introduced as explanatory of the Holy Church. Originally the word simply meant universal, but here its meaning is not so much that the Church is everywhere as that it is for every one and so has universal scope, as in the Ignatian phrase, "wheresoever Jesus Christ is there is the catholic church." In time there emerges the distinction between the catholic church and the heretical sects, and then the phrase comes to denote a particular visible organisation. Luther, one may note, translates the word "Christian," and in the Lutheran branch belief is declared in the Christian Church. (*c*) "The communion of saints" is also an addition which belongs to the fifth century. This article does not belong to Eastern creeds; but later it appears to have come into Gaul. The original meaning could scarcely have been what is a popular interpretation—the fellowship of believers with one another. The Reformers thus take it as a definition of the Church. Nor does it seem satisfactory to take the phrase

[1] 1 Pet. iii. 11; Acts viii. 37.
[2] Acts ii. 38; viii. 16; x. 48; xvii. 5.
[3] St. Matt. xxviii. 19.
[4] Vespers in Holy Pasha.

as a communion in holy things. The article seems to point to a heavenly fellowship hereafter or a present fellowship with the saints departed. (*d*) One also notes that the article, "the resurrection, of the flesh," which we mistranslate the "resurrection of the body," is rendered somewhat differently in the East as the "resurrection of the dead." [1]

Three points therefore we note about this baptismal confession. (*a*) There is a constant change and development. Local churches would have their own formularies. (*b*) The singular "I believe" is used because it is a baptismal creed. (*c*) Its associations are with the instruction for Baptism and not with the Eucharist. This creed becomes associated with the Lord's Prayer and the Decalogue as what it was needful for all to know. It found its way into the ritual of the Reformed Church through its use in the daily services of Prime, Matins, and Compline. Thus as a popular creed it enters the liturgy of the Scots Kirk. The popularity of this creed in the mediæval Church is attested by the fact that it might be said in the vernacular when the Mass or Nicene Creed was recited.[2] The reformed use of this creed was as we saw probably derived from the service of Prime, and this practice has one precedent in the Mozarabic Rite which uses this creed on Palm Sunday in Mass.

(2) The Nicene Creed follows the same general Trinitarian scheme as the earlier creed. We need not deal with its origin as a combination of the original creed of Nicæa and the creed of some local church, perhaps Jerusalem. It was probably used in the East as a baptismal confession in some regions, and this may account for the singular "I believe" being found in many of the Eastern liturgies.[3] However, other [4] rites preserve the original plural "we believe." In the fourth century it was the test of the orthodoxy of the ordained, but from the sixth century onward it became part of the service in the Mass in the West and of the liturgy in the East. It therefore became associated with the eucharistic Celebration.

[1] Russian and Coptic Liturgies.

[2] The Lay Folks' Mass Book. Cf. Bodington, *Books of Devotion*, p. 115.

[3] Liturgies of St. James, St. Mark, St. Chrysostom.

[4] Coptic, Nestorian, Armenian, Syrian Uniat, Abyssinian Jacobite.

(3) Of the Athanasian Creed little need be said. It is not strictly a creed at all, but a song about a creed. Nor has it ever had widespread acceptance. We do not find it in the liturgies of the East. Its harshness is not quite so great as the translation in the Anglican Prayer Book suggests, for the words "qui vult ergo salvis esse, ita de Trinitate sentiat," which are rendered "he therefore that will be saved, must thus think of the Trinity," might equally be translated "he therefore that would be saved; let him thus think of the Trinity." [1] Yet even with all possible softening of its damnatory clauses, it remains alien to the modern mind and antipathetic to the Christian mood of to-day. These two facts, therefore, that we can hardly speak of it as belonging to the worship of the Universal Church and that it sounds crudely vindictive to modern ears, allow us to set it aside as a creed for the liturgical use of this generation.

It is a commonplace to say to-day that a creed is something to be sung, not said. The Te Deum answers this test, and there are other great hymns which sound the same note. Indeed there are those who hold that the declaratory element in worship can be best uttered through the great objective hymns of Christendom. The question to which we have to address ourselves, however, is this. Was the instinct of the Church right in seeking a credal statement additional to its praise in the worship of God? The forms which have survived (the Apostles' and the Nicene Creeds) seem so remote from the modern mind that their use in worship has been questioned. It is not possible for an intelligent worshipper to step into a world of alien thought without difficulty. The suggestion of unreality is fatal to the spirit of worship, and to say a creed which is not our belief detracts from that sincerity of mood which is the salt of worship. But if we regard a creed not as the statement of our theological position but as the witness of the Church, we could perchance find a way whereby we might preserve the tradition of the past not as a cramping fetter but as the testimony to a great experience. "A creed religious or political," said Professor Walter Raleigh, "is the voice of the community rather than the expression of individual character." It is because

[1] Cf. Dowden, *The Workmanship of the Prayer Book*, p. 114.

the communal voice should sound in public worship that there is an argument for the liturgical use of the creed. Dr. Gore is surely right when he says: "I cannot help thinking that we should make the purpose for which the creed is recited in public worship more evident if we were to say it in the form in which the council proclaimed the Nicene Creed, saying not 'I believe' but 'we believe,' which would mean, this we acknowledge to be the Catholic faith to which through all failures of faith we intend to unite ourselves."

Yet such a statement about the nature of a creed does not remove the perplexity. There is a real difficulty about our generation confessing in the language of a far-off generation unless we frankly admit the inadequacy of all creeds. On the other hand, all modern attempts to make a confessional statement by their vagueness of expression and cautious timidity result in what is of little value for subscription and of no value for any liturgical purpose. Such an atmosphere is not the atmosphere of devotion. In worship what we wish to say is that we walk the same great highway of life as did the followers of Christ who live no longer in this life of time. Only by using the speech and the thought of an age other than our own are we freed from cramping hesitations and timid dubieties. Yet we must bear in mind that we are using a creed for another purpose than its original intention. It is not as a complete summary of the faith that we use it in worship; it is not as a test of orthodoxy that it is recited in a service; it is as an assertion of spiritual unity with bygone eras and as the affirmation that our faith is not something we have discovered but is something given by God.

However, in using a creed we must never forget its inadequacy. It is not simply that the words of the Apostles' and Nicene creeds are inadequate. These creeds are inadequate for two inevitable reasons. The first is that of necessity they leave out much that belongs to our past. They themselves were the result of development and this development has been arrested. The Articles, for example, on Christ do not deal sufficiently with the actuality of the Incarnation—with the words and doings of Jesus. These great statements are like unfinished statuary, for the Grace and Guidance of God have been with His Church since the days these were framed. Such additions to these creeds should be made in the worship of the Church, but they are to be made not by altering the Creed but by expressing these further affirmations of faith in the other declaratory elements in worship. In her praise and in the teaching of the sermon the Church is amplifying and expanding the articles of the historic Creed.

The second reason of inadequacy is deeper. There is no language that can declare the " unspeakable gift of God." The attempt to make a creed quite comprehensible and intelligible fails to satisfy our religious instinct. We cannot utter what the Love of God and the Grace of Christ meant to any age not our own except through the expressions of that age. It is simply not true to say that we can express what Christianity meant to the first century or to the fourth in the thoughts of the twentieth. We can say what Christianity means to the twentieth century, and we ought to do so in the language of the twentieth century. But when we seek to " stand under the open Hand of God " and to link ourselves with all God's Love has meant, then we must needs use thoughts and forms which do not belong to our day. The very aloofness of these thoughts, the strangeness of the expressions minister to our sense of the wealth and mystery of God's revelation. A creed ought to make us feel the mystery of God's revelation. It is not enough to say that there is mystery in the Faith. A liturgical creed must make us experience this mystery. The great symbol of Nicæa can be riddled with criticism, but it at least makes us feel the mystery of our Faith.

There is I know the peril of permitting ourselves to be blind to the truth revealed in God's world to-day. Every form of art runs the risk of seeming inaccurate to standards that do not belong to it, and worship is the noblest form of art. What we are seeking is not accuracy but appreciation. When we use a creed in worship, then we ought to realise what we are doing. We are not submitting our minds to the fetters of a dead tradition, but we are emancipating our souls from the limitations of our circumstance and our lot, that we may receive an enhancing of life through the remembrance and contemplation of what God's Grace has meant.

Therefore I would argue that the Nicene Creed has its place in Divine Service if we recognise why it is there and what its purpose is. Thereby the Creed becomes an act of faith and its presence enriches public worship.

II. The second declaratory element in the Divine Service is the lection of Holy Scripture. We have seen that scriptural lessons were taken over by the Church from the synagogue and were an essential part of the Liturgy of the Catechumens. At first the number of lessons and the amount read were not fixed; and when these were determined there was great variety in the number of lessons. The *Apostolic Constitution* [1] has five, and evidence of this extended use is found in Eastern rites [2] and in the Roman Mass.[3] Eventually the number became three. From the place of the lessons in the Liturgy of the Catechumens we see their instructional function. In Scotland the reader's service which was preliminary to the service of preaching consisted of scripture reading and prayer, and had the same object of edification through instruction. We also find the use of a lectionary in the office of the Hours. These readings from Scripture derive from the vigil services of the past. These lessons were taken from Scripture, the writings of the Fathers, and the lives of the saints. Thus the practice of reading canonical lessons is a firmly established tradition in Church Worship.

But what of to-day? The attitude to the Bible has greatly altered since the days of the Reformation. Are lessons to be exclusively confined to the canon of Scripture? In certain churches in America and elsewhere we see a tendency to depart from this strict observance. Precedent for this might be found in the mediæval breviary and in the usage of the early Church before the canon of the New Testament was fixed. Writings doubtless were used in public worship in the early days which have not found a place in the canon. Yet such a modern innovation fails to appreciate that the canon was the result of experience and was the sure affirmation of the Church that within these pages is the message of revelation. We must therefore insist that no writings of any kind can

[1] Chap. viii. [2] Syrian, Coptic, Abyssinian, Nestorian.
[3] Lent and Ember Days.

have the authority and the value of Scripture, and that the message of the Bible must be given a paramount and unique place in our service. The instructional value of other writings can be recognised by means of the sermon, but Scripture stands alone. This is not to deny the worth and the inspired character of other books for we may not limit the revelation of God to men, but the place of Scripture is unique and unrivalled.

While the place of the Bible for edification and instruction remains supreme there is a difficulty caused by our new attitude to Scripture. Not all the Bible is the Word of God, and unlike our forefathers we acknowledge there are passages in the Bible that are not only pre-Christian but sub-Christian. The contention that the whole Bible needs no interpreter has been proved untrue. Certain passages are clearly inappropriate for public worship because they are not in accord with the clearest and fullest revelation. But there are also passages which if they are interpreted are of value, but without an exposition they may give rise to erroneous views of God and His Grace. The old Scots habit of interlarding the Scripture lesson with exposition, while objectionable in practice, was not wholly worthless in its object. There are great passages in the Old Testament and stirring narratives which do not clearly announce their spiritual lessons. The duty therefore of preaching from such lessons is very obvious or at least explaining their meaning somewhere in the service. The interpretation of Scripture is a most urgent need. Some have sought to make clearer the meaning of Holy Writ by the use of modern translations. I acknowledge the worth of these and they have a real supplementary value. Yet since public worship has need of a special and liturgical speech to invoke the deepest associations, it seems a real loss to depart from the accepted and hallowed words. Unquestionably some passages need to be explained at times, but we must beware of disturbing the atmosphere of devotion by the use of language unredeemed from the commonplace and divorced from devotional associations.

III. The Sermon is the third declaratory element in worship. I would dissociate myself wholly from all those who depreciate the place of the sermon in public worship. Undoubtedly the Reformers erred in their liturgical endeavours. We do not, however, correct their mistakes and omissions by ignoring the one thing which was of real worth in their thought. The place of the sermon is very important. It is fruitless to discuss what is the most important element in worship. Probably we would all more or less agree that it is prayer. But the truth is the Divine Service is a living unity. It is bootless to discuss whether the hand or foot is the more important part of the body; both are needed and both belong to the body. So the preaching of the word and the offering of the soul are both integral parts of the public worship. The sermon therefore has an assured place in the complete service; and it also has a primary place in that type of incomplete service whose purpose is edification by instruction.

Preaching has had various characteristics in the history of Church worship in accordance with the different functions it has fulfilled. In the first days preaching must have taken two forms. The missionary preaching was the advocacy of this new faith to those who had to be awakened to their need and won to its power; but the preaching in the little assemblies of the believers would be a less premeditated form of speech. "In the missionary gatherings, the speaking was the decisive factor, for it was through it that the Word of God was brought home to men with power. But in Worship proper the preaching does not seem to have had this all-prominent place." [1] In later times preaching became more formal in its expression and more instructive in its character. It was the medium for the exposition of high doctrine as well as the delineation of the Christian life. That preaching fell into abeyance is an undoubted fact; yet we have not to wait until the age of the Reformers to find preaching exercising a potent influence. The Franciscan and Dominican preachers of mediæval times show how the sermon became a very human and telling instrument in devotion. Through threat of judgment and by word picture, by an appeal to humour and through denunciation of evil practice, by the use of conversational dialogue and the abundant employment of illustration, the sermon linked worship to the lives and circumstances of men. Dr. Owst [2] has pointed out that two types of sacred discourse correspond

[1] Macdonald, *Christian Worship in the Primitive Church*, p. 86.
[2] *Literature and Pulpit in Mediæval England*.

to the Miracle play and the Morality play. The first deals with scriptural scenes and episodes in the lives of Christ and of the saints, and uses the greatest freedom of imagination in seeking to make such scenes real. This lets us see how the sermon uses the appeal to the dramatic sense. The second type expounds the Creed and the Paternoster and the Ten Commandments, personifying the various virtues and vices. In this we recognise the instinct that makes the abstract concrete and adorns the universal with the vivid directness of the particular. The teaching is largely based on allegory, and the barb of satire and the spear of terror are thrust home by story and example. Entirely unhistorical these methods may be, but they are not without their effect. Nor can this preaching be accused of dealing with far-off things remote from the life of the common man. A social gospel was enunciated that brought near the Day of Judgment to the political and social conditions of the time. In the Lutheran and reformed churches preaching received a new emphasis as the proclamation of the Word, but here too the sermon was the thing which brought home to man's breast the message of God's Presence.

We may not therefore limit the scope of preaching by the restrictions of a narrow view of its function. One obvious lesson from the past is that preaching has played many parts. It has been both teaching and exhortation, and many means it has employed to further these ends. Sometimes preaching has to be as in the early days the preparation for, and the supplement to, the worship offered in prayer and in sacrament. "Praying is the end of preaching," says George Herbert. Sometimes preaching is mainly instructive, the explanation of Scripture or the expounding of the great doctrines and truths about God and life. Sometimes preaching is an appeal to the will, and edification has a practical issue. "My test of the worth of a man as a preacher," says St. Francis de Sales, "is when his congregation go away saying, not 'What a beautiful sermon,' but 'I will do something.'" Sometimes preaching is direct exhortation; sometimes it deals with the ethical issues of this generation, sometimes its appeal is indirect through cleansing the emotions or enlightening the mind. In these ways preaching is concerned with the Word of God as revealed to man, at times explaining it, that is, expository or doctrinal preaching; at times pointing out its consequences in the life of nations and of men—that is, ethical preaching; at times creating the mood of worship—that is, devotional preaching. But preaching also is evangelical—that is, not preaching about the Word but proclaiming the authentic Word of God's revelation.

Thus I would claim for the sermon an importance, not as the substitute for symbolic worship or the offering of devotion, but as the necessary accompaniment that enlightens the mind, creates the mood of worship, and stirs the will to action. To this new age which so clamorously seeks, preaching has a message to give, but by no restraint of habit or convention must it be shackled. If we are to build a worship catholic and free it is largely through preaching that the new atmosphere must be created and the new spirit called into being. In this the sermon must be the servant of the spirit of worship. Amid these days so filled with promise and so fraught with peril, preaching never had a greater part to play in proclaiming the Faith nor a more urgent duty than to call forth the spirit of worship.

With one remark I would close. A distinguished scholar has said that "the ritualist and the puritan conceptions of worship will probably always exist side by side, for they represent two opposite conceptions of religion which can never entirely blend." [1] Doubtless it is true that there are two opposite conceptions of religion. I have argued that there is the mystical approach through the ascent of man's spirit and the revelational approach through the descent of the Divine. But I have also argued that these two approaches are not antagonistic but complementary. If then the ritualist could learn the truth which the puritan asserts, and the puritan become aware of what the ritualist means, the foundation would be laid for the Universal Church. To put it otherwise, the Protestant temper and the Catholic spirit are fundamentally not opposites but complementary. The peril of Protestantism is individualism; the danger of Catholicism is institutionalism. The virtue of Protestantism is its assertion of freedom; the virtue of Catholicism is its affirmation of corporate unity. The standard

[1] Dill, *Roman Society from Nero*, p. 603.

in Protestantism is the historical life of Jesus; the standard in Catholicism is the historical development of God's purpose. Protestant worship tends to speak only to the faith conscious of God; Catholic piety recognises also the wider ministry of God. The Protestant outlook makes worship the expression of what man knows of God's Will and Grace; the Catholic view makes worship the instrument for creating the sense of God's Grace and the appreciation of His presence. But these are not ultimately contradictory. Only in an institution can a man be free and only by the spirit of freedom can an institution live. The historical development can only be judged by the spirit of Christ's teaching, but the meaning of that spirit can only be appreciated through its development in history. Worship can only be the instrument of Grace when it is the expression of faith and the expression of faith attains its goal by becoming the instrument of Grace. The march of history has shown us these two tempers at war, but have we not transcended the division that cripples both? And can we not dream of a Church universal and catholic, evangelic and free, whose worship will contain all that the spirit of man in its strange pilgrim quest has learned from the Grace and Guidance of the Eternal Father?

INDEX OF AUTHORS

INDEX OF SUBJECTS

PRINTED BY MORRISON AND GIBB LTD., EDINBURGH AND LONDON

THE KERR LECTURESHIP.

THE "KERR LECTURESHIP" was founded by the TRUSTEES of the late Miss JOAN KERR of Sanquhar, under her Deed of Settlement, and formally adopted by the United Presbyterian Synod in May 1886. In the following year, May 1887, the provisions and conditions of the Lectureship, as finally adjusted, were adopted by the Synod, and embodied in a Memorandum, printed in the Appendix to the Synod Minutes, p. 489.

On the union of the United Presbyterian Church with the Free Church of Scotland in October 1900, the necessary changes were made in the designation of the object of the Lectureship and the persons eligible for appointment to it, so as to suit the altered circumstances. And at the General Assembly of 1901 it was agreed that the Lectureship should in future be connected with the Glasgow College of the United Free Church. From the Memorandum, as thus amended, the following excerpts are here given :—

II. The amount to be invested shall be £3000.

III. The object of the Lectureship is the promotion of the Study of Scientific Theology in the United Free Church of Scotland.

The Lectures shall be upon some such subjects as the following, viz. :—

A. Historic Theology—

(1) Biblical Theology, (2) History of Doctrine, (3) Patristics, with special reference to the significance and authority of the first three centuries.

B. Systematic Theology—

(1) Christian Doctrine—(*a*) Philosophy of Religion, (*b*) Comparative Theology, (*c*) Anthropology, (*d*) Christology, (*e*) Soteriology, (*f*) Eschatology.

(2) Christian Ethics—(*a*) Doctrine of Sin, (*b*) Individual and Social Ethics, (*c*) The Sacraments, (*d*) The Place of Art in Religious Life and Worship.

Further, the Committee of Selection shall, from time to time, as they think fit, appoint as the subject of the Lectures any important Phases of Modern Religious Thought or Scientific Theories in their bearing upon Evangelical Theology. The Committee may also appoint a subject connected with the practical work of the Ministry as subject of Lecture, but in no case shall this be admissible more than once in every five appointments.

IV. The appointments to this Lectureship shall be made in the first instance from among the Licentiates or Ministers of the United Free Church of Scotland, of whom no one shall be eligible who, when the appointment falls to be made, shall have been licensed for more than twenty-five years, and who is not a graduate of a British University, preferential regard being had to those who have for some time been connected with a Continental University.

V. Appointments to this Lectureship not subject to the conditions in Section IV. may also from time to time, at the discretion of the Committee, be made from among eminent members of the Ministry of any of the Nonconformist Churches of Great Britain and Ireland, America, and the Colonies, or of the Protestant Evangelical Churches of the Continent.

VI. The Lecturer shall hold the appointment for three years.

VII. The number of Lectures to be delivered shall be left to the discretion of the Lecturer, except thus far, that in no case shall there be more than twelve or less than eight.

VIII. The Lectures shall be published at the Lecturer's own expense within one year after their delivery.

IX. The Lectures shall be delivered to the students of the Glasgow College of the United Free Church of Scotland.

XII. The Public shall be admitted to the Lectures.
